VICTORIAN BLOOMSBURY

Also by S. P. Rosenbaum

THE BLOOMSBURY GROUP: A Collection of Memoirs,
Commentary, and Criticism

VICTORIAN BLOOMSBURY

The Early Literary History of the Bloomsbury Group

Volume 1

S. P. Rosenbaum

St. Martin's Press   New York

823
R

First published in the United States of America in 1987

Printed in Hong Kong

ISBN 0-312-84051-9

Library of Congress Cataloging-in-Publication Data
Rosenbaum, S. P. (Stanford Patrick), 1929–
Victorian Bloomsbury: the early literary history
of the Bloomsbury Group.
"Volume 1."
Bibliography: p.
Includes index.
1. Bloomsbury group.   2. English literature – 20th
century – History and criticism.   3. English literature –
19th century – History and criticism.   4. University of
Cambridge – History – 19th century.   5. Cambridge
(Cambridgeshire) – Intellectual life.   6. Bloomsbury
(London, England) – Intellectual life.   7. London
(England) – Intellectual life.   I. Title.
PR478.B46R67   1986   823'.912'09   86-3940
ISBN 0-312-84051-9

This history is dedicated to

Naomi Black

Contents

PART FOUR   CAMBRIDGE WRITINGS

Acknowledgements

Though *Victorian Bloomsbury* is in no way an authorised literary history of Bloomsbury's early years, nor even for that matter an unauthorised one, it could not have been written without the unremitting co-operation and kindness of a considerable number of people, some of whom were members of the Group themselves or closely related to them. Many of those who have helped me over the years I now cannot thank, but in gratitude and memory I make no distinction here between the living and the dead.

I was fortunate to be able to talk and correspond about Bloomsbury and its works with three of the original members of the Group: E. M. Forster, Leonard Woolf and Duncan Grant. I also benefited from conversations with David and Angelica Garnett and with James and Alix Strachey. But above all it has been Quentin Bell, the one figure in Bloomsbury fully an artist and a writer, who has helped me longer and more often than anyone else.

In writing on Virginia and Leonard Woolf I am much indebted to Anne Olivier Bell and her excellent edition of Virginia Woolf's diary. With E. M. Forster I have been kindly helped by his biographer, P. N. Furbank, and his editor, Oliver Stallybrass. Michael Holroyd, Anne Wilson and Paul Levy of the Strachey Trust have been very helpful in providing access to Lytton Strachey's extensive unpublished writings. Desmond MacCarthy's papers were made available to me along with much helpful advice by Dermod MacCarthy, David and Rachel Cecil, Chloe MacCarthy and Desmond MacCarthy. Julian Fry, Pamela Diamand and Frances Spalding have provided illuminating information about Roger Fry, and Frances Spalding has also helped me valuably with Vanessa Bell's life and letters. I have benefited from Donald Moggridge's knowledge of Keynes and his papers. Trekkie Parsons has kindly given me access to Leonard Woolf's papers, and Angelica Garnett to Vanessa Bell's papers.

A number of libraries and librarians have been indispensable for the research in *Victorian Bloomsbury*. Of great assistance with most of the Bloomsbury writers have been A. N. L. Munby of King's College, Cambridge, and Lola Szladits of the Berg Collection in the New York Public Library. In addition to these two great archivists, I am considerably indebted to Elizabeth Inglis, and John Burt as well, for repeated help with the papers of Virginia and Leonard Woolf at the University of Sussex Library. I have also been assisted with the Charleston Papers and the papers of E. M. Forster and Roger Fry at King's by Peter Croft and particularly the Modern Archivist, Michael Halls, with his detailed knowledge of the collection. Penelope Bullock and Marion Stewart, formerly of the King's College Library, were also very helpful. The assistance of Leila Luedeking of the Washington State University Library has been invaluable. Rosemary Graham and Trevor Kaye of the Library at Trinity College, Cambridge, assisted me with the papers of Clive Bell, and A. E. B. Owen of the University of Cambridge Library kindly provided copies of G. E. Moore's papers, to which Dorothy Moore gave me access before they were sold to that library. Judith Allen has been helpful with Keynes's papers in the Marshall Library at Cambridge, and Ellen Dunlap of the Humanities Research Center, University of Texas, with the various Bloomsbury-related collections there. I am also very grateful to the staff of the British Library for help with the extensive Strachey papers and with manuscripts of Virginia Woolf, J. M. Keynes, E. M. Forster and Duncan Grant, and to the British Broadcasting Script Library for broadcasts by and about Bloomsbury. The Robert H. Taylor Collection of the Princeton University Library gave me access to its Strachey papers. And back home I am very much obliged to the staff of the University of Toronto Libraries, in particular to Richard Landon and Christina Duff Stewart. I have also benefited from the excellent Bloomsbury collection of Mary Jackman at Victoria College, and from the help of the college librarian, Robert Brandeis.

Various other institutions have provided financial assistance of one kind or another for study, research and writing. For these I thank the Carnegie Foundation for the Advancement of Teaching; the Guggenheim Foundation; the Social Sciences and Humanities Research Council of Canada, and its predecessor, the Canada Council; and, finally, the Connaught Fund, the Office of Research Administration and the Department of English at the University of Toronto.

The undergraduate and graduate students I have been fortunate to teach at Toronto have helped me think about the literary history of Bloomsbury for nearly twenty years now. Some of them, such as Linda Hutcheon, Donald Laing and John Stape, have gone on to publish their own work on Bloomsbury, from which I have profited.

This history could not have been written without the preliminary labour of a number of biographers and editors whose work is acknowledged through frequent references in my text. There are few references, however, to the books of a group of bibliographers that have been invaluable for this history: B. J. Kirkpatrick's third revised editions of *A Bibliography of E. M. Forster* and *A Bibliography of Virginia Woolf*, Donald A. Laing's *Clive Bell: An Annotated Bibliography* and *Roger Fry: An Annotated Bibliography*, Michael Edmonds's *Lytton Strachey: A Bibliography*, and J. Howard Woolmer's *A Checklist of the Hogarth Press, 1917–1938*.

To Richard Garnett I am obliged for a thorough and thoroughly helpful reading of *Victorian Bloomsbury* and a copy of *Cornishiana*. Also thoroughly helpful was the meticulous copyediting of Graham Eyre.

Many other people have given aid, comfort, criticism, and facts of various kinds. It is a pleasure to go over their names again: Peter Allen, Noel Annan, Henry Auster, Barbara Bagenal, John Beer, John W. Bicknell, Kenneth Blackwell, Elizabeth Boyd, R. B. Braithwaite, Stuart Brown, J. E. Chamberlin, Terri Cherney, Ralph Cohen, Kathleen Coburn, S. J. Colman, Susan Dick, David Dowling, Leon Edel, Valerie Eliot, J. W. Graham, Carolyn Heilbrun, Elizabeth Heine, Judith Herz, Barbara Howard, Heather and J. R. de J. Jackson, James McConkey, Andrew McNeillie, Michael Millgate, Nigel Nicolson, Richard Outram, Anthony d'Offay, Frances Partridge, Elizabeth Richardson, Paul Roche, Bertrand Russell, John Slater, George Spater, Anne Synge, Joanne Trautmann Banks, Ian Watt.

Parts of *Victorian Bloomsbury* have been published in different form in *New Literary History* and *The Times Higher Education Supplement* as well as the following collections: *Intellect and Social Conscience: Essays on Bertrand Russell's Early Work*, ed. Margaret

Moran and Carl Spadoni; *Virginia Woolf: Centennial Essays*, ed. Elaine K. Ginsberg and Laura Moss Gottlieb; and *Virginia Woolf: New Critical Essays*, ed. Patricia Clements and Isobel Grundy. I am grateful to their editors for permission to use this material.

For permission to quote from *The Letters of Virginia Woolf*, ed. Nigel Nicolson and Joanne Trautmann, from *The Diary of Virginia Woolf*, ed. Anne Olivier Bell and Andrew McNeillie, from *The Collected Essays of Virginia Woolf*, ed. Leonard Woolf, and from the memoirs published in *Moments of Being*, ed. Jeanne Schulkind, I am grateful to Quentin Bell, the Hogarth Press, and Harcourt Brace Jovanovich, Inc. For permissions to quote from unpublished papers of Clive Bell in the library at Trinity College, Cambridge, I am grateful to Quentin Bell. The Provost and Scholars of King's College, Cambridge, and the Society of Authors as literary representatives of the Estate of E. M. Forster have granted permission to quote from unpublished texts of Forster. For permission to quote from unpublished papers of Lytton Strachey in the British Library, the Berg Collection of the New York Public Library, the Humanities Research Center at the University of Texas, and the Strachey Trust, I am grateful to that Trust. Pamela Diamand has kindly granted me permission to quote from Roger Fry's unpublished papers at King's College, Cambridge, and Trekkie Parsons permission to quote from Leonard Woolf's papers at the University of Sussex library. Henrietta Garnett has kindly allowed me to quote from Duncan Grant's unpublished papers. The Royal Economic Society has granted permission to quote from unpublished material in the Keynes Papers at the Marshall Library in Cambridge. The Permissions Committee of the Bertrand Russell Archives at McMaster University, Hamilton, Ontario, has allowed me to quote from Russell's papers. And I am grateful to Sir Rupert Hart-Davis and Eva Reichmann, copyright-holder, for permission to quote from an unpublished letter of Max Beerbohm's at the University of Sussex library.

Finally there are the unsayable debts of love and gratitude that I owe to my family – Dorothy and Harry Rosenbaum, Susanna and Samuel Rosenbaum, Max and Michal Black, and the person to whom this history must be dedicated.

Toronto

S.P.R.

Explanation of References and Abbreviations

Note numbers in the text refer to substantive notes at the end of the book. References to books or papers given in parentheses in the text refer to the Bibliography listed after the notes. These parenthetical references are of two types.

(1) The most frequently cited writers and books are given by initials only, with an oblique or slash separating author and title; volume and page numbers follow. Periodical writings by these frequently cited authors are given short titles after the oblique. References to collections of papers are indicated by a 'p' and initials indicating their location; unpublished-letter citations include dates when known.

(2) Other references give the author's last name, a short title when there is more than one work by an author of that name, then volume and page numbers.

References omit indications of authors or works when they are supplied by the context. (All citations are given in the Bibliography.)

Examples of references:

LS/*PM*, p. 45	Lytton Strachey, *Portraits in Miniature*, p. 45.
VW/*D*, II 123	*The Diary of Virginia Woolf*, vol. II, p. 123.
10.viii.05, LW/pT	Unpublished letter by Leonard Woolf, 10 August 1905, Leonard Woolf papers, Texas
DM/'Irish Plays', p. 252	Desmond MacCarthy, 'The Irish Plays', p. 252

Laing, *RF*, p. 237   Donald A. Laing, *Roger Fry: An Anno-
                           tated Bibliography of the Published Writ-
                           ings*, p. 237

ABBREVIATIONS

1   *Bloomsbury authors and works*

CB   Clive Bell
     A   *Art*
     OF   *Old Friends*
     PB   *Pot-Boilers*
     pTC   Papers, Trinity College, Cambridge

VB   Vanessa Bell
     pAG   Papers in possession of Angelica Garnett

EMF E. M. Forster
     AE   *Albergo Empedocle and Other Writings*
     AH   *Abinger Harvest*
     AN   *Aspects of the Novel*
     CB   *Commonplace Book*
     GLD   *Goldsworthy Lowes Dickinson*
     HE   *Howards End*
     LJ   *The Longest Journey*
     M   *Maurice*
     MT   *Marianne Thornton*
     pKC   Papers, King's College, Cambridge
     2CD   *Two Cheers for Democracy*

RF   Roger Fry
     L   *Letters of Roger Fry*
     LL   *Last Lectures*
     pKC   Papers, King's College, Cambridge

JMK John Maynard Keynes
     CW   *Collected Writings*
     pKC   Papers, King's College, Cambridge
     pML   Papers, Marshall Library, Cambridge

DM   Desmond MacCarthy
       C   *Criticism*
       E   *Experience*
       H   *Humanities*
       M   *Memories*
       P   *Portraits*
       pC   Papers, Lord David Cecil

LS   Lytton Strachey
       BC   *Books and Characters*
       CC   *Characters and Commentaries*
       EV   *Eminent Victorians*
       LFL   *Landmarks in French Literature*
       LSH   *Lytton Strachey by Himself*
       LVWLS   *Virginia Woolf and Lytton Strachey: Letters*
       pBL   Papers, British Library
       PM   *Portraits in Miniature*
       pP   Papers, Princeton University Library
       pST   Papers, Strachey Trust
       pT   Papers, University of Texas
       RIQ   *The Really Interesting Question*
       SE   *Spectatorial Essays*
       SS   *The Shorter Strachey*

LW   Leonard Woolf
       AD   *After the Deluge*
       BA   *Beginning Again*
       DAW   *Downhill All the Way*
       E   *Essays*
       G   *Growing*
       PP   *Principia Politica*
       pS   Papers, University of Sussex
       S   *Sowing*
       WV   *The Wise Virgins*

VW   Virginia Woolf
       BP   *Books and Portraits*
       CE   *Collected Essays*
       CSF   *The Complete Shorter Fiction of Virginia Woolf*
       CW   *Contemporary Writers*

D	*The Diary of Virginia Woolf*
HH	*A Haunted House and Other Short Stories*
JR	*Jacob's Room*
L	*The Letters of Virginia Woolf*
LVWLS	*Virginia Woolf and Lytton Strachey: Letters*
MB	*Moments of Being*, second edition
pNY	Papers, New York Public Library
pS	Papers, University of Sussex
RF	*Roger Fry*
RO	*A Room of One's Own*
3G	*Three Guineas*

2   *Other authors, works, periodicals*

DNB	*Dictionary of National Biography*
MH/*LS*	Michael Holroyd, *Lytton Strachey*
MH/*LSBG*	Michael Holroyd, *Lytton Strachey and the Bloomsbury Group*
OED	*Oxford English Dictionary*
PE	G. E. Moore, *Principia Ethica*
PNF/*EMF*	P. N. Furbank, *E. M. Forster*
QB/*VW*	Quentin Bell, *Virginia Woolf*
RFH/*JMK*	R. F. Harrod, *J. M. Keynes*
SPR/*BG*	S. P. Rosenbaum (ed.), *The Bloomsbury Group*
TLS	*The Times Literary Supplement*

Introduction

The works and days of the Bloomsbury Group have been attracting commentary of one kind or another for three quarters of a century now. Virginia and Leonard Woolf, Vanessa and Clive Bell, Lytton Strachey, E. M. Forster, John Maynard Keynes, Roger Fry, Duncan Grant and Desmond MacCarthy have been recognised as writers, artists and thinkers whose work shaped modern English fiction, biography, criticism, economics, aesthetics, painting and decoration, and whose lives could be taken, for good or ill, as models of modern living.

Written attention first began to accumulate around Bloomsbury in the form of reviews, essays, satires and memoirs. They were followed by biographies, bibliographies, autobiographical essays, letters, diaries, collected editions, manuscript editions, and an apparently endless series of critical studies. More is now known about Bloomsbury's life and work than of any other group in literary history. Yet among the many books on Bloomsbury there remains an incongruity. The books devoted to the interrelated lives of the Group have had little to say about their works, although these are now the principal justification for studying the Group. If Bloomsbury had written or painted nothing of enduring value, their lives would not continue to interest us the way they do. On the other hand, the books that have been devoted to the Group's writing (the situation is different with their painting) have had practically nothing to say about how these writings are connected with those of the other members, even though it is the interconnectedness of these writings that makes the Group's work something quite different than the sum of its individual achievements.

The intention of *The Early Literary History of the Bloomsbury*

Group is to describe a historical sequence of Bloomsbury's early interconnected texts in order to interpret them analytically and comparatively. E. M. Forster's famous epigraph for *Howards End*, 'Only connect . . .', could serve as a motto for the enterprise. *Victorian Bloomsbury*, the first half of this literary history, examines the intellectual, family, and Cambridge origins of the Group, often as these are reflected in the Group's autobiographical and undergraduate writings. The second half, *Edwardian Bloomsbury*, will describe the literary beginnings of Old Bloomsbury (as they later liked to refer to themselves) during the years between the end of their formal education and the beginning of the apocalyptic First World War.

There is a justifiable scepticism today about the traditional assumptions of literary history – about the causal relations of historical conditions and creative processes, about the critical significance of sources, about the logic of influences. Some of these assumptions can be avoided and others set forth with some precision in Bloomsbury's literary history by concentrating on the analysis and comparison of a chronological series of interrelated texts. For Bloomsbury's is a special kind of literary history. It is not primarily the record of evolving forms, styles, conventions, themes; it is not the history of a period, a country, or – despite the Library of Congress's disposition to classify books on Bloomsbury as literary topography – a place. The principal materials of Bloomsbury's literary history are a series of texts written over a period of sixty or seventy years by a close group of friends. When these texts are examined chronologically, the private and public circumstances and conditions that accompanied their composition become more apparent. The literature of Bloomsbury can be examined in other ways, of course, just as there can be other kinds of history written about the Group's place in twentieth-century English culture. But any history of Bloomsbury must realise the centrality of writing in their achievements, just as any literary history must refer, implicitly at least, to the temporal order of its texts. The freedom of criticism depends upon the recognition of chronological necessity.

The premises of the early literary history of the Bloomsbury Group are further explained in sections of this introduction having to do with the nature of Bloomsbury, the range of its texts, their kinds of interconnection, and the periods into which Bloomsbury's writing may be divided.

II

The Bloomsbury Group was a collectivity of friends and relations who knew and loved one another for a period of time
extending over two generations. Because friendships – especially
those that developed out of their shared education at Cambridge
– were the original and enduring bonds of the Group, Bloomsbury is a difficult entity to define. Polemical misrepresentations
of the Group's membership or purposes and essentialist
definitions that have futilely sought commonly held beliefs of the
Group have resulted from time to time in denials of the Group's
existence. I have tried to show in *The Bloomsbury Group: A
Collection of Memoirs, Commentary, and Criticism* how the Group
described themselves and were seen by their contemporaries. It
is fairly clear now that the problems of defining Bloomsbury
have as much to do with preconceptions about the nature of
artistic or intellectual groups as with the elusive character of the
Bloomsbury Group itself.

Bloomsbury was closer to being a modern movement than a
traditional school, although neither term applies to it very
accurately.[1] G. E. Moore and Roger Fry profoundly affected the
Group's thought and art but they were not its masters. No
doctrine was taught in Bloomsbury. 'We had no common theory,
system, or principles which we wanted to convert the world to',
Leonard Woolf asserted in the clearest account of Bloomsbury
that has been written by one of its members (*BA*, p. 25). Because
Bloomsbury was not a school of writers, artists, or intellectuals,
the term 'circle' that is sometimes used to identify the Group is
too restrictive, as is the term 'set', which applies essentially to
social relations. The looser notion of 'group' seems more accurate. Bloomsbury's associations included philosophical, artistic,
literary, political, economic and moral affinities in addition to
their friendships, but the affinities accompanied the friendships
rather than the other way round. As a cultural group Bloomsbury has been described as a fraction by association with, rather
than in programmatic opposition to, the English upper middle
class (Williams, p. 60). But like an avant-garde movement
Bloomsbury sometimes defined itself in terms of opposition to
various cultural establishments or to other avant-garde movements; it also rejoiced in change and experiment and sought an
artistic, intellectual and familial milieu – but not in the Victorian

family way. Virginia Woolf's writing can be difficult, yet no one
in Bloomsbury practised the 'linguistic hermeticism' that often
characterises avant-garde writing (Poggioli, p. 37). A belief in
the common reader underlies Bloomsbury's prose. Nor did the
Group maintain any little magazines, as avant-garde movements
appear to do.[2] Bloomsbury could be said to have a press, but it
published little of E. M. Forster's work, none of Lytton
Strachey's, and many of the Hogarth authors had nothing at all
to do with Bloomsbury.

The difficulty of mapping a network of friendships is another
reason why Bloomsbury is difficult to define. Friends of the
friends were not necessarily members of the Group. It was not
obvious from the outside who belonged, and this allowed their
enemies to associate all sorts of unlikely people with Bloomsbury. The Group's easiest defence was simply to deny their
existence as a group. With the publication of Bloomsbury biographies and autobiographies the membership of Bloomsbury
along with the complex nature of their associations became clear.
Other difficulties in defining the people in Bloomsbury have to
do with the 'marriage and death and division' that Swinburne,
an early favourite poet of Bloomsbury's, says 'make barren our
lives' ('Dolores', ll. 159–60). The membership of the Group
altered somewhat with marriages of one kind or another, with
the coming of the younger generation, and with the dying of the
older. Perhaps the simplest way of identifying the members of
the Bloomsbury Group is to look at the Memoir Club that was
founded in 1920 to commemorate – ironically and otherwise –
Old Bloomsbury. Whether the Group came together in Cambridge undergraduate discussion societies or during the early
years of the new century in that district of West Central London
from which the Group took its name, the papers of the Memoir
Club and other autobiographies of the members agreed that Old
Bloomsbury ended with the First World War.

Originating in shared past experiences, the Memoir Club
provided a continuing basis for the New Bloomsbury that lasted
more or less through the Second World War. The last meeting
was in 1956. According to Leonard Woolf the initial members of
the Memoir Club, in addition to himself and his wife, were
Vanessa and Clive Bell, Lytton Strachey, John Maynard
Keynes, Duncan Grant, Roger Fry, E. M. Forster, Saxon
Sydney-Turner, Adrian Stephen, and Desmond and Mary

MacCarthy[3] (*DAW*, p. 114). There is room for qualification and disagreement in this as in all Bloomsbury lists, but for the purposes of literary history the only writer missing from Leonard Woolf's list who was intimately associated with Bloomsbury is David Garnett, and he did not become involved with Bloomsbury until the First World War.

It is worth emphasising that Leonard Woolf's list includes a very important writer who is sometimes left out of Bloomsbury accounts because he was not closely involved with the Group during its Edwardian years. For purposes of literary if not personal history, E. M. Forster is crucial to Bloomsbury. His novels and essays influentially embodied Bloomsbury values, and his achievements were of considerable significance for Virginia and Leonard Woolf as well as for Lytton Strachey and Desmond MacCarthy. Forster's significance together with Bloomsbury's is sometimes ignored by feminist interpretations of Virginia Woolf that emphasise the influence of other women upon her. But Virginia Woolf herself was quite clear on the importance of a group for an artist's development. In a public dispute with Desmond MacCarthy over the intellectual status of women, she argued that among the necessary conditions for a Shakespeare was 'that he shall have had predecessors in his art, shall make one of a group where art is freely discussed and practised, and shall himself have the utmost of freedom of action and experience' (*D*, ɪɪ 341). The women artists such as Vita Sackville-West or Ethel Smyth that Virginia Woolf knew outside the Bloomsbury Group did not give her such an opportunity. And of course within the Group was the most important woman in her life, her sister the artist–matriarch Vanessa Bell.

Other writers of the younger generation who became closely associated with Bloomsbury in various ways, and therefore also have some place in its later literary history during the Georgian years and into the 1930s include James and Marjorie Strachey, Arthur Waley, Francis Birrell, Gerald Brenan, Raymond Mortimer, F. L. Lucas, John Lehmann and, of course, Julian and Quentin Bell. But it should be noted that some writers who had a close relationship with one or two people in Bloomsbury were not considered to be members by the Group or themselves, despite what the writers of reviews or surveys sometimes say. The Sitwells were not Bloomsbury, though polemical outsiders lumped them together. Vita Sackville-West and her husband

Harold Nicolson were closer, but neither their Hogarth Press books, which interested Bloomsbury, nor Virginia's affair with Vita should obscure the considerable differences in class, education and values between them and Bloomsbury. The relations of Bertrand Russell and T. S. Eliot with Bloomsbury are again different. Russell's philosophy and social criticism, Eliot's poetry and literary criticism influenced Bloomsbury deeply; both were at times good friends with various members, but neither was associated throughout his career in the manner of intimate friendship that characterises Bloomsbury's relations. Then there is Lady Ottoline Morrell – always a special case, but she was not really a writer; of her Virginia Woolf remarked that when the history of Bloomsbury came to be written (she thought it would be a good subject for Strachey's next book) a chapter or at least an appendix would have to be devoted to her (*MB*, p. 199).

'Division' in Bloomsbury has sometimes affected definitions of the Group. Because, as Leonard Woolf said, they had no commonly held theory, system or principles, it has been assumed that there was no intellectual basis for the Group. Such an assumption has been reinforced by the unsparing criticism that the members directed at one another's life and work. This mutual criticism, along with the mutual admiration that the Group is often accused of, is among the most important kinds of interconnection a literary history needs to trace in Bloomsbury's writings. As for the lack of common ideas, Leonard Woolf himself also wrote in a passage cited above that 'the colour of our minds and thought had been given to us by the climate of Cambridge and Moore's philosophy' (*BA*, p. 25). This colour changed at least its hue when Bloomsbury encountered in Edwardian London the political climate of suffragism, socialism, pacifism, and the aesthetic climate of post-impressionism. None of these can be considered a defining characteristic of Bloomsbury, but this does not mean that Bloomsbury fails to manifest a clear similarity of convictions about philosophy, art and society. There is, in Wittgenstein's metaphor, a family resemblance between members of the Bloomsbury Group that appears not in their common features but in their overlapping and criss-crossing similarities (*Investigations*, I 67). A literary history of the Bloomsbury Group needs to trace this family resemblance in their writings.

Another philosophical comparison that can clarify the nature of the Bloomsbury Group is G. E. Moore's notion of an organic whole. For Moore it is a whole that bears no regular relation to the sum of its parts (*PE*, p. 27). Moore applied his idea to the assessment of value, but it is relevant to Bloomsbury's writings: they have a value as a whole for Bloomsbury's literary history that has no regular relation to their intrinsic value as works of literature. Leonard Woolf's novels, for instance, or Desmond MacCarthy's reviews are not among the monuments of English fiction or criticism, but in the literary history of Old Bloomsbury they are invaluable.

Neither Wittgenstein's nor Moore's analogies should be taken to imply unanimity in Bloomsbury, however. There is, alas, no convenient term for referring only to some of the individuals in Bloomsbury. 'Bloomsberries' will not do, and 'members' (though sometimes unavoidable) unfortunately suggests some kind of dues-collecting organisation. But 'Bloomsbury' can be a collective noun taking either the singular or the plural, and I have tried to discriminate between the two depending upon whether the emphasis is on the group itself or on the individuals comprising it. One further point about the term 'Bloomsbury': used as a noun or as an adjective in this history, it refers, unless otherwise indicated, to the members of the Bloomsbury Group and not to the district or its other inhabitants.

The nature of the Bloomsbury Group is truly remarkable only in one aspect. There are innumerable groups without leaders or goals, that are based on friendship and whose membership is not easily defined (Boissevain, pp. 170–205). Here, for example, is a description of a group in a novel talked about in Cambridge at the beginning of Bloomsbury's history: 'Oh yes; not a formal association nor a secret society – still less a "dangerous gang" or an organization for any definite end. We're simply a collection of natural affinities . . .' (Henry James, *The Awkward Age*, ch. 10). What makes the Bloomsbury Group more than simply a collection of affinities is the work they achieved. Their lives are best understood, finally, as they are enacted in and through their work. The work was not, of course, exclusively literary: painting and political economy were as important as literature in Bloomsbury. Yet the early literary history of Bloomsbury may be the most comprehensive way of beginning the study of their achievements, depending on how widely we construe the primary materials of literary history, that are its texts.

III

The terms 'text' and 'writing' may suggest some kind of automatic activity purged of human origins, yet they include more types of writing and beg fewer questions about form or purpose than the word 'work' does. Often the terms are interchangeable, but the greater inclusiveness of 'text' or 'writing' is especially important for Bloomsbury literary history. The history of English literature includes Donne's sermons, Burton's anatomy, Gibbon's history, Johnson's biographies, Lamb's essays, Ruskin's art criticism, yet in the twentieth century much modernist literary theory has insisted that a crucial disjunction exists between works of poetry, drama and fiction, on the one hand, and what is defined merely negatively as non-fiction, on the other. Whatever such a separation does for the freedom of criticism elsewhere, it obscures the understanding of Bloomsbury's literary achievement. The literary history of Bloomsbury, Old and New, is to an unusual extent a history of prose. Except for Lytton Strachey, the members wrote little poetry or drama, and none of them published much of it. To dichotomise their writing into fictive and non-fictive categories and then to interpret the former as proper literary works and the latter as something else leads to the misinterpretation of both. Thinking of Bloomsbury's works simply as texts or writings helps to avoid this split.

I am not trying to suggest that there are no distinctions between fiction and non-fiction in Bloomsbury. There are many distinctions, but they cannot be adequately subsumed under some kind of binary figural–referential system. One of the most salient features of Bloomsbury's modernism, ironically enough, is their mixture of genres in writing and painting. Forster's essays – even very early ones – sometimes have fictional settings and characters, and there are essay chapters in his novels. Perhaps the most widely read of all Bloomsbury books today, Virginia Woolf's *A Room of One's Own*, synthesises the forms of lecture, short story, critical essay, polemical tract, mystical meditation, research paper, and even literary history. To ask whether it is fiction or non-fiction seems pointless, yet the work is often misinterpreted by readers assuming it has to be one or the other. As for her novels, recent feminist criticism has shown the incompleteness of older critical interpretations that failed to see how her significant forms expressed deeply felt cognitive contents. Revaluation still awaits the biographies of Lytton Strachey. Whether he was a historian, a satirist or a fabricator has exercised his critics, but there has been little analysis of the literary means he used to obtain the pervasively ironic ends of his texts, whether they be biographies, essays or letters. Strachey's imagery and syntax, his use of clichés and indirect discourse, the structure and rhythm of his narrative are all part of his careful literary intention. Even in Bloomsbury studies Strachey is not much discussed as a writer; the frequent quotations from his writing present, however, a literary voice as distinctive as his physical one. Voice is an interesting and complex literary feature of the writing of Strachey, Forster, and Virginia Woolf. Useful comparisons are to be made here, but they cut right across fictive and non-fictive boundaries.

One consequence of the hierarchical division of prose into fiction and non-fiction is the reluctance or inability of many modern readers to respond to literary beauty except in forms of exalted fiction. Bloomsbury took beauty in writing more seriously and less seriously than is now fashionable. They expected it in great fiction but they also welcomed it in essays, biographies, histories. Nor did they feel any incompatibility between beauty and humour in writing. Bloomsbury's prose has been described as aiming at 'a beautiful amusingness' (Furbank, 'Bloomsbury Prose', p. 161). Those who deplore the frivolous aestheticism of Bloomsbury's literary art might well agree. For Bloomsbury, however, there was no reason why prose in almost any form could not be beautiful and funny and serious at the same time. Contemporary taste does not seem to be as catholic as Bloomsbury's, but if readers of Bloomsbury's writings clothe their literary inhibitions in evaluative theories of genre, they will be unable to interpret the Group's texts properly. Kenneth Clark once observed that, in Roger Fry's company, 'the proper answer to Tolstoy's "What is Art?" was the counter-question, "What isn't?"' (RF/*LL*, pp. x–xi). In the company of Bloomsbury's writings, the answer to the question 'What is literature?' ought to be, 'What isn't?' And involved in this answer are matters having to do with the purposes of writers and the expectations of readers – with form, organisation, style, imagery, and the blending of fiction, drama, poetry, history, autobiography and criticism. The literariness of a Bloomsbury text may depend in the final analysis on that fundamental ethical distinction that Bloomsbury, following Moore, made between ends and means: writing is literary for Bloomsbury if it is worth reading for its own sake, apart from or in addition to its usefulness as a means to truth or goodness.

The authors of Bloomsbury works that raise such considerations are not only Virginia Woolf, E. M. Forster and Lytton Strachey. They also include Leonard Woolf, Clive Bell, Roger Fry, Desmond and Mary MacCarthy, and John Maynard Keynes. Their novels, memoirs, biographical essays, letters and criticism are not major writings in the literary history of Bloomsbury. Yet, when they are recognised *as* writers, their texts can be related to others in Bloomsbury, including the Group's greatest works of fiction. Thus a wide conception of what constitutes a Bloomsbury literary text enhances rather than diminishes Bloomsbury's literary value.

IV

Reasons, he said, in Aesthetics, are 'of the nature of further descriptions', . . . and all that Aesthetics does is 'to draw your attention to a thing', to 'place things side by side'.   (Moore, 'Wittgenstein's Lectures', p. 315)

The primary reason for a literary history of the Bloomsbury Group is to be found in the interrelatedness of its texts. They are interconnected analogously and contiguously: they resemble each other in various ways and are juxtaposed in various contexts. Connections by analogy and by contiguity are both very relevant to the interpretation of these texts, as a short description of the principal interrelations will suggest.

The network of interconnections formed between Bloomsbury's writings is most obvious, perhaps, in the dedications of a number of their works. Leonard Woolf dedicated *The Village in the Jungle* to Virginia Woolf and *The Wise Virgins* to Desmond MacCarthy. Virginia Woolf dedicated *The Voyage Out* to Leonard Woolf and *Night and Day* to Vanessa Bell. Lytton Strachey dedicated *Queen Victoria* to Virginia Woolf (she asked him to use more than just her initials lest someone think the dedicatee 'some Victoria Worms or Vincent Woodlouse' – *L*, II 456) and *Books and Characters* to John Maynard Keynes. Virginia Woolf dedicated *The Common Reader* to Strachey; later she regretted not having dedicated *To the Lighthouse* to Roger Fry. Clive Bell dedicated *Civilization* to Virginia Woolf, and Forster dedicated his Rede lecture on Virginia to Leonard Woolf. These dedications display interrelations that go beyond friendship to the meanings of the works themselves. So do the Bloomsbury novels where the partial resemblance of characters to members of the Group signifies more than just in-jokes.

The interconnectedness of Bloomsbury's texts begins, of course, in the friendships of their authors, friendships that developed out of shared backgrounds, experiences and convictions. That development is basically the subject of *Victorian Bloomsbury*. All the individuals in Bloomsbury except Clive Bell came from professional upper-middle-class families, several of which were very large. The wealth of these families has been exaggerated, but several of the Group's members did have enough independent means not to have to work very steadily for a living; eventually Strachey, Virginia Woolf and Forster all became financially successful through their writing. In religion the Victorian partriarchies and matriarchies from which Bloomsbury descended were in a general sense evangelical puritans – general enough to take in Quakers and even Jews, that is. In politics they were liberal. Their Bloomsbury offspring reacted strongly against the Victorian family as a means of social organisation and made their inherited puritanism compatible with atheism and their liberalism complementary to socialism. Crucial for these adaptations was the philosophy that constitutes the intellectual foundation of Bloomsbury and makes its literary history something of a philosophical history as well, as the Cambridge chapters that follow show. Two of Bloomsbury's fathers were Cambridge utilitarian philsophers, and all the men of Bloomsbury but Duncan Grant went to Cambridge, where all but Bell were members of what now must be the most famous student society in the world, the Cambridge Apostles. Through the Apostles, Cambridge philosophy in general and G. E. Moore's philosophy in particular influenced Bloomsbury deeply and permanently. This influence appears in the epistemological, ethical and aesthetic interconnections of their writings: Bloomsbury's writers were commonsense realists in theory of perception, consequentialists and pluralists in ethics, formalists and

eclectics in aesthetics. Their rationalism was qualified by a
quasi-neo-Platonic mysticism that might be traced back to the
Cambridge Platonists, and their aestheticism, which became
post-impressionist under Roger Fry's guidance, never subordinated love or truth to art. The importance of Cambridge
philosophy for Bloomsbury's writing is to be found not so much
in their topics as in their assumptions – assumptions about the
nature of consciousness and its relation to external nature, about
the irreducible otherness of people that makes isolation unavoidable and love possible, about the human and non-human
realities of time and death, and about the supreme goods of
truth, love and beauty. The philosophy also underlies Bloomsbury's criticisms of capitalism, imperialism and war, of
materialistic realism in painting and literature, and of sexual
inequality, discrimination and repression.

The social and philosophical lines along which Bloomsbury's
works are interconnected can be illustrated quite specifically.
The significance of private rooms as symbols of consciousness
in the writings of Forster and Virginia Woolf is strikingly similar. Moore's means–ends analysis of ethics is reflected in the
metaphors of journeys that appear in the titles of a number of
Bloomsbury works. The settings of Bloomsbury novels in Cambridge, London and the country, the money the characters have,
the books they read, the paintings and sculptures and buildings
they contemplate, the discussions they pursue, the points of view
through which these are rendered are all interrelated in social
and intellectual implications.

Sometimes entire texts are related to others in Bloomsbury.
Forster's Edwardian novels *A Room with a View* and *The Longest
Journey* are female and male *Bildungsromane* related directly to
Virginia Woolf's pre-war *The Voyage Out* and post-war *Jacob's
Room*. Keynes's *The Economic Consequences of the Peace* is something
of a sequel to Strachey's *Eminent Victorians*. Virginia Woolf's
Flush is partly a parody of Strachey's Victorian biographies. Her
A Room of One's Own is partly a response to Forster's *Aspects of the
Novel*, and a pageant play similar to his *England's Green and
Pleasant Land* became the centre of her *Between the Acts*.

A different kind of interconnection, but one just as important
for the interpretation of Bloomsbury's texts, is to be found in the
Group's extensive, reflexive mutual criticism. The reception of
their work began in Bloomsbury, and Bloomsbury's judgements

were the ones taken most seriously. For the interpreter of the Group's writings, this criticism is frequently the most interesting that exists on their works. Often it is not the most favourable, but such criticism is directed more consistently to the basic concerns, achievements and difficulties of the texts being commented upon. The Group's mutual criticism is of two different kinds, personal and public. The personal is to be found in letters and diaries, and some of this is not only personal but private, confided to a diary or written in a letter to someone other than the author. The public literary criticism that Virginia and Leonard Woolf, Forster, MacCarthy and Clive Bell wrote of the Group's works is only partly known because comparatively little of Bloomsbury's extensive journalism has been collected. Yet this criticism, because it is sympathetic without being adulatory, often makes the most important discriminations. It was certainly among the most careful criticism they wrote.

Besides direct commentary, Bloomsbury's literary criticism exhibits other textual interrelations. Sometimes individuals in the Group reviewed the same books or wrote on the same authors or subjects. The various possibilities for comparison here include disconnection as well as connection. Silence was one of Bloomsbury's most effective critical reactions, and they did not spare one another in the use of it. There are also the interpretative comparisons suggested by contiguities of space and time. In all the criticism that has now been devoted to Virginia Woolf's work, no one that I know of has yet looked carefully to see what Leonard Woolf was writing in his weekly literary columns for the *Nation* in the 1920s while his wife was writing her essays and novels. Then there are the decades of weekly reviews MacCarthy wrote for the *New Statesman* and *The Sunday Times*. The literary history of Bloomsbury cannot be told apart from the innumerable periodical writings of the Woolfs, Forster, MacCarthy, Strachey and Keynes – writings that were shaped from the very beginning by the conditions of literary journalism in early-twentieth-century England.

As important were the conditions of book publication that affected Bloomsbury's works. The history of the Woolfs' Hogarth Press is inseparable from the later history of Bloomsbury. Unlike almost all modern authors, Virginia Woolf published her major novels unedited. The dustjackets that were designed for them by Vanessa Bell and the blurbs that were written by Virginia or

Leonard Woolf are significant comments on these texts. Vanessa Bell's designs in particular are, in Henry James's phrase, optical echoes of the books that a literary history should listen to ('Prefaces', p. 333). Throughout Bloomsbury's writings there are relations of picture and text that should be noticed. And, of course, the 500 or so works that the Hogarth Press published are potentially relevant to the writings of their publishers. In this way Katherine Mansfield, Middleton Murry, T. S. Eliot, Robert Graves, Herbert Read, John Crowe Ransom, Conrad Aiken, Edith Sitwell, Edwin Muir, Gertrude Stein, H. G. Wells, Christopher Isherwood and C. Day Lewis, among many others, became part of Bloomsbury's literary history, as did translations of Tolstoy, Dostoevsky, Chekhov, Rilke and above all Freud, whose more rational and moral psychology was preferred to Jung's.

The interrelations of Bloomsbury's texts distinguish its literary history from other modern kinds, which are mainly concerned with single authors, movements or genres. But the Group's literary history has also to do with these, for Bloomsbury is itself an interacting part of modern English literature. This becomes clearer when Bloomsbury's texts are examined in their chronological sequence.

V

To describe Bloomsbury's texts in their temporal order is to go against Bloomsbury's own inclinations. 'Time, all the way through, is to be our enemy', wrote Forster in *Aspects of the Novel*, and most of Bloomsbury would have agreed with his formalistic dictum, 'History develops, Art stands still' (pp. 5, 13). The historian of literature, Lytton Strachey said in an early essay, 'is little more than a historian of exploded reputations. . . . His business is with the succeeding ages of men, not with all time . . .' (*BC*, p. 139). Yet Strachey's first book was actually a literary history. So was Virginia Woolf's last projected one; in some ways she was more of a formalist than Forster, yet she knew there was no escaping history for women writers.

When Bloomsbury's texts are looked at through 'the succeeding ages' of men and women, it is possible to describe not only how they developed in relation to one another but also how they were connected with contemporary events, including the publication of other works. Nor do the ages of Bloomsbury have to be imposed by the literary historian. The 'periodisation' of Bloomsbury's early literary history divides quite simply into Victorian and Edwardian phases because of the way the personal lives of the Group intersected with the historical changes of their time. *Victorian Bloomsbury* begins with the intellectual and familial origins of Bloomsbury and then examines the Cambridge literary and philosophical education that so influenced the Group, including Virginia Woolf, whose higher education took place in the library of the eminent Victorian man of letters who happened to be her father. Bloomsbury's earliest, often unpublished writings and later autobiographical recollections are used wherever possible to reflect their Victorian experience. Between Bloomsbury's coming of age around the turn of the century and the start of the First World War lies the period of time usually identified as Edwardian. The literary beginnings of Old Bloomsbury during these years are diffuse but illuminating, and they include all but one of Forster's novels, Leonard Woolf's two novels, Virginia Woolf's first novel, Desmond MacCarthy's Court Theatre drama criticism, Lytton Strachey's introduction to French literature, Clive Bell's most influential book, *Art*, and the early literary journalism of Virginia Woolf and Strachey (not to mention his unpublished poems and plays). Among the historical issues that affected Bloomsbury's writing during their Edwardian years were anti-imperialism, women's suffrage and post-impressionism.

The subsequent literary development of Bloomsbury includes most of the novels, biographies, essays and lectures on which their reputations rest, but, without a detailed knowledge of Bloomsbury's ante-bellum literary history, the illuminating interrelations of these later texts as well as their connections with other modern writing cannot be thoroughly understood. For example, in what Virginia Woolf liked to think of as Georgian Bloomsbury she and Lytton Strachey published works displaying their respective but interrelated revolts against Victorian and Edwardian fiction and biography. Lady Ottoline Morrell's Garsington and the founding of the Hogarth Press also brought Bloomsbury into relation with such basic modernist works as *Women in Love*, *Ulysses* and *The Waste Land*, and their responses to them were conditioned by Old Bloomsbury values. In the 1920s

Forster and Virginia Woolf wrote what are considered to be their major works, whose interrelatedness derives in an important degree from Edwardian and even Victorian associations. And it was during the twenties that the Apostles Desmond MacCarthy and Leonard Woolf became competing literary editors of the *New Statesman* and the *Nation* (which Keynes controlled). In the 1930s Bloomsbury attracted increasing attention. The deaths of Strachey and Fry led to the reconsideration of their careers, while the literary and political significance of Forster and Virginia Woolf for younger writers began to be more apparent. Keynes became a world figure, which drew attention to the Bloomsbury values he had been expressing in various essays; Desmond MacCarthy, who had first established himself as an Edwardian drama critic, succeeded Edmund Gosse on *The Sunday Times* to become the most influential newspaper critic of the day. MacCarthy continued to write actively through the 1940s, Forster through the 1950s, Leonard Woolf through the 1960s, and the posthumous publication of various editions of Bloomsbury novels, essays, memoirs, letters and diaries, which has proceeded through all the Group's centenaries, continues to reveal the connections between Bloomsbury's early and later literary history.

VI

The justification for such a detailed study of the early literary history of a group whose writings now span almost a century depends finally on both extrinsic and intrinsic considerations. Extrinsically, *Victorian Bloomsbury* and its sequel *Edwardian Bloomsbury* appear warranted by the Group's relevance to modern English literary and cultural history. We are well into the third generation of the twentieth century, yet with a very few exceptions there are still no thorough literary histories of the time. Modern literary study continues to exhibit what Roman Jakobson has diagnosed as a 'contiguity disorder'. Our literary studies are preoccupied with what he calls the metaphoric pole of verbal process – with the similitudes of literature; the metonymic pole of contiguity, of spatial and temporal context, remains unattractive (Jakobson, pp. 81–2). Most of the modern contextual studies of literature have been critical biographies. The theory of their literary history has been of the great-man variety: the earlier twentieth century is called the age of Joyce or Lawrence, Eliot or Pound. (Even a great-women theory of literary history would be an improvement on these simplifications: the failure of historians and anthologists of modernism to recognise until quite recently the movement for the emancipation of women as a fundamental characteristic of modernism shows what can happen when historical contexts are ignored.) The Bloomsbury Group is a good place for metonymic literary study. The way their texts can be ordered in space and time brings out the contiguities so important to the comprehensive interpretation of them. The fact that prose was their medium reinforces the metonymic character of the Group's writings, including Virginia Woolf's. The discontiguous similarities must also be brought out, of course, and here the usefulness of having a group of works to compare becomes apparent.

The density of the Bloomsbury Group's interrelations and the scope of their connections with English culture make their extended literary history an invaluable part of twentieth-century literary history. Because we can now know so much about the lives and works of the Group through its texts, we can also learn much, directly and indirectly, about other writings of the time, including those of the great men that most of our literary history has so far been organised around. But the literary history of Bloomsbury is not a microcosm of the history of modern English literature: without poetry, it could not be. Here again, however, contiguities are needed as well as analogies, and Bloomsbury's writings connect at innumerable points with the poetic history of its time.

Intrinsically, the justification of Bloomsbury's early literary history must rest largely on the worth of their later creative achievement. Good literary history is not just the history of masterpieces, but it ought to be more than the history of exploded reputations. Ultimately the value of a literary history of the Bloomsbury Group may depend upon our response to certain kinds of value aesthetically embodied in their texts. Bloomsbury's writing combines two broadly different clusters of value, one of which is usually sacrificed to the other in much modern literature. The terms for these kinds of value are necessarily vague, but one of them could be identified as rational. It can be recognised by a profound belief in truth, analysis, pluralism, toleration, criticism, individualism, egalitarianism and secularism. The other cluster of values is harder to label, but it has to do with the visionary. It is to be discovered in an equally profound faith in intuition, imagination, synthesis, ideality, love, art, beauty, mysticism and reverence. How these two different types of value complement each other in Bloomsbury's writing can be seen in some of their most familiar texts – Virginia Woolf's *A Room of One's Own* and *To the Lighthouse*, Forster's *A Passage to India* and 'What I Believe'. They also appear in such diverse works as Strachey's *Eminent Victorians*, Fry's *Vision and Design*, Clive Bell's *Civilization*, Keynes's 'My Early Beliefs', and Leonard Woolf's *Sowing*.

The ways in which these two kinds of value complete each other in Bloomsbury's literary history allow us to read their work as we can read the work of very few of their contemporaries, without finding our responses inhibited by the presence of the positivistic or authoritarian attitudes that appear when only one of these types of value is asserted. But, in order to read Bloomsbury's writing well, it is necessary to accept a wide notion of what a Bloomsbury literary text is, to see the ways in which these texts can be interrelated, and to understand the historical sequence in which they developed. Then we may be able to interpret both the rational and visionary significance of Bloomsbury writing.

Part One
Origins

1 Intellectual Backgrounds

I

Bloomsbury was born and bred Victorian. The rational and visionary significance of the Group's writing has its origins in Victorian family, school and university experience. The Group's literary history begins with this experience, particularly as it is reflected in their autobiographical texts. But the Group's Victorian upbringing and education were moulded by certain intellectual attitudes that need to be described first, and here intellectual and literary history are not easily separable. Bloomsbury's writings in all their forms are related in important ways to Victorian beliefs about religion, philosophy, politics and art. Therefore the literary history of Bloomsbury is, among other things, the story of how their writings transmuted these beliefs into modern convictions about ultimate reality, knowledge, society and value. Of course there were other crucial sources, in French, Russian, American and especially eighteenth- and early-nineteenth-century English culture – sources which obviously influenced Victorian culture too – but in the literary history of Bloomsbury it is Victorian evangelicalism, utilitarianism, liberalism and aestheticism out of which the Group's habits of thought and feeling grow.

None of these terms is very precise. All need considerable qualification before they can be used to describe the strands of religious, philosophical, political and artistic thought that constitute Bloomsbury's intellectual backgrounds.

II

'Our religion', wrote John Maynard Keynes in the celebrated memoir of his early beliefs, 'closely followed the English puritan tradition of being chiefly concerned with the salvation of our own

21

souls.' By religion Keynes meant 'one's attitude towards oneself
and the ultimate', as distinguished from morals, which had to do
with 'one's attitude towards the outside world and the intermediate' (*CW*, x 436–7). This distinction is an important and
controversial one in Bloomsbury's history; it shows just how far
Bloomsbury moved from its Victorian origins. The English
puritan tradition was certainly present in Keynes's own background, for his grandfather had been a minister in Bunyan's
church. The puritan tradition in which Keynes locates Bloomsbury is essentially evangelical puritanism. But, in its extended
sense, the tradition can also be applied to the Hebraism of
Bloomsbury's most puritanical member, Leonard Woolf. But
Bloomsbury's puritan context is most manifest in two remarkable religious groups to which a number of Bloomsbury's ancestors belonged: the Clapham Sect and the Society of Friends.

Both E. M. Forster and Virginia Woolf had great-grand-
fathers who were active members of that early-nineteenth-
century upper-middle-class collectivity of reforming Anglican
evangelicals whose undying achievement was the abolition
of slavery in the British Empire, and whose revolutionary
methods of organising social dissent through their writings and
public meetings were radically influential. Forster's description
of Clapham could almost serve as a definition of Bloomsbury: 'It
was not a closed sainthood, there were no entry tests, no esoteric
hush-hush, but the members of it shared so many interests that
they hung together, and lived as near to each other as they could'
(*MT*, p. 35). Forster was critical of Clapham because it did not
go on to interest itself in the abolition of industrial slavery and
because its religious impulses were more moral than mystical.
Again this helps to define the distance between Clapham and
Bloomsbury.

The evangelical character of the Clapham Sect was an essential aspect of its influence. G. M. Young has well described the
Victorian heritage of evangelicalism in words that illuminate its
relation to Bloomsbury:

> On one of its sides, Victorian history is the story of the English
> mind employing the energy imparted by Evangelical convic-
> tion to rid itself of the restraints which Evangelicalism had laid
> on the senses and the intellect; on amusement, enjoyment, art;
> on curiosity, on criticism, on science.   (Young, p. 5)

In Bloomsbury this riddance was continued, as the Group divested itself of the restraints that the Victorians had maintained on religious, ethical, political and artistic ideas. Among the characteristics of the Group that they appear to have inherited from their evangelical forebears, however, were outspoken truth-telling, social nonconformity, a quest for moral and aesthetic salvation, self-reliance on intuitive ideals, and a contempt for luxury.

The Quakers, with their legacy of the inner light, pacifism, simplicity, asceticism, nonconformity, a strong sense of group identity and perhaps also a sense of persecution, were present in Bloomsbury's religious background through the family of Roger Fry. After G. E. Moore (whose mother had been a Quaker), Fry was the most important influence on Bloomsbury's early intellectual development, and the intuitive formalism, the pacifism, the group feeling and the mysticism of various members of Bloomsbury suggest connections with Quakerism, though Fry himself was not a believer or an observer. But Fry's relatives were not the only Victorian Quakers among the families of Bloomsbury. The sister of that puritan agnostic Leslie Stephen was a widely read Quaker author at the end of the nineteenth century. (Women were allowed to be more prominent and effective among Quakers than in Clapham.) The subtitle of one of Caroline Emelia Stephen's books, 'Thoughts on the Central Radiance', could describe the mystical meditations in some of Virginia Woolf's fiction. Her aunt called her religious belief 'rational mysticism', a phrase that fits the mystical experiences in her niece's novels and in Forster's as well. But there were also fundamental differences here: Caroline Emelia Stephen's mysticism is introvertive, arising from an inner light, whereas the sources of the visionary moments that Mrs Dalloway, Mrs Ramsay, and even Mrs Moore experience are extrovertive, coming from external nature.[1]

For all the significance of evangelicalism in the intellectual origins of Bloomsbury, it must not be forgotten that they sought a secular salvation. Almost all the members were not just Victorian agnostics, like a number of their fathers and mothers, but modern atheists. It has been ·suggested that Bloomsbury rejected the evangelical notion of original sin for an eighteenth-century faith in reason and the perfectibility of man (Annan, *Stephen*, p. 161). But we do not have to return to the eighteenth century for the ethical antecedents of Bloomsbury's transformation of evangelical puritanism. They are clearly present in the nineteenth-century utilitarianism that Bloomsbury adapted.

III

The importance of utilitarianism in the philosophical backgrounds of the Bloomsbury Group has generally been overlooked. Bentham and his followers formed a group very different from the Clapham Sect or the Society of Friends, yet it was a group whose ideas did more than either of them to form the minds of Bloomsbury. For readers of English literature the writings of Dickens and Carlyle have often discredited one of the most influential, liberating modern moral theories. The utilitarian ethical environment which the Keyneses, the Stephens and the Stracheys grew up in was created not so much by Bentham's hedonistic calculus as by John Stuart Mill's reconciliation of the values of Bentham's thought with those of Wordsworth and Coleridge. Leslie Stephen and John Neville Keynes were utilitarian philosophers. And Moore's *Principia Ethica* together with his later *Ethics* are works of moral philosophy belonging to the utilitarian tradition, though they also owe something to the Victorian intuitional moralists. Moore, John Neville Keynes and the Cambridge Apostles were all strongly influenced by Henry Sidgwick, whose achievement as an ethical thinker may be second only to Mill's in the Victorian period. Through the work of Mill, Sidgwick, Stephen, Keynes and finally Moore, the rationality of utilitarianism – its valuing of common sense and clarity, its eschewing of metaphysics and mysticism – became part of Bloomsbury's way of thought.

Yet utilitarianism in Bloomsbury underwent a transformation almost as extensive as its evangelicalism. It was the utilitarianism, in fact, that fundamentally changed the evangelicalism. Bloomsbury retained one of the two basic tenets of Victorian utilitarianism but not the other. Moore called one of his chapters in *Ethics* 'Results the Test of Right and Wrong', and this concisely summarises what has been called the 'consequentialism' that Moore and Bloomsbury retained from utilitarianism (Braithwaite, p. 243). 'Consequentialism' is a more exact, if inelegant, term than 'utilitarianism' to describe Bloomsbury's nineteenth-century ethical heritage. But Moore and his disciples were all agreed in rejecting Bentham's calculus of pleasure and pain. In place of the hedonistic ends of Bentham's and Mill's ethics, Moore substituted a plurality of goods together with an intuitional concept of good as an indefinable property. This, of course, affected utilitarian calculations: good as an indefinable rather than a hedonistic property does not lend itself in the same way to calculations of the greatest good for the greatest number.

Bloomsbury's consequentialism is rooted in the essential distinction of *Principia Ethica* between good as a means and good as an end in itself. The distinction is engrained in the Group's thinking and writing. With it Strachey and others were able to reduce those large Victorian notions of duty and virtue to their proper size as matters having to do with the right means to good ends. And Virginia Woolf would use the distinction to argue in her feminist criticism that value in women's work must not be confined to the instrumental; as she wrote at the end of *A Room of One's Own*, 'Do not dream of influencing other people, I would say, if I knew how to make it sound exalted. Think of things in themselves' (p. 167). The language here and elsewhere in Bloomsbury is paradoxically Kantian; the distinction between means to ends and ends in themselves turns finally into one between appearance and reality.

The presence of words relating to means and ends in the titles of various Bloomsbury works, sometimes expressed in metaphors of travel, shows how significant Moore's means–ends analysis of ethics was for Bloomsbury's work. Think of *The Longest Journey*, *Howards End*, *Landmarks in French Literature*, *The Voyage Out*, *The Economic Consequences of the Peace*, *A Passage to India*, *To the Lighthouse*, *Landmarks in Nineteenth-Century Painting* or *The Journey Not the Arrival Matters*. The basic distinction in *Principia Ethica* between instrumental and intrinsic value is probably more important for an understanding of Bloomsbury's ethics than the book's Ideals of aesthetic enjoyments and personal relations.

Keynes thought Bloomsbury forsook Moore's ethical means for his ends, but Leonard Woolf and others have effectively denied this (LW/*S*, pp. 144ff.; Braithwaite, pp. 237–46). Keynes was nevertheless right when he pointed to the presence of neo-Platonism in Moore's thought and in Bloomsbury's (*CW*, x 436ff.). The only philosophical tradition comparable to utilitarianism in the intellectual backgrounds of Bloomsbury is

Platonism. (Virginia Woolf's godfather James Russell Lowell described Emerson as a 'Plotinus Montaigne' (p. 39); Moore as interpreted by Bloomsbury might be described as a Platonic Mill.) The centre of value in Bloomsbury's literary texts is ultimately an intuitive awareness of an unanalysable good. And this good brought back into Bloomsbury's ethics something of the mysticism, if not the metaphysics, that the Group's utilitarianism excluded.

The contemplative life that Bloomsbury so valued was not particularly admired in the active ethics of the utilitarians. This brings us to the Victorian sources of Bloomsbury's political convictions. But before sketching them it is important to note that there was an essential epistemological dimension to the philosophical sources of Bloomsbury's ethics. Utilitarianism often combined with an empirical philosophy of mind from which Bloomsbury's ideas about the nature of consciousness are descended. The philosophical Realism of G. E. Moore and Bertrand Russell rejected British and German (but not necessarily Greek) Idealism and substantially changed the theory of knowledge of Mill and others. Bloomsbury's epistemological assumptions were derived from this philosophical Realism, with its dualistic analyses of perception into acts and objects of consciousness. Forster is clearly a philosophical Realist in his fiction. In the writings of Virginia Woolf the representation of states of mind and their shifting sense- and self-perceptions belong to a tradition of philosophical psychology that focused on the associations of sense-experience. It is a tradition that connects, among others, Locke, Hume, Mill and William James – a tradition evident in Virginia Woolf's so-called stream-of-consciousness techniques and with links to continental phenomenology.[2] This philosophical context also helped to make Freud's psychology more available to Bloomsbury.

IV

The importance of Bloomsbury's utilitarianism has not been much remarked upon, perhaps because it has been considered part of the Group's liberalism – and everyone knows that Bloomsbury was liberal. Liberalism is a political and economic philosophy often accompanied by utilitarian ethics. Its intellec-

tual spirit has been well described in various essays by Bloomsbury's most famous liberal, John Maynard Keynes. His account,
for example, of the intellectual tradition of Malthus's work is also
an account of the liberal background of Bloomsbury's work:

> It is profoundly in the English tradition of humane science – in
> that tradition of Scotch and English thought, in which there
> has been, I think, an extraordinary continuity of *feeling*, if I
> may so express it, from the eighteenth century to the present
> time – the tradition which is suggested by the names of Locke,
> Hume, Adam Smith, Paley, Bentham, Darwin, and Mill, a
> tradition marked by a love of truth and a most noble lucidity,
> by a prosaic sanity free from sentiment or metaphysic, and by
> an immense disinterestedness and public spirit. There is a
> continuity in these writings, not only of feeling, but of actual
> matter.' (*CW*, x 86)

The continuity of feeling and matter in liberalism, as distinct
from utilitarianism, centres around the values and requirements
of individualism, but here the political and economic aspects of
liberalism can become confused. The rational individualism of
political liberalism consorts with economic philosophies ranging
from *laissez-faire* capitalism to socialism. In trying to identify
which strain of liberalism affected the formation of Bloomsbury's
political convictions, the best touchstone again is the work of
John Stuart Mill. Bloomsbury came to change Mill's liberalism
almost as much as its inherited Victorian religious and
philosophical beliefs. The direction of the change was socialist
rather than conservative, though not Marxist.[3] Keynes again
illustrates this development of Bloomsbury's liberalism; in 1926
he succinctly defined 'the political problem of mankind' as
having 'to combine three things: economic efficiency, social
justice, and individual liberty' (*CW*, ix 311).

That ideal combination was the basis for Leonard Woolf's,
Lytton Strachey's and E. M. Forster's condemnations of the
imperialism that nineteenth-century liberalism had helped to
foster. Strachey and Forster also used liberal assumptions to
argue for a *laissez-faire* sexuality. And in the writings of Virginia
Woolf the two come together in her recurrent exposure of sexual
imperialism. Virginia Woolf's feminism is liberal in origin. It is
not a coincidence that the most influential feminist work written

is still probably John Stuart Mill's *The Subjection of Women*. But in
her awareness that the liberty of the individual must be pro-
tected from the encroachments of patriarchal institutions, be
they families or armies, Virginia Woolf is also a very modern
feminist.

   Mill's liberalism influenced Bloomsbury not only because he
applied the principles of individual liberty and critical toleration
more widely than any other liberal thinker, but also because he
recognised some of the emotional and imaginative shortcomings
of nineteenth-century utilitarianism and liberalism. The liberal
tradition's continuity of feeling that Keynes honours also produced philistinism. Individual liberty was a means, not an end in
itself, and the inadequacy of liberalism's ends is a Bloomsbury
theme that goes back to Matthew Arnold as well as Mill. Arnold
does not belong to Keynes's tradition of humane science, yet he
is a significant Victorian influence on Bloomsbury, though not as
important as Mill.

   In Bloomsbury, Arnold's as well as Mill's criticisms of liberalism are most apparent in the fiction and criticism of E. M.
Forster. Liberal democracy, said Forster in his well-known
essay, deserved two cheers because its values were various and
because it allowed criticism; only love got three cheers, and it
was a private as well as an artistic, but not a political, state
(*2CD*, pp. 65–73). Forster is Arnoldian in his realisation of the
lack of coherence and fraternity in liberalism that so bothered
such unliberal critics of Mill as Carlyle and that other Stephen,
Sir James Fitzjames Stephen. For Forster and Bloomsbury,
social cohesion lay not in patriarchies but in tolerant co-
operation, personal relations and aesthetic experience. Art, said
Forster in another famous essay, was 'the one orderly product
which our muddling race has produced' (*2CD*, p. 90). The title
of that essay was 'Art for Art's Sake', and this brings us to the
last of the Victorian backgrounds of Bloomsbury's intellectual
assumptions.

                                    V

Aestheticism requires even more explanation and qualification
than evangelicalism, utilitarianism or liberalism in the intellectual origins of Bloomsbury. Yet no other term conveniently sums

up the nineteenth century's concern with the value of art, a concern so important in the development of the Group. It has been widely assumed that Bloomsbury's view of art as an autonomous activity of very great potential value was basically a modern extension of the *fin-de-siècle* aestheticism of Walter Pater in particular, but also of Swinburne, Wilde, Whistler, Symonds, Beerbohm and other English aesthetes. There are certainly important connections between the writing of these men and Bloomsbury, but there were other, equally influential sources, which Bloomsbury transformed as thoroughly as they modified their religious, philosophical and political inheritance.

Bloomsbury's aestheticism, like so many aspects of modernism, is Romantic in origin, of course. The formalistic, autotelic aesthetics of Roger Fry and Clive Bell go back to Kant's *Critique of Judgement*, which separated disinterested aesthetic experience from the exigencies of practical and pure reasons. Bell's influential doctine of significant form also clearly owes something not just to Moore's ethics but also to Plato's theory of forms: the significant form of a work of art is an indefinable, intuited Platonic idea behind the representational surface. In the later nineteenth century the direct and indirect sources of Bloomsbury's ideas about art appear to be principally French. The Group's admiration of French culture's devotion to art is summarised by Lytton Strachey at the end of his first book, *Landmarks of French Literature*:

> The one high principle which, through so many generations, has guided like a star the writers of France is the principle of deliberation, of intention, of a conscious search for ordered beauty; an unwavering, an indomitable pursuit of the endless glories of art.   (p. 247)

Even more influential on Bloomsbury's aestheticism than French literature was French painting. The close association of the arts of writing and painting is one of the primary characteristics of the Bloomsbury Group. In Virginia Woolf's work, though not in Forster's, art approached the condition of painting rather than, as Pater thought, of music. When Virginia Woolf stated in her modernist manifesto 'Mr Bennett and Mrs Brown' that 'on or about December, 1910, human character changed',[4] and therefore the novel changed, she was alluding with that very

specific dating to Roger Fry's first post-impressionist exhibition
(*CE*, I 320). Virginia Woolf's impressionism has been widely
noted, but it has not been sufficiently recognised that her mature
work was post-impressionist in being both visionary and
designed.

The source usually given for Virginia Woolf's impressionism
is Walter Pater's *The Renaissance*. His emphasis on knowing one's
impression as it really is, on living for moments of aesthetic
ecstasy, has illuminated her work for many readers. Pater's great
accomplishment, along with Swinburne's and the Pre-
Raphaelites', has been described as the purifying of Ruskin's aesthetics by ridding it of moral bias (Bloom, pp. xxx–i). This
aesthetic purification was continued by Bloomsbury, but it is an
oversimplification to locate the origins of the Group's artistic
convictions only or even mainly in the work of Pater and other
English aesthetes.[5] Bloomsbury's aesthetics developed out of
puritan, utilitarian Cambridge rather than Anglo-/Roman
Catholic Idealist Oxford. Pater's sceptical, even solipsistic, epistemology, and the Idealist implications of Wilde's theory that
nature imitates art were refuted for Bloomsbury by the
common-sense philosophical realism of Moore, which gave to
Bloomsbury's aesthetics a solidly logical underpinning. It is true
that Moore's ethics resembles Pater's aesthetics in several
respects: both relied upon an intuitional ideal, valued aesthetic
experience for its own sake, thought of that experience primarily
in terms of perception, and were unconcerned with its temporal
dimensions. But there is a crucial difference between Pater's
aesthetic attitude and Moore's – a difference that clearly limits
the aestheticism of Pater and others for Bloomsbury.

Moore's Ideal in *Principia Ethica* was twofold not single: personal relations were at least as important as aesthetic experience
– and love was more important. In Bloomsbury's aesthetics,
therefore, love was not subsumed under art. In his memoir on his
early beliefs Keynes wrote that he and his friends at Cambridge
had sterilised human experience by classifying it as aesthetic
experience. There is little conformation of this in Bloomsbury's
Cambridge writings; still, Keynes reveals here how aware later
Bloomsbury was of the dangers of aestheticism. Forster in his
fiction and essays is vigilantly critical of the aestheticising of love
that characterised the undeveloped heart of a certain kind of
English man or woman. Yet, Forster, Strachey and, in her

different way, Virginia Woolf clearly do continue the aesthetes' use of their art as a weapon of social revolt against the sexual authoritarianism of their time. Sex and art were combined in the martyrdom of Oscar Wilde, and the lesson was not lost on Bloomsbury.

The use of the moment in the novels of Forster and Virginia Woolf is also quite different from the Paterian moment in the conclusion to *The Renaissance*. Its function, when ecstatic, is not simply an end in itself but also a means to the enhancement of ordinary daily experience for Bloomsbury. And sometimes in Bloomsbury's novels the structured moments of vision were desolating. ('Moments of Vision' was a phrase Virginia Woolf took from a poet much admired in Bloomsbury, Thomas Hardy – *D*, III 105.) Yet there is a difference in tone, mood and style between Bloomsbury's texts and those of the Victorian aesthetes. Traces of *Weltschmerz* can be found in Strachey's or Leonard Woolf's writings, but Bloomsbury's pessimism is tougher, more modern, than the tender-minded religious glooms of Pater or Swinburne. 'Modern literature,' wrote Virginia Woolf in 1927, 'which had grown a little sultry and scented with Oscar Wilde and Walter Pater, revived instantly from her nineteenth-century languor when Samuel Butler and Bernard Shaw began to burn their feathers and apply their salts to her nose' (*CE*, II 223). There is, however, a kinship between the well-made essays of Strachey, Forster, Bell, Keynes, MacCarthy and Virginia Woolf and those not just of Macaulay, Arnold and Stephen, but of Pater, Wilde and especially Beerbohm too. But the greatest writer of prose at the end of the nineteenth century in England was Henry James. His relationship to French and Victorian aestheticism is, like everything else about him, complex. If one is looking for anxieties of influence among the novelists and critics of the Bloomsbury Group, he is surely a most important precursor. James's moral aestheticism is finally the best clue, in both its achievements and its limitations, to Bloomsbury's literary aestheticism.

Even so, the influence of Victorian aestheticism on the Group's ideas about the purpose and value of art cannot truthfully be reduced to the influence of one writer. Roger Fry, the chief source of Bloomsbury's aesthetics, studied painting in Italy and France in the 1890s and knew such aesthetes as John Addington Symonds. The ideas of William Morris were also influential on his development, as the Omega Workshops disclose, and behind Morris is the complex influence of Ruskin, which impinges on Bloomsbury in a number of places, the last being the Group's enthusiasm for Proust. Virginia Woolf's father had an anaesthetised aesthetic sense, but through her mother she was connected to the world of the Pre-Raphaelites. And in her own relationships she associated with the families of Victorian aesthetes: Pater's sister began teaching her Greek, and Symonds's daughter may have been her first love.

In *Art* Clive Bell thanked both the aesthetes and the French impressionists for awakening the aesthetic conscience dormant since before the Renaissance. They both taught that the significance of a work of art lay in itself and not in the external world (p. 183). Unlike Fry, Bell did not believe this significance held true for literary works of art because words had meanings that paint did not. Fry argued for the unity of the arts, and thought the first fruitful work in aesthetics had been done by Tolstoy. For all the perversity of *What Is Art?*, its expressive, emotive, socially aware aesthetics permanently influenced Bloomsbury's aesthetics. Fry and Bell agreed, however, with the utterly un-Tolstoyan literary formalism expressed by A. C. Bradley in his 1901 inaugural lecture as the Oxford Professor of Poetry. 'Poetry for Poetry's Sake' is perhaps the best statement of the transformation that Victorian aestheticism underwent in the literary history of Bloomsbury. In some respects Bradley was a latter-day representative of the Oxford aesthetic tradition; his brother was the famous Oxford Idealist, and the lecture cites Arnold and Pater in the course of its argument. But that argument contains an analysis of art for art's sake that carefully qualifies it. Bradley distinguishes between two meanings of the phrase: art as an end in itself, and art as 'the whole or supreme end of human life' (p. 5). Forster made the same distinction nearly half a century later and joined Bradley in upholding the first and completely rejecting the second. Here is the most basic difference in doctrine between Bloomsbury and the aesthetes. Bradley does not talk about love, but it was love that ultimately restricted the role of art in Bloomsbury. Bradley went on in his lecture to analyse what he called heresies of separable form and content, arguing that in evaluating poetry the recognition of both aspects, as he called them, are necessary, 'So that what you apprehend may be called indifferently an expressed meaning or a significant form' (p. 19). It is interesting, in the light of how this last phrase became famous as a formalist theory of painting, that it was first used as a description of literature.

VI

Every man naturally exaggerates the share of his education due to himself. He fancies he has made a wonderful improvement upon his father's views, perhaps by reversing the improvement made by the father on the grandfather's. He does not see, what is plain enough to a more distant generation, that in reality each generation is most closely bound to its nearest predecessors. (L. Stephen, *Hours*, II 214)

The religious, philosophical, political and artistic backgrounds of Bloomsbury's convictions can be resolved into four very general traditions of Western thought. The ultimate origins of the Group's religious ideas were Protestant, not Catholic. Empiricism rather than rationalism was their primary philosophical tradition. They were democratic not authoritarian in their fundamental political assumptions. And they were more romantic than classical in their basic aesthetic attitudes.

The usefulness of such generalising is to be found in the outline this chapter offers of how these traditions descended to Bloomsbury through the Victorian period. Leslie Stephen's observations on the influence of the previous generation apply to the generation that succeeded his own. Bloomsbury was closely bound by its inherited evangelicalism, utilitarianism, liberalism and aestheticism, though each of these intellectual traditions was transformed in the Group's development. They modified Victorian evangelicalism with atheism and utilitarianism with Platonism; their liberalism was qualified by pacifism and their aestheticism by love. To understand the intellectual backgrounds of Bloomsbury, it is essential to recognise each of these different traditions as well as the changes that were made in them.

But it is even more important to be aware of how the evangelical, utilitarian, liberal and aesthetic origins interacted in Bloomsbury – of how it is possible to speak, for example, of the evangelicalism of liberals or the aestheticism of utilitarians. The

strongest claim that can be made for the significance of Bloomsbury's intellectual sources is that the ignoring of any one of them
will affect our understanding of the others and therefore of the
whole that the intellectual origins of Bloomsbury's literary history comprise.

To be more specific about the intellectual influences that
shaped the literary history of Bloomsbury, it is necessary to turn
to the intellectual historian and literary biographer who was
Bloomsbury's single most influential Victorian predecessor, Leslie Stephen himself. Then, in the chapter on Bloomsbury's
literary visions of family and school life that follows, Leslie
Stephen's remarks on generational influence will have to be
modified: the improvements made upon the views of Bloomsbury's mothers and grandmothers will have to be included along
with those of the fathers and grandfathers. That Bloomsbury's
intellectual origins were almost entirely masculine is, of course,
part of the situation to which the movement for the emancipation
of women called attention.

2 Leslie Stephen

I

Leslie Stephen has been described by his grandson as 'in a sense the father of Bloomsbury' (Q. Bell, *Bloomsbury*, pl. facing p. 32). He was not only the actual father of the author and the painter who formed Bloomsbury's nucleus; he was also an eminent Victorian man of letters whose moral philosophy, intellectual histories, literary criticism and biographies reveal, when compared with Bloomsbury's writings, many of the fundamental continuities and discontinuities between nineteenth- and twentieth-century English literature.

T. S. Eliot regarded Virginia Woolf as having 'a kind of hereditary position in English letters' ('VW', p. 203), and Leonard Woolf, another outsider, recalled how her father's talk 'enabled one to catch a last glimpse of that incredibly ancient London literary world of ladies and gentlemen which went right back to Thackeray and Dickens, to Mr and Mrs Carlyle, to Mill and Huxley' ('Coming', p. 34). As editor of the *Cornhill* Stephen first published Henry James's *Daisy Miller*, *Washington Square* and 'An International Episode', Thomas Hardy's *Far from the Madding Crowd* (slightly bowdlerised) and *The Hand of Ethelberta* (though his editorial timidity lost his magazine *The Return of the Native*), as well as essays by Stephen himself, Matthew Arnold, Robert Louis Stevenson and John Addington Symonds, and poetry by Browning, Meredith and Henley (Maurer, pp. 67–95). Stephen's first wife was a daughter of Thackeray. James Russell Lowell stood as an agnostic equivalent of godfather to Virginia.[1] Meredith portrayed Stephen as the austere Vernon Whitford – 'Phoebus Apollo turned fasting friar' – the least egoistic of the characters in *The Egoist*. And Thomas Hardy compared him in a poem to the Shreckhorn, which Stephen was the first to climb, finding the mountain like Stephen's personality 'In its quaint glooms, keen lights, and rugged trim' (*Poems*, p. 322).

It is the glooms more than the lights or the trim that mark the image of Stephen's personality for readers who know him only through his daughter's often misinterpreted portrait of Mr Ramsay in *To the Lighthouse*, from her recollections in 'A Sketch of the Past', or through the *Mausoleum Book*, the grief-stricken domestic autobiography that Stephen wrote for his children after the death of his second wife. Almost no one mentions that his daughter's first portrait of him, in F. W. Maitland's *The Life and Letters of Leslie Stephen*, begins with the recollection of the 'perfectly equal companionship' between him and his children (p. 474). Stephen's later overwhelming fatherhood is part of the Victorian family life that will be described through Bloomsbury's memoirs in the next chapter. But in the special case of Leslie Stephen it is important to observe the distinctions Virginia Woolf carefully made in the recently recovered revised draft of 'A Sketch of the Past', which includes a hitherto unknown account of Stephen.[2] In articulating her ambivalent feelings toward her father at the end of her life, Virginia Woolf distinguished three kinds of fathers in him: there was 'the writer father', whom she could always get a critical hold of through his books; 'the sociable father', whom she never really knew; and 'the tyrant father', from whom she and Vanessa suffered for seven years. The tyrant father has dominated the discussions of Stephen's influence on his daughter, yet for her and for Bloomsbury the most enduring father was the one always present through his books. 'A Sketch of the Past', because it was about the past, concentrates less on Leslie Stephen as a writer – 'the man's Leslie Stephen' Virginia Woolf called him – and more on the tyrant who was the daughters' Leslie Stephen. Yet even there, in the revised draft, Virginia Woolf makes some important observations about the significance of her father's criticism for her own, as we shall see. Leslie Stephen's influence on Virginia Woolf cannot be properly understood apart from those writings of his that she could approach directly, all her life, without the mediations of memory. After all, she was the writer father's writer daughter.

Since the rediscovery of Virginia Woolf as a major modernist, little attention has been paid to her literary and intellectual heritage by the interrelated kinds of proliferating criticism devoted to her. Formalist analyses of her fiction continue to be mainly synchronic in their assumptions; psychological investigations, for all their biographical scrutiny, take place in largely ahistorical contexts; and feminist criticism for the most part shuns the principal traditions of literature and ideas in which she developed, because they were masculine. Though these critical emphases have provided valuable understanding of Virginia Woolf's art, life and thought, they have also served to diminish her achievement by treating her work as if literary and intellectual history were irrelevant to it. That the daughter of the leading Victorian intellectual and literary historian should have her writing insulated from that history by her critics is ironic. Yet understanding how Leslie Stephen's deeply ambivalent daughter responded to her father's work is not easy. The personal dimensions of 'that immensely important relationship' are likely, as she said, to queer the angle of vision (*MB*, p. 108). She did not write very much directly about her father's work, and brief comparisons of the extensive critical and biographical essays that both wrote often do not go very far beyond the kinds of generalities Max Beerbohm amusingly offered in a letter to Virginia Woolf about *The Common Reader*: 'You certainly are very like your Father. With great differences of course. What I mean is that if he had been a "Georgian" and a woman, just so would he have written' (30.xii.27, VW/pS).

Through the Bloomsbury Group, however, there is available a wider context in which at least some of the meanings of Leslie Stephen's work for his daughter's writings and those of her friends can be examined. He would have been horrified at the twist of history that made him a kind of father to that extended family of writers and artists that formed around his children early in this century. But Stephen's work influenced not only his daughter's criticism, biographies and polemics, but also the literary and historical writings of Leonard Woolf, the biographies of Lytton Strachey, the essays of Keynes, the criticism of MacCarthy, and the biographical and critical writings of Forster. The writer father was significant for Bloomsbury as a Victorian moral philosopher and historian of ideas, as a literary historian and critic, and – perhaps most important – as a

biographer. Each of these aspects of Stephen's achievement
deserves to be considered separately as part of the intellectual
backgrounds of Bloomsbury's literary history.

II

Leslie Stephen's moral philosophy permeates his literary work.
He valued literature most for its expression of ideas and its
revelation of the author's character. This intellectual and biographical interest in literature is continued in much of Bloomsbury's writing, but with differences that can be better appreciated by looking first at some of Stephen's ethical ideas.

The father of Bloomsbury began adult life as a Cambridge don
and a clergyman. He ceased to believe in God and was troubled
by the problem of evil. 'The potter has no right to be angry with
his pots', he wrote later. 'If he wanted them different, he should
have made them different. The consistent theologian must
choose between the Creator and the Judge' (*Science*, p. 267).
With his lost faith, Stephen had to resign his fellowship, so he
came to London to be a man of letters. Some years later, shortly
after the death of his mother, he decided to resign formally the
office of priest in the Church of England by signing an official
document. How symbolic for the literary history of Bloomsbury
that Stephen asked not some lawyer, philosopher or friend to
witness his signature, but a contributor to the *Cornhill*, which he
was then editing. Thus it happened that on 23 March 1875,
Thomas Hardy ceremonially witnessed Leslie Stephen's renunciation of the priesthood (F. Hardy, pp. 105–6).[3]

As an essayist in London, Stephen followed Huxley and
championed agnosticism, which for him meant that 'the natural
man can know nothing of the Divine nature' (*Apology*, p. 8). The
content and form of Stephen's essays are well described by the
title he gave to a collection of them: *Essays in Freethinking and
Plainspeaking*. These were qualities Bloomsbury valued and displayed in their writings. Though members of the Group were
atheists more than agnostics, they nevertheless cared for religious emotion more than Stephen, who seems to have experienced
it only in the mountains. Stephen's arguments for the limits of
human knowledge were familiar truths to Bloomsbury, yet
neither he nor his heirs were really sceptics. It was the scepticism

of believers about the common-sense workings of the world that he exposed in a characteristic essay (*Apology*, pp. 42–85). Stephen's writing clearly belongs to that English and Scottish tradition of humane science described by Keynes as having a continuity of feeling from Locke to Moore.

Though Stephen's loss of faith was not, apparently, a prolonged agony, his agnostic disbelief in an afterlife was sorely tried by grief. The tombstone of his father bore the inscription, 'Be strong and of a good courage; be not afraid, neither be thou dismayed: for the Lord thy God is with thee whithersoever thou goest' (L. Stephen, *Fitzjames Stephen*, p. 170). His son was strong, courageous, unafraid, but the deaths of his wives dismayed him terribly; he knew he could not know whether the Lord God was with him or not. Bloomsbury were aware they lacked the awesome energies of the Victorians, but at least they were able to accept death without the sentimental excesses of nineteenth-century grief that they grew up with. Still, there was something admirable in this grief. After reading Maitland's biography, Lytton Strachey quoted to Keynes 'one rather magnificent thing' that Stephen had written after the death of Virginia's mother (6.xii.06, JMK/pKC). Stephen wrote,

> I have often thought, in reading about Swift, for example, that the saddest of all states of mind was that in which a man regrets that he has loved because his love has brought sorrow. That is 'the sin against the Holy Ghost' – to blaspheme your best affections, which are your Holy Ghost. . . .' (Maitland, p. 430)

For Bloomsbury too, one's best affections were one's Holy Ghost.

It was Wordsworth, Stephen recorded in the *Mausoleum Book*, who taught him the transmutation of sorrow into strength (p. 71). 'The great aim of moral philosophy', he said in his well-known essay on Wordsworth's ethics, 'is to . . . end the divorce between reason and experience . . . ' (*Hours*, II 279). Wordsworth had suggested to him how this might be done through the transformation of primitive instincts into reasoned convictions. Here Stephen thought he found the beginnings of an ethical philosophy that could reconcile the great rival nineteenth-century schools of ethical thought, the utilitarians and the intuitionalists. In a book that he hoped would be his *magnum opus* Stephen tried to expound this reconciliation. In *The Science of Ethics* Stephen's sympathies are largely with the utilitarians. He considered himself a follower of Mill, who of course had also derived profound consolation from Wordsworth. 'Read Mill' was the injunction of his Cambridge friends to the unenlightened, just as 'Read Moore' was in Bloomsbury's Cambridge (L. Stephen, *Impressions*, p. 76). Stephen could not follow Wordsworth and assume there was a divine order regulating the growth of early impulses into rational understanding, but he agreed that obedience to the 'stern lawgiver' Duty was required by the change. Stephen's duty came from Darwin rather than God.

From Darwin Stephen took the idea that duty, a fundamental concept for the intuitionalists, could be fitted into utilitarianism through the idea of evolution. The individual's growth from instinct to reason resembles society's evolution, and the chief means of this change in the individual is the family. For Stephen the family is that 'immediate and primitive relation which holds men together' (*Science*, p. 128). This intuitive principle evolved from a utilitarian struggle for happiness, which illustrates how the ideas of the utilitarians and the intuitionalists could be reconciled through evolution.

Victorian and modern moral philosophers have between them pretty well demolished *The Science of Ethics*. Henry Sidgwick noted that all the problems of utilitarian ethics re-emerge in Stephen's goal of maximising society's general welfare, and furthermore, that Stephen had not offered adequate reasons for concluding that society's welfare necessarily coincides with the individual's happiness. Most relevant for Bloomsbury, Sidgwick also objected that many highly cultivated pleasures, such as aesthetic ones, have little or nothing to do with the social evolution on which Stephen based his ethical science (Sidgwick, *Methods*, pp. 471–3). G. E. Moore does not mention Stephen in *Principia Ethica*, but his attack on Herbert Spencer's evolutionary ethics applies equally to Stephen's. All that survival of the fittest ultimately means, says Moore, is 'the survival of the fittest to survive', and who knows, he adds at the end of the Victorian era of progress, whether evolution is not just a prelude to involution (*PE*, pp. 48, 57).

There is no record of anyone ever having read *The Science of Ethics* in Bloomsbury. Moore's combination of consequentialism and intuitionalism is very different from Stephen's, and Bloomsbury quite rejected Stephen's family-centred ideal. Something of the distance between Stephen's notion of family life as an immediate, primitive relation holding men together and Bloomsbury's non-monogamous idealisation of personal relations can be gauged from an essay on Godwin and Shelley in which Stephen discusses the 'anti-matrimonial theory' in Shelley's poem *Epipsychidion*. The same poem and theory that gave E. M. Forster the title and one of the organising ideas for his novel *The Longest Journey*. Stephen quoted the lines in which Shelley attacked

> that great sect
> Whose doctrine is that each one should select
> Out of the world a mistress or a friend,
> And all the rest, though fair and wise, commend
> To cold oblivion

as 'the shrill tones of a conceited propagator of flimsy crochets, proclaiming his tenets without regard to truth or propriety' (*Hours*, III 87). Stephen's own shrillness here, along with his criteria of truth and propriety, makes him remote from Bloomsbury.

Leslie Stephen's familial science of ethics also included, however, the liberal idea of individual freedom, and this connects him directly to Bloomsbury. The proprieties of personal conduct in Stephen's family and society limited one's freedom, his daughter recalled in the only essay she published on her father, 'yet if freedom means the right to think one's own thoughts and to follow one's own pursuits, then no one respected and indeed insisted upon freedom more complete, than he did' (*CE*, IV 79). (But this did not mean that sons and daughters were allowed the same amount of freedom: Stephen was not prepared to follow all the way Mill's views on the subjection of women.[4]) The liberal tradition that Leslie Stephen's work continued for Bloomsbury can be illustrated by contrasting it with his brother's writing. James Fitzjames Stephen's conservative criticism of Mill in *Liberty, Equality, Fraternity* is more widely read today than any text of Leslie's; in it Fitzjames argued that the imperfectibility and inequality of man required a cohesive society with more restrictions on the individual's liberty that Mill or Leslie Stephen allowed for.

Leslie Stephen's liberalism was also a characteristic of his

literary criticism. In 'Thoughts on Criticism by a Critic' he
argued that the critic must show a liberal toleration, though he
should not be an aesthetic sceptic (*Men, Books*, pp. 230–1). The
differences become clear here between the tradition of humane
science that links three centuries of philosophical thought and
that other tradition of literary and philosophical criticism going
back to Samuel Johnson and continuing through Coleridge to
Carlyle, Ruskin and even Matthew Arnold. Both traditions
influenced Bloomsbury, but the Group are unusual in the history
of modern English literature because their intellectual attitudes
were moulded more by the first than by the second. The differences between these traditions are not simple or absolute, however. Maitland, the great historian who wrote Stephen's biography, called his subject a Thackerayan because of his worship of
the family and his somewhat cynical attitude toward other things
(pp. 169–70). (Stephen signed a series of articles for the *Cornhill*
as 'A Cynic'.) Noel Annan, Stephen's intellectual biographer,
called him a Wordsworthian and showed how he was a Millian
and a Darwinian too (*Stephen*, pp. 92, 175ff., 198ff.). Stephen had
more respect for Carlyle as a man than for any of his contemporaries, including Mill, whom he found a little unmanly; yet
Carlyle's attacks on what he called the utilitarian 'pig philosophy' did not, Stephen drily observed, 'represent my own pre-
judices' (*Studies*, III 109). And, although Carlyle influenced
Stephen's practice as a biographer, his reactionary puritanism
repelled him – though not his brother, whom Carlyle made his
executor. Because of Leslie Stephen's aesthetic insensitivity,
Ruskin meant less to him than Carlyle, yet Stephen was grateful
for Ruskin's writings about the Alps. Arnold, of course, was an
important critical influence, but it was his poetry that Stephen
really admired. 'Philistine', he thought, was a name given to
mankind by a prig (Maitland, p. 170).

The change from Stephen's moral earnestness and Darwinian
social faith to Bloomsbury's celebration of personal relations and
aesthetic experiences has been widely noticed and frequently
deplored. But it is arguable whether this was a greater change
than that from the devout providential belief and government
service of Sir James Stephen to the agnosticism and literary work
of his son Leslie. In terms of literary history, Bloomsbury owed
more to Leslie Stephen than he inherited from his ancestors and
their circle.

III

It was in literary and especially intellectual history that Stephen's interests in philosophy, literature and biography came together. His two-volume *History of English Thought in the Eighteenth Century* and his three-volume *The English Utilitarians* remain important analytic expositions of two centuries of English philosophical, religious and political ideas. Leslie Stephen was not just a practising liberal utilitarian philosopher: he was the historian of that philosophy, and in his intellectual histories Bloomsbury could find a record and an example of the philosophical tradition from which they descended. For Stephen the interest of this tradition was in its relevance for his agnosticism; his history of eighteenth-century ideas has been called a tract for the times in its investigation of how that century's free thinking prepared for the advent of evangelicalism (Bicknell, Stephen, pp. 103–20). For Bloomsbury Stephen's advocacy of the eighteenth century was an important legacy; it was the century, he wrote, 'as its enemies used to say, of coarse utilitarian aims, of religious indifference and political corruption; or, as I prefer to say, the century of sound common sense and growing toleration, and of steady social and industrial development' (*English Literature*, p. 58). Bloomsbury preferred to say that too, but they were prepared to accept more of that century's literary expression than Stephen was allowed by his Victorian sensibilities.

Maynard Keynes in some of his essays and Leonard Woolf in *After the Deluge* wrote intellectual history in the wake of Stephen's work. As has been noted, Stephen was the historian of the intellectual tradition in which Keynes located his own work and the lives of the economists he wrote about. Leonard Woolf, whose work and temperament resembled Leslie Stephen's more than did any one else's in Bloomsbury, tried in his intellectual history to describe the connections between communal ideas and actions in Europe between the French Revolution and the First World War. Because of its poor reception the work is unfinished, and one of the reasons for this reception is that Leonard Woolf's analysis of what he called 'communal psychology' is confined too much to the ideas of individuals instead of the functions of class structures. In this he was following Stephen's practice, if not his theory.[5] Stephen had argued in the Introduction to the *History of*

Thought in the Eighteenth Century that the immediate causes of
change in the history of ideas 'are to be sought rather in social
development than in the activity of a few speculative minds'
(I 11). Stephen did not really write such a history; he was
concerned with changes in logical conditions rather than social
ones, but he recognised the limitations of his account, as one
might expect in a follower of Darwin.

  Though he was a historian of philosophy, Leslie Stephen was
not a philosopher of history, nor was Bloomsbury much
interested in a subject that seems to attract philosophical Idealists and Materialists rather than Realists. A good deal of history
was read, early and late, in Bloomsbury. MacCarthy, Forster,
Bell and Strachey all specialised in history at Cambridge, and
Virginia Woolf read it extensively under her father's tutelage,
chose historical subjects (religion, women) for her very early
writing, and even taught the subject briefly at a college for
working men and women. But basically the interest in history for
Bloomsbury was biographical and, in two different senses, literary. 'Human beings are too important to be treated as mere
symptoms of the past', Lytton Strachey proclaimed in the Preface to *Eminent Victorians*. 'They have a value which is independent of any temporal process – which is eternal and must be felt
for its own sake' (p. viii). This Bloomsbury conviction, derived
among other things from Moore's ethics, led to the realisation in
Bloomsbury that Stephen's most important contribution to English historiography was the *Dictionary of National Biography*.

  Literary history for Bloomsbury meant not simply the history
of literature, which for them was essentially the history of
writers, but also literature as history. Strachey wanted all history
to approach the condition of literature, and his models were
historians such as Thucydides, Tacitus, Gibbon and Michelet.
But when he wrote his manual of French literary history
Strachey seemed more under the influence of Macaulay than of
anyone else as he grouped France's literary landmarks around
the antitheses of rhetoric and realism (*LFL*, pp. 201–2). Forster
shared Strachey's conviction that history was a branch of literature, but literary history he dismissed as usually an evasion of
the arduous necessity of coming to terms with texts (*AN*, p. 8).
His ahistorical view of the novel is an aspect of Bloomsbury's
formalism, which left the Group uninterested in many of
Stephen's essays in literary history. Clive Bell wrote to Lytton

Strachey after reading his father-in-law's most important single work of literary history, the late lectures on eighteenth-century English literature and society, that he wondered what Stephen thought literary artists were trying to do (6.iv.08, LS/pBL). Yet *English Literature and Society in the Eighteenth Century* may have helped Virginia Woolf to realise how social conditions shaped literature (Hill, pp. 356–9). Stephen said his interest in the history of literature was both philosophical and social: to appreciate a great writer fully, he felt, it was necessary to distinguish between his individual characteristics and those resulting from his times and their 'existing stage of social and intellectual development' (*English Literature*, p. 5). The evolution of English literary history accorded well with Stephen's Darwinian ideas, and Virginia Woolf was not slow to see the feminist implications of a theory of literary history that was at least rudimentarily aware of the conditions affecting literary production. In works such as *A Room of One's Own*, where she explores the social and intellectual conditions affecting the development of women's writing, Virginia Woolf seems to owe something to her father's ideas; but how much she owed can be overstated. The context of Virginia Woolf's literary criticism is more often the socially anonymous common reader than the socially conditioned writer, which brings us to the significance of Leslie Stephen's literary criticism for Bloomsbury.

IV

To read what one liked because one liked it, never to pretend to admire what one did not – that was his only lesson in the art of reading. To write in the fewest possible words, as clearly as possible, exactly what one meant – that was his only lesson in the art of writing. All the rest must be learnt for oneself.   (*CE*, IV 80)

Virginia Woolf's 1932 centenary description of Leslie Stephen's teaching in the arts of literary criticism appropriately emphasises his integrity and lucidity as a critic. He set moral and rhetorical standards not just for his daughter but for all the writers of the Bloomsbury Group. Yet 'all the rest' that had to be learnt by oneself included a great deal that inevitably lead to

profound differences between Stephen's criticism and Bloomsbury's.

The most fundamental of these differences has to do with the
nature and value of aesthetic experience. In Bloomsbury it was
part of the *summum bonum* both for its own formal sake and also in
combination with other kinds of experience. Stephen found art
for art's sake a canting doctrine, 'which would encourage men to
steep themselves in luxurious dreaming, and explicitly renounce
the belief that art is valuable, as it provides a worthy embodi-
ment for the most strenuous thought and highest endeavour of
the age' (*Apology*, p. 124). Stephen attacked Pater's claim at the
end of *The Renaissance* that art proposed only to give the highest
quality to our moments for the sake of those moments, and he
argued that art could not be independent of moral concerns.[6] Yet
Stephen did not, as is sometimes claimed, equate moral and
aesthetic standards: he only said they were not independent of
each other (*Hours*, I 100). Pater, of course, is a moralist in *The
Renaissance*, especially with his recommendations about what
success in life ought to be. Stephen's quarrel with him – and with
Bloomsbury, could he have known it – was first of all a moral,
not an aesthetic, one. They differ over the value of aesthetic
contemplation. 'To recommend contemplation in preference to
action is like preferring sleeping to waking . . .', Stephen wrote in
'Wordsworth's Ethics' (*Hours*, II 293). Pater might have agreed
with this preference; Bloomsbury would not have. Bloomsbury
did not disagree with Stephen that literature could have instrumental moral value; they only thought its intrinsic worth more
important.

Yet there are deep aesthetic disagreements between Leslie
Stephen's literary criticism and Bloomsbury's. At the end of his
life, with a dozen or so volumes of literary biography and
criticism to his name, Stephen expressed his dislike of the whole
business in his lectures on eighteenth-century literature and
society: 'In some sense I am ready to admit that all criticism is a
nuisance and a parasitic growth upon literature. The most
fruitful reading is that in which we are submitting to a teacher
and asking no questions as to the secret of his influence' (*English
Literature*, p. 4). Criticism had evolved, Stephen went on, from
the judicial to the historical, which was the aspect of criticism
that most interested him. Bloomsbury would have added that
criticism then evolved into the aesthetic. (After that, one might

argue, it became analytic.) 'The whole art of criticism', Stephen
wrote earlier of the judicial critic Dr Johnson, whom he loved,
'consists in learning to know the human being who is partially
revealed to us in his spoken or his written words' (*Hours*, II 3).
The historical critic, by exploring the intellectual and social
background of literature, helps the reader to know the author. So
little did Stephen regard aesthetic, analytic criticism, that he was
even willing in theory to do away with literature. In a lecture
replying to Matthew Arnold's criticism of his essay on Wordsworth's ethics, Stephen said, 'literature may be sufficiently
regarded as simply one form of personal intercourse. It is a
subordinate question whether I know a man through his books,
or hear him discourse with me *vivâ voce*, or talk to him in ordinary
society . . .' ('Moral Element', p. 39). For all their valuing of
personal relations, Bloomsbury never went that far. The highest
praise that Stephen can give an author is to say that he is
'lovable' – and it always seems to be a 'he'. 'Manly' echoes
through his criticism as a term of praise. Female authors can be
charming and are sometimes praised for being feminine but they
really could not be considered lovable by Leslie Stephen. (Yet
privately Stephen wrote to his wife that he thought it 'womanly'
to be a writer, something more in Virginia's line than in his son
Thoby's – Love, p. 156.) And twice in his criticism Stephen
expresses the desire to horsewhip his authors – Laurence Sterne
for his behaviour and Jonathan Edwards for his sermons (*Hours*,
I 311, III 148).

The critical implications of Stephen's personal conception of
literature appear in his concern with the biographical, social and
intellectual aspects of literature, and in his avoidance, for the
most part, of technical or affective literary analyses. As a critic of
poets Stephen almost always defers to his predecessors for
discussions of their poetry; with writers of prose he is more
willing to talk about style or characterisation, narration and
setting. Even here Stephen remains very general. Strachey, in an
essay that anticipates *Eminent Victorians*, saw the essential weakness of the Victorian age as 'its incapability of criticism':

When Dryden or Johnson wrote of literature, they wrote of it
as an art; but the Victorian critic had a different notion of his
business. To him literature was always an excuse for talking
about something else. From Macaulay, who used it as a

convenient peg for historical and moral disquisitions, to Leslie
Stephen, who frankly despised the whole business, this singular tradition holds good.   (*CC*, pp. 188–9)

A similar complaint might be levelled against the Bloomsbury
critics, including Strachey. When it is not about writers,
Bloomsbury's literary criticism is usually concerned with readers, but there is comparatively little attention given to analysing
the writing itself. Strachey and Virginia Woolf agreed with
Stephen about the greatness of Sainte-Beuve, who sought literary understanding by focusing on the backgrounds of authors. In
one important respect, however, Bloomsbury critics were capable of talking about literature far more than Leslie Stephen was,
and that had to do with feeling.

The experience of aesthetic emotion is as central to Bloomsbury's thinking about art as their formalism is. Indeed feeling is
the confirmation of the value of form. Leslie Stephen, like his
father, regarded himself as a skinless man almost incapable of
discussing his vulnerability. He was a sentimentalist and suffered from those English inhibitions anatomised by Forster as
the undeveloped heart. Virginia Woolf thought Cambridge had
atrophied her father's sensibility, and connected his unaesthetic
attitude with his agnostic lack of imagination (*MB*, p. 146; *D*,
III 246). She owes much to her father's literary criticism, to its
historical range, its style, its integrity, and its emphasis on
literature as the expression of personality and character, but, as
a reader valuing the imaginative expression of feeling, she owes
him little. As late as 1937 she complained to her diary about
Stephen's denial of feeling, of passion, in Congreve's plays. She
had gone to her father's writings, as was her custom, to see what
he had to say about the author she was currently reading, and
was shocked at what he said in the *DNB*. Stephen found an
'absence of real refinement of feeling' in the plays and described
their atmosphere as 'asphyxiating'. She found, on the contrary,
more feeling in *Love for Love* than in all of Thackeray, and
thought the play's indecency often only honesty (*D*, v 97).

In the revised typescript of 'A Sketch of the Past' Virginia
Woolf described the influence of her father's criticism in this
way: 'I always read an *Hours in a Library* by way of filling out my
ideas, say of Coleridge, if I'm reading Coleridge; and always find
something to fill out; to correct; to stiffen my fluid vision.' And,

after this important statement of an indebtedness that extended to Stephen's biographical studies and articles, she proceeded to generalise about her ambivalence toward her father as a writer. (She said she had been reading Freud, and the sexual metaphor of Stephen's influence perhaps supports this.) His was not a subtle, imaginative or suggestive mind, but it was a strong one whose limited view of the world's humbug vices and domestic virtues she admired and even envied. Her father was not the kind of writer she had a natural affinity for, 'yet just as a dog takes a bite of grass, I take a bite of him medicinally, and there often steals in, not a filial, but a reader's affection for him; for his courage, his simplicity, for his strength and nonchalance, and neglect of appearances' (pp. 115–16). These last qualities do not get noticed in discussions of Stephen's influence, yet they are a part of the lessons he gave his daughter in the arts of reading and writing.

Desmond MacCarthy defended Stephen from the disparagement of Arnold Bennett and maintained that the virtue of his criticism was 'that there is so much intellectual hard work in it. . . . His criticism was never impressionistic and he never relied on his sensibility alone' (*H*, p. 195). But, MacCarthy pointed out in the Leslie Stephen lecture that he gave on Stephen himself in Cambridge in 1937, this made for critical limitations as well. MacCarthy called Stephen 'the least aesthetic of noteworthy critics' (*Stephen*, p. 11):

> Stephen himself was deficient in the power of transmitting the emotions he had derived himself from literature; he seldom, if ever, attempted to record a thrill. But he excelled in describing the qualities of authors, whether he summed up for or against them; and this is a most important part of the critic's function.' (p. 45)

MacCarthy's lecture was basically sympathetic to Stephen, but nevertheless it brought down the wrath of *Scrutiny* in the form of a rejoinder by Q. D. Leavis. She described MacCarthy as a leftover decadent of the 1890s who thought critics should record thrills instead of analysing literary works. (Q. D. Leavis, 'Stephen', pp. 404–15). *Scrutiny*'s polemics belong to the literary history of Bloomsbury in the 1930s, but, in considering Leslie Stephen's significance as a critic in the backgrounds of the

Group, it is worth noting that the difference between Stephen's and Bloomsbury's literary criticism is not one of analyses versus thrills. Certainly Virginia Woolf, Forster, Strachey and MacCarthy were more concerned with aesthetic feeling in their criticism than Stephen, but to a disinterested observer it should be clear that Stephen's unanalytic interest in literature as an expression of personality is more closely related to Bloomsbury's literary criticism than to the Leavises'.

Stephen's overriding moral judgements in his criticism do, of course, make it part of the Victorian critical tradition *Scrutiny* admired and sought to continue; but his dislike of critical analysis does not. He is closer to the conclusions of E. M. Forster, for example, who maintained at the end of his career that there was no 'first-class *raison d'être* for criticism in the arts' – only love could provide that, love not for the artist (which Stephen was willing to give) but for the art (*2CD*, p. 118). MacCarthy's criticism, as will become clear later in this history, was in fact as much concerned with moral judgements as with aesthetic experiences. The relation of a work of literature to life, 'the extent to which it ministered, in one way of another, to all human good' that he says was Stephen's critical criterion was also his own (*Stephen*, p. 47). And MacCarthy's respect for Stephen's work as a model of criticism was such, according to the *DNB*, that he once disbanded a collection of critical articles because it fell below the standard Stephen set in *Hours in a Library*.

Two other features of Leslie Stephen's literary criticism connecting him with Bloomsbury remain to be mentioned: like Stephen the Bloomsbury critics were primarily critics and almost exclusively writers of prose; and very prominent in the forms of prose they criticised and wrote was biography. Virginia Woolf's was a prose inheritance. Among the leading English and American novelists who were her contemporaries – Joyce, Lawrence, Faulkner, Hemingway, Fitzgerald – she was the only one who appears to have written no verse at all outside of the doggerel in her last novel. One might expect to find at least some kind of juvenile experiments with poetry at the beginning of her career, but instead she seems to have written, together with Thoby, for their family newspaper the *Hyde Park Gate News* a prose satire, influenced by *Punch* (QB/*VW*, 1 30) entitled *A Cockney's Farming Experiences*, and a sequel of him as a paterfamilias, as well as a very romantic tale of a young woman on a ship that she sent secretly and unsuccessfully to her favourite weekly, the popular *Tit-Bits*, which Vanessa and she read in Kensington gardens while eating Fry's chocolate (VB/*Notes* [p. 11]). Under Leslie Stephen's guidance she also appears to have written some history and then criticism. In finally becoming a novelist – with a romantic novel that begins with a young woman on a ship – she turned to the one major form of modern prose that her father had never attempted to write. (After his death Virginia Woolf once dreamt of showing her father a novel she was writing and hearing him snort with disapproval – *L*, I 325.) Leslie Stephen's criticism of fiction has been described, however, as one of his enduring critical achievements, blind as he was to some of the greatest eighteenth- and nineteenth-century English novels (Annan, *Stephen*, pp. 317, 330–2).

As a critic Stephen is more interested in, more comfortable with, prose than poetry, and the same can be said for Bloomsbury. This is one reason why critics in the Group focused on the same two centuries of writers that Stephen does; Strachey and Virginia Woolf were perhaps more sensitive to sixteenth- and seventeenth-century writing than Stephen, and of course they wrote about the literature of their own century, but nevertheless there is a critical continuity between Stephen's and Bloomsbury's criticism of eighteenth- and nineteenth-century novelists, historians, essayists, autobiographers and especially biographers that should become clear in the course of the Group's literary history. What will also emerge is a striking connection between Stephen and Bloomsbury in the practice of biography. The biographical texts of Leslie Stephen may have been the most enduring part of his heritage for Bloomsbury.

V

The separation of Leslie Stephen's achievements as a critic and a biographer is one that Bloomsbury would have made sooner than Stephen. There are no clear methodological differences between the essays he published under the title *Hours in a Library* and those called *Studies of a Biographer*. Yet by distinguishing between critical and biographical essays it is possible to see beyond the disagreements about the social morality of authors or

the aesthetic character of their work to how Bloomsbury continued Stephen's strongly biographical interest in literature. As
much as Stephen, members of the Group studied what MacCarthy called the 'Natural History of Authors' (*Stephen*, p. 46). The
biographical essays of Virginia Woolf, Forster, Strachey, Mac-
Carthy and Leonard Woolf are usually shorter than Stephen's
because of the changed conditions of periodical journalism, and
as a result they appear more neatly turned and even contrived
than Stephen's more judicious and sometimes prolix studies.
(Keynes's biographical essays written for journals rather than
newspapers are closer in form to Stephen's.) In an essay on
biography Virginia Woolf began with the definition of Sidney
Lee's – her father's successor as editor of the *Dictionary of National
Biography* – that biography was 'the truthful transmission of
personality', which she symbolised in the images of granite and
rainbow (*CE*, IV 229). There is more granitic truth in Stephen's
leisurely essays and more rainbow personality in Bloomsbury's.
But, despite these differences in form and emphasis, there is,
from time to time, a remarkable similarity in tone between
Stephen's biographical essays and some of the longer ones
Lytton Strachey wrote, either for journals or as chapters of
Eminent Victorians. In yet another Leslie Stephen lecture, the next
to be delivered after Desmond MacCarthy's, J. Dover Wilson
pointed out how 'the limpid style, the irony, the appetent smile
with which Strachey exhibits to the reader the moral tumour
before he lances it, all are to be found in essay after essay of
Leslie Stephen's volumes' (Wilson, pp. 20–1). If Lytton
Strachey is the debunking father of modern biography, Leslie
Stephen is one of the grandfathers.

In *English Literature and Society in the Eighteenth Century* Stephen
described the British essay as a lay sermon (p. 44). It continued
to be so for Stephen, Strachey, Forster and the Woolfs, though
the doctrines preached were of different religions. As a Victorian
and an admirer of Carlyle, Stephen was a hero-worshipper. He
used Carlyle's life of Sterling as a model for his full-length
biographies of Henry Fawcett and Fitzjames Stephen. Except for
them, however, Stephen's biographies are not lay saints' lives.
Of the twin plagues of biography, which he once identified as
hagiography and iconoclasm (*Hours*, III 341), Stephen was more
susceptible to the second, though not as much as Bloomsbury
was. In biography as elsewhere he was – to use a metaphor of his

daughter's that comes at the end of one of her last important essays – an eminent Victorian trespasser whose advice to walkers (and writers) was, 'Whenever you see a board up with "Trespassers will be prosecuted", trespass at once' (*CE*, II 181).

Bloomsbury biographers happily followed him, but to see this more clearly it is useful to distinguish between the four biographical genres in which Stephen wrote. There was the periodical essay, the man-of-letters monograph, the full-dress authorised life, and the biographical-dictionary article. We have been mainly discussing the first of these. The second has no parallel in Bloomsbury's work, though they knew of Stephen's studies of Johnson, Pope, Swift, George Eliot and Hobbes. The biographies of Fawcett and Fitzjames Stephen are in the same genre as Forster's *Goldsworthy Lowes Dickinson* and Virginia Woolf's *Roger Fry*. None suffers from that other plague of Victorian biography, elephantiasis. All are lucidly written. In all there is that close personal relationship between author and subject that has made much of the best English biography into a form of autobiography. But for Stephen the closeness of the relationships makes emotional demands that the inhibited biographer cannot meet. His biographies of his friend and his brother are utterly reticent lives. Fitzjames's private life is treated with such decorum that it comes as a surprise to find him suddenly with a wife and seven children. Reticence, however, is also a problem with Forster's and Virginia Woolf's modern biographies; they are much closer to Stephen's in the absence of any explicit discussion of their subjects' sexuality than they are to the full-frontal biography of today. But what Bloomsbury felt as a necessary constraint, Stephen experienced more as a comforting decency.[7] The main difference, however, between Stephen's and Bloomsbury's full-length biographies lies in their moral purpose. The sole stated aim of *The Life of Henry Fawcett* is to bring his character to bear on the reader's (p. 468). 'Sympathetic appreciation . . . is essential to satisfactory biography', Stephen wrote in the Preface to the biography of his brother (p. vi) where he is described on the title-page as Fitzjames's brother. This is true of Forster's and Virginia Woolf's biographies too, but they are more detached, more detailed about the feelings if not the emotional experiences of their subjects. The pieties of Victorian friendship have gone underground in their books, along with the moral purpose.

The art of Victorian biography as found in the works of Leslie
Stephen was most pervasively present to the writers and readers
of Bloomsbury in the *Dictionary of National Biography*. The *DNB*
was begun the year of Virginia Woolf's birth, and she liked to
joke about what it cost her nervous system: 'It gave me a twist of
the head. . . . I shouldn't have been so clever, but I should have
been more stable, without that contribution to the history of
England', she wrote in her diary in 1923 (II 277). Year by year,
from 1884 until 1900, the future members of Bloomsbury grew
up with this vast serialised biographical chronicle of England. As
the first and most important editor of the *DNB*, and the author of
378 of its lives, Stephen 'set the stroke' in Maitland's phrase
(p. 371). Stephen tried to keep down the number of clergymen in
the dictionary, for example, and several saints, such as Alban
and Asaph, had to wait for the supplement to get in. As editor he
felt sorely tried by 'the susceptibilities of a most fretful and
unreasonable race of men, the antiquaries' (*Mausoleum Book*,
p. 86). Most of the biographical essays on writers in the original
edition were written by Stephen, and he thought the *DNB* would
make a pretty good introduction to English literary history when
it was finished (*Men, Books*, p. 32). By his critical lights it is; his
lives of the poets, novelists and essayists are long on moral and
short on aesthetic analysis. (In thirty-six columns on Alexander
Pope, for instance, there is no mention of his art of the couplet.)
    Stephen's stamp on the *DNB* is a matter, then, of emphasis,
treatment, tone, as well as selection of subjects and their biographers. In announcing the beginning of the dictionary, he put
its ideal of style as follows:

> I have been asked whether anything in the way of 'literary
> style' is to be admitted. If style means superfluous ornament, I
> say emphatically, No. But style, and even high literary ability,
> is required for lucid and condensed narrative, and of such
> style I shall be anxious to get as much as I can. ('New
> Biographica', p. 850)

He would have got a good deal from Bloomsbury could they
have contributed.
    The unofficial motto for the *Dictionary of National Biography*,
suggested by one of the contributors and accepted by Stephen,
was 'no flowers by request' (*Impressions*, p. 163), and Thoby

Stephen as a child is supposed to have described it as the 'contradictionary' (Boyd, *Bloomsbury*, p. 35). Stephen's own biographer said Stephen established in the *DNB* a school of portraiture in black and white, and thus made it a central Victorian source for modern critical biography (Maitland, p. 372). Strachey called the *DNB* 'one of the most useful books in existence' ('Frock-Coat', p. 10) and Stephen himself regarded it as 'one of the most amusing works in the language' (*Studies*, I 12). Virginia Woolf mocked the *DNB* along with other aspects of biography in *Orlando* (p. 275) but kept her father's set in her workroom and used it repeatedly in her essays. Indeed, all Bloomsbury relied on the *DNB* for their critical and biographical writings. It is Stephen's most important work in the Victorian background of the Group and epitomises his achievement for them, drawing as it does on his skills as an editor, critic, intellectual historian, essayist and trespasser.

It has been suggested by a modern critic that Murray's great *Oxford English Dictionary* is the nineteenth-century equivalent to Gibbon's eighteenth-century epic *The Decline and Fall of the Roman Empire* (Kenner, p. 366). The *Dictionary of National Biography* is a closer analogue. The similarities are in story and moral rather than in structure or style. For Bloomsbury the *DNB* became a kind of Victorian epic tracing prophetically, if unknowingly, the development and decline of the British empire, whose fall Bloomsbury lived through and wrote about in their biographies, essays and novels. For Virginia Woolf the *DNB* traced the decline of the patriarchy, whose fall she regretted not witnessing; the dictionary demonstrated again that 'the history of England is the history of the male line, not the female', as she wrote in 'Women and Fiction' (*CE*, II 141). 'The lives of the obscure', which most women's were, the *DNB* excluded almost by definition, and this gave the first editor's daughter an opportunity to include a few among the essays of the common reader that she saw herself to be.

VI

One last kind of writing by Leslie Stephen needs to be noted for the example it provided to Bloomsbury, and that is autobiography. The Stephen family tradition of domestic autobiography begins with Leslie's grandfather's *The Memoirs of James Stephen Written by Himself for the Use of his Children* and continues through Leslie's *Mausoleum Book* to Virginia Woolf's 'Reminiscences', written for her infant nephew Julian Bell, and her unfinished 'A Sketch of the Past' (*MB*), on down to Leslie's grand-daughter Angelica Garnett and her recent exorcistic *Deceived with Kindness: A Bloomsbury Childhood*. James Stephen's memoirs are a theodicy justifying God's ways to his children; his autobiographical purpose, he says, is to instruct and improve, not to entertain or interest (p. 235). Yet the account of his passionate youth in the late eighteenth century ('It has been said that no Man can love two women at once; but I am confident this is an error' – (p. 305) is more lively reading, for all its providential moralising, than the agnostic, grief-stricken *Mausoleum Book* that Leslie Stephen began as an outlet for his incapacitating grief over the death of Julia Stephen in 1895. The *Mausoleum Book* too was written for his children, but there is little Protestant self-examination here; Leslie Stephen still avoids the inner life, taking satisfaction in the reticence that he is convinced will prevent any adequate biography of him from being written. One result of this reticence is that his grief and guilt at Julia's death (he kept thinking of Carlyle) are maudlin.

In the last year of his life Leslie Stephen published some public reminiscences about Cambridge, the *Cornhill*, the *DNB* and the Victorian world of letters in general; they are anecdotal and drily humorous, neither as moving nor as exasperating as the *Mausoleum Book* with its theme of 'the terrible havoc made by death' (p. 61). Twenty years later the Woolfs republished them and talked of publishing the *Mausoleum Book*, which members of the Memoir Club were allowed to read; in the end it was left unpublished, though after Virginia's death Leonard did print an edition of James Stephen's hitherto unpublished memoirs.

Bloomsbury continued the clear distinction Leslie Stephen made between private and public autobiography. Their private memoirs written for the Memoir Club, while not always ironic, often mocked the genre of the sentimental Victorian autobiography. (After the death of Julian Bell, Virginia Woolf, like her father, turned in her grief to memorial autobiography but wrote only a fairly short, unsentimental sketch – QB/*VW*, II 255–9). The various kinds of autobiography that members of Bloomsbury wrote throughout the Group's literary history are among the best ways of understanding how their private experience shaped the writings that make up that history. Nowhere is this truer than in their Victorian family and school recollections.

3 Some Victorian Visions

I

Lytton Strachey's response in *Eminent Victorians* to the over-whelming materials of Victorian history was to try,

> through the medium of biography, to present some Victorian visions to the modern eye. They are, in one sense, haphazard visions – that is to say, my choice of subjects has been deter-mined by no desire to construct a system or to prove a theory, but by simple motives of convenience and of art. It has been my purpose to illustrate rather than to explain.   (p. vii)

Strachey's motives of convenience and art are, in fact, far from simple, but his method of using biography as a medium for presenting some Victorian visions can be used to approach Bloomsbury's Victorian visions through the medium of auto-biography. The Bloomsbury writers were preoccupied with Vic-torianism throughout their careers. (Forster once remarked, 'Victorianism may not be an era at all. It may be a spirit biding its time' – *AE*, p. 116.) In their autobiographies they provided glimpses of the Victorian world that conditioned their modern attitudes. These autobiographies lack detachment and com-prehensiveness, yet taken together they have considerable scope. Most are memoirs, concentrating on past experiences of memor-able people and events, but intermingled with these reminis-cences are elements of the confessional and the educational autobiography. The tone of many of the memoirs is self-consciously ironic, for their writers were aware of the memoirs their Victorian progenitors had written. James Stephen's *Memoirs*, Leslie Stephen's *Mausoleum Book*, Lady Strachey's 'Some Recollections of a Long Life', Sir Edward Fry's family

autobiography, the 'Recollections' of Forster's great-aunt
Marianne Thornton – these lay behind the memoirs Bloomsbury
wrote, particularly those they read to the Memoir Club.

The eminence of the Victorians who were Bloomsbury's
ancestors added to the interest and to the irony of Bloomsbury's
memoirs. With the exception of Clive Bell, whose family, according to his son, 'drew its wealth from Welsh mines and ex-
pended it upon the destruction of wild animals' (Q. Bell, *Bloomsbury*, p. 19), Bloomsbury's family origins were of the professional
upper middle class, and most of their families belonged to that
new Victorian class that Noel Annan has described as the
'intellectual aristocracy'. The *Dictionary of National Biography*,
founded by the most eminent of Bloomsbury's ancestors,
includes not only Virginia Woolf's father, grandfather, great-
grandfather, aunt, uncle and various cousins, but also Lytton
Strachey's father, uncle and godfather, E. M. Forster's great-
grandfather and great-grand-uncle, Roger Fry's father and uncle,
and Mary MacCarthy's father. Not distinguished enough for the
DNB but certainly an intellectual aristocrat was Keynes's father,
a philosopher and university administrator. And eminently
respectable Victorians were Leonard Woolf's father, a Queen's
Counsel; Duncan Grant's father, a major; Saxon Sydney-
Turner's father, a doctor; and E. M. Forster's father, an
architect. Eminent autobiographical material was also to be
found in the lives of Bloomsbury's mothers and aunts, as
Elizabeth Boyd has shown. The Pattle sisters and their daughters (the ancestors of Julia Stephen), Caroline Emelia Stephen,
Lady Strachey, Blanche Warre-Cornish (Mary MacCarthy's
mother), Florence Ada Keynes – all were formidable women,
and, if the range is extended to include those remarkable sister-
hoods, the Frys and the Stracheys, there may be, person for
person, more distinguished women in the families of Bloomsbury
than there were distinguished men.

Autobiographies of one kind or another by more than half of
the members of Bloomsbury have now been published. Some
sixty years separate the first from the last of them. Except for
Leonard Woolf's and Mary MacCarthy's (and David Garnett's
in New Bloomsbury), these autobiographies are either essays or
fragments. The Memoir Club origins of most of them has
determined their form and often their points of view and their
tones. Roger Fry's brief memoirs are embedded in Virginia

Woolf's biography of him. Virginia Woolf's own autobiographies, apart from her diary, consist of two long fragments and three short Memoir Club papers; one of these fragments, 'A Sketch of the Past', is being recognised in its fully recovered state as one of her most important pieces of writing. Two Memoir Club papers of Vanessa Bell's on Virginia's childhood and Old Bloomsbury have been published and others used in her biography. J. M. Keynes and Lytton Strachey each left only two carefully written Memoir Club essays, though both also left various kinds of brief diaries. Clive Bell published a book of essays on his old friends; his other memoirs have been considered unpublishable for various reasons. Desmond MacCarthy's *Memories* contains Memoir Club fragments of various lengths. And E. M. Forster edited with commentary his own letters from India and then wrote the 'domestic biography' of his great-aunt, in which his own memoirs figure, but these were written toward the end of his career; earlier he kept a diary of short entries and then later converted an inherited commonplace book into a book of autobiographical and critical observations.

Forster once wrote in an essay entitled 'Recollectionism' that he could not manage chronology, that memory alters and thus destroys what it remembers. Yet he practised writing recollections and not just for the money they brought in, recalling the past gave 'mental balance' – 'the present is so heavy and so crude and so vulgar that something has to be thrown into the opposite scale, or one will live all lopsided. I throw in my own past' (p. 405). Virginia Woolf used different metaphors to say something similar in 'A Sketch of the Past':

> The past only comes back when the present runs so smoothly that it is like the sliding surface of a deep river. Then one sees through the surface to the depths. In those moments I find one of my greatest satisfactions, not that I am thinking of the past; but that it is then that I am living most fully in the present. For the present when backed by the past is a thousand times deeper than the present when it presses so close that you can feel nothing else, when the film on the camera reaches only the eye.' (*MB*, p. 98)

Bloomsbury's recollections – despite their differences in form, tone, time, occasion – all helped their writers to relate the present to the past and the past to the present. Their Victorian visions illustrate, if they do not explain (to use Strachey's distinction), how Bloomsbury came to regard their nineteenth-century origins. For explanations, their autobiographies would have to be supplemented with their fiction, biographies, criticism – in other words, with practically all the writings of the Group's literary history. There is a sense, however, in which that history begins not with their early writings but with the autobiographical texts in which the Group recollected their Victorian growing-up.

II

When Queen Victoria died, Roger Fry was twenty-four, Desmond MacCarthy twenty-three, E. M. Forster twenty-two, Lytton Strachey and Leonard Woolf twenty, and Virginia Woolf and Mary MacCarthy eighteen. Only Fry's childhood was spent in the full glare of the period, though Virginia Woolf and Lytton Strachey grew up in families more or less contemporary with Fry's. Sir Edward Fry was actually ten years younger than Sir Richard Strachey and only five years older than Sir Leslie Stephen. Virginia Woolf felt that Vanessa, Thoby, Adrian and herself were not Stephen's children but his grandchildren; the same might be said of Lytton Strachey and in a way of Forster, whose dominating great-aunt was born in the eighteenth century. The longevity of Bloomsbury's parents is quite extraordinary. Fry's parents died at ninety-one and ninety-eight, Strachey's at ninety-one and eighty-eight; Leslie Stephen died at seventy-three and Francis Warre-Cornish at seventy-six. Leonard Woolf's and E. M. Forster's fathers died young but their mothers lived on into their eighties, and both of Keynes's parents survived him, living into their nineties. Throughout much of their adult lives, Bloomsbury had to contend with the living presence if not the influence of their parents. In addition to being long-lived, Bloomsbury parents were also very fertile. Roger Fry had six sisters and one brother, Lytton Strachey five brothers and five sisters. Virginia Woolf grew up in three families all at once, with one retarded half-sister from her father's first marriage, one half-sister and two half-brothers from her mother's first marriage, and one full sister and two full brothers

– seven of them in all, with an age range of fifteen years. Mary
MacCarthy and Leonard Woolf each had eight siblings. For
these five families the average number of children is more than
nine. The families of the other members of the Group were
smaller, with three of them being only children.

The large upper-middle-class Victorian family is for Virginia
and Leonard Woolf, for Lytton Strachey, Roger Fry and Mary
MacCarthy, the essential Victorian experience, and it explains
much about the lives that the Group led when they grew up.
They had, for example, a total of ten children – half the number
of the original Group itself. The large and lasting Victorian
establishments of Bloomsbury's childhood and adolescence
preoccupy their autobiographical visions. In some of them the
ancestral homes appear as symbols of the patriarchies and
matriarchies they contained. Houses, together with their rooms,
gardens and districts, remain as important symbols of consciousness in Bloomsbury's writing and painting. It is not simply
fortuitous that the Bloomsbury Group came to bear the name of
a district of London. Around 1900, five of the Victorian households in which the members of the Group had grown up were
located in the Kensington area of London. The early history of
Bloomsbury might be described as a progress from Kensington
to Bloomsbury, from the respectable inhabitants living around
Kensington Gardens, that is, to the middle-class bohemians of
Bloomsbury. Architecturally it was a progress from High Victorian houses and what a character in one of Leonard Woolf's
novels calls 'the red horror of West Kensington' to 'the superb
fadedness of Bloomsbury' with its Georgian squares (*WV*, p. 45).
But in this change there were also continuities of urban nature
and cultural institutions: the green squares, the British Museum,
the University of London and the Slade School replaced Kensington Gardens, the Albert Hall, the Imperial Institute and the
Natural History Museum.

Among the memoirs of Bloomsbury there are visions of four
Kensington Gardens households in which the Frys, Woolfs,
Stephens and Stracheys lived. (Desmond MacCarthy left no
record of his Kensington youth.) These, along with recollections
of E. M. Forster and Mary MacCarthy, illustrate in literary
non-fiction the Victorian family backgrounds of Bloomsbury.

III

Roger Fry's family did not move to Bayswater in order to be near Kensington Gardens until Fry was at Cambridge. After he had come down, he wrote to Lowes Dickinson about the reek of his family's 'Nomian atmosphere':

> When every member of a family has a moral sense that makes them as rigid as iron and as tenacious as steel and when they have got through this same moral sense a feeling of the superlative necessity of doing everything in common because of the family tie, you may imagine that the friction is not slight. (VW/*RF*, p. 63)

The house itself was flamboyant, pretentious and uncomfortable for Fry, unlike the small eighteenth-century house in Highgate where he had grown up and in whose garden his first two great emotional experiences of passion and disillusionment had occurred. The passion was for poppies in a garden that became 'the imagined background for almost any garden scene that I have read of in books', Fry wrote in a Memoir Club paper. He worshipped his poppies more than anyone, including Jesus but excluding his father. Disillusionment came when he picked one of the buds for his mother during a botany lesson and was gravely reproved for it. 'The shock of that confused experience was still tingling fifty years later', Virginia Woolf commented in her biography, where this garden scene is used as a motif, and later she speculated that it was one of the unanalysable elements behind the 'moments of vision' that helped make Fry a painter (pp. 15–16, 161). In such a comment Virginia Woolf reveals the affinities between her creative experience and Fry's.

That Roger Fry's first disillusionment was connected with his mother explains something of its severity and permanence. Virginia Woolf described her as living between the two worlds of Quaker inhibition and the upper middle-class judiciary. It was not until late in her life, after her husband's death, that her son felt able to discuss anything with her. 'It shows what a portentous pressure my father exercised over her', he concluded (VW/ *RF*, p. 261) – a conclusion that is to be found in other Bloomsbury family memoirs too. Still, Fry's mother dominated his sisters, none of whom married and only two of whom managed even to leave home.

Sir Edward Fry was an archetypal Victorian father. His son thought him more a puritan than a Quaker. Nowhere in the childhood experience of Bloomsbury was the moral law observed with greater strictness than in the Fry household. Once when he was ten, Fry wrote in one of his memoirs, the family lessons were interrupted by a summons from his mother:

> For lessons to be interrupted it must be grave, it might – it probably would be, a criminal case – so peculiar were the intricacies of the moral code – one might quite well have committed an act of whose enormity one was still unconscious. My mother was seated gravely with an inscrutable air – no it was not criminal – it was solemn but we were not in disgrace – how quickly and surely we had learned to read the hieroglyphics on a face on which so much depended!   (VW/*RF*, p. 27)

The occasion was the announcement that the government had confirmed what his family knew all along: Edward Fry was a judge of the law. Father became Mr Justice Fry outside the home as well as inside. Father as judge superseded the image of father as skater, which is Roger Fry's most vivid vision of his father. In another Memoir Club paper, written, Virginia Woolf cautioned her readers, 'for friends who took a humorous rather than a reverential view of eminent Victorians', Fry depicted his father's passion for skating. There was no style in it, 'the way he scuttered along with legs and arms and long black coat tails flying out at all angles and the inevitable top hat to crown it all'. Skating was the only thing he ever allowed to interrupt work, and when there was skating he was 'all laughter and high spirits and there seemed no danger of suddenly finding oneself guilty of moral obliquity'. There was one difficulty, though. The nature of Victorian skates made men with chairs who fitted the skates very desirable, but the moral law decreed they were not to be paid. The theory behind the law held that money was 'a coefficient of virtue', and this made the loafing skate-fitters into some foreign, almost criminal species of being:

> It is impossible to exaggerate the want of simple humanity in which we were brought up or to explain how that was closely

associated with the duty of philanthropy. To pay these poor men who after all were trying to do a piece of work – to pay them a decent tip was truckling to immorality. . . . (VW/*RF*, pp. 20–2)

No one in Bloomsbury knew better than Roger Fry what he owed to 'that grand Victorian vice of saving' (VW/*RF*, p. 28). It allowed him to become an independent art critic and painter by remaining dependent upon his father's support. (A legacy from his chocolate-manufacturing uncle allowed Fry to start the Omega Workshops.) But Fry would certainly have agreed with Bloomsbury's economist that the Victorian vice of saving, which Keynes described as the non-consumption of the cake that the labouring and capitalist classes had co-operated to bake, gathered around itself 'all those instincts of puritanism which in other ages has withdrawn itself from the world and has neglected the arts of production as well as those of enjoyment' (*CW*, ii 12). In rejecting Victorian puritanism, Bloomsbury followed Keynes and made spending into a virtue; then they dedicated themselves to the production of art and the values of enjoyment. This change involved a devaluation of the importance of family. 'I've always hated families and patriarchalism of all kinds. . . . I have so little family feeling, so little feeling that it's by the family that one goes on into the future' (VW/*RF*, p. 281). These words, quoted by Virginia Woolf to illustrate what she said was one of Fry's most persistent theories, could have been said by many members of the Group, including the qualification added by his biographer that the theory broke down when it came to his relation with his sister Margery. Throughout Bloomsbury there were intense selected relationships between brothers and sisters – Virginia and Vanessa, Lytton and James Strachey – but there was little sense of the need to maintain close, emotional relationships between all siblings. Leonard Woolf was distant from most of his brothers and sisters; even in smaller families, such as the Keyneses, brothers and sisters were not close to one another. The cohesiveness of the Bloomsbury Group derived from and endured through family relationships, but it did not necessarily include even the closest relatives of the members. This too is part of the legacy of their Victorian families.

Fry's father appears to have felt in his own life something of the discontinuity that his son observed between the skater and the judge. The alarming puritan father and judge actually preferred botany to the law and retired as soon as he could to pursue his scientific hobby, while undertaking special government missions until he was very old. It must have been a great disappointment that his son finally chose art over science. Fry left no autobiographical account of the consequences of this decision, but there is a letter, used in the best dead-pan Bloomsbury way by Virginia Woolf, in which Fry's father was assured by his son not to worry, because the only nudes he would be painting at Cambridge were male. According to his art-teacher, men as a rule have better figures than women in England and therefore are 'more useful to practise drawing on' (*RF*, p. 59). After Bloomsbury such Victorian innocence became impossible.

IV

Like Roger Fry's father, Leonard Woolf's was a graduate of the University of London (nonconformists and non-Christians were not admitted to Oxford or Cambridge until 1871), a Queen's Counsel, and the head of a large family living near Kensington Gardens. Leonard Woolf calculated in *Principia Politica*, which includes some political autobiography, that in 1890 a barrister with a wife and nine children employed nineteen people – eight for general domestic work, two for the care of infants, and seven for the education of the older children: 'standards of social value were implicit in this arrangement and from the earliest years my contact with human beings made me unconsciously conscious of these standards and of the class distinctions to which they were attached'. The house of this establishment was divided into strata which reflected the family hierarchy, the servants occupying the lower and upper extremities of the structure and the family living on the comfortable middle floors (pp. 31–2). In these features of the large, professional upper-middle-class Victorian family, Leonard Woolf's resembled Roger Fry's. Yet there were also some fundamental differences separating the Woolfs from the Frys and all the other families of Bloomsbury. Though he was a member of the same general class, Leonard Woolf thought of himself as an outsider because his family had no roots in it; they had 'only recently struggled up into it from the stratum of Jewish shopkeepers' (*BA*, p. 74). A significant part of Leonard

Woolf's influence on Virginia Woolf may have come from this sense of being an outsider, for, though her upbringing was certainly that of an insider, she came to see herself as a writer and a woman whose values were not those of her society's.

Leonard Woolf's *Sowing* gives the fullest finished picture of childhood in Bloomsbury's autobiographies. He re-created in old age a childhood that on weekdays was spent in a matriarchy and on Sundays in a patriarchy. His father's moral law was simpler and more humane than Edward Fry's; all that was required, his father explained in the words of Micah, was 'to do justly, and to love mercy, and to walk humbly with thy God'. In practice it was a little more complicated than that, for Sidney Woolf – intelligent, high-strung, with a violent temper and a 'terrific' code of personal behaviour – found it impossible to suffer fools mercifully. He died at forty-seven of the overwork that seems to have killed so many Victorians, and Micah's words became his epitaph (pp. 25–6). From the age of eleven Leonard Woolf grew up in a matriachy seven days a week. By fourteen he had become an unbeliever and began to acquire the deep scepticism that is 'the religion of all sensible men' (*S*, p. 50). That phrase is the title of an article by Leslie Stephen reprinted in *An Agnostic's Apology*, and it identifies one of the several important similarities between Leonard Woolf and his father-in-law. In one significant way Leonard Woolf retained his Jewish heritage, however. He felt, in contrast to Fry and others in Bloomsbury, including Virginia Woolf, that he was without a sense of sin. This helps to explain the astringent plainness of his autobiography. Leonard Woolf was not, as he said in another context, one of Rousseau's latter-day disciples; there is little of the confessional mode in his autobiography. The only point of autobiography, he argues, while explaining that there must be no concealment,

> is to give, as far as one can, in the most simple, clear, and truthful way, a picture, first of one's own personality and of the people whom one has known, and secondly of the society and age in which one lived. To do this entails revealing as simply as possible one's own simplicity, absurdity, trivialities, nastiness. (*G*, p. 148)

The pictures that Leonard Woolf's autobiography gives us are characterised by simplicity more than any other quality. And, if there is no concealment in them, there are surprising blanks. How little we are told in his early volumes about his eight brothers and sisters. Yet how apt is the classification of his own personality: 'the human caterpillar and chrysalis, infant and boy, emerges as butterfly or moth; in my own case, I may perhaps be said to have emerged as that appropriately named variety of moth, the Setaceous Hebrew Character' (*S*, pp. 78–9). *Setaceous* means having the form of a bristle. Leonard Woolf knew how prickly he was.

Leonard Woolf's picture of his mother is in contrast to that of his father: she was physically tough and psychologically soft. To some extent she conformed to the matriarchal archetype of the Victorian age in which a long widowhood was shadowed by an apotheosised husband. Her son criticised the unreality of the dream world in which Mrs Woolf lived with 'nine perfect children worshipping a mother to whom they owed everything, loving one another, and revering the memory of their deceased father' (*S*, pp. 32–3). Bloomsbury's writings throughout their history are concerned with reality as a standard of judgement. In their family visions the criticism of the unreality of Victorian life keeps recurring. Just what they meant by this standard should become clearer in the following Cambridge chapters. When Leonard Woolf threw doubt on his mother's optimism, she was distressed, and he came to feel she loved him the least of all her children. Yet her psychological softness was not incompatible with a common sense that led her to gamble her capital on her children's education in the hope that they would become successful enough to support her afterwards, which they did. The financial insecurity that followed the death of her husband left a deep mark on Leonard Woolf and may even be seen in his feeling a lack of maternal love. His most intense autobiographical visions have to do with security, and, as with so many of Bloomsbury's recollections, they are associated with places as much as people.

Both sets of Leonard Woolf's grandparents lived in Blooms-bury, but he too grew up in Kensington, where, in the gas-lit nursery at night, with the sound of cab horses clopping past outside, Leonard Woolf experienced what he describes at the end of his life as his 'Platonic idea laid up in heaven of security and peace and civilization' (*S*, p. 55). But outside there were horrors: Jack the Ripper, drunks, appalling slums, bloody unemployment riots. Fear and politics – the Hobbesian title of a pamphlet he wrote in 1925 – were always connected in Leonard Woolf's mind. As a socialist he admits in his autobiography that he has to condemn bourgeois family life, 'its snugness and smugness, snobbery, its complacent exploitation of economic, sexual, and racial classes'. From such a life came the philistinism that he renames 'spiritual suburbanism' and finds attacked in English novels written between 1890 and 1914 – novels including Forster's, and his own *The Wise Virgins*. Yet, as he experienced it in Kensington, the social (as opposed to the economic) value of that bourgeois life was, he insists, very high (*S*, p. 36). Other members of the Group might not go that far, but, as already seen in Roger Fry's memories, there was in Bloomsbury a basic ambivalence toward nineteenth-century middle-class family life.

After Leonard Woolf's father died, the family moved across the river to the London district of Putney. This fall in fortune taught Leonard Woolf to accept fatalistically 'instability and the impermanence of happiness' (*S* 86). The lessons of death for Virginia Woolf were different. Leonard Woolf's fatalism was also nourished by moments of 'cosmic despair' similar perhaps to some of her experiences. One such moment was a garden scene very different from Roger Fry's, in which, as a child in a grimy spider-covered garden at home, Leonard Woolf was overwhelmed with *Weltschmerz* (*S*, p. 40). Bloomsbury's was, after all, a *fin-de-siècle* childhood.

V

Leonard Woolf, E. M. Forster and Lytton Strachey all were raised, more or less, in matriarchies. Forster was one year old when his father died. He grew up an only child too much noticed by adults, as he says in the autobiographical section of his great-aunt Marianne Thornton's biography. All the adults seem to have been women, either Thorntons or in-laws of Thorntons because Forster's mother was dependent upon them for support. Marianne Thornton was the principal matriarch of the Thornton clan, and it is of her that Forster has left some Victorian visions. He was her favourite nephew. The legacy of £8000 that she left him made his writing-career possible: 'her love', he wrote at the end of his biography of her, 'in a most tangible sense followed me beyond the grave' (*MT*, p. 289) – as did the love of Caroline Emelia Stephen, for her niece, Virginia Woolf, to whom she left the means for a room of her own. The high-mindedness of the Thorntons, of which Forster's legacy was a manifestation, figured significantly in his own life, Forster believed, but his heart lay with his mother's family, who were artistic rather than intellectual (pp. 250–1). Throughout his writing Forster sought to connect heart and mind. His biography of a Thornton is dedicated to his mother.

As with other Bloomsbury recollections, Forster's autobiographical writings are about places as much as people. Two houses are the influential settings of these texts and of the double vision he came to write about. The first is Battersea Rise on Clapham Common, another Queen Anne house that was expanded by Marianne Thornton's father, one of the leaders of the Clapham Sect. The heart of the house was not the drawing-room, as in the Victorian establishments of Kensington, but the oval library with its Adam mantel and ceiling; from its bow windows one looked out to a spacious garden and a beautiful tulip-tree. Forster could not actually remember Battersea Rise, which was torn down for a housing-development in 1907, but its spirit of place presides over his biography. Marianne Thornton's departure from it in 1852 is described by her great-nephew as tragic for her and infuriating for him. What infuriates Forster is that she had to leave on account of 'the cruelty and stupidity of the English law in matters of sex' (p. 192). It is a familiar Bloomsbury theme. Her brother Henry Sykes Thornton had gone into exile with an illegal bride, his deceased wife's sister, and to the horror of his relatives this meant abandoning the family home. Forster's persona intervenes here as the omniscient, commenting biographer to sympathise with the family because he too had been deprived of a house once (p. 188). The allusion is to the house, designed by his father, which Forster had to leave after his mother's death; but as a child he had been dispossessed once before, of the other house of his memoirs.

From the time he was four in 1883 until he was eleven, Forster lived in a Hertfordshire farmhouse that he made, along with its wych-elm, the centre of *Howards End*. The importance of Rooks-nest, as the house was called, is made clear in a Memoir Club fragment on memory that Forster wrote in the 1930s. Again with the disclaimer that he had lost his memory, Forster explained that, if he had been allowed to stay at Rooksnest, 'I should have become a different person, married, and fought in the war'[1] (Colmer, p. 3). More plausibly, in *Marianne Thornton* he recalled how his impressions of the house still glowed in his mind, 'not always distinguishably, always inextinguishably' (p. 270). Forster's Victorian visions here and elsewhere are spatial rather than temporal, paradoxical as that may be. He summed up this absorption in timeless impressions at the end of his *Commonplace Book* in 1956, when he wrote, apropos of his lack of belief in an afterlife, 'my great extension is not through time to eternity, but through space to infinity: here: now: and one of my complaints against modern conditions is this – they prevent me from seeing the stars' (p. 305). Time remained the enemy in art and life for Forster and, in different ways, for Bloomsbury too. Virginia Woolf also preferred infinity to eternity, and her childhood impressions in Cornwall parallel Forster's in Hertfordshire.

The influence of Rooksnest owed something to that of Battersea Rise, however. Just after he describes the inextinguishable impressions of the latter, Forster goes on to say that they 'have given me a slant upon society and history. It is a middle-class slant, atavistic, derived from the Thorntons, and it has been corrected by contact with friends who have never had a home in the Thornton sense, and do not want one' (*MT*, p. 270). The results of the slant and its corrections pervade Forster's accounts of his Clapham ancestors. Marianne Thornton's enlightened banker and economist father Henry Thornton taught her that economy had to do not with saving but with the right distribution of property. Keynes would have assented, and indeed it has been said that all but one of the key elements in Keynes's theory can be found in Thornton's *An Enquiry into the Nature and Effects of the Paper Credit in Great Britain*, which was published in 1802 (Hicks, pp. 174–88). Forster wrote a brief essay on Henry Thornton in 1939 and commented on the relation of this book to Thornton's other, more popular work, *Family Prayers*. Thornton's life is almost a parable of religion and the rise of capitalism. Forster is amusing on the way the Thorntons connected these worlds. He respects their philanthropy but is critical of their indifference to the unseen, comparing them unfavourably to the Quakers in this respect. (But then he did not know Fry's family, though he visited Caroline Emelia Stephen, a friend of his aunt's, at Cambridge.) Forster complains that, for the Thorntons, 'poetry, mystery, passion, ecstasy, music don't count' (*2CD*, p. 188).

In *Marianne Thornton* Forster's critical views of Clapham were both moral and socio-economic. He finds modern belief more spiritual than Clapham's 'solid possession' of hopes for immortality, less emotionally self-indulgent (p. 29). The pietistic threnodies that accompanied Thornton death-bed scenes appear to have disgusted Forster more than any other feature of their religious belief; here certainly there was no lack of passion. But of their class behaviour Forster's autobiographical writings, like Leonard Woolf's, express a mixture of approval and disapproval. These abolitionists did much good, and that is why Forster says he lacks moral indignation while criticising Clapham's failure to realise that industrial slaves wanted freeing too (p. 54). Class interests more than moral law appear to have preoccupied Marianne Thornton's family; the illegality of marriage with one's deceased wife's sister exercised them far more than its biblical immorality. Class interest more than moral law appear to have preoccupied Marianne Thornton's family: the illegality of marriage with one's deceased wife's sister exercised them far more than its biblical immorality. Class was an important motive behind Marianne Thornton's educational zeal. It was necessary to have a supply of useful servants and governesses, but more important, Forster thinks, and more admirable, was 'her dislike of ignorance and her eighteenth-century faith in reason' (p. 224). This Thornton interest in education became part of her great-nephew's heritage. 'I neglected no one's education', he writes of himself as a child, thinking of his relationship with a garden boy at Rooksnest whose name he preserved in his fiction. For his part, this boy, associated with the other house of Forster's childhood, did not neglect Forster's education either, probably doing 'more than anyone towards armouring me against life' (*MT*, pp. 274–5).

Marianne Thornton died when Forster was eight, in the year of Queen Victoria's jubilee. She had rebuked Forster and his mother for being too republican to celebrate it; in a sense she stood for the Queen in Forster's family as Leonard Woolf's mother did in his. Forster's autobiographical visions of Marianne Thornton and of his own childhood at Rooksnest appear more benign on the whole than Bloomsbury's usual view of the period. This is no doubt partly owing to Forster's having written it in his seventies, which was the age Marianne Thornton had reached when her great-nephew became aware of her. Recollecting her life and his childhood may have helped Forster balance his present life and times against hers. In the aftermath of the Second World War the Victorian period had its attractions. Forster cannot say he truly loved his great-aunt when he was a child, but, after tracing 'the unfoldings of her good life', his vision of her is finally one of love (p. 287).

VI

Before returning to Kensington and the extraordinary Stephen and Strachey *ménages* there, it is useful to glance first at some Victorian visions of Bloomsbury's family backgrounds at Eton and Cambridge.

The opening paragraph of the least known of Bloomsbury's published autobiographies, Mary (or Molly, as she was called) MacCarthy's *A Nineteenth-Century Childhood*, identifies the similarities and differences between her Victorian family and those of other members of the Group: 'I was born in the 'eighties into a sheltered, comfortable, upper middle class, religious and literary circle.' The sheltered sense of class was shared with other Victorian families in which Bloomsbury was growing up, but the religion and the culture were somewhat different. The Warre-Cornishes, whose name is disguised as Kestrell in Mary Mac-Carthy's autobiography,[2] ranged from Broad to High Church, which befitted the family of the Vice-Provost of Eton. Their literary interests were more modern; Maurice Baring was the chief ornament of their circle. They were closer, in other words, to the Stephens and the Stracheys than to the Frys, Woolfs or Thorntons. 'Our elders, after all,' Mary MacCarthy wrote toward the end of her recollections, 'had won all their refined and graceful art and sounded the high, noble note of poetry and symbolism, through rebellion against Philistine ugliness and the narrow terrors of an outworn evangelical creed' (pp. 99–100).

The Victorian visions of *A Nineteenth-Century Childhood* are not as heavily framed with the present as so many Bloomsbury autobiographies are. The Warre-Cornishes were not so visited with death as the Stephens were. The focus of Mary MacCarthy's memoir is softer, more nostalgic, less ironic. Her father, for example, shared the financial anxieties of Leslie Stephen and others of their class; even though they had a legion of servants and a country home, the children were brought up to believe they were 'gravely poor' (pp. 4ff.) But the scenes in which the family account book was gone over (its title of 'Le Grand Livre' mocked its seriousness) are not comparable to Stephen's rages over the weekly household expenses, except as manifestations of an irrational attitude toward money.

The kinder tone of Mary's MacCarthy's autobiography is partly the result of its predominant child's point of view, whereas in Virginia Woolf's late memoir it interacts with the remembering adult's vision. Virginia Woolf reviewed *A Nineteenth-Century Childhood* in *The Times Literary Supplement* and alluded to *Eminent Victorians* in describing the book's point of view: 'Bulky, vigorous, and voluble, not so very eminent, full of agreeable eccentricities and dashed with a whimsical radiance – such are the Victorians if you lie with Mrs MacCarthy on the schoolroom floor' ('Schoolroom', p. 609). The child's-eye view of late-nineteenth-century upper-middle-class life in an academic community has been memorably rendered in Gwen Raverat's *Period Piece: A Cambridge Childhood* – not a Bloomsbury autobiography, though her sister married Maynard Keynes's brother Geoffrey and Virginia Woolf was friends with her and her husband, Jacques Raverat. *Period Piece* is a fuller and funnier autobiography than *A Nineteenth-Century Childhood*, but the genre, the period, the class and many of the conclusions are the same.

The gentler mood of Mary MacCarthy's reminiscences contrasts not with Gwen Raverat's but with Virginia Woolf's, in the attitude toward the situation of women in the Warre-Cornish family. Nowhere in the families of Bloomsbury was the inferior status of females more obvious than in the Eton household of the Vice-Provost. His daughter's reaction, however, is more one of annoyance than bitterness or envy at the way her freedom was restricted. Schoolmaster though he was, Francis Warre-Cornish appears to have been the mildest of Bloomsbury's Victorian fathers. The family, again, was something of a matriarchy, and there are stronger resemblances between Mary MacCarthy's mother and the other ancestral matriarchs of Bloomsbury. Kindly, detached, absent-minded, even elusive, Blanche Warre-Cornish had such a reputation for originality of wit and eccentricity of behaviour that a collection of her sayings was compiled and privately printed by Robert Gathorne-Hardy in the 1930s under the title *Cornishiana*. (To a daughter travelling in Africa she wrote urging her to console herself every morning by remembering, first, that she was an Englishwoman; second, that she was born in wedlock; and, third, that she was on dry land – Benson, p. 156.) In her daughter's memoirs, however, Blanche Warre-Cornish is a shadowy figure, and there is no intimation of her conversion to Roman Catholicism in the 1890s. More memorable in *A Nineteenth-Century Childhood* is the vision of a relative whom Mary MacCarthy shared with Virginia Woolf – the novelist and memoirist Annie Thackeray Ritchie, who was Mary's aunt by marriage, the sister of Leslie Stephen's first wife, and the daughter of Thackeray. The story of how she took her young niece along for support on the day she persuaded the Dean of Westminster Abbey to allow a sculptor to trim the marble whiskers of her father's bust in Poets' Corner is a lovely illustration of the peculiarities of Victorian ancestor worship. The 'charming impressionist writing' of Annie Thackeray Ritchie (*NC*, p. 85) is also related to the prose of her niece's memoir and perhaps to Virginia Woolf's as well.

Finally, the vision of Queen Victoria herself is nowhere more omnipresent in Bloomsbury memoirs than in Mary MacCarthy's. The proximity of Windsor Castle to Eton added an almost feudal unreality to the setting of the Warre-Cornish household, which is described in *A Nineteenth-Century Childhood* in terms of a game of chess: 'The white queen, bishops, knights, and pawns of Camelot, flanked by the Castle towers, stand arrayed, and facing them are the powers and the pawns and the red battlements of Eton' (p. 64). The last scene of the memoir is the funeral procession of the White Queen, which Eton was allowed to watch at Windsor.

VII

Among the Etonians watching Victoria's funeral was another future member of the Group. The Queen's death coincided with Maynard Keynes's maiden speech in College Pop on the barely carried resolution that woman was not more fitted to rule than man (G. Keynes, 'Early Years', p. 34). Sexual equality in the ability to govern was manifest in Keynes's own family, his father becoming the chief educational officer in the university, and his mother the first woman mayor in the city, of Cambridge. Maynard Keynes left no memoirs about his home or school life; 'My Early Beliefs', although it does touch upon the puritan background of his family, is about his education at King's. His brother Geoffrey, however, did write a memoir of Maynard's early years as well as a full-length autobiography finished in his nineties. Geoffrey Keynes notes that his brother had an immense respect for John Brown, his mother's father, who was a Congregationalist minister at Bedford, the biographer of John Bunyan (one of his predecessors there), and a distinguished scholar of English and American puritanism' (G. Keynes, *Gates*, pp. 12–13).[3] The Keyneses gave their children a nonconformist religious education, but their own beliefs may be reflected in their giving up church-going when the children were grown.

Maynard Keynes was born and raised in a semi-detached house on the outskirts of Cambridge that his parents lived in all their long married life. According to his brother, the house was 'unmistakably and inevitably Victorian in character'. Despite Morris wallpaper and prints of Raphael and Reynolds, plus some insignificant oil paintings,

> our home surroundings afforded no aesthetic stimulus of modernity or novelty to our expanding consciousness, but Maynard was fully able to get the best out of his contacts with our academic society. Home was, then, all middle-class comfort and security without luxury. . . . (G. Keynes, 'Early Years', pp. 26–7)

Unaesthetic middle-class comfort and security recur as basic values in the families of Bloomsbury, but with Maynard there was also a clear continuity of intellectual interests between himself and his father. John Neville Keynes was, like his son, not only a Cambridge don and administrator; he was also a logician and an economist. His *Studies and Exercises in Formal Logic* (1884) was considered to be one of the best works on traditional logic, and his *The Scope and Method of Political Economy*, published when Maynard was seven, remained for many years the standard work on the subject (Harrod, p. 10). There is, in fact, a distinct parallel between the Keyneses and the Stephens in the work of parent and child, generation gaps notwithstanding. Another parallel is suggested by Keynes's first biographer. After quoting from a diary entry in which J. N. Keynes regrets that his son's departure for Eton means they will no longer work together in his study, Harrod notes the similarity to the lives of that pair of father-and-son economists, James and John Stuart Mill (p. 13).

VIII

The most extensive and intensive autobiographical Victorian visions of Bloomsbury are to be found in the posthumously published writings of Virginia Woolf. The revised version of 'A Sketch of the Past', written at the end of her life, together with a much earlier substantial fragment entitled 'Reminiscences', three Memoir Club Papers, eleven volumes of published letters and diaries, and a half-dozen fragmentary and still unpublished early diaries constitute an extraordinary autobiographical *oeuvre* which can be further supplemented with her sister's Memoir Club papers. Her earliest diary, kept for a year when she was fifteen in 1897, was begun along with diaries by Vanessa and Adrian as a kind of family group project, and at the end of the year she could write, 'Here is a volume of fairly acute life (the first really *lived* year of my life) ended locked & put away' (DeSalvo, p. 78). Though interesting as a record of her extraordinary reading, it is otherwise unremarkable as a literary document, its allotted daily page filled with various doings and happenings, until the illness and death in July of her half-sister Stella. The entries then become movingly sparse. At the end of the one dated 15 July 1897, for example, she writes how Stella 'came to me before breakfast in her dressing gown to see how I was. She only stayed a minute; but then she was quite well. She left me and I never saw her again' (pNY). There is considerable literary skill in the diarist's use of retrospection and understatement here.[4]

Virginia Woolf's diaries and letters are basic resources for Bloomsbury's literary history; it is the memoirs, however, that most vividly represent the Victorian visions recurring variously in her fictions. As a Victorian memoirist, Virginia Woolf was preceded in her family not only by her father but also by Annie Thackeray Ritchie. Her step-niece owes little to her sentimental novels, though some readers have detected an influence in the prose of Mrs Ritchie's volatile non-fiction (Q. Bell, *Bloomsbury*,

pp. 26–7). Leslie Stephen thought she had a genius for sympathy
(*Mausoleum Book*, p. 12), some of which may be reflected in the
portrait of the enthusiastic but scatty Mrs Hilbery in *Night and
Day*. In her obituary of Annie Thackeray Ritchie, published the
same year as this novel, Virginia Woolf honoured her as 'the
un-acknowledged source of much that remains in men's minds
about the Victorian age. She will be the transparent medium
through which we behold the dead' ('Lady Ritchie', p. 123).[5]
Virginia Woolf's memoirs are not transparent. They lack the
sentiment, sympathy, and enthusiasm of her aunt's; they are
more ironic and more profound.

The visions of Virginia Woolf's memoirs to be looked at here
focus first on her parents and then on her homes. Her mother
died when Virginia was thirteen; her father died at seventy-two,
when she was twenty-two. These facts help to explain why her
memories of her mother are more idealised than those of her
father. The tragedy of Julia Stephen's death, Virginia Woolf
wrote in her last memoir, was that it made her unreal (*MB*,
p. 95). Unreality shadows life throughout Bloomsbury's Victorian visions, but nowhere more than in the death-ridden
Stephen family. The very happy first marriages of both Virginia
Woolf's parents ended with the early deaths of their spouses, and
the presence of children from these marriages in the new household was a reminder of death and the remoteness of past families.
Leslie Stephen's brilliant nephew J. K. Stephen died mad in his
early thirties, three years before Julia died. Two years after her
death Stella, whom J. K. Stephen had loved, died after three
months of marriage. Seven years later Leslie Stephen died, and
two years after that, Thoby Stephen. The mourning that followed the death of Virginia Woolf's mother increased her unreality. 'Lugubrious' is a recurrent adjective in Bloomsbury family
memoirs. The Queen's grief set the pattern. One of Virginia
Woolf's psychological critics, Mark Spilka, has argued that she
had a quarrel with grief. The absence of grief she felt at her
mother's death may suggest a wider failure of feeling, as it does
for example in *Mrs. Dalloway*, but there were other reasons
besides psychological ones for Virginia Woolf's and Bloomsbury's revulsion with nineteenth-century mourning. They
rejected its religious content, manifested in the pious orgies
Forster recounts from Thornton deathbeds. They found in the
sentimentality of the grief, as shown also be Leonard Woolf's

mother, a different kind of failure of feeling. In the Stephen household the exaggerated grief was agnostic. Both of Virginia Woolf's mother's husbands were clergymen; the death of the first also killed his wife's religious faith, and the agnostic writings of the second led to her interest in him. With Julia Stephen's death in 1895 there began, Virginia Woolf wrote in her early memoir for Julian Bell, 'a period of Oriental gloom' in which Stephen's lamentations 'passed the normal limits of sorrow, and hung about the genuine tragedy with folds of Eastern drapery' befitting a Hebrew prophet (*MB*, p. 40). At dinner their faces loomed like Rembrandt portraits, Vanessa Bell recalled (pAG).

The unreality that came with death and grieving in Virginia Woolf's Victorian visions was also counteracted by very different private intimations of intense reality. Death in the family meant 'that the Gods (as I used to phrase it) were taking us seriously. . . . If life were thus made to rear and kick, it was a thing to be ridden. . . . So I came to think of life as something of extreme reality' (*MB*, p. 137). After her mother's death Virginia Woolf experienced two 'moments of being', as she described these mystical manifestations of reality. One was of blazing light at Paddington Station, which contrasted with the mourning gloom at home. The other was the sudden understanding of a poem: 'I had a feeling of transparency in words when they cease to be words and become so intensified that one seems to experience them; to foretell them as if they developed what one is already feeling' (p. 93). This literary moment of being is part of a theory of creativity whose formulations in 'A Sketch of the Past' make that memoir one of Virginia Woolf's most enlightening texts. Before going on with her family memories, it is important to observe the connections being made in it between death, unreality, the moment, writing, and the past.

The central notion in these connections is conveyed again by that indefinable, evaluative term 'reality'. The discrimination of reality was an essential moral activity for Bloomsbury in their lives and their works. One of the functions of a literary history of Bloomsbury, therefore, is to describe the meanings given to 'reality' in their writings. In 'A Sketch of the Past' Virginia Woolf digresses to outline an aesthetic psychology or philosophy (she uses both words) to account for the intense, even mystical, experiences of reality she calls 'moments of being'. These moments, she believes, are the origin of her ability to write, and they are to be separated from the 'many more moments of non-being' – the nondescript, unconscious 'cotton wool' of daily life – in which they are embedded. Moments of being come as shocks. When Virginia Woolf was young, she thought of them as blows from a real enemy hidden behind the cotton wool of appearance. ('A fin in the waste of waters' is a later formulation in her diary and *The Waves*.) Many of these moment–shocks 'brought with them a peculiar horror and a physical collapse', yet others were ecstatic experiences. As she grew up, Virginia Woolf came to think of these moments as revelations of a pattern of reality behind appearance, in which all human beings were connected, as in a work of art. But there was emphatically no creator. In her own writing, Virginia Woolf says, she tries to make real the experience of a moment of reality by putting it into words: 'It is only by putting it into words that I make it whole; this wholeness means that it has lost its power to hurt me. . . .' (*MB*, pp. 70–2). The making of literary wholes is later identified in 'A Sketch of the Past' with the recollection and re-creation of scenes, and she wonders again. 'Is this liability of mine to scene receiving the origin of my writing impulse?' (*MB*, p. 142). If it were the origin, it also seems related to the voices she heard from these scenes and from others – voices that signalled the onset of madness. But, to return to moments of being, the giving of literary form to them also entailed for the novelist those moments of non-being that fill up life and fiction. Some novelists had been able to combine both kinds of moments in their work, but Virginia Woolf felt she had not been able to. This is her last word in the critical argument that she began with *Mr. Bennett and Mrs. Brown*.

The intense momentary consciousness of reality amid every-day moments of non-being is further connected by Virginia Woolf with the remembrance and writing of things past. In revising 'A Sketch of the Past' she carefully maintained the juxtaposition of disastrous events happening in 1939 and 1940 with the nineteenth-century family visions she was sketching. She hoped the present would give her a literary form, a platform from which to view the past. It does, and the form is like a diary. Indeed, she comments on her memoir in the diary she is keeping at the same time, noting that 'the platform of time' allows her two angles of vision, as a child and as a fifty-eight-year-old woman (*D*, v 281). In another revealing simile, quoted at the beginning of this chapter, Virginia Woolf likens the appearance of the present and the reality of the past to the depths of a river over which the surface slides. 'What is there real about this?' she says to Leonard Woolf in her memoir about the disintegrating present of July 1939:

> 'Shall we ever live a real life again?' 'At Monk's House', he says. So I shall write this . . . partly in order to recover my sense of the present by getting the past to shadow this broken surface. Let me then, like a child advancing with bare feet into a cold river, descend again into that stream. (*MB*, p. 98)[6]

'We are sealed vessels afloat upon what it is convenient to call reality', Virginia Woolf wrote in yet another metaphor that also appears elsewhere in her writing; 'at some moments, without a reason, without an effort, the sealing matter cracks; in floods reality' in the form of scenes from the past (p. 142). Yet the waters of reality still contained the enemy. A year and a half after the last date in 'A Sketch of the Past', Virginia Woolf drowned herself.

IX

Until she wrote *To the Lighthouse*, Virginia Woolf says she was obsessed by her mother. Julia Jackson Duckworth Stephen's beauty and sadness, her spirited and unremitting philanthropy, her subservient devotion to her husband – these are the main features of her daughter's vision of her. All the lives that she touched on appeared to form a pattern while she was involved in them, yet, her daughter continues in her early memoir, glancing perhaps at her own life and that of her sister, Julia Stephen 'was no aesthetic spectator collecting impressions for her own amusement' (*MB*, p. 35). One of her activities was to teach her children their lessons, and as a teacher Virginia found her difficult; she was quick-tempered and unsparing of everyone except her husband. 'Although there were certain matters which seem to us now decided by her too much in a spirit of compromise, and exacted by him without strict regard for justice or mag-nanimity', her daughter continues, 'still it is true whether you judge by their work or by themselves that it was a triumphant

life, consistently aiming at high things' (p. 34). The accents here
are surprisingly Victorian, while the criticism of injustice is quite
muted. Later in 'Reminiscences', Virginia Woolf describes her
mother as 'ruthless in her ways, and quite indifferent, if she saw
good, to any amount of personal suffering' (p. 42). And it was
characteristic of the Victorian woman Julia Stephen was that her
daughters, especially the eldest, Stella, suffered more than her
sons. When Leslie Stephen once complained that she treated
Stella more harshly than her brothers, she replied simply that
Stella was part of herself. The repressive raising of females in the
Stephen family owes much, directly and indirectly, to their
mother. She was their first teacher, and it appears from the
selfless, tragic image of Stella Duckworth in Virginia Woolf's
memoirs that the principal domestic lesson to be learned was
how to be the Angel in the House.

The Angel in the House is the title of a long poem by Coventry
Patmore that celebrates married, spiritual, Victorian love by
describing how the female of the title mates her sensitive soul to
her husband's rational one. Patmore was a close friend of Julia
Stephen's mother; she tried to interest her new son-in-law in
Patmore's poetry and was offended by the violence of his
response. (Stephen characteristically thought Patmore's religios-
ity made him an effeminate poet – Maitland, pp. 314–15.)
Virginia Woolf invoked Patmore's title to identify a Victorian
phantom of the house that made professions for women such as
writing impossible. The angel in the house

> was intensely sympathetic. She was immensely charming. She
> was utterly unselfish. She excelled in the different arts of
> family life. She sacrificed herself daily. If there was a chicken,
> she took the leg; if there was a draught she sat in it. . . . Above
> all – I need not say it – she was pure.

The purity most inhibited the writer, for it denied her a mind of
her own, interposing doubts about the propriety of what she was
writing. 'Killing the Angel in the House was part of the occupa-
tion of a woman writer', Virginia Woolf concludes – but not in a
memoir. The angel is a phantom from a speech given in 1931
that was the kernel of *The Years* and *Three Guineas* (*CE*, II 285–6).
This phantom haunts the development of a literary vocation,

which we have seen is central to Virginia Woolf's memoirs, but she is rather faint in the idealised portrait of Julia Stephen.

The reality of Julia Stephen is a problem in autobiographical form as well as content for her daughter. The difficulty with memoirs, Virginia Woolf observes at the beginning of 'A Sketch of the Past', is that 'they leave out the person to whom things happened. The reason is that it is so difficult to describe any human being. So they say: "This is what happened"; but they do not say what the person was like to whom it happened' (*MB*, p. 65). Unlike her 'Reminiscences', which is partly restricted by the child for whom the reminiscing is being done, 'A Sketch of the Past' tries to solve the difficulty by being self-conscious, which helps to explain why it is so concerned with writing and reading. Virginia Woolf's relation to her mother is crucial for 'A Sketch of the Past', and this, of course, brings in the whole question of influences, which is so crucial to literary history. What Virginia Woolf says about it has been misrepresented recently by critics wishing to confine the influences on her essentially to women, so it is best to use her own words. Julia Stephen, says her daughter.

> was one of the invisible presences who after all play so important a part in every life. This influence, by which I mean the consciousness of other groups impinging upon ourselves; public opinion; what other people say and think . . . has never been analysed in any of those Lives which I do so much enjoy reading, or very superficially.

The invisible presence of her mother, she continues, 'should be more definite and more capable of description than for example the influence on me of the Cambridge Apostles, or of the influence of the Galsworthy, Bennett, Wells school of fiction, or the influence of the Vote, or of the War' (pp. 80–1). It should be, but it is not. Why the influence of Julia Stephen is not more definable in 1939 than the influence of groups such as Bloomsbury, the Apostles, Edwardian novelists, the suffragists, is the result of two things. The first is that Virginia Woolf feels she has, psychoanalytically as it were, eased her mother's influence by expressing it through *To the Lighthouse*. The other reason, which brings us back to the subject of her Victorian visions, appears to be that her mother's presence lacked reality. 'Central' is the

word Virginia Woolf thinks is closest to the feeling she had of
her, but this meant 'that one never got far away from her to see
her as a person'. The demands of her family made her only 'a
general presence rather than a particular person to a child of
seven or eight' (*MB*, p. 83). The most vivid moments of memory
her daughter has of her are associated with her death.

> For what reality can remain real of a person who died forty-
> four years ago at the age of forty-nine, without leaving a book,
> or a picture, or any piece of work – apart from the three
> children who now survive and the memory of her that remains
> in their minds? There is the memory; but there is nothing to
> check that memory by; nothing to bring it to ground
> with.'   (p. 85)

The question here about the posthumous reality of her mother
obviously relates to the enduring reality of Virginia Woolf's
father, who left a shelf of books and the *Dictionary of National
Biography* in which his daughter could ground her visions of him.
Julia Stephen did, however, leave some writing behind, both
published and unpublished. In addition to a correspondence
with Leslie Stephen that Virginia Woolf read at the end of her
life and was much moved by, three essays in manuscript and
nearly a dozen stories by Julia Stephen survive.[7] The most
interesting of the essays is a defence of agnostic women that
argues for equality of religious belief, but happily accepts their
inferiority in politics and the professions. Some of the essay's
ironic touches, when directed, for example, against the supposedly more tender mercies of Christian nurses who believe in
hell, or against the supposedly greater civic responsibility of
Christian men, will remind some readers of Leslie Stephen's
ironic humour or Virginia Woolf's. Two manuscripts on the
servant question are firm, even complacent, defences of the
status quo in middle-class family life. Julia Stephen argues that
the current arrangements unite the interests of householders and
servants more satisfactorily than any other system by providing
the former with domestic service and the latter with economic
security.

   The sexual and social assumptions of Victorian patriarchy
also fill the animal and class fables that Julia Stephen wrote. All
those involving people take place in upper or upper-middle-class

families, with their butlers, maids, nurses, pages, cooks and gardeners. The narratives of young children's misadventures offer moral instruction about being thoughtful of others, not hurting animals, and so on. The children are usually boys and even all the animals seem male. Clearly present in the stories is that strong sense of middle-class family security that Leonard Woolf remembered and valued. In one of Julia Stephen's stories, for example, a young boy and girl play at being a crossing-sweeper and cat's-meat seller while their parents are off at a philanthropic meeting. After the children lose their money, they become frightened by the realities of the roles they were playing; this allows a little social commentary along with the author's implicit criticism of parents who appear more intent on reform than on raising their children properly. As works of fiction, Julia Stephen's stories are smoothly written and about as interesting and imaginative as Virginia Woolf's two slight children's stories.[8]

Except for a brief *DNB* article on Julia Margaret Cameron, who preserved her niece's beauty among unforgettable photographic images that influenced Bloomsbury's Victorian visions, the only text Julia Stephen published was a privately printed pamphlet on domestic nursing entitled *Notes from Sick Rooms* that appeared when Virginia was one year old. The nurse desiderated in these notes is no Stracheyan Florence Nightingale. There is no evangelical passion, no reforming ambition in the common sense, the humour and the compassion with which the author treats such subjects as the mysterious origin of bed crumbs or the assumption of visitors that any illness also affects the ears or the brains of the sick.

But the writings, the photographs, the lessons, the early memories were insufficient. Virginia Woolf's mother is not an invisible presence that her daughter could envision beyond the fictiveness of Mrs Ramsay, in an autobiography.

X

Ambivalence rather than unreality characterises the descriptions of Leslie Stephen in his daughter's various visions of him in her letters, diaries and essays, in *The Voyage Out* and *To the Lighthouse*, in Memoir Club papers, 'Reminiscences', and 'A Sketch of the

Past'. At the beginning of the account of Stephen to be found in
the revised version of the 'Sketch', Virginia Woolf noted that it
was only the other day, while reading Freud for the first time,
that she discovered 'this violently disturbing conflict of love and
hate is a common feeling; and is called ambivalence' (*MB*,
p. 108). In her case the natural ambivalence of a daughter's
feelings for her father was increased by his extensive literary
legacy, his divided domestic personality, and the disconnections
of the Victorian households of Virginia Woolf's childhood and
adolescence. It is hardly surprising, given these complications,
that Leslie Stephen's influence on his daughter provokes con-
troversies among her interpreters.

In a Memoir Club paper on Virginia Woolf's childhood,
Vanessa Bell remembered that, when they were very young,
Virginia once asked her sister whom she liked best, her mother
or her father. Vanessa, disturbed by the propriety but also
stimulated by the freedom of the question, replied her mother,
but Virginia 'went on to explain why she, on the whole, preferred
my father', her answer being more critical than Vanessa's surer,
simpler response (VB/*Notes*, p. 7). Much later, in her centenary
essay on her father, Virginia Woolf agreed with James Russell
Lowell's assessment of him as 'the most lovable of men' – a
quality that made him 'unforgettable' (*CE*, IV 80). And almost
the last thing in 'A Sketch of the Past' is the recollection of a
loving visit to his study to return a book:

> Rising he would go to the shelves, put the book back, and ask
> me gently, kindly: 'What did you make of it?' Perhaps I was
> reading Boswell; without a doubt, I would be gnawing my way
> through the eighteenth century. Then, feeling proud and
> stimulated, and full of love for this unworldly, very disting-
> uished and lonely man, whom I had pleased by coming, I
> would go back to the drawing room and hear George's patter.
> There was no connection. There were deep divisions. (*MB*,
> pp. 157–8)

Virginia Woolf's affection for her father requires emphasising,
because in her complex vision of him love is sometimes obscured
by anger, disgust, even hate. Julia Stephen was the indirect
cause of some of these feelings, for she cultivated her husband's
dependence upon herself and would have approved of its transfer

to her daughter Stella after her death. Stella, who appears to have lacked her mother's intelligence and spirit, bore the additional burden of her stepfather's remorse for his selfishness towards his dead wife. 'I was not as bad as Carlyle, was I?' Virginia heard him ask Stella, whom she thought might never have heard of Carlyle (p. 41). After Stella's death Leslie Stephen was 'quite prepared to take Vanessa for his next victim'. He appeared as some kind of monster, claiming one angel of the house after another, a 'tyrant of inconceivable selfishness, who had replaced the beauty and merriment of the dead with ugliness and gloom'. This was his daughter's judgemental vision just five years after his death. She admits it was unjust, the consequence in part of the wide difference in age between his daughters and himself. A mother or an older sister should have intervened to spare them, 'but again, death spoilt what should have been so fair' (p. 56).

Returning to the memories of her father in 1940, Virginia Woolf is more circumstantial and analytic. She realises that the difficulties Leslie Stephen raised over Stella's engagement were prompted by jealousy. What made matters so bad was his unawareness of this. Fresh from her biography of Roger Fry, Virginia Woolf applied to her father Fry's equation of civilisation and awareness, and concluded that her father was uncivilised. Nothing was so dreadful for the individual or those around him, she concluded, as egotism (pp. 146–7). For seven years Vanessa and Virginia confronted the tyranny of their father's domestic egotism. Wednesdays were the worst.

> On that day the weekly books were given him. Early that morning we knew whether they were under or over the danger mark – eleven pounds if I remember right. On a bad Wednesday we ate our lunch in the anticipation of torture. The books were presented directly after lunch. He put on his glasses. Then he read the figures. Then down came his fist on the account book. His veins filled; his face flushed. Then there was an inarticulate roar. Then he shouted . . . 'I am ruined.' Then he beat his breast. Then he went through an extraordinary dramatisation of self pity, horror, anger. (p. 144)

Stephen did not like Virginia to witness these scenes with Vanessa and was ashamed of them afterwards. ' "You must think me", he said to me after one of these rages – I think the word he used was "foolish". I was silent. I did not think him foolish. I thought him brutal' (p. 146). Vanessa Bell's account of these ordeals is more detailed and sympathetic. She was quite willing to fiddle with the books in order to reduce some of the outbursts, and she later recognised what an aggravatingly silent young woman she must have been. Storms and silences were the chief means of communication between a daughter for whom life apart from people was almost entirely visual, and a father with so little interest in art that in all his visits to the Alps he never once went down into Italy (pAG).[9]

The puritan foundations of sound saving and careful expenditure on which the essential economic security of Bloomsbury's Victorian households rested (and which Keynesian economics would criticise in the next century) appears in most of the family memoirs. Its success was demonstrated in the economic independence of the Stephen sisters, Fry, Clive Bell and Forster. But the violent anxiety that Leslie Stephen suffered over his household accounts, and made his daughters suffer with him, had more than an economic cause, Virginia Woolf is at pains to show in 'A Sketch of the Past'. As she tries to explain her father as domestic tyrant, the ambivalences in her sketch reappear. They can be seen in the metaphor she introduces in her revised text to give form to her memories. Leslie Stephen's type is 'like a steel engraving, without colour, or warmth or body; but with an infinity of precise clear lines' (*MB*, p. 109). The image doubles the pictorial analogy of the memoir she called a sketch, and is used later as a metaphor for Cambridge's influence on her father. But when Virginia Woolf begins to describe Stephen's temper – how he was indulged as a child and later hoped to be a Victorian genius, licensed like Carlyle or Tennyson for self-centred misbehaviour, and how, knowing that he had only a good second-class mind, he became despondent and hungry for compliments – then the Cambridge steel engraving takes on the colours of a painting.

Involved with the frustrated aspirations of genius was Stephen's characteristic Victorian assumption that a woman's role, which Vanessa refused to play, was to be 'part slave, part angel' (p. 146). Leslie Stephen's tantrums never occurred while men were present; his biographer Maitland refused to believe he even had a temper. Stephen himself may not have believed it. He was unconscious of his egotistical brutality, his daughter thought, because of the disparity between his strong critical and enfeebled imaginative powers. Ultimately this disparity goes back to the puritan inheritance of the Stephens. Early in 'A Sketch of the Past' Virginia Woolf describes her father as 'spartan, ascetic, puritanical. He had I think no feeling for pictures; no ear for music; no sense of the sound of words' (p. 68). (But Stephen's love for the sound of ,poetry, large amounts of which he easily memorised and repeatedly recited out loud to himself, suggests some exaggeration in her account.) Virginia Woolf wondered in this context if her own love of beauty were affected by 'some ancestral dread' that she relates to her sense of shame and fear about her body. And this is connected with her dislike of self-conscious actions such as looking in a mirror – a characteristic she shared with her grandfather[10] – or posing for painters, sculptors or photographers. More importantly, she associates these puritan vestiges with the traumatic experiences of incestuous fondling that she was subjected to by her half-brother Gerald when she was a small child (pp. 68–9).

In her memoir Virginia Woolf thought, however, that the discrepancy between Stephen's critical and creative faculties was more immediately the result of Cambridge's unaesthetic education compounded with the sustained mental exertions required of a nineteenth-century professional author. Stephen could analyse thought in the best Cambridge way – Keynes confirmed this to her – but his analysis of character was crude and conventional. By the time he was sixty-five, 'he was a man in prison, isolated. He had so ignored, or disguised his own feelings that he had no idea of what he was; and no idea of what other people were' (p. 146).

Yet he was the most lovable of men, capable of considerable moral delicacy. When the issue of marriage with a deceased wife's sister raised its head again in Bloomsbury's families – this time with Stella's widower, Jack Hills, and her half-sister Vanessa – George Duckworth led the attack but got no support from the author of *The Science of Ethics*:

he, with that backbone of intellect which would have made him, had we lived to be at ease with him, so dependable in serious relations, had said simply; she must do as she liked; he was not going to interfere. That was what I admire in him; his dignity and sanity in the larger affairs; so often covered up by his irritations and vanities and egotisms.   (p. 142)

XI

Virginia Woolf's late memoir offers here again the explanation which she finally used to resolve her conflicting visions of Leslie Stephen. He was too old and his children too young to live at ease with one another.

> Two different ages confronted each other in the drawing room at Hyde Park Gate. The Victorian age and the Edwardian age. We were not his children; we were his grandchildren. . . . But while we looked into the future, we were completely under the power of the past. Explorers and revolutionists, as we both were by nature, we lived under the sway of a society that was about fifty years too old for us. It is this curious fact that made our struggle so bitter and so violent. For the society in which we lived was still the Victorian society. Father himself was a typical Victorian. George and Gerald were consenting and approving Victorians. So we had two quarrels to wage; two fights to fight; one with them individually; and one with them socially. We were living say in 1910; they were living in 1860.   (*MB*, p. 147)

This conflict in age and ages is presented in Virginia Woolf's autobiographical texts through visions of places as well as people. Like Fry, Leonard Woolf and Strachey, Virginia Woolf represents houses, their settings and rooms as symbols of the lives that were lead in them. 22 Hyde Park Gate is described as a model of Victorian life. Cage images recur in metaphors sometimes of grim prisons, sometimes of absurd circuses or zoos. Here is a scene of life with father around 1897:

> It was like being shut up in the same cage with a wild beast. Suppose I, at fifteen, was a nervous, gibbering, little monkey, always spitting or cracking a nut and shying the shells about, and mopping and mowing, and leaping into dark corners and then swinging in rapture across the cage, he was the pacing,

dangerous, morose lion; a lion who was sulky and angry and injured; and suddenly ferocious, and then very humble, and then majestic; and then lying dusty and fly pestered in a corner of the cage. (*MB*, p. 116)

Continuing to describe the cage of 22 Hyde Park Gate, Virginia Woolf switches to the image of a family body. The tea-table was its heart, the bedroom its sexual, birth and death centre, and the study at the top of the house the family's brain. There was also a room of one's own. Virginia Woolf's description of her first such room exhibits once more the ambivalence of her Victorian visions. The room was divided into living and sleeping halves, and they too fought each other as she retreated there in a rage with her father, read herself into an ecstatic trance, was interrupted by the family, studied Greek, and 'first heard those horrible voices . . .'. That room – she now imagines some occupant thinking who has read her work – explains a great deal about the person who wrote *To the Lighthouse*, *A Room of One's Own* or *The Common Reader* (*MB*, pp. 123–4).

Toward the end of 'A Sketch of the Past' Virginia Woolf develops the idea of 22 Hyde Park Gate as a machine in which the inhabitants had to follow the routines of the Victorian game of manners. There was little time for personal work between the obligations of breakfast and the social pressures that began after lunch, mounted at tea with callers, increased through the formal-dress dinner, and culminated in the parties to which George Duckworth dragged his half-sisters. The machine game of Victorian life had its advantages for social intercourse; it allowed the communication of things that would have been inaudible if spoken straight out. But for the writer, especially the woman writer, Virginia Woolf found that this angelic social behaviour was harmful: 'when I read my old *Literary Supplement* articles, I lay the blame for their suavity, their politeness, their side-long approach, to my tea-table training' (*MB*, pp. 147–50).[11] The disconnection in the machine that was the Victorian home separated the social conventionality of the drawing-room from the intellectual work of Stephen's study, and this did not help the education of a writer either. Practically no relation existed between the hoops of Victorian society that George Duckworth was flying through and the visits of Meredith, James, Watts, Sidgwick, Symonds, Haldane, Burne-Jones and Lowell.

The experience of their greatness was in their presence, not in how they behaved or what they said. 'But it never exists now. I cannot remember ever to have felt greatness since I was a child' (p. 158).

The revised version of Virginia Woolf's last memoir breaks off with this sentence, but it might be concluded with a passage near the end of her diary that emphasises again the memoir's two intersecting angles of view, the child's and the adult's. These are Virginia Woolf's last, Yeats-like words of tranquillity on her parents:

> How beautiful they were, those old people – I mean father & mother – how simple, how clear, how untroubled. I have been dipping into old letters & fathers memoirs. He loved her – oh & was so candid & reasonable & transparent – & had such a fastidious delicate mind, educated, & transparent. How serene & gay even their life reads to me: no mud; no whirlpools. And so human – with the children & the little hum & song of the nursery. But if I read as a contemporary I shall lose my childs vision & so must stop. Nothing turbulent; nothing involved: no introspection.   (*D*, v 345)

XII

The symbolic significance of Virginia Woolf's Victorian home is further described in two of the papers she wrote for the Memoir Club in the early 1920s. The tone of these papers is very different from the long autobiographical fragments written fifteen to twenty years before and after. One of the papers is very similar to Lytton Strachey's memoir of Lancaster Gate and may in fact have influenced it. Another unpublished Memoir Club paper by Vanessa Bell on the same subject resembles both of them.

The Stephen and Strachey houses still stand across Kensington Gardens from each other, and both, as Strachey said of his, were crowning symbols of the Victorian family system. Virginia Woolf's Memoir Club paper entitled '22 Hyde Park Gate' begins with the indispensability of folding doors in a Victorian drawing-room to separate tea-table chat from agonised confessions. How could life have been carried on without them, she asks the club members. 'As soon as dispense with water-closets or bathrooms as with folding doors in a family of nine men and women, one of whom into the bargain was an idiot' (*MB*, p. 164). Despite its title, Virginia Woolf's paper is actually about George Duckworth's unhappy (for both of them) efforts to introduce her into Victorian society at the turn of the century, and she ends with an ironically sensational revelation that George was both his sisters' lover. With Virginia this amounted to cuddling when she was in bed. In Vanessa's memoir of Hyde Park Gate, however, George Duckworth appears as a chaperone-*cum*-nursemaid, rather than an incestuous half-brother. He supplemented Leslie Stephen's meagre allowance with everything from jewels and dresses to a horse for riding in Rotten Row. George accompanied Vanessa on the rides and to the evening parties, the Sunday calls (including one to Mrs Humphry Ward, who seems to have been trying to continue George Eliot's salon) and the country weekends – most of which her younger sister escaped (pAG).

Virginia Woolf's Hyde Park Gate memoir is continued in a paper entitled 'Old Bloomsbury', which was also the subject of one by Vanessa Bell. At the beginning of her memoir Virginia alludes again to the scene of George's cuddling, but does not suggest it was incestuous. Then she offers a fuller vision of an extended Victorian family's house in which such goings-on were possible:

> It was a house of innumerable small oddly shaped rooms built to accommodate not one family but three. . . . To house the lot of us, now a storey would be thrown out on top, now a dining room flung out at bottom. My mother, I believe, sketched what she wanted on a sheet of notepaper to save the architect's fees. (*MB*, p. 182)

The cupboards and wardrobes were filled with the possessions of the past – 'filth-packets' the Stracheys called them in their house. 'The place seemed tangled and matted with emotion. . . . The walls and rooms had in sober truth been built to our shape. We had permeated the whole vast fabric . . .' (p. 183). Virginia Woolf thought she could write the history of every mark on her room's wall. What might have been said in that unwritten history may be guessed at through the contrast 22 Hyde Park Gate offered to that other Victorian house of her childhood,

Talland House at St Ives in Cornwall, the house she enshrined in
To the Lighthouse. There the most important of her early memories
began, memories evoked again in *The Waves* and finally in 'A
Sketch of the Past'. 'If life has a base that it stands upon', she
wrote at the beginning of her final attempt to recapture the
ecstatic past of early childhood,

> if it is a bowl that one fills and fills and fills – then my bowl
> without a doubt stands upon this memory. It is of lying half
> asleep, half awake, in bed in the nursery at St Ives. It is of
> hearing the waves breaking, one, two, one, two, and sending a
> splash of water over the beach; and then breaking one, two,
> one, two, behind a yellow blind. It is of hearing the blind draw
> its little acorn across the floor as the wind blew the blind out.
> It is of lying and hearing this splash and seeing this light, and
> feeling, it is almost impossible that I should be here; of feeling
> the purest ecstasy I can conceive.

And once again in her memoirs she reverts to analogies of visual
art to convey her vision. If she were a painter, she says, her first
impressions would be painted 'in pale yellow, silver, and green'
(*MB*, pp. 64–6). The contrast between the two Victorian household worlds of Virginia Woolf's childhood can be seen in colour
and light alone. The colours of memories at Talland House were
offset by the steel-engraved father of Hyde Park Gate, where the
Watts tradition of black, gold-lined woodwork and red velvet
favoured by Julia Stephen prevailed. Only outside the house, in
Kensington Gardens, was there beauty comparable to the setting
of Talland House.

XIII

That the most famous critic of the Victorians should have
devoted his only family memoir to a house rather than his
parents illustrates again the significance of place in Bloomsbury's Victorian visions. Lytton Strachey's Memoir Club paper
'Lancaster Gate' reads in part like a continuation of Virginia
Woolf's '22 Hyde Park Gate'. Both papers end in sexual encounters with relatives in bedrooms. Both focus on the drawing-room
– 'the riddle of the Victorian Age', Strachey called it (*LSH*,

p. 20). Both houses were huge, dark and badly designed; there was only one bathroom in each, though the Stephens had three water-closets to the Stracheys' one, according to these memoirs. Both houses, in brief, moulded the lives of their occupants. The meaning of personal history, Strachey maintained, was to be found not in love, work or mortality (he was luckier in his family history than Virginia Woolf in hers) but in the atmosphere of existence. And it was just the atmosphere of Lancaster Gate that revolted Strachey. Like Forster's and Virginia Woolf's, his memories disclose that the lives of his family were as entangled in their houses as the souls in their bodies. Such an idea would have been dismissed by Victorian fathers, Strachey continues, because they were more concerned with the mental, moral and social implications of surroundings rather than with their actual nature:

> The notion that the proportions of a bedroom, for instance, might be significant would have appeared absurd to them. . . . Our view is different. We find satisfaction in curves and colours, and windows fascinate us, we are agitated by staircases, inspired by doors, disgusted by cornices, depressed by chairs, made wanton by ceilings, entranced by passages, and exacerbated by a rug. (p. 16)

The hyperbole here is Strachey's response to the dowdiness of his home. Yet 'few things could be imagined more terrible', he added later, 'than a *smart* Lancaster Gate' (p. 24). Hyde Park Gate could never be called smart, but Virginia Woolf did not picture it as dowdy or disordered as Strachey's. To him and his innumerable siblings nosing into the corners of their house,

> the full incorrectitude of the place stood revealed. Visitors, perhaps, might not particularly notice, but *we* knew by heart all the camouflaged abysses, taking a sardonic delight in the ruthlessness of the introspective realism with which we plumbed and numbered 'filth-packet' after 'filth-packet' – for such was our too descriptive phrase.

The sardonic delight and the introspective realism of nosing out filth-packets continued on into Strachey's biographies. At Lan-

caster Gate he wondered if the whole house were not 'one vast
filth-packet, and we the mere *disjecta membra* of vanished generations, which Providence was too busy or too idle to clear away'
(pp. 25–6). There are times in his writing, too, when Strachey
appears to wonder if the same might not be true of the entire
Victorian age.

In the midst of Lancaster Gate's chaos, however, there was
still vitality. Strachey thought that 'the same vitality, the same
optimism, the same absence of nerves, which went into the
deliberate creation of ten children, built the crammed, high,
hideous edifice that sheltered them' (p. 20). By the time he was
growing up, Strachey found this vitality coming from his mother
rather than his father, who was sixty-two when Lytton was born.
Sir Richard had been a distinguished Indian administrator and
scientist, but, when Leonard Woolf visited the family in 1902,
Lytton's father was spending all his time reading novels by the
fire while family life swirled around him.

In her obituary of Lady Strachey written for the *Nation and
Athenaeum* in 1928, Virginia Woolf commented on her wide
literary culture: 'She had her hands upon the whole body of
English literature, from Shakespeare to Tennyson, with the large
loose grasp that was so characteristic of the cultivated Victorian.' This culture and energy were indeed characteristic of
the finest Victorian women, and Virginia Woolf found it easy
to 'imagine how, had she been a man, she would have ruled
a province or administered a Government department' (*BP*,
p. 208). When he was thirty-six and in the midst of writing
Eminent Victorians, Strachey assured his mother, 'if I ever *do* do
anything worth doing I'm sure it will be owing to you much
more than to anyone else' (MH/*LS*, p. 631). But later to the
Memoir Club Strachey stressed his mother's vague immaterial-
ity and eccentricity, which noticeably affected the conventionality of Strachey family life. In religion, for example, where the
Stracheys like the Stephens were agnostics, Lytton's mother had
all her children christened, 'but she never went to Church –
except in the country, when she went with the utmost regularity'
(*LSH*, p. 24).

The Stracheys' unconventionality is attributed by Lytton to
their class. Like the rest of Bloomsbury's families they were
upper-middle-class professionals, but with a penchant for government service. They differed more importantly from the Frys,
Woolfs, Thorntons, Warre-Cornishes, Keyneses and Stephens in

their aristocratic origins, which went back to the eighteenth century and before. Strachey family history was longer than any one else's in Bloomsbury, and an account of a voyage to Bermuda by one ancestor probably influenced Shakespeare's *The Tempest*. The aristocratic origins of the Stracheys might also help to explain their differences from a number of Bloomsbury families – though not the Stephens or the Warre-Cornishes, perhaps – in the manner in which the Stracheys' middle-class professionalism was, in Lytton's words, 'interpenetrated by intellectualism and eccentricity'. He thought that this mixture resulted in 'the peculiar disintegrating force of the Strachey character' (*LSH*, p. 25). But, with all its disintegration, the Strachey household did not exhibit the kind of disconnection Virginia Woolf remembered feeling in the Stephen household.

There is another Strachey memoir of a kind, though not strictly speaking a Bloomsbury memoir, in which the Strachey parents resemble other Bloomsbury parents a little more than in 'Lancaster Gate'. The anonymous, fictionalised autobiography *Olivia* by Lytton Strachey's second eldest sister, Dorothy Bussy, the distinguished translator of André Gide, was dedicated to the memory of Virginia Woolf and published by the Hogarth Press in 1949. In it Olivia describes her parents as militantly agnostic yet completely unsceptical about the Victorian ideals of work, self-sacrifice and good manners. Like Sir Edward Fry, Olivia's father would not have dreamt of subjecting moral laws to the minute scrutiny he gave as a scientist to the laws of nature. Dorothy, who was sixteen years older than Lytton, attributed her mother's vitality and vagueness to her Victorian ability to keep experience at bay. 'Married at eighteen, and the mother of thirteen children, she was', her daughter imagined, 'completely unaware of her senses.' The statement is not easy to believe, even in an autobiography of schoolgirl love, but that was how she seems to have appeared to her children. And it is similar, finally, to the criticism that Fry made of his parents, Forster of the Thorntons, and Virginia Woolf of her father. Despite their varied intellectual interests, there was

a curious, an almost anomalous lack – an insufficient sense, that is – of humanity and art. With all her love of literature and music and painting, with all her vivid intelligence, my mother, I think, never felt them otherwise than with her mind. (*Olivia*, pp. 13–14)

XIV

Bloomsbury's autobiographical Victorian visions are focused much more on family than school life. The reasons for this depend upon the sex of the memoirist. For the men of Bloomsbury the most important formative experiences outside their families happened to them at university, not school. This differentiates them from many of their contemporaries, as well as from writers, such as Isherwood, Auden and Orwell, who grew up in the 1920s. As for the women of Bloomsbury, only one attended a school at which the kind of sentimental education described in Dorothy Bussy's *Olivia* was possible. Mary MacCarthy was sent from her Eton home to a very High Church school, whose education she remembered almost entirely in terms of religious rituals or schoolmate friendships. Of her finishing-school in Berlin she writes nothing in *A Nineteenth-Century Childhood*.

Virginia Woolf and Vanessa Bell never went away to school. Virginia's health was clearly one of the causes for her being kept at home. Another was their mother's lack of enthusiasm for the higher education of women; she had even signed an anti-suffrage petition arguing that women had enough domestic duties to take care of without needing the vote too (*MB*, p. 120). Leslie Stephen believed women should be better educated and accorded his daughters the theoretical freedom to choose their careers, but the education of his sons left little or no money for this. His daughters were taught at home first by their mother and after her death by their father. Later on Virginia read some Greek and German with him, and remembered his characteristic method of teaching languages: 'He put all grammar on one side, and then, taking some classic, made straight for the sense' (Maitland, p. 476). One consequence of the Stephen daughters being taught at home was the neglect by agnostic parents of their religious education. E. M. Forster once evoked 'the spiritual shallows' of his schooling with a story of the shock and missionary zeal caused in him by a schoolmate who did not know the meaning of Good Friday ('How I Lost', p. 263). Neither did Virginia Stephen. Vanessa recalled that her young sister once had to be removed from a singing-class, shrieking with laughter, after another child had explained what the crucifixion was (*Notes*, p. 9).

In her memoir of Virginia's childhood Vanessa also recalled how nerve-racking the arithmetic lessons of her father were for both teacher and pupils. The result was that all their lives the daughters of this Cambridge mathematician counted up on their fingers. Virginia Woolf later had Greek lessons from Clara Pater and then Janet Case; she also did some Latin and Greek as well as history at King's College, London, while Vanessa studied painting first in South Kensington and then at the Royal Academic Schools. That grubby and shabby world of art students, she remembered, allowed her to be interested in shapes and colours alone, and therefore had no connection with her home life (pAG). Vanessa agreed with Virginia, however, that they were both uneducated,

> if by education is meant learning things out of books. If she had none, however, I had less, for she did at least teach herself or get herself taught Greek, and was given books to read by my father which may, for all I know, have had educational value. (*Notes*, p. 8)

The dryness of Vanessa Bell's qualification should not obscure the enormous value of having Leslie Stephen and his books as one's teacher and library of English literature and history. Virginia Woolf recollected for her father's biographer how Stephen had read to the family such writers as Stevenson, Hawthorne, Shakespeare, Thackeray (he broke off in the middle of *Vanity Fair* because it was 'too terrible'), Carlyle, Austen, and especially Scott; and for poetry there was Milton, Wordsworth, Arnold, Meredith, Kipling and others. Stephen's capacity for memorising poetry was extraordinary, and Virginia could not separate many great English poems from the memory of father and his ideas: 'I hear in them not only his voice, but in some sort his teaching and belief' (Maitland, pp. 474–6). As for her own reading at home, she remembered her father saying, 'Gracious child, how you gobble!' when she would ask for another volume and be reminded that anything worth reading was worth reading twice (*L*, IV 27). The fare she gobbled is set forth in some detail in her earliest extant diary, and it shows how she ate her way through eighteenth- and nineteenth-century English history, biography, and fiction, and sampled the sixteenth and seventeenth centuries as well (pNY). But reading by oneself was not enough. All her life Virginia Woolf regretted that she had not attended school, for, never having 'competed in any way with children of my own age, I have never been able to compare my gifts and defects with other people's' (*MB*, p. 65). Her resentment of this lack of education was one of the chief sources of Virginia Woolf's feminism. Yet for a genius this lack might also have been an advantage, as those who have had their gifts devalued by formal education will appreciate.

In 1938, during the Spanish Civil War, Virginia Woolf argued in *Three Guineas* that women such as she had, in effect, been declassed by their lack of capital and education – the two prime characteristics, she says, of the bourgeoisie. (She goes back to *Pendennis*, a novel by her father's first father-in-law, for the phrase 'Arthur's Education Fund' that she uses to describe the familiar situation of the sons absorbing the family's financial resources in their education and the daughters being left without education or money.) Women like herself are not, she says, of the middle class, they are merely 'educated men's daughters' (*3G*, pp. 10–12, 265), E. M. Forster also related school education to class, but in a way that suggests, again, that there were advantages as well as disadvantages to being informally educated in late-nineteenth-century England. In 'Notes on the English Character', which he wrote in 1920 and then used as the opening essay in *Abinger Harvest* fifteen years later, Forster argued that the undeveloped heart of England was the middle classes, and the undeveloped heart of the middle classes was the public-school system (*AH*, pp. 3–5). Applied to Victorian literature, the argument needs some refinement, for the protagonists of the two greatest Victorian autobiographies each suffered acutely from undeveloped hearts, yet neither Mill nor Ruskin was educated at an English public school. In *The Longest Journey* and then again in *Maurice* – the fullest treatments of public-school education in Bloomsbury's writings – Forster developed some of the implications of this criticism in Edwardian life, but it was not until the First World War that he realised, along with Lytton Strachey in his *Eminent Victorians* portrait of Dr Arnold, the national and international harm this system had helped to cause. Virginia Woolf does not write of men's undeveloped hearts, but her feminist arguments lead straight from the limitations of the English public school and university education to the values of compassionate pacifism.

XV

Forster went to Tonbridge School, Clive Bell to Marlborough, Keynes to Eton, Strachey to Leamington College, Thoby Stephen to Clifton, Duncan Grant to St Paul's – but none cared to remember them outside of fiction. Only Roger Fry, Desmond MacCarthy and Leonard Woolf wrote recollections of their Victorian school experiences, but all illustrated the influential pedagogical priorities of Thomas Arnold's Rugby. As quoted in *Eminent Victorians*, these were, 'first, religious and moral princi-ple; secondly, gentlemanly conduct; thirdly, intellectual ability' (p. 188). The results of these priorities were not entirely what the morally energetic but intellectually confused Christian of Strachey's biography wanted; the old emphasis on classical grammar remained, and to it was added the worship of athletics and good form. Strachey's portrait of Arnold is less sympathetic, closer to caricature, than his portraits of other eminent Vic-torians, perhaps because the consequences of Arnold's ideas for the minds and bodies of late-Victorian schoolboys were more obvious to Strachey and his friends than the influence of a priest, a nurse or a soldier.

Roger Fry's education away from home began symbolically enough with gifts of a watch from his father and a Bible from his mother. His experiences at preparatory school had left him, he told the Memoir Club, with 'a morbid horror of all violence between men so that I can scarcely endure the stimulation of it on the stage'. As head of school Roger was forced to witness the headmaster's sadistic floggings, and the images of these in his memoirs that Virginia Woolf quotes are disgusting:

> There was a wild red-haired Irish boy, himself rather a cruel brute, who whether deliberately or as a result of the pain or whether he had diarrhoea, let fly. The irate clergyman instead of stopping at once simply went on with increased fury until the whole ceiling and walls of his study were spattered with filth. (VW/*RF*, p. 33)

It was some time before Fry understood through erections his repressed sexual responses to these beatings, though Virginia Woolf could not include this explanation in her quoted account (RF/pKC).[12] Fry remembered with astonishment how his daily

Bible readings failed to affect his total immunity from sexual comprehension. Disturbing to him in a different way was the apparent hypocrisy of his parents to school beatings; they had told him there would be none, yet he could not doubt that they knew about them. Fry himself was never beaten – 'I was of such a disgustingly law-abiding disposition' – and perhaps that was sufficient for his parents' consciences. As for the headmaster, he seems to have been fond of Fry and bequeathed him a copy of Dr Arnold's sermons (VW/*RF*, pp. 32–5).

The public school Fry attended was the recently established Clifton, whose first headmaster was a well-known disciple of Arnold's. Distinguished masters were teaching there, and later Leslie Stephen, who had suffered at Eton, sent Thoby to Clifton. However, Fry's time at public school was largely but not completely wasted, Virginia Woolf wrote, because of Clifton's 'good form, its Christian patriotism, and its servility to established institutions' (p. 43). The presence of Fry's schoolmate Jack McTaggart made the years at Clifton almost worthwhile. (Another schoolmate was Graf Harry Kessler, who loved Clifton in his memoirs and included Fry among his friends.) An atheistic idealist at Cambridge, McTaggart was an atheistic materialist at Clifton, but he tactfully concealed this from his Quaker friend. McTaggart's intellectual brilliance, spiritual depth and obvious bad form led to a friendship with Fry that was continued at Cambridge among the Apostles and for the rest of their lives. Yet McTaggart's intensely conservative loyalty to all his institutions did not influence his friend. Fry remained as resolutely antagonistic to the English public-school system and its values as Forster.

Desmond MacCarthy's school memoir typically treats anecdotally and digressively only his first two days at Eton. It contrasts with Fry's and Leonard Woolf's because like Keynes he enjoyed his time there. But MacCarthy's vision of Eton is not all that different from Fry's of Clifton or Leonard Woolf's of St Paul's. His education, like Fry's, did not for the most part come from his teachers. 'In spite of having been at Eton and Cambridge,' he begins his Memoir Club paper on his youth, 'I regard myself as a self-educated man, so little have I owed to those who tried to teach me. . . . At school I was educated by the boys, at Cambridge by my friends – and myself' (*M*, p. 205). What the boys taught him at Eton was worldly knowledge of games and sex. His father's only advice was not to go about with older boys because it was not good form. (As for following good form himself, MacCarthy's father horrified his son by turning up on parents' day in a cap!) The headmaster's solemn advice to the new boys was to 'shun the abomination in our midst', and he told them of a father who had wished his son dead rather than tainted with this abomination. Despite some temptations, Mac-Carthy avoided it, but without restricting very much his sexual education at Eton:

> If I were a novelist, I should have no difficulty whatever in describing the mingled feelings of apprehension and exhilaration in a virtuous maid waiting upon a group of dazzling young swells: I should only have to recall my experiences as a fag.   (*M*, pp. 211–12)

The Bloomsbury character of MacCarthy's memories of Eton appears in a review he once wrote of Percy Lubbock's *Shades of Eton.* They were contemporaries, but so different were their recollections that in a sense they were not at the same school. 'His Eton is composed entirely of masters and traditions, mine of boys and places' (DM/*E*, p. 153). The pieties of Lubbock's remembered shades are absent from MacCarthy's memoir, which is dominated by lunatic boys he knew there. The anecdotes about them begin humorously and end sadly.

Another contemporary of MacCarthy's at Eton was, of course, his future wife. In a different sense she was not at the same school either. Had she and other daughters of educated men been students there, the abomination, the piety, the madness of the place might well have been diminished.

Keynes attended Eton six years after MacCarthy, and was a colleger instead of an oppidan. He left no memoir of his triumphant academic and social successes there, but in his mother's memoir glimpses are to be seen of him with his daily new white tie and fresh boutonnière – which provoked F. R. Leavis's comment that this descendant of Bunyan-chapel ministers was apparently attending Vanity Fair ('Keynes and Currency', pp. 398–9).

XVI

At St Paul's Duncan Grant studied mathematics and history preparing to follow his father in an army career, until Lady Strachey persuaded his parents that he was better off at the Westminster School of Art. For Leonard Woolf, however, St Paul's was where his education in the strict sense began – and also ended, five years later, with his winning a classical scholarship to Cambridge. Before he went to St Paul's, Leonard Woolf spent two years at a preparatory school, where his education too consisted chiefly in learning about cricket and sex. From the former he learned to play games seriously and with style. From the latter he recoiled with disgust; the school had the atmosphere of a brothel until his brother and he, as successive heads of school, cleaned the place up. Preparatory school also taught Leonard Woolf how to make himself acceptable as a 'swot', in which he was assisted by his setaceous Hebrew character.

The central theme of Leonard Woolf's educational memories in *Sowing* is the traditional English contempt for intelligence and intellectuality. He found the origins of this attitude, which had made England the most philistine country in Europe, in the public school, and his view supplements Forster's indictment of the institution's inadequate emotional education. Leonard Woolf's response to its anti-intellectualism was to develop what he called his carapace, but he admired those, such as G. E. Moore, Virginia Woolf and even Forster himself to a certain degree, who had enough of the 'silly' in them to survive without shells (pp. 71–2). Of those, such as MacCarthy, who were able to charm their way through school without having their minds or their hearts atrophy, Leonard Woolf says little in his rather grim memoir.

The education of Leonard Woolf at St Paul's was in what he calls 'classical fanaticism' (p. 77). He was better at mathematics, enjoying it more perhaps than Greek or Latin, yet almost his entire public-school effort was channelled into making the grammar, syntax and vocabulary of those languages 'part of the permanent furniture of my mind' (p. 75). It was a training rather than an education, devoted to means rather than ends in themselves, for its overriding purpose was to turn boys into scholars who would promote the greater glory of St Paul's by winning scholarships at Oxford and Cambridge. One sympathetic master recognised Leonard Woolf's intelligence from his English essays and encouraged him to read widely and develop his own judgement. And there was also an exclusive debating-society at St Paul's that, like the Apostles, brought Leonard Woolf into contact with older members for the purpose of frank, thoroughly intellectual discussion, but only of politics, not of the arts. G. K. and Cecil Chesterton were among the members Leonard Woolf remembered debating with, as was Edmund Clerihew Bentley. Compton Mackenzie was another contemporary, who later told Leonard Woolf that he had put him into one of his novels (LW/'Coming', p. 30). It was not *Sinister Street*, which deals extensively with St Paul's but embodies the customary sentimental, intellectually limited if not completely anti-intellectual, Victorian and Edwardian attitudes toward the public school. *Sinister Street* owes nothing to its predecessor *The Longest Journey*.

So thorough and deadening was the classical training at St Paul's that Leonard Woolf says he was a better classical scholar before going to Cambridge than afterwards. Still, his education seems to have been better than MacCarthy's or Fry's. No one at Clifton suspected Fry of any latent artistic talent. In all of Bloomsbury's school visions, however, the prevailing attitudes of anti-intellectualism, sexual brutality, religious hypocrisy, and class discrimination are unmistakable. Only personal relationships with an occasional schoolmate, or more rarely a teacher, redeemed something of value in their school education.

XVII

'For a long time now,' Mary MacCarthy wrote in the 1920s of her Eton family memories, 'the sound of crashing and smashing of glass has been in my ears. It is the strong, rose-coloured glass of the nineteenth century conservatories cracking up.' 'The detached biographess', as she calls herself, can only murmur at the devastation, 'Stones for bread! Stones for bread!' (*NC*, p. 18). The other detached Bloomsbury biographers and biographesses whose Victorian visions have been described and compared in this chapter found more than stones in modernism. They did not share her regret at the passing of the nineteenth century's rose-coloured unrealities. Leslie Stephen in an essay on his

beloved Scott thought that 'one thing is pretty certain, and in its
way comforting; that, however far the rage for revivalism may be
pushed, nobody will ever want to revive the nineteenth century'
(*Hours*, I 158). Most of Bloomsbury would have taken comfort in
this too. There may have been some nostalgia for the age's
vitality, simplicity and security, but there was also great relief at
having got free from the tyranny of moral and economic law that
governed the unaesthetic households of the patriarchies and
matriarchies in which they grew up. And some women of
Bloomsbury were more ready for change than the men. Virginia
Woolf described herself and her sister as by nature 'explorers
and revolutionists' (*MB*, p. 147). Even those men of Bloomsbury
who were not so revolutionary would still have exulted with
Leonard Woolf when they arrived at Cambridge and

> found ourselves living in the springtime of a conscious revolt
> against the social, political, religious, moral, intellectual, and
> artistic institutions, beliefs, and standards of our fathers and
> grandfathers. We felt ourselves to be the second generation in
> this exciting movement of men and ideas. The battle, which
> was against what for short one may call Victorianism, had not
> yet been won, and what was so exciting was our feeling that we
> ourselves were part of the revolution, that victory or defeat
> depended to some small extent upon what we did, said, or
> wrote.   (*S*, p. 160)

At Cambridge the men encountered directly, the women
indirectly, the ideas, works, and personalities of some of the first
generation of rebels against Victorianism. Bloomsbury's literary
and philosophical education there is the foundation of their
literary history and needs to be carefully described.

Part Two
Cambridge: Literary Education

4   History and Classics at King's and Trinity

The significance of Cambridge in the literary history of Bloomsbury is difficult to overemphasise. For twenty years, from 1885,
when Roger Fry came up, to 1905, when Maynard Keynes went
down, Cambridge moulded the minds of the Group, including
those who were not educated at Cambridge. Cambridge was
where the Victorian religious, philosophical, political and
aesthetic beliefs of home and school became transformed into
Bloomsbury's distinctive modernist convictions.

In 1903, the year of *Principia Ethica*, Leslie Stephen reminisced
about the traditions of the university to which he had been sent:

> Cambridge has for the last three centuries inclined to the less
> romantic side of things. It was for Puritans against Cavaliers,
> for Whigs against Jacobites, and down to my time was
> favoured by 'Evangelicals' and the good 'high and dry' school
> which shuddered at the development of the 'Oxford Move-
> ment'. . . . We held that our common sense enabled us to
> appreciate [Newman] only too thoroughly by the dry light of
> reason and to resist the illusions of romantic sentiment. That
> indeed was the merit of Cambridge in the eyes of those who
> were responsible for my education.   (*Impressions*, pp. 13–14)

What remained of the Oxford Movement toward the end of the
nineteenth century probably did not bother those responsible for
the education of Bloomsbury's men, but the puritan associations
of Cambridge would have been congenial to nonconformist
families such as the Frys, the Keyneses and even the Woolfs.
Cambridge puritanism continued to colour the education of
Bloomsbury but morally rather than religiously. The only part

109

members of the Group willingly took in the religious life of the university and its colleges was to attack it. The earnest agnosticism of Sidgwick and even of Stephen hardened into an indifferent agnosticism almost indistinguishable from atheism. Stephen had been a member of the celebrated Cambridge Society for Psychical Research, which Sidgwick, Myers and others founded in 1882; Bloomsbury's attitude toward such matters was summarised by Forster's description of the SPR as 'that dustbin of the spirit' (*GLD*, p. 102). Yet Bloomsbury's atheism was quite compatible with a strong, at times mystical, response to what Forster liked to call the unseen.

One manifestation of Cambridge puritanism was the longer, more bitter struggle for female equality in education there than at Oxford. Virginia Woolf has immortalised the attitudes toward women at Cambridge in the late 1920s. Her ambivalence about Cambridge values, so clear in her filial feelings, recurs throughout her writings and is related not just to her feminism, but also to her beliefs about truth and knowledge, personal relations and beauty. The intellectual light of Cambridge had a mystical significance for her, yet she detested the egotistical brutality that could accompany Cambridge truth-telling. She envied the critical spirit of Cambridge and deplored its creative cost. Still, Bloomsbury's Cambridge was an improvement on Leslie Stephen's, because it could combine puritan integrity with a high valuation of personal and aesthetic emotion. Of H. T. J. Norton, an Apostle, mathematician and close Bloomsbury associate, Virginia Woolf once wrote to her sister, 'I felt a kind of reverence for him, as the representative of old Cambridge, as we knew it, in the days of "personal emotions"; I must say I think it probably the highest type in the world, and it solves all my religious feelings' (*L*, II 292). That was at the end of the war, but a few years later, in her 'Old Bloomsbury' memoir, she would describe Norton as 'the essence of all I mean by Cambridge; so able; so honest; so ugly; so dry' (*MB*, p. 198).

To those in Bloomsbury who went to Cambridge, its cloisters, as Lytton Strachey said in *Eminent Victorians*, had 'ever been consecrated to poetry and common sense' (p. 15). In the literary history of Bloomsbury this consecration manifested itself through the Group's dominant, interrelated interests in literature and philosophy at Cambridge. Beyond the Greek and Latin classics, however, neither literature nor philosophy was formally studied there by anyone of the Group. Most read history or classics at Cambridge and got what literary education they could from them. They supplemented this education through literary lectures and societies, the writing of English essays for various prizes, and a wide extra-curricular reading, especially of modern works. The description of this literary education is the subject of Part Two of Bloomsbury's Victorian literary history.

II

When Leslie Stephen went up to Cambridge in 1850 the only subjects to be studied for the tripos or honours examinations were classics and mathematics. Shortly afterwards triposes were established in the natural sciences and in the moral sciences, as philosophy was characteristically described at Cambridge. By the end of the century there were triposes in theology, law and history; economics did not become a tripos subject until 1903, and English not until 1919. Except for Fry, who read natural sciences, and Keynes, who read mathematics, all the members of Bloomsbury took either the history or the classics tripos. The state of historical and classical studies at Cambridge around the turn of the century bears on the literary history of Bloomsbury and needs to be described, particularly at the two colleges in which all the Cambridge men of Bloomsbury were educated and from which almost all the Apostles came.[1]

One way of viewing the Cambridge origins of Bloomsbury is to distinguish between those who went to King's College and those who went to Trinity. Roger Fry, E. M. Forster, and Maynard Keynes were the Kingsmen of Bloomsbury. In the mid nineteenth century King's had, as it were, joined the University of Cambridge by selecting its members from other schools than just Eton, and by making them take the university examinations, from which they had hitherto been exempt (though all had been required to take honours examinations, there being no pass men at King's). By the end of the century King's was still a small, intimate college, closely tied to Eton and preoccupied with the importance of teaching and the study of classics. Cambridge's other great subject, mathematics, had more or less been ignored at King's, because of the college's freedom from the tripos. By the time Roger Fry came to King's it was possible to do natural sciences there, but the college was hardly known for its scientists as Trinity was. An exception was Karl Pearson, a former wrangler of King's, whose *Grammar of Science* later appears to have influenced Fry's thinking. King's also had a fellow, J. H. Middleton, who was Slade Professor of Art and later director of the Fitzwilliam Museum; his influence helped Fry to shift to art from science, in which he obtained first-class honours. Fry's Apostolic friendships with Lowes Dickinson at King's, and McTaggart, now at Trinity, also helped him move from science to art, but there was little at Cambridge to attract him to painting. The climate of Cambridge in the 1880s 'was not altogether favourable to the growth of the aesthetic sense', Clive Bell understated in his memoir of Fry (*OF*, p. 67). Beyond literature the only art cultivated with any intensity was music. Forster, Dickinson and G. E. Moore were all passionately interested in music, and the greatest artist at Cambridge during Moore's undergraduate years in the 1890s was his Trinity friend the composer Ralph Vaughan Williams (who later married a Fisher cousin of the Stephens). Even when most of Bloomsbury were up at Cambridge at the end of the century, only Clive Bell appears to have been particularly attracted to painting.

E. M. Forster's studies at King's were more typical of Bloomsbury's than Fry's. He read classics, won the College Latin-verse prize twice, took only second-class honours, and then stayed up a fourth year to read history, which King's had begun to emphasise together with classics. One of Forster's classics tutors at King's was the Apostle Nathaniel Wedd. To him more than anyone else at Cambridge – more even than to Dickinson, whose considerable influence for Forster and Bloomsbury will be described later – Forster said he owed whatever awakening had happened to him (*GLD*, p. 61). Wedd's reputation at King's was as a teacher and a personality rather than as a scholar like Walter Headlam, whom Forster also knew at King's. (Headlam, considered by some to be King's most brilliant classicist, was one of Virginia Woolf's early admirers and in gratitude for her criticism dedicated his translation of Aeschylus's *Agamemnon* to her – *L*, I 259.) Wedd was known as a radical and a blasphemer; he read Baudelaire, taught Dickinson to swear, and later turned Tory. George Santayana, who was at King's the year before Forster came up, sympathised with Wedd's 'pagan satirical view of life' while finding Dickinson 'a romantic Puritan' (*My Host*, pp. 22–4). There are traces of both temperaments in Forster. Wedd awakened Forster not just to the classics but to writing, to life. 'He said in a sort of drawling voice "I don't see why you should not write", and I being diffident was delighted at this remark and thought, after all why shouldn't I write? And I did' ('Forster on his Life', p. 11). As important as this suggestion was Wedd's teaching 'that we all know more than we think' (EMF/*LJ*, p. 300). This was a revelation for Forster, who thought he knew less than he pretended, and it became a central theme in his writing.

When Forster shifted to Bloomsbury's other subject at Cambridge, he thought his history tutor would be Dickinson, but he was 'dished' by yet another notable history don at King's: 'So once a fortnight I read aloud about Wallenstein or Louis XIV to the handkerchief which covered O. B.'s face, and Dickinson's power to teach remained unknown to me, except as far as I have heard of it from others' (*GLD*, p. 85). Oscar Browning's outrageousness made even his initials famous at Cambridge:

O. B., oh be obedient to nature's stern decrees!
For if you were not singular, you'd soon be too obese.

This brilliant couplet, attributed to J. K. Stephen but apparently by G. A. Falk,[2] sums up the gross singularity of a homosexual Falstaff whose vitality, wit and snobbery made him controversial at Eton, Cambridge and beyond. Virginia Woolf pilloried him in *A Room of One's Own* for asserting that university examinations demonstrated that the most intelligent women were inferior to the most stupid men, and then extolling the high-mindedness of stable boys (p. 81). Desmond MacCarthy, who was reading history at Trinity, became friends with Browning through Eton and the Apostles, learning from him to avoid the public-school confusion of good with good form. Browning he thought embodied 'the heart of a University, "learning, laughter, and love of friends"' (DM/*P*, p. 38). Lowes Dickinson declared flatly in his autobiography that Oscar Browning 'is the largest figure Cambridge has known, in my time, inspired with the maieutic passion. But as a researcher! The two things seem hardly compatible' (p. 151). This familiar antithesis of teaching and scholarship explains to some degree why so many of Bloomsbury's Cambridge teachers are unknown today, while famous

Cambridge scholars of the time seem not to have affected the Group very much. But the incompatibility is frequently exaggerated, then as now. Browning hoped to found a history school at Cambridge, and, although Forster found him 'viewy and careless' as a historian compared with Dickinson (*GLD*, p. 72), he appears to have improved the teaching of history in Bloomsbury's Cambridge. Many years later, while reviewing a snobby, sexist book on Cambridge, Forster quoted Browning to show that enlightening the minds of students requires generosity and warmth, without which education becomes senseless. (He also quoted without attribution the beautiful description of the light of Cambridge in *Jacob's Room* [p. 40] and commented ironically, 'How splendidly these words express our faith! How unlucky that they should have been written by a woman!' [*2CD*, pp. 345–7].)

A history school was developed at Cambridge during Forster's time by a researching historian whose liberalism and scholarship are still remembered. Lord Acton became Regius Professor of History and a fellow of Trinity College in 1895. Forster and perhaps others of Bloomsbury attended his lectures on the French Revolution. Forster was still quoting Acton from his lecture notes forty years later ('Every villain is followed by a sophist with a sponge' – *CB*, p. 171). Bloomsbury's liberalism owes much to Cambridge history, for it was the principal form in which they studied political economy. The reality of the past and its significance for the present and the future are fundamental Bloomsbury beliefs, expressed most memorably perhaps in Forster's English novels.

III

Acton has taken us from King's to Trinity and a very different intellectual and educational environment. The difference between a King's education and a Trinity one could be described by William James's account in *Pragmatism* of tender- and tough-mindedness. This may more or less have been what J. T. Sheppard, a friend of Bloomsbury and future provost of King's, meant in a 1903 Apostle paper entitled 'King's or Trinity?' For Sheppard the King's state of mind stressed moral character, whereas the Trinity attitude concentrated on intellectual pursuits; King's valued human beings, while Trinity cared only for things of the mind.[3] The distinction is, of course, a tender-minded King's one which Sheppard applied only to the Apostles, but it does help to define more clearly some basic differences within the Bloomsbury Group, such as Forster's and even Fry's dissimilarities. 'King's or Trinity?' was an attempt to describe states of mind rather than individuals, and Sheppard recognised that there were Kingsmen with Trinity states of mind and vice versa. Keynes is partly an example, for he also conformed to his own distinction between the austerity of Trinity states of mind and the pleasurableness of King's ones (*CW*, x 441). Strachey inhabited both states and colleges in his extended Cambridge career, and even Leonard Woolf, almost a pure Trinity type, found on his return from Ceylon that he was 'still a native of Trinity and King's, a Cambridge intellectual' (*BA*, p. 20).

In contrast to the intimacy of King's, with its emphasis on teaching, Trinity was the largest college in Cambridge and intellectually the most distinguished in England. The education offered by it and like-minded colleges to honours students in the mid nineteenth century was bluntly set forth by Leslie Stephen: 'Our plan was not to teach any one anything, but to offer heavy prizes for competition in well-defined intellectual contests', the contests being confined to mathematics and classics (*Sketches*, p. 89). Yet by the end of the century Trinity had become the home of an extraordinary number of world-famous research dons – not just classicists and mathematicians, but also historians, scientists and philosophers. In the two or three decades before the First World War there were at Trinity eleven members of the Order of Merit and seven Nobel-prizemen (G. M. Trevelyan, *Trinity*, p. 114). King's had none of either. At the turn of the century Trinity fellows were involved in three remarkable intel-lectual revolutions all taking place in Cambridge at the same time, in physics, anthropology and philosophy. Only the last affected Bloomsbury directly when they were undergraduates.

Between Desmond MacCarthy's matriculation in 1894 and Adrian Stephen's in 1902, seven future members of Bloomsbury attended Trinity College. Thoby Stephen, Clive Bell, Saxon Sydney-Turner, Lytton Strachey and Leonard Woolf came up together in 1899. All the Bloomsbury men at Cambridge except maybe Fry and Keynes wanted to be writers according to Leonard Woolf (*S*, p. 159). They knew the great writers who had

helped consecrate Cambridge's cloisters to literature, starting
with Erasmus and including Marlowe, Milton, Marvell, Dryden,
Gray – and in the nineteenth century Wordsworth, Coleridge,
Byron, Tennyson and Thackeray. After Balliol had rejected
Strachey and Trinity accepted him, his mother wrote, 'I think
you are to be congratulated on the change, especially as it is a
sign from above that you are to be a poet – the coming man in
that line could never have been allowed to be anywhere but at
Cambridge' (MH/*LS*, p. 131). Strachey's friends would have
hopefully agreed. And, as the only places in the honours curriculum where it was remotely possible to study the art of writing
were history and classics, Strachey, MacCarthy, Bell and Adrian
Stephen all read history, while Thoby Stephen, Leonard Woolf
and Sydney-Turner read classics. Both these Trinity subjects
and their dons are worth looking at in Bloomsbury's Cambridge
literary education.

History in one form or another was written by Leonard and
Virginia Woolf, Clive Bell, Strachey, Forster and Keynes. They
read the great British historians Clarendon, Gibbon, Hume,
Macaulay and Carlyle, and some, such as Strachey and Bell,
knew Michelet too. Virginia Woolf was widely read in English
history and used the Oxford historians Freeman and Green for
her classes at Morley College (QB/*VW*, 1 203). Yet the predominant conception of history in Bloomsbury remained biographical. In the Cambridge of Virginia Woolf's *Jacob's Room*,
Jacob writes an essay on the Carlylean topic 'Does History
consist of the Biographies of Great Men?' (p. 37). In Bloomsbury's practice, if not theory, it sometimes seems to. Desmond
MacCarthy thought Strachey's work was not really historical
because it was not concerned with causality. And Leonard Woolf
argued, in the most sustained historical work to come out of
Bloomsbury, that history was about the past of human beings
living in communities (*AD*, 1 vii, 46ff.). But in the writings of
Virginia Woolf and Forster as well as Strachey and even Keynes,
the past is best understood through the lives of individuals.
Virginia Woolf came to reject the *Dictionary of National Biography*'s
concentration on famous males, and Strachey would interpret
eminence ironically, but the *DNB* remained as influential as
Gibbon or Macaulay on Bloomsbury history. Strachey's conception of history included a theory of value, derived from Moore,
that locates intrinsic value in essentially atemporal states of

mind. In his writings about the past, and in Forster's and Virginia Woolf's too, the emphasis is thus on character and personality in history rather than on causality and chronology.

Ten years before *Eminent Victorians* Strachey reviewed a volume of the *Cambridge Modern History* that Acton had planned before his death. Strachey honoured Acton's liberalism in *Eminent Victorians*, using it to criticise Cardinal Manning (pp. 89ff.), but one of Strachey's unpublished aphorisms complains that Acton was regarded as 'a nobleman of industry, and therefore . . . a historian' (Merle, p. 913). The modern-history volume he found boring; it had been partly written by one of Strachey's history-teachers at Trinity, Stanley Leathes, and Strachey thought it fell between the stools of minutely descriptive narrative, such as Macaulay's, and broadly outlined historical conditions, as in Michelet (*SE*, p. 116). Acton was succeeded as Regius Professor by J. B. Bury, who became a fellow at King's. In his inaugural lecture Bury propounded a scientific conception of history which Strachey criticised in an essay society paper to be discussed later with his Edwardian essays. Throughout his writings Strachey maintained that history's value was as an art not a science, reaffirming in a late essay on his beloved Gibbon that 'History is not the accumulation of facts, but the relation of them' (*PM*, p. 160).

Yet there was at Cambridge when Strachey was up a historian, a Trinity man, an Apostle whom Acton described as the ablest of English historians. F. W. Maitland's great work in the history of law is hardly artistic. (Neither for that matter is his last book, *The Life and Letters of Leslie Stephen*, yet Virginia Woolf agreed with her father in thinking him a genius who 'made everybody else seem clumsy and verbose' – *L*, 1 271.) Maitland's legal history belongs to the tradition of Cambridge Whig history, tracing as it does the evolution of law, yet its greatness lies not in Maitland's relation of facts but in the ones he chose to accumulate and generalise about.[4]

Finally there was at Trinity during Bloomsbury's time there another, much younger Apostle historian whose work clarifies, mainly by contrast, the ideas of history that Bloomsbury developed at Cambridge. George Macaulay Trevelyan was named after his great-uncle, the historian that Leslie Stephen found to epitomise Cambridge in his clarity, energy and limited intellect (*Sketches*, p. 95). G.M.'s brother the poet R.C. was much closer to Bloomsbury, but it was George Trevy, as he was called, who opposed Strachey's influence in the Apostles before leaving Trinity (he would return much later as Master) to write the kind of artistic history that he felt inhibited from doing by the critical nature of Cambridge historical scholarship (G. M. Trevelyan, *Autobiography*, p. 21). Bloomsbury did not think highly of Trevelyan's widely read histories: Strachey thought his Whig history too optimistically uncritical, and in *A Room of One's Own* Virginia Woolf derided his treatment of women, but she used him later as a source in *Between the Acts*.

Desmond MacCarthy's degree in history was *aegrotat* (a pass given because of illness). Clive Bell, to his tutor's annoyance 'and George Trevelyan's amusement', was awarded only a second (*OF*, p. 139); Trinity still offered him a studentship, and he went off to do research on the Congress of Verona in London and then Paris, where his aesthetic interests superseded his historical ones. Strachey, also to his tutor's annoyance, obtained but second-class honours and then spent the next two and a half years mostly in Cambridge and London writing his unsuccessful fellowship dissertation on Warren Hastings. What was the loss to history, what the gain to criticism, aesthetics and biography, that Bloomsbury abandoned academic historical research?

IV

Just how one assesses the teaching and study of classics during Bloomsbury's time at Trinity varies according to whether one considers the rather dispiriting academic attainments of Saxon Sydney-Turner, Thoby Stephen and Leonard Woolf, or the distinguished work of the fellows who continued Trinity's great tradition of classical scholarship, which stretched back centuries to Porson and Bentley.

Sydney-Turner was the best classical scholar in Bloomsbury. An accomplished translator with a facility for minor verse and puzzle-solving, he was devoted to opera, especially Wagner's, and was the only member of Bloomsbury to compose music, none of which has survived. After a first at Cambridge he went into the Civil Service and spent most of his career in the Treasury. Both Leonard and Virginia Woolf wrote character sketches of him that portray his scholastic uncreativeness.

Leonard Woolf depicted him as a cocooned Aristotle who covered up the present with the past (*S*, pp. 116–9). For Virginia Woolf he was 'one of our great men' who somehow never did anything with his greatness (pS). Her unpublished sketch reads like a Cambridge representation of the moral paralysis afflicting Joyce's Dubliners. Fond as she was of him, she saw his life as another judgement on Cambridge truth-telling, which could make one into an egoist without generosity or imagination, as she wrote to Vanessa, urging her to impress the lesson upon her children (*L*, ɪɪ 303).

Thoby Stephen attained second-class honours in classics at Trinity and then went on to study law. Leonard Woolf finally obtained a second as well, to the disappointment of the college authorities, and then did poorly in the Civil Service examinations. He thought the reason for his unsatisfactory performance at Cambridge was that he had spent his time voraciously reading Greek and Latin (and French and English) instead of perfecting his skills in writing them. Surviving among Leonard Woolf's papers are some lists of classical authors he read as an undergraduate. Included are Homer, Hesiod, Aeschylus, Sophocles, Euripides, Aristophanes, Theocritus, Sappho, Herodotus, Thucydides, Plato, Aristotle, Demosthenes, Xenophon, Plautus, Terence, Lucretius, Catullus, Propertius, Virgil, Ovid, Horace, Lucan, Juvenal, Cicero, Livy and Tacitus (pS). Yet Leonard Woolf had no regrets about his having been a better classical scholar when he came up to Trinity than when he went down. Literature was one of three passions he shared with his Trinity friends. In an undergraduate paper entitled 'Classical Education and Literature' he took the familiar Bloomsbury line that literature or literary feeling could not be taught, because it developed out of one's view of life; nevertheless, a knowledge of Greek literature showed how Greek were the roots of English literature, a comparison that enabled one to contrast, say, Greek pessimism with the ravings of a Carlyle (pS). Leonard Woolf's two other undergraduate passions were for friendship and truth (*S*, p. 159). Their classical context was something Forster and Strachey responded to strongly as well, in different ways, as did their Apostolic teachers. Classical studies were one of the sources, for example, of Moore's influential insistence on verbal exactitude.

Clearly, however, the classical teaching of Trinity did not stimulate Leonard Woolf and his friends in the same way as that of King's had stimulated Forster. Yet it is somewhat surprising that, in the hundred pages of autobiography that Leonard Woolf devotes to Cambridge, he never refers to any of the any Trinity classical dons, some of whose work he must have read. There was R. C. Jebb, for one, the Regius Professor of Greek and Cambridge MP, whose edition of Sophocles the *DNB* described as 'the most completely satisfactory commentary on a classical author that has been written in the English language'. Jebb was also the author of a popular translation of Theophrastus's *Characters* that Forster based his 'The Cambridge Theophrastus' pieces on, and that Leonard Woolf, Strachey and maybe Virginia Woolf too used, along with La Bruyère, in their character-writing and biographies. (Jebb was something of a character himself: 'All the time he can spare from the adornment of his person, he devotes to the neglect of his duties' was Sidgwick's Theophrastrian description of him – Russell, *Portraits*, p. 64.)

Jebb's successor was Henry Jackson, OM, an Apostle and Vice-Master of Trinity who influenced G. E. Moore deeply, introducing him to the works of Plato and Aristotle (Moore, 'Autobiography', pp. 19–20). Jackson's work on Plato may have encouraged Bloomsbury's Platonic susceptibilities. An even more influential classical scholar at Trinity during Bloomsbury's years there was yet another Apostle, A. W. Verrall, a specialist in Euripides, whose tragedies he convincingly interpreted as rationalistic in intention. *Euripides the Rationalist* (1895) was read and appreciated by Bloomsbury at Cambridge. Forster's two 'tragic interiors' written for a King's magazine (see Chapter 12) satirised Verrall's interpretation by applying it to Aeschylus. Strachey wrote enthusiastically to his mother about Verrall's book and hoped to write a tragedy influenced by it (25.xi.03, pT). According to Edward Marsh, a contemporary of Moore's, an Apostle and later the editor of *Georgian Poetry*, Verrall was one of the first dons in Cambridge to teach classics as works of art (Hassall, *Marsh*, p. 40). This ability was recognised when in 1911 Verrall was elected to the first professorship of English literature to be established at Cambridge. It was, of course, completely characteristic of the Cambridge attitude toward the teaching of English at this time that the first professor should have been a classicist.

Trinity's most famous classicist at the beginning of the twentieth century was the author of *The Golden Bough*, James Frazer.

He has been ranked with Trinity physicists such as Thomson and Rutherford, or Trinity philosophers such as Russell and Moore, as a maker of the modern mind. Frazer's expansion of his 1890 'study of magic and religion', as it was subtitled, into a vast modern descriptive classification of primitive magical and religious practices, accompanied by Victorian evolutionary and agnostic explanations, was the most important work being done in religious studies while Bloomsbury was at Cambridge. Frazer's detached, ironic attitude toward his material would have been congenial to Leonard Woolf, Strachey and others – though it was not to Wittgenstein, who found in Frazer a lack of reverence that he also found missing in Bloomsbury (Wittgenstein, 'Remarks on Frazer'; JMK/*CW*, x 447–8). But there is no evidence that any members of the Group read Frazer's work at Cambridge.

Another brilliant Cambridge classicist, whose work derived directly from Frazer's, was neither an Apostle nor a fellow of Trinity or of King's. Yet Jane Ellen Harrison's work was perhaps better known in Bloomsbury than that of any Cambridge classicist or historian. She had been a lecturer in classical archaeology at Newnham since 1898. Fry and McTaggart heard her lecture on Greek art at Clifton, she later recalled in an autobiography published by the Hogarth Press (*Reminiscences*, p. 54). Fry once paid her the highest of Cambridge compliments in saying she had a 'really Apostolic mind' (VW/*RF*, p. 92). By the time of *A Room of One's Own* Virginia Woolf considered her famous enough to be referred to only by her initials (p. 26). Her first major book, *Prolegomena to the Study of Greek Religion*, appeared in 1903, the *annus mirabilis* of Cambridge philosophy. There she argued that Greek religious ritual needed to be studied apart from its literary expression, a study that would, however, lead to a better understanding of Greek literature. In 1913 she published a popular account of the relation of Greek art and ritual in the same Home University Library series in which Russell, Moore and Strachey had all published introductions to philosophy, ethics and French literature the year before. *Ancient Art and Ritual* was quite likely the book that made the new anthropology familiar to Bloomsbury. And their sympathetic interest was returned; in her brief bibliography, Harrison cites Fry's 'Essay on Aesthetics' as 'the best general statement on the function of Art known to me' (p. 254).

V

By indirection, then, through history and classics at King's and Trinity, the vernacular literary education of Bloomsbury was carried on. It proceeded directly as well, but outside the curriculum, at public lectures, through literary societies and essays, and of course in the modern reading that Bloomsbury did in their own rooms.

5 English Literary Lectures, Reading and Essays

I

The study of English literature at Cambridge had been advocated as early as 1867 by no less a figure than Henry Sidgwick, who suggested it might replace compulsory Greek. A chair of Anglo-Saxon had been created in 1878. But English was not established as a tripos subject until after the First World War. For those interested in the literature of their own country there were in the late nineteenth and early twentieth century at Cambridge a lecture series in the subject, various reading-societies devoted to English works, and prizes awarded by colleges and the University for English essays of one kind or another.

The Vice-Master at Trinity College in Bloomsbury's time was Aldis Wright, 'our greatest Shakespeare scholar since Edmund Malone', according to D. Nichol Smith in the *DNB*. Wright had been nineteenth wrangler in 1854, when Leslie Stephen was twentieth and Clerk Maxwell only second (Annan, p. 28). Wright neither tutored, lectured, nor even suffered very gladly undergraduates and is not to be found among the members of the Trinity Shakespeare Society whose photograph appears in Leonard Woolf's autobiography (*S*, p. 97). He had coedited the enduring Globe Shakespeare edition with George Clark, whose bequest to Trinity resulted in the well-known Clark lectures in English literature – at the time, were the closest thing to institutional instruction in the subject that Cambridge offered. The first lectures were given in 1884 and the lecturer was Leslie Stephen. Forster and MacCarthy were among his successors, but not his daughter, who declined to perform in a university that treated women so inequitably.

As Clark lecturer Stephen continued to be a mid-Victorian

don and was contemptuous of his subject and his audience. 'I shall have to go to Cambridge three times a week', he wrote to Charles Eliot Norton, 'to talk twaddle about Addison and Pope to a number of young ladies from Girton and a few idle undergraduates', who included the son of the Prince of Wales. Stephen complained that the female student did not understand that the purpose of study was to do well in examinations and therefore 'lectures are a vanity and a distraction' (Maitland, pp. 380, 382). Yet Stephen was not unsympathetic to the study of English literature. A lecture so entitled was given by him three years after he resigned his Clark lectureship, and was subsequently published in his old magazine, the *Cornhill*. He reiterated there his critical belief that the purpose of studying a man's writings was to make a friend of the author, and he expressed again his conviction that the analysis of literary form was a barren exercise. In the matter of literary judgement, Stephen's emphasis on sincerity also appears antiquated now, but for other, more depressing reasons:

> There are, I think, two rules in this matter. Never persuade yourselves that you like what you don't like. . . . Sham liking is far worse than honest stupidity. But, again, do not presume to think that your dislike to an accepted masterpiece proves it not to be a masterpiece. (*Men, Books*, p. 38)

This kind of critical integrity was honoured by the Bloomsbury critics, if not always practised by them.

In a rather coy aside in his lecture, Stephen recommended a certain biographical dictionary that, when finished, would offer 'a pretty full introduction to English literary history' (p. 32). It did so for Bloomsbury, more indeed than the lectures on literature they heard or read at Cambridge and later. Yet Stephen on the study of English literature had nothing to say about its teaching, apart from some reservations about the relevance of classical and philological studies. The debate about the place of English literary studies in the universities that was carried on by the Victorians revolved around the usefulness of these subjects as prerequisites, the basic question being whether English could be made a serious enough discipline for academic study (Gross, pp. 167–89). The question continued to interest Bloomsbury in the twentieth century. Given what dons did in their academic pursuits, Bloomsbury was persuaded that on the whole it was probably not worthwhile to teach and study English at university – a persuasion that enraged some Cambridge critics in the 1930s.

Stephen would have relished the irony of the honour that his university did his memory by establishing in his name a literary lectureship in 1905. Bloomsbury had all gone down by then, but in later years Strachey came back to deliver the Leslie Stephen lecture on Pope, MacCarthy to give it on Stephen himself, and Forster to devote it to Virginia Woolf after her death.

II

Stephen resigned his Clark lectureship after the first of the three years he was to hold it. His successor was Edmund Gosse, who remained until 1890 in spite of having his published lectures ridiculed by Churton Collins for their methods and their mistakes. Collins, alliteratively skewered for ever by Gosse's friend Tennyson as 'a Louse on the Locks of Literature' (Charteris, p. 197), helped establish English literature as an academic subject at Oxford. There in the early years of the century were lecturing two very different professors of English literature, with whose work Bloomsbury was familiar.

A. C. Bradley was Oxford Professor of Poetry from 1901 to 1905, and, as has already been noted (pp. 32–3), his inaugural lecture, 'Poetry for Poetry's Sake', influenced the articulation of Bloomsbury's later formalism. In the 1920s both Clive Bell and Roger Fry cited Bradley's lecture in arguing with I. A. Richards, and in the 1940s Forster was still echoing Bradley's literary formalism. The Shakespearean criticism of Bradley, which continues to be read, owes something to Hegel in its theory of tragedy, as one might expect from the brother of F. H. Bradley. Bradleyan Idealism was not of much interest to the philosophical Realists of Bloomsbury, but they found his psychological analyses of Shakespeare's characters stimulating, if incomplete. Forster, Virginia Woolf and many others, such as Arnold Bennett, would have agreed with A. C. Bradley that character was the most important aspect of drama and fiction. For Bloomsbury, however, there was also the crucial question of form, which was not taken sufficient account of in Bradley's analyses of character.

In the book on Shakespeare that he began shortly before he died, Lytton Strachey was trying to go beyond psychological to dramatic necessity in analysing *Othello* (*CC*, pp. 308–15).

The other Oxford English professor was Walter Raleigh, a Kingsman and Apostle who succeeded Bradley at Liverpool, then Glasgow, before accepting a new Oxford chair of English literature in 1904. At Cambridge in 1898 Raleigh had given the Clark lectures on letter-writers, Milton and courtesy literature, but his connection with Bloomsbury came first through a cousin of his wife's, Lytton Strachey, who before coming to Cambridge spent two years at Liverpool studying, among other subjects, English literature. At Liverpool 'Uncle Raleigh' was a very popular lecturer and the author of books on the English novel (thirty years later Forster still thought this study a work of genuine scholarship – *AN*, p. 5), on Robert Louis Stevenson (a formative influence on Raleigh's own ideas about life and literature) and on style. Strachey in his Liverpool diary noted that the book on Stevenson was 'quite good, but nothing remarkable, as indeed how could it be' (*LSH*, p. 92). The reservation appears to concern not Raleigh but Stevenson, whom Bloomsbury generally disliked. Raleigh's *Style*, published in 1897, is in date as well as deed a *fin-de-siècle* work. Lyrical rather than expository or analytic, its discussions are abstract and figurative, the aim being to exhibit style while talking about it. This is the first sentence: 'Style, the Latin name for an iron pen, has come to designate the art that handles, with ever fresh vitality and wary alacrity, the fluid elements of speech.' The style of everything from epic poetry to legal briefs is mentioned, but without attention to the genres that condition style.

Around 1900 Raleigh was becoming recognised, according to the *DNB*, 'as the most original and stimulating of the younger critics'. He made a strong impression on Strachey at Liverpool, but it faded at Cambridge, where unaffected candour, analysis and the plain style went together. After his death in 1922, Virginia Woolf wrote in a review of Raleigh's letters that 'it would be difficult to find a single remark of any interest whatsoever about English literature', for he was a professor of literature yearning to be a professor of life, and he confused the two because, she thought, he never tried himself to be a writer (*CE*, I 314). MacCarthy, however, who knew Raleigh from Apostle meetings, found the artist in him spent in brilliant talk (*P*,

p. 218) – a judgement sometimes made about MacCarthy by his friends. Both views are more plausible than Q. D. Leavis's unfavourable comparison of Raleigh to Stephen (Gross, p. 182). Although Stephen's unaesthetic, moralistic integrity is obviously very different from Raleigh's self-conscious brilliance, there are still some clear similarities between them. Raleigh has been recognised as an early anti-academic academic. Stephen was an earlier one who admired Raleigh's books on Milton and Stevenson, and shared with him the suspicion that literary study was somehow unmanly. In both there was for Bloomsbury a confusion between the values of art and those of life. A. C. Bradley, with his psychologising of Shakespeare's drama, was closer to Bloomsbury in the refusal to subordinate either art or life to the other.

III

The lack of an English tripos at Cambridge may have saved Bloomsbury from Anglo-Saxon, Middle English and other philological weariness of the literary spirit, but that does not mean they were completely unread in earlier English literature. Bloomsbury's extensive undergraduate reading was not confined to modern authors or even English ones. In addition to Greek and Latin authors, they all read French literature – Montaigne, Pascal, Molière, Racine, Voltaire, Rousseau, and the great nineteenth-century novelists and poets. Some read Dante in Italian and Goethe in German. More English literature was read than anything else, of course, beginning with the Elizabethans. The Clark lectures for 1900, delivered by the *DNB* author Canon Ainger, were devoted to Chaucer, but there is little indication that Bloomsbury read much medieval English literature. The Elizabethan and seventeenth-century writers Bloomsbury read included considerably more than Shakespeare and Milton. Strachey developed a passion for Pope and took his friends with him (CB/*OF*, p. 29). All read the Romantic poets (though not much Wordsworth), Austen, Scott, Dickens, Thackeray, the Brontës, George Eliot, Carlyle and Ruskin. Leonard Woolf remembered reading Fielding and Richardson because he felt he ought to, and Austen, Peacock and the Brontës because he liked them; but Thackeray and Dickens 'meant nothing to us or rather they stood for an era, a way of life, a system of morals against which we were in revolt' (*S*, p. 165). Leonard Woolf's 'we' does not include all of Bloomsbury, for Thackeray obviously meant many things to the Stephens, who also liked Scott. Other English authors had a special appeal for some of the members of Bloomsbury. Surtees, for instance, was enjoyed by Clive Bell, MacCarthy and, most likely, the Stephens.

Bloomsbury's quite extraordinary undergraduate knowledge of English literature may partly explain why so many of their degrees were undistinguished. Clive Bell has recorded, in an unpublished memoir on the Cambridge origins of Bloomsbury, his astonishment at how much English literature his Trinity friends had read – not just Strachey, who had studied the subject at Liverpool, nor the Stephens, who had the run of their father's books, but also Leonard Woolf and Sydney-Turner, who appeared to be familiar with the lesser Elizabethans and with such figures as Burton, Browne and Beddoes (pTC). In his published memoir on Bloomsbury, Clive Bell lists some of the 'trifles' consumed by his friends and himself along with milk punch, whisky and 'gloomy beef-steak pies': Jonson's *Barth-olomew Fair*, Milton's *Comus*, Shelley's *Prometheus Unbound* and *The Cenci*, and Browning's *The Return of the Druses* (*OF*, p. 26). These works were read out loud at the meetings of a reading-club called the Midnight Society. It met on Saturday evenings after yet another play-reading group called the 'X' Society, which devoted itself to the reading of drama by other playwrights than Shakespeare, to whose works still another reading-group was devoted, the Trinity Shakespeare Society, to which Leonard Woolf, Thoby Stephen, Strachey and perhaps others in Blooms-bury belonged.

A copy of the rules of the 'X' Society, printed in 1902, survives in Leonard Woolf's papers and gives some idea of the nature of these literary societies. Literature in Greek, Latin, Sanskrit or Hebrew is excluded, and the minutes of the discussions following the readings are to be kept in rhyming verse; the Society was limited to Trinity undergraduates, but visitors were allowed (pS). Leonard Woolf still remembered at the end of his life the aesthetic and intellectual pleasures of reading in the 'X' Society *The Duchess of Malfi*, *Volpone*, *The Maid's Tragedy* and *The Way of the World* (*S*, p. 163).

The significance of Cambridge reading-societies in the literary history of Bloomsbury extends considerably beyond their fare. Clive Bell believed that the story of the Bloomsbury Group began when Strachey, Leonard Woolf, Thoby Stephen and he founded the Midnight Society in the autumn of their first year at Trinity (*OF*, pp. 129–31). But neither Clive Bell nor Thoby Stephen belonged to *the* Society, the Cambridge Apostles, deeply influenced though they were by Apostolic philosophy. Leonard Woolf shows in *Sowing* that the Apostles figured more importantly than any other Cambridge group in the formation of Bloomsbury (pp. 155ff.). Only there did the future members of Bloomsbury who were at King's and Trinity come together to discuss literary questions as well as religious, moral, political and aesthetic ones. King's, of course, had its own literary societies such as the Apennines, a discussion club to which Fry, Forster and Keynes all belonged. In the gatherings of all these groups was formed one of Bloomsbury's strongest bonds, the sharing of literary experience through reading, writing and discussion. In Bloomsbury's Edwardian years, for example, the Group formed a play-reading society in London, and midway through their careers they came together in a new kind of reading-society at which, for over a quarter of a century, the members read their memoirs to one another.

How important to the literary development of Bloomsbury was the literature they read and discussed together at Cambridge can perhaps be gauged by the experience of the one writer in the Group who did not go to Cambridge. Whether it was because of her health, her lack of schooling, or her parents' indifference to the higher education of women that Virginia Woolf did not go to college, the consequences of her disqualification are apparent in her conviction that she was uneducated. Greek lessons and lectures at the University of London were not enough, nor was the greedy reading she did in her father's library. 'I don't get anybody to argue with me now, and feel the want', she wrote in 1903 to Thoby, who, after her father, appears most to have stimulated her thinking about what she was reading: 'I have to delve from books, painfully and all alone, what you get every evening sitting over your fire and smoking your pipe with Strachey etc. No wonder my knowledge is but scant' (*L*, i 77). In other letters she would ask about Shakespeare's characters and plots, and Marlowe's and Jonson's. She treasured family gifts of Dante (in Italian, from Caroline Emelia Stephen),

Montaigne, Bacon, Johnson's *Lives of the Poets*, Lockhart's life of Scott, Mackail's *Select Epigrams from the Greek Anthology*, which was Thoby's present for her twentieth birthday, and Fitzgerald's *Rubáiyát*, another gift from Thoby. But the craving for sustained, serious literary talk with her contemporaries remained. When she was finally able to have it, in Edwardian Bloomsbury, Virginia Woolf brought to literary discussion not just a greater depth of reading in all but recent English literature than any of her Cambridge contemporaries, but also a more independent sensibility, formed in the loneliness of her self-education, that eventually led her to question whether literary study at a university was worth doing after all.

Some idea of the books Virginia Woolf was delving into when she might have been at college is given in 'Hours in a Library', published in 1916. The title of the essay, like the library, was her father's. 'The great season for reading', she says, 'is the season between the ages of eighteen and twenty-four. The bare list of what is read then fills the heart of older people with despair.' She lists the works from an 'orgy of reading' indulged in six months by 'someone' at the age of twenty. Included are all of Meredith's, Peacock's and Ibsen's writings, most of Jane Austen's, and selected works by Fielding, Hardy, Webster, Tourneur, Browning, Shelley, Spenser, Congreve, Shaw, Milton and Browne. This reader has literary arguments as well, in which the Greeks are opposed to the moderns, romance to realism, Racine to Shakespeare. The same reader mounts a defence against someone who has adopted Pope rather than Browne as a hero, and is persuaded maybe by another to purchase Voltaire in eighty-nine octavo volumes (*CE*, II 34–6).

There seem to be allusions here to Lytton Strachey's advocacy of Pope and Leonard Woolf's taking Voltaire to Ceylon, which suggests the literary arguments described may have taken place after Bloomsbury came down from Cambridge. The influence of Cambridge on her, which first came through Leslie Stephen, was then renewed. Years later she summed up once again her mixed feelings about that influence in a letter to Ethel Smyth:

> Much though I hate Cambridge, and bitterly though I've suffered from it, I still respect it. I suppose that even without education, as I am, I am naturally of that narrow, ascetic,

puritanical breed – oh what a bore; and its too late now. It
cant be helped. (*L*, IV 155)

IV

Among the papers of Leonard Woolf, Roger Fry, E. M. Forster,
Maynard Keynes and Lytton Strachey are to be found various
undergraduate and postgraduate essays written for literary
societies at Cambridge or for prizes offered by King's, Trinity or
the University. Often on English literature, these essays are
worth glancing at for what they reveal through their subjects and
critical assumptions about the Cambridge literary education
that Virginia Woolf missed.

More of Leonard Woolf's undergraduate writings have survived than have any other Bloomsbury writer's (pS). The longest
is a largely illegible rough draft of an essay on Byron done in
1902; its gist is reflected in Strachey's judgement that Leonard
Woolf had satisfactorily demolished that Trinity poet's poetic
claims (28.ix.02, pT). A shorter paper on Browning found him to
be a great dramatic poet, a thinker, and – strangely for Leonard
Woolf – an optimist. Elsewhere Lucretius, a favourite Bloomsbury author, is praised in an essay as a great poet, thinker,
scientist and satirist. Two undergraduate papers are on education: one, already referred to (see p. 119), is about classical
education; the other presents a dialogue of the dead at Trinity
between Bacon and Johnson in which science and classics are
opposed. An essay on pastoral poetry declares it to be neither a
criticism of life nor a representation of ordinary men's thoughts
but an expression of ideal beauty; Theocritus is the great poet of
the pastoral, which is becoming extinct as poets such as Burns,
Keats and Tennyson confine themselves to the landscape of their
own country. Two essays discuss style, one being an Apostle
paper that defines style as a function of imagination rather than
thought. And there is a book review of some Shakespearean
studies by the redoubtable Churton Collins that criticises his
deduction of Shakespeare's thoughts from his characters' and
rejects Collins's conclusion that Shakespeare was an optimist.
Leonard Woolf's contempt for optimism was long-lived.

Also to be found among Leonard Woolf's Cambridge papers

are essays on history, government and philosophy. The most interesting of these for Bloomsbury's literary history is an English essay of some twenty pages on mysticism. An ambitious piece of undergraduate writing with quotations and sources in English, French, German and Greek, it may well have been the work for which Leonard Woolf was awarded the Trinity English essay prize in 1901. The essay is valuable for its indication of the general direction Bloomsbury's non-theistic, mystical impulses would take. Mystics are defined by Leonard Woolf as those seeking to explain man's relation to the Final Cause through the soul instead of through reason. The two types of mystic are thinkers who consciously reflect on the soul and poets who unconsciously recognise its beautiful workings. Plato and the neo-Platonists are the greatest mystical thinkers; among the moderns, Swedenborg, Novalis and Emerson stand out. Maeterlinck is the latest of the true poetic mystics, not Symbolists like Rimbaud with their meaningless assemblages of words. Leonard Woolf's view of mysticism is thus secular but not modernist. He argues characteristically that scepticism rather than belief is the natural result of the mystical questioning of rationality, and sees this borne out in Christianity's persecution of mystics such as Eckhart and Boehme. Swedenborg's Platonic doctrine of correspondences, in which nature mirrors the infinite, is good mysticism for Leonard Woolf, but his mystical visions are not. And, while great thinkers like Hegel may herald mysticism as a means to the infinite, most true mystics regard their experiences as sufficient in themselves.

Leonard Woolf's essay on mysticism obviously predates the influence on him and his friends of Moore and other Apostolic philosophers, who would not find mysticism and logic as incompatible as Leonard Woolf did in 1901. The difference is even clearer in a related document among Leonard Woolf's papers. This is a syllabus on mysticism 'for contributors only' to a book proposing to deal 'exhaustively with the subject of mysticism'. A brief preface by the general editor, Leonard Woolf, sets forth two points for general agreement to ensure the book's unity: one is a description of mysticism almost the same as that given in his essay; the other explicitly assumes that the soul is higher than reason by virtue of its direct relation to the infinite. The syllabus divides the book into three parts. The editor is to do the first, on 'The Soul of Mysticism'. The second or historical section is to be done by Sydney-Turner or someone called Angus, with Strachey helping out on English, American and French mysticism, and Bella Woolf, Leonard's eldest sister, writing on the future of mysticism. The third part is to have sections on mysticism and the arts, Leonard Woolf doing its relation to literature, Sydney-Turner the relation to music, and Strachey that to art. Also marked for the use of contributors are copies of a chronological list of mystics written by Leonard Woolf in red and black ink.[1]

Nothing came of this collaborative project by a group of Cambridge men and one woman relative on a subject that continued to interest Bloomsbury. The essay, syllabus and lists all appear to date from around 1901, and are therefore the earliest texts in the literary group history of Bloomsbury.

V

In Leonard Woolf's essay on mysticism there is only a brief reference to William Blake as one of the great poetic mystics. Blake, however, is the subject of what appears to be the only specifically literary undergraduate essay of Roger Fry that apparently has survived, though he also wrote papers on Jane Austen, George Eliot and James Russell Lowell (VW/*RF*, pp. 45–6). Fry's attitude toward Blake was ambivalent, early and late. His student essay finds Pope a greater poet, Gainsborough a greater painter, and Blake a greater man; the lyrics are supreme but much of the rest of Blake's writing was too subjective, too philosophical, because he thought nature a spiritual hindrance (pKC). Fry together with Strachey in their Edwardian reviews of Blake's drawings and poetry agreed on the greatness of his poetry but expressed misgivings about a mysticism that dispensed with worldly joys.

Forster once inherited an original copy of Blake's *Songs of Innocence*, which he later gave to King's. His two surviving undergraduate English papers, both written for the college essay prize, are on more conventional subjects, however (pKC). They reveal more clearly than Leonard Woolf's how the history of English literature was viewed at the beginning of the century in Cambridge by another would-be writer. The essay entitled 'The Relation of Dryden to Milton and Pope' presents the relation as a literary myth of decline and renewal in the history of English poetry: the great poetry of the classical renaissance, culminating in Milton, was corrupted by Dryden, destroyed by Pope and revived by the Romantics, including Tennyson. Forster apolog- ises for his unfashionably low opinion of Dryden, but cites Macaulay in support of his contention that Dryden's work reveals a distaste for nature. (For Pope he lists Leslie Stephen's as the most useful discussion.) The essay shows a greater famil- iarity with English poetry than with literary history. Forster's account of English poetry's decline was pretty much received opinion (but not by Strachey, who liked Pope), against which T. S. Eliot directed the influential criticism he collected for the Hogarth Press under the title *Homage to John Dryden* in 1924.

Forster's second essay won him the prize. Its topic, 'The Novelists of the 18th Century and their Influence on Those of the 19th', is as soaked in chronology and the play of influences as his first paper. Both are fine undergraduate examples of the 'pseudo-scholarship' he would mock in the 1920s when he returned to give the Clark lectures on the novel. Letters and dramas influence the eighteenth-century novel's development; Smollett influences Dickens; Fielding influences Thackeray; Goldsmith and Sterne influence modern novelists. There is not much surprising here, but the recognition of Sterne's influence is prescient. Significantly, Forster preferred Goldsmith. An epi- graph from *Tom Jones* supports Forster's claim that there are no rules in novel criticism beyond those of human nature – a critical position Forster would continue to maintain in *Aspects of the Novel* after he had written six of them. But, when he came to Dickens's novels in his essay, Forster complained that they were all episodic, except for the masterpiece *A Tale of Two Cities*.

Forster's view of Dickens now appears grotesquely antique, but it was shared in Bloomsbury and by many cultivated Vic- torian readers. Leslie Stephen, for example, was uncharacteristi- cally critical of *Bleak House* in the *DNB* (perhaps because of its attack on the work of his father and his brother, Fitzjames, who detested Dickens). Maynard Keynes, who was compelled for some reason to write an undergraduate essay on Dickens, is not far from Forster's opinion; he criticises Dickens's humour and sentimentality, finding only *A Christmas Carol*, *The Pickwick Papers* and *A Tale of Two Cities* completely successful. Keynes actually prefers Mrs Gaskell to Dickens (pML).

Keynes's criticism of Dickens shows little awareness, oddly

enough, of one feature of his fiction on which Keynes wrote an interesting undergraduate essay. The occasion for 'Shall We Write Melodramas?' is not revealed in the paper. Its concern with reality is Apostolic, but the essay seems too long and impersonal to have been written for that society. The answer to the title's question is yes, because stage melodramas allow us to transcend the limitations of realism. Keynes puts his point in a typical paradox: realism in the theatre is quite incompatible with 'a realistic treatment of that which really matters'. The real drama of our lives is played out only before God; in plays we can only 'seek by signs and symbols to make known the workings of the spirit' – signs and symbols that melodramas provide in their form and content (pML). Dickens could have provided Keynes with some good illustrations of the spiritual uses of melodrama. But he was not read in this way – not even by Virginia Woolf. Her Bloomsbury concern with the realistic representation of states of mind so lamentably lacking in 'realistic' fiction is curiously foreshadowed in Keynes's paper.

At Eton Keynes had been interested in medieval Latin poetry, and at King's he wrote a long paper on Abelard for the Apennines in which reason and love are opposed to piety and morality (Skidelsky, p. 113). The most substantial undergraduate essay he wrote, however, was a long discussion of the political doctrines of Edmund Burke, which won the University English essay prize in 1904. Though it is not really a literary essay, the analysis of Burke's doctrines as concerned with means not ends shows the strong influence of *Principia Ethica* on Keynes the year after its publication. One of Keynes's biographers has even argued on the basis of this essay that Keynes used Burke's politics to supplement Moore's ethics (Skidelsky, p. 154).

VI

Lytton Strachey's various, extensive Cambridge papers belong more appropriately to the chapter on Bloomsbury's Cambridge writings or with his Edwardian essays, but two papers he wrote for prizes at Cambridge should be noted with the Group's English essays. The first, on Warren Hastings, was later expanded by Strachey into his fellowship dissertation; it differs from many of his later biographical essays in defending an eighteenth-century imperialist instead of exposing an eminent Victorian. The mature finish of the essay's style contrasts with the antithetical oversimplifications of its analysis.

Strachey's other essay, a postgraduate one, was written in 1905 for the Le Bas essay prize. 'English Letter Writers' is an even more polished performance than 'Warren Hastings'. When the essay was posthumously published, Virginia Woolf thought it was an amazing performance for someone not twenty-two to have written, 'not as thought but as cabinet making – putting little bits of wood side by side in their right places'. And she added 'That is why one gets so sick of essay writing' (*L*, v 98). The essay has no clear argument, no conclusion; instead there is an elegantly framed series of extracts primarily from eighteenth-century letter-writers. Strachey's critical commentary on his specimens is more moral than literary, referring usually to the writer's character or sometimes the age's. Steele's letters are better than Addison's because he was capable of domestic love; Swift is a great epistolary artist partly because he felt deep affection; Walpole's sensitivities rather than cold-heartedness kept him from writing great prose; Byron's marvellous letters suggest he should have written novels instead of poems or plays even though his egoism rendered him incapable of friendship. Leslie Stephen would not have admired either the style or the judgements of 'English Letter Writers', but he might have approved of its method.

It is hardly surprising that Strachey's essay did not win the prize. Again, its thin matter contrasts with the elaborate manner. Browne, Gibbon and Macaulay appear to be influencing Strachey's style, and so perhaps is Walter Raleigh, whose Clark lectures on letters were delivered while Strachey was studying with him at Liverpool. Strachey's prose did not grow plainer as he developed, but it became less self-consciously flamboyant. Yet there are also continuities with his later writing. The accents of *Eminent Victorians* are quite audible in the ironic exaggeration and rhetorical questions of passages such as the following on Lord Chesterfield's letters to his son:

> It is difficult to conceive a fate more terrible than that which condemned the young Stanhope to the weekly bombardment of his father's packet. . . . The grave was the one refuge from such a persecution; but who could tell that the grave itself

would be safe? Might not a letter from Lord Chesterfield
follow one even there, with instructions as to how one should
deport oneself in that situation? (*CC*, pp. 28–9)

'English Letter Writers' is a more accomplished piece of prose
that anything else Bloomsbury wrote at Cambridge. Yet it
resembles their student essays on English literature by being
notable less for critical acumen than for the scope of reading it
demonstrates. What none of these essays reveals, however, is the
nature and extent of the Group's education in modern literature
during their Cambridge years.

6 Modern Reading

I

At the end of the nineteenth century, living or recently deceased authors were apparently not considered appropriate subjects for Cambridge University public lectures, reading societies, or essay prizes. Undergraduate Bloomsbury also favoured the ancients to the moderns in the battle of the books, if one can judge from a literary game that Leonard Woolf, Strachey and Sydney-Turner used to play at Trinity. The game consisted of ranking the world's great or popular authors in a tripos list. A 1901 honours list, referred to by Leonard Woolf in a letter to Strachey, put Shakespeare and Plato at the very top, and gave them fellowships; the Book of Job was a close third (20.iii.01, pT). A complete 1902 list in Leonard Woolf's papers at Sussex has no modern authors at all in the first division of the first class, which contained Job, various Greeks, Lucretius, Dante, Heine, and others in addition to the English authors Spenser, Shelley (both of whom won the prize for English poetry), Milton, Browne and Keats. Francis Bacon (first class, second division) won the English essay prize. The list continues through the three divisions of the three classes, down to the 'ploughed' modern authors Marie Corelli and Kipling – the poet, not the prose writer. The highest ranked modern author was Robert Browning, placed in the first class, second division.

Yet it is clear from Bloomsbury's letters, diaries and autobiographies that they read avidly in modern literature during their Cambridge years. The history of their writing entails a history of this reading, for it was ultimately with the literature of their own time that they had to compare their own work. To describe Bloomsbury's reading of more or less contemporary poetry, fiction, drama and essays at the end of the nineteenth and the beginning of the twentieth century without resorting to a

138

catalogue, or a tripos list, is not easy. But some account is needed of this last measure of their Cambridge literary education.

II

Of the great recently dead English poets, Browning was preferred by Bloomsbury to Tennyson (second division, second class), not just because of the Laureate's establishment pieties. Like Eliot, Pound and other modernists, members of the Group were interested in Browning's dramatisations of states of mind. Swinburne was ranked below him but above Tennyson in Leonard Woolf's list; 'Dolores', 'The Garden of Proserpine', 'Hymn to Proserpine' and 'Hertha' were among the poems that Strachey, Sydney-Turner, Clive Bell and Leonard Woolf chanted to one another at night in Trinity's cloisters. Forster also liked and quoted Swinburne, whose rhythms and paganism were irresistible to the literary young at the turn of the century. Sixty years later Leonard Woolf, who occasionally used to see Swinburne around Putney, still preferred his poetry, but conceded it may have been overestimated at Cambridge (*S*, pp. 167–71). Bloomsbury came to agree with the middle-aged MacCarthy's Moorean judgement that Swinburne's 'command of means is so great, his mastery over metre and rhythm so astounding, that he often loses sight of his end' (*H*, p. 173). Fitzgerald's *Rubáiyát* was also recited in Trinity's cloisters, along with a poem by an exceedingly obscure Swinburnean poet. Charles Elton achieved literary immortality by having one of his unpublished poems memorised by Strachey and Leonard Woolf; Virginia Woolf heard them speak it and used the poem with its refrain 'Luriana, Lurilee' in *To the Lighthouse* (Boyd, 'Luriana').

A greater nineteenth-century poet than Swinburne was another alternative to Tennyson for Bloomsbury. He is missing from the tripos list, which indicates it may not have expressed Bloomsbury's mature Cambridge enthusiasms. Walt Whitman also had little or no effect on the verses Bloomsbury wrote at Cambridge, yet along with Emerson, Melville and Henry James he was an essential American author for the Group. (One of the unfortunate disconnections of literary history is that until 1930 Virginia Woolf knew nothing of America's other great nineteenth-century poet, Emily Dickinson.) Lowes Dickinson's friend Edward Carpenter publicised Whitman in England; thus Fry read him enthusiastically in the 1880s and thought he had converted his family too (*L*, I 109). It was later that Bloomsbury discovered the French Symbolists, and Mallarmé became for Fry the Cézanne of poetry. Whitman's poetry, like Swinburne's, appealed to the Group for its sense as well as its sound, for the conjunction of love and democracy in his poems, and for their freedom from Victorian moral and literary conventions. Virginia Woolf would quote from the Calamus poems in her first novel, and Forster take the title of a later poem for his last.

Another alternative to Tennyson, not as un-English as Whitman or as decadent as Swinburne, was George Meredith. Among the later-nineteenth-century writers that Bloomsbury enjoyed, Meredith underwent the greatest change in the history of their literary opinions. Forster, MacCarthy, Virginia Woolf and others admired him in the 1890s and found him unsatisfactory in the 1920s. His novels may have been more highly regarded than his poems because of their wit, but Meredith's expression of 'the joy of earth', as one of his early volumes of poems is entitled, and the proto-Lawrentian attitudes of the sonnet sequence *Modern Love* led to his being taken seriously as a writer and thinker by Cambridge undergraduates. G. M. Trevelyan called his 1906 study *The Poetry and Philosophy of George Meredith* and acknowledged Desmond MacCarthy's great help. Forster found wisdom in Meredith's poetry and quoted from it in *Howards End* (p. 315). Later, in *Aspects of the Novel*, he came to feel that, like Tennyson, 'through not taking himself quietly enough [Meredith] strained his inside' (p. 62). The contrast was with Hardy, one of the most admired of living English writers in Bloomsbury, whose poetry, however, was virtually unknown during their Cambridge period.

A more contemporary poet whom Bloomsbury read at university published his first famous volume in 1897. A. E. Housman did not become Professor of Latin at Trinity College until 1911, though Virginia Woolf, who did not altogether like his poetry, remembered Thoby Stephen enjoying his fierce scholarly polemics (*L*, VI 33). Forster was the most enthusiastic reader of *A Shropshire Lad* in Bloomsbury. Strachey liked it too, as the other budding Group poets must have. The classicism of Housman's and Swinburne's verse forms was more congenial than Whitman's free American verse. Forster, for one, responded to more than the classical elegance of Housman's forms or his melancholy celebration of natural beauty. In a Memoir Club paper on his encounters with Housman at Cambridge in the 1920s, Forster wrote of how his self-awareness had been helped in realising from the poetry that Housman had loved a man (pKC). The conjunction of nature and male love in Housman's poems made them touchstones in Forster's Edwardian novels.

The later nineteenth-century English poetry that Bloomsbury read at Cambridge was not confined to individual volumes of poetry. Palgrave's *Golden Treasury*, published in 1861 and dedicated to Tennyson, provided Virginia Woolf with one of her moments of illumination just after her mother's death. It was the most popular anthology of the time but included no living poets. Palgrave was partially supplanted by a four-volume collection edited by Mr Humphry Ward in 1880 and then in 1900 by the most familiar of all modern anthologies of English poetry, Quiller-Couch's *The Oxford Book of English Verse*. 'Q' did not make a very good selection of nineties poets, having no Dowson, Johnson, Symons or, of course, Wilde, but there were poems by Dobson, Henley, Francis Thompson (ranked with Swinburne in Leonard Woolf's tripos list), Stevenson, Newbolt, Davidson, Yeats, 'AE', Binyon and naturally the ploughed Kipling. Whatever the attitude toward Kipling at Trinity and King's, he was heard if not read around Hyde Park Gate, for Leslie Stephen knew a number of his and Newbolt's poems by heart.

Two poets in the *Oxford Book of English Verse* were of personal interest to some of the members of Bloomsbury. One was Sturge Moore, the elder brother of G. E. Moore. It can be assumed that at least some of his poetry and criticism were read in Bloomsbury. (Leonard Woolf once received a letter in Ceylon from G. E. Moore characteristically objecting to the kinds of statements his brother made in a book on Dürer – LW/*S*, pp. 139–40.) Fry, for one, had various not always amiable associations with Sturge Moore. Fry was also related through marriage to Robert Bridges, who undertook to help him by discussing beauty with Fry's parents. Fry kept in touch with Bridges about aesthetic matters in poetry, and in 1896 was shown some manuscripts of a poet friend of Bridge's, Gerard Manley Hopkins. They included 'The Windhover', which Fry quoted in correspondence with his good friend the poet R. C. Trevelyan (*L*, I 165). Through Bridges, Fry was among the earliest to recognise Hopkins's

greatness – and he always shared his enthusiasms with Bloomsbury. Virginia Woolf agreed with him about Hopkins; years
later, after his poems were published, she wrote to Janet Case
that she would like to have written 'Heaven-Haven' (*L*, II 415).

One other poet should be mentioned – a Stephen who has
received surprisingly little attention in Bloomsbury biographies
and criticism, though he is still anthologised in collections of
light verse. Cambridge seems to have been full of Stephens in the
latter half of the nineteenth century. Sir James Stephen was
Regius Professor of Modern History there after his retirement
from the Colonial Office; his sons Fitzjames and Leslie went to
Trinity College and to Trinity Hall (where Leslie became a
fellow) and his daughter Caroline Emelia settled at the Porch.
Fitzjames's daughter Katherine was Vice-Principal of Newnham
when Thoby was at Trinity, and his son was the famous J. K.
Stephen of Eton and King's – athlete, Apostle, scholar, lawyer
and poetic wit – who died insane, apparently of a head injury, in
1892. In his last years J. K.'s madness disrupted his uncle's
household, for he was in love with Stella Duckworth. When
Roger Fry came up to King's in the 1880s, J. K. Stephen was a
fellow of the college. Desmond MacCarthy knew of his fame at
Eton and once compared him to Oscar Wilde, another large-
sized wit; the resemblance ended there, for J. K. was no aesthete
but a proud philistine whose humour was inseparable from a
'crashing common sense' (DM/*P*, p. 252).[1] Leonard Woolf too
observed the 'Stephenesque' characteristics of good looks, large-
ness, Johnsonian common sense, and lapidary modes of expression. 'Monolithic' was the word he gave to these qualities as he
found them in Leslie, Fitzjames, Katherine and J.K., in
Vanessa, Virginia and, most familiarly, Thoby (*S*, pp. 123–4,
183–5).

What now survives of J. K. Stephen's verse is his parodies of
Wordsworth, Whitman and Browning, and above all his 'To
R. K.':

> Will there never come a season
> Which shall rid us from the curse
> Of a prose that knows no reason
> And an unmelodious verse:
> . . .
> When there stands a muzzled stripling,
> Mute, besides a muzzled bore:

> When the Rudyards cease from kipling
> And the Haggards Ride no more.
> (*Lapsus Calami*, p. 3)

Stephen's debt to C. S. Calverley is acknowledged in the first poem of his first collection; their poetry along with Praed's constitutes something of a Cambridge tradition of comic verse, to which the little light verse that was written in Bloomsbury, chiefly by Clive and Julian Bell, belongs.

III

George Meredith, Thomas Hardy, Samuel Butler and Henry James were the later-nineteenth-century writers of fiction in England that most interested Bloomsbury while they were at Cambridge. Meredith, Hardy and James were the accepted classics among living authors, Virginia Woolf recollected from her hours in Leslie Stephen's library, though none had the influence of a Carlyle, Ruskin or Tennyson (*CE*, ii, 36). Before looking at these novelists, however, some note needs to be taken of several other respected writers of fiction who did not attract or sustain Bloomsbury's attention as these four did. Robert Louis Stevenson, for example, was given a high second class in the Trinity–Bloomsbury world authors' tripos of 1902, the year of Leslie Stephen's book on him. Under the influence of Raleigh's book, Strachey at Liverpool thought Stevenson better than Ruskin (*LSH*, p. 94). By the 1920s Leonard Woolf found Stevenson's posthumous reputation had fallen more sharply than anyone else's (*E*, pp. 39–40), but he continued to enjoy the daydream fiction of Stevenson, and so did MacCarthy, but not Virginia Woolf or Forster, who does not even mention him in *Aspects of the Novel*. Joseph Conrad's writings were not much read during Bloomsbury's undergraduate years, though they were later. Virginia Woolf found his prose self-conscious (*CE*, i 303) but continued to think about his writing. Forster described his genius as a vapour (*AH*, p. 135), and Leonard Woolf recalled that, while his friends respected Conrad's writing, he 'had no contact with or message for our generation' (*BA*, p. 123). Neither did Kipling. Bloomsbury was repelled by his imperialism while recognising the acuteness of his representation of Anglo-Indian life. Leonard Woolf wondered if the society he encountered in

Ceylon had moulded or been moulded by Kipling (*G*, p. 46). Whatever the answer, it seems clear that Kipling and Conrad both contributed to the moulding of Leonard Woolf's Far Eastern writing.

Before Conrad's and Kipling's fiction, everyone in Bloomsbury read Pater's *Marius the Epicurean*. It had been one of Virginia Woolf's favourite books (*MB*, p. 182), for here was a historical novel quite unlike those of Scott she had been brought up on – a novel that concerned itself, as its subtitle declares, with 'sensations and ideas' instead of the passionate events of historical romance. Pater's preoccupation with subjectivity and isolation interested Virginia Woolf and others in Bloomsbury, as Conrad's did later, but again there were misgivings about his style. When Forster read *Marius* he was repelled by its hushed, lifeless tones and fatal lack of vulgarity (PNF/*EMF*, I 132). In their maturity it was Pater's essays that interested Bloomsbury more than his fiction.

Among the many other later-nineteenth-century novelists Bloomsbury read, George Gissing was admired more for his realism – psychological and social – than for his art. George Moore's criticism and memoirs were enjoyed more than his novels. ('George Moore is not a good name for a novelist', Virginia Woolf wrote in an early review of his *Avowals*, where Moore plays with the names of novelists; 'and now we recollect that it is above all things a philosophic name' [*CW*, p. 144]. She was distressed that the *TLS* cut out her expression of strong affection for him [*L*, II 396].) H. G. Wells's early science fiction attracted little interest in Bloomsbury at the time, but later Forster would parody it. Nor were there any women novelists that could be read alongside Meredith, Hardy, Butler or James. Annie Thackeray Ritchie was naturally read by the Stephens, but they said little about her sentimental fiction. Still, she was better fare than Mrs Humphry Ward. 'What is the peculiar mixture of commonplace banality, snobbishness, arrivism and boastfulness which makes her hit the bull's eye of British middle-class taste with such amazing skill each time?' Vanessa Bell asked her sister after reading her memoirs during the war (Spalding, *VB*, p. 166).

Though George Meredith's poetry was ostensibly taken more seriously than his fiction in Cambridge – probably the result of a genre bias – it was the humour, the feminism and the love of nature in novels such as *The Ordeal of Richard Feverel* and especially *The Egoist* that appealed to Forster, Virginia Woolf and Strachey. Forster, in a paper on the three generations he had lived through, believed *The Egoist* captured the mood of hope without faith that the young around 1900 felt (pKC). Meredith's detached Comic Spirit flourished in free, rational, civilised discourse that mocked sexual sentimentality and inequality. This was congenial to Bloomsbury. Meredith was also valued as a literary descendant of his father-in-law, Thomas Love Peacock. Nevertheless, Forster's dismissal of Meredith in *Aspects of the Novel* was definitive for Bloomsbury and others. Writing later, Leonard Woolf agreed with Forster about Meredith's phoneyness, but still honoured him as a rebel against Victorianism (*S*, p. 166). Virginia Woolf had reviewed Meredith's achievement around the time she was evolving her first modernist fictions in 1918; she continued to regard him a great writer rather than a great novelist (*CE*, i 236). The reason for this was not Meredith's phoneyness, but more likely the authenticity of some of his Russian contemporaries. Turgenev, Tolstoy, Dostoevsky, and finally Chekhov had all been appearing in French and then English translations in the latter part of the nineteenth century. For Virginia Woolf and her friends these Russian writers embodied a conception of fiction 'larger, saner, and much more profound' than the English (*CE*, i 233). No modern literature was more important for Bloomsbury's modernist development than the novels, stories and plays of these men. In this respect, the most influential literary parent in Bloomsbury after Leslie Stephen was a second-generation one, as it were: Constance Garnett, the mother of David, whose translations were the principal means through which Bloomsbury encountered nineteenth-century Russian literature. But this was after Bloomsbury had finished their Cambridge literary education.

Hardy's tragedies wore better than Meredith's comedies for Bloomsbury. For Forster, Hardy gave a literary endurance to bleak Dorset that outlasted Meredith's fluffy, lush Surrey (*AN*, p. 62). Both authors were part of the literary greatness that Virginia Woolf felt surrounded by as she grew up in Leslie Stephen's house. The controversial receptions of *Tess of the D'Urbervilles* and *Jude the Obscure* were important literary events of the 1890s that revealed to young Bloomsbury the moral limitations of Victorianism. Reading *Tess* around 1903, Virginia Woolf noted in a little essay on reading in the country that

Hardy was writing about the brutality of social conventions (pNY). After his death she would describe him as 'the greatest tragic writer among English novelists' (*CE*, 1 263). Hardy's conviction that a novel was an impression, not an argument, was also preferred by her to the philosophy that was not 'consumed' in Meredith's novels but didactically obtruded to the detriment of both the philosophy and the novel (VW/*CE*, 1 230). Finally, Hardy's poetry came to mean more to Bloomsbury not only than Meredith's poetry but even than Hardy's own novels. This is partly a consequence of the shape of his career. Hardy was a Victorian novelist but essentially a twentieth-century poet.[2] Strachey resolutely disliked his novels yet quickly recognised the significance of *Satires of Circumstance* when he reviewed it in 1914. The title of Hardy's next volume of poems, *Moments of Vision*, Virginia Woolf never forgot. In valuing both Hardy's poetry and fiction over Meredith's, contemporary judgement continues in accord with Bloomsbury's mature opinion.

Samuel Butler was a Cambridge man, but not, for once, a King's or Trinity Apostle. His influence even as a novelist was more intellectual than literary on Bloomsbury. Forster thought he had learned how to mix up the actual with the impossible from *Erewhon* (*2CD*, p. 215); from *Erewhon Revisited* he took the theme of a lost natural brother for *The Longest Journey*. Such was Forster's interest that, while writing *Maurice* under the influence of Edward Carpenter and Butler, he signed a contract for a critical study of Butler, though he never wrote it (PNF/*EMF*, II 3). The importance for Bloomsbury as a whole of the posthumous *The Way of All Flesh*, published in the same year as *Principia Ethica*, was enormous. More than any other contemporary work it smashed the moral, religious and educational icons of the Victorian patriarchy. Butler attacked a different kind of idealism from that refuted by Moore's philosophy, but the basis of his criticism was still common sense; without this firm ground, Butler saw Victorian morality floundering in a swamp of hypocrisy. Butler's interest in the unconscious has no parallel in Moore. It was part of the ethical basis on which Butler and his follower George Bernard Shaw rejected Darwin. Bloomsbury thought vitalism bad philosophy and remained Darwinian, though Butler's notions about the unconscious influenced Forster. Virginia Woolf liked Butler's criticism of the joyless Victorian professional man, which she would echo in the memoirs of her father, but she did not think highly of Butler as an artist, calling him an amateur novelist (*CW*, pp. 29, 34). *The Way of All Flesh* she listed as one of the books heralding the change of human character in 1910 (*CE*, I 320), but she refers more in her writings to his notebooks than to his novels.

Leonard Woolf, not surprisingly, admired Samuel Butler's work, particularly his ironic treatment of resurrection arguments in *The Fair Haven* (*E*, pp. 48–52). Forster too enjoyed Butler's dry irony, preferring it to Swift's savage indignation (*AN*, p. 128). But the member of the Group upon whom Butler had the greatest effect was Desmond MacCarthy. As a child he had met Butler and later visited him in London. After Butler's death MacCarthy published extracts from the notebooks in the *New Quarterly* and much later in *Life and Letters*. He also wrote of Butler from time to time in his various literary columns. Mac-Carthy thought that the most comprehensive description of Butler was as 'a humorous philosopher' (*C*, p. 2). The comic irony of his philosophy complemented Moore's, which so deeply influenced MacCarthy. Butler's critique of Victorian idealism insisted, for example, on the importance of money: 'he would have no blaspheming against Mammon', says MacCarthy (p. 8). This honest and frank materialism was something of a revelation to Forster and Virginia Woolf, not to mention Shaw. Oddly enough, however, the only Bloomsbury author who did not write on Butler is the one who is most often associated with him. Lytton Strachey once offered to write on him for the *Edinburgh Review* but was not asked to (*MH/LS*, p. 540). When he read *The Way of All Flesh* he found it 'cheering' (*MH/LS*, p. 529), and thought the notebooks amusing, intelligent, well written; yet he complained to Virginia Woolf about Butler's unaesthetic view of life and his 'rubbishy science and philosophy' (*LVWLS*, p. 47). The aesthetic judgement is a little odd, given Butler's enthusiasms for Handel and Bellini (the subject of Fry's first book), but Strachey regretted the absence of panache in him. Perhaps he sensed a repressed homosexuality in Butler, and that may have also inhibited Forster's plans for a critical study of him. Despite their diverse qualifications, all Bloomsbury found Butler's work stimulating, which illustrates again the Group's intellectual cohesion.

IV

Henry James illustrates it too, but with him the task of epitomising Bloomsbury's modern reading at Cambridge and later becomes practically unmanageable. His work, particularly the late novels that were appearing at the beginning of the century, exhibited the limits of the art of fiction for the would-be novelists of Bloomsbury before they read the Russians or their own modernist contemporaries. Associated with James's work for the Group were various kinds of personal connections. 'He loomed up in my young days almost to the obstruction of his works', Virginia Woolf recalled much later (*L*, v 392). Leslie Stephen had published him in the *Cornhill* and been his host in London and Cornwall. When Gerald Duckworth set up as a publisher in 1898, James's *In the Cage* was included in his first list – together with his stepfather's *Studies of a Biographer*, a Strindberg play and Galsworthy's first novel. (Gerald Duckworth & Company is an overlooked source of literary modernism for Bloomsbury as well as an important predecessor of the Hogarth Press.) James followed the lives of the Stephens through their funerals and weddings, wrote them letters of condolence, and privately deplored the husbands and friends of Sir Leslie's daughters. MacCarthy knew James during the Edwardian years, and wrote to him almost apologetically of his infatuation with his books (DM/pC). Forster met him through Sydney Waterlow, who lived near James at Rye and introduced his Cambridge friends to him, including G. E. Moore; when James first met Forster he thought he was Moore (PNF/*EMF*, i 164).

At Cambridge, under the influence of *The Awkward Age*, *The Sacred Fount*, *The Wings of the Dove* and *The Ambassadors*, Leonard Woolf felt he and his friends lived in 'a Jamesian phantasmagoria', where subtle psychological, moral and aesthetic distinctions were refined through oblique conversation. Two of these conversations are preserved in Cambridge parodies that Leonard Woolf published later in *Sowing*; one is intensely opaque, the other ridiculous for the Jamesian form in which such un-Jamesian subjects as a cat with worms and a woman rat-killer are discussed. Strachey too wrote dialogues parodying James, and Virginia Woolf mocked his talk in her early letters. The impact of late James on Leonard Woolf and at least his Trinity friends went even further. Together with Strachey

Leonard Woolf invented a 'method' that incorporated techniques of James, Socrates and Moore. It was a pre-Freudian psychoanalytic third degree applied, sometimes with devastating results, to the psyche of a friend like Sydney-Turner, whom Leonard Woolf used to think of as a character in an unwritten James novel (*S*, pp. 106–16). James's analyses of moral and aesthetic impressions made the connection between his art and Moore's philosophy inevitable for Bloomsbury at Cambridge and afterwards. When he finished reading *The Golden Bowl* in Ceylon, Leonard Woolf wrote to Strachey, 'Did he invent us or we him? He uses *all* our words in their most technical sense & we cant have got them all from him' (QB/*VW*, 1 177). This was the same Wildean question Leonard Woolf asked in Ceylon about Kipling. MacCarthy also connected the influences of James and Moore at Cambridge. His celebrated Apostle paper on the change of personal relations in the society took its title and theme from *The Awkward Age* (see pp. 171–2), and, in his recollections of James's importance for himself and his friends as a novelist of distinctions, he used the ethical language of *Principia Ethica* (*P*, pp. 165–6).

A generation later MacCarthy still thought James's 'philosophy' a sound one, if too exclusive in what it left out (*P*, 165–6). Keynes in his memoir of Cambridge said the same thing of Moore's philosophy. Roger Fry had found James unresponsive to the paintings of the second post-impressionist exhibition (LW/*S*, pp. 108–9), but continued to regard him as the greatest novelist of his time. Virginia Woolf and E. M. Forster were less constant in their admiration. For her fourth book review, the clerical *Guardian* sent Virginia Woolf *The Golden Bowl* in 1905, and she gave her opinion that 'there is no living novelist whose standard is higher, or whose achievement is so consistently great' ('James's Latest', p 339). In 1913, she and MacCarthy were the only members of Bloomsbury to subscribe to a seventieth-birthday tribute to James (James, *Letters*, IV 665–8). And in 1918, two years after his death, she reviewed a good critical study of James, and distinguished between three Jamesian sects: those who preferred the early works, those who liked the later ones, and a third group (to which she herself belonged), 'the fickle Jacobeans', who admired the work of both periods but also suffered lapses amounting to contempt for some of his writing. She eloquently summarized James's significance as 'a priest of the art of writing in his lifetime, he is now among the saints to whom every writer, in particular every novelist, must do homage' ('Method', p. 655). Part of her own homage took the form, according to David Garnett, of keeping a signed photograph of him on her writing-desk at Asheham (p. 125). But several years earlier she wrote to Strachey that she was disabusing Leonard of his admiration for James and wanted to know what merit Lytton found in him: 'I read, and can't find anything but faintly tinged rose water, urbane and sleek, but vulgar, and ... pale. ... Is there really any sense in it? I admit I can't be bothered to snuff out his meaning when it's very obscure.' She adds that she is beginning Dostoevsky's *The Insulted and the Injured* (*L*, II 67). Leonard Woolf did come to feel that he and his friends had overvalued James at Cambridge, and that, unlike Butler, Hardy or even Meredith, James was not an ally in the revolt against Victorianism (*S*, p. 166). When Virginia Woolf reviewed James's letters in 1920, she deplored the dilettantism that found Ibsen ugly and common, Hardy vile, Dostoevsky a jumble and Stevenson wonderful (*CE*, I 282–5). The next year she tried to call James's ghost stories lewd in *The Times Literary Supplement*, but the editor would not allow it (*D*, II 151). At the end of her life, however, it was James she thought of, quoting for consolation in her penultimate diary entry his injunction to observe perpetually (v 357–8).

Forster was the only member of Bloomsbury who did not show himself to have been under James's spell at Cambridge. Yet *The Ambassadors* helped him to complete his first novel. In *Aspects of the Novel* Forster attacks James for imposing too much pattern on his fiction – a view Virginia Woolf criticised and then more or less adopted in her abortive 'Phases of Fiction' book on the novel. Forster's *Commonplace Book* reveals that he disliked what he took to be James's homosexual reticence. 'My ability to write fuck may preserve me from too close contact with H. J.', he added later while thinking of writing a middle-aged novel, and in old age Forster recorded his enjoyment of James's earlier novels such as *The Princess Casamassima* (*CB*, pp. 23, 33, 42, 190).

The Bloomsbury Group as a whole were fickle Jacobeans, then. They revolted against the English social milieu in which James moved. They disliked the absence of plain speaking, the reticent indirections, of his late writing and talk. Yet as epistemological drama the fiction of Henry James, especially the late work, is closer in its moral, aesthetic and even social values to the fiction of Forster and Virginia Woolf than anyone else's in Victorian England. Were there finer novels about the situation of women for Virginia Woolf to read than *The Portrait of a Lady* or *The Bostonians*? Could Forster find the international theme better embodied anywhere else in contemporary fiction? Was there a critic whose sensitive perceptions and firm standards were closer than James's to the kinds of criticism Bloomsbury would write? Certainly not Walter Pater, on the one hand, or Leslie Stephen, on the other. The conclusion is difficult to escape that the fickleness of Bloomsbury's reactions to James was a natural consequence of their effort to assimilate his complex influence without being overwhelmed by it. They criticised everything in James's art and character from nationality to sexuality, yet no other nineteenth-century writer's achievement interested them more.

V

The only modern playwright whom Bloomsbury read as attentively as they read James at the turn of the century had to be translated for them. Leonard Woolf described how exciting it was to encounter in Henrik Ibsen's plays a dramatist who gave aesthetic pleasure while attacking the hypocrisies of nineteenth-century society (*S*, pp. 163–4). (The impact of Chekhov on Bloomsbury came after Cambridge.) Roger Fry thought *Pillars of Society* Shakespearean (*L*, I 122). *John Gabriel Borkman* was read in the Midnight Society. Forster used Peer Gynt as a pseudonym in a Cambridge essay contest, and on the centenary of Ibsen's birth called him a great romantic, like Beethoven (*AH*, p. 84). Virginia Woolf might have agreed; she once contrasted Forster's divided artistic self with Ibsen's fusing of realism and mysticism (*CE*, I 346–7). But Virginia Woolf has less to say about the drama in her criticism than about any other major literary form, and nothing really about Ibsen's depiction of women in nineteenth-century bourgeois society. It was Maynard Keynes, surprisingly enough, who saw *A Doll's House*, *The Master Builder*, *Hedda Gabler* and *Rosmersholm* as 'a continuous commentary on the emergence of the modern woman', and who in the 1930s helped finance productions of them as vehicles for Lydia

Lopokova's acting and also to see how well Ibsen's plays were wearing (Arundell, p. 131).

Desmond MacCarthy, Bloomsbury's best drama critic, saw Ibsen as 'the dramatist of the future' even at the end of the First World War. He too appreciated Ibsen's use of beautiful symbolism to express revolutionary ideas, but believed it was his 'theatre of the soul' that made him important, not Ibsen's advocacy of social reform (*H*, pp. 60–5). But perhaps the most revealing assessment of Ibsen in the early literary history of Bloomsbury came from a source almost as unlikely as that of Keynes in their later literary history. Clive Bell, while he was formulating his ideas about significant form in the wake of the second post-impressionist exhibition, reviewed a book on Ibsen for the *Athenaeum* in which he compared Ibsen with Cézanne. Ibsen also had sought the thing-in-itself, the essential reality of form, which lies beyond the concerns of most literature. But Ibsen was not as great as Cézanne. His symbolism was unconvincing, and not just because he was a dramatist instead of a painter; Ibsen 'lacked the imagination by which alone one arrives and remains in the world of reality'. Yet at least his plays revealed 'a new world, in which moral values were real and convincing', for they showed the truth of right feeling as opposed to the herd-instincts of the state known as 'Morality and Idealism' (*PB*, pp. 28–40). Bell's language here has been encountered before – in Leonard Woolf's and Desmond MacCarthy's discussions of James, for example – and it will reappear in the chapters that follow on Bloomsbury's philosophical education at Cambridge.

The attack on Idealism, the necessity of respecting reality, also attracted Bloomsbury to George Bernard Shaw's plays. In *Sowing* Leonard Woolf quoted from the preface in which Shaw explained the general onslaught on idealism in plays like *Arms and the Man*. This was a message that made him 'one of our leaders in the revolutionary movement of our youth', even though he lacked the poetic imagination of a truly great dramatist such as Ibsen (*S*, pp. 164–5). Strachey, in the midst of trying to write one of his plays, wrote to Leonard Woolf, 'If only Bernard Shaw had been screwed up a peg higher, it would have been worthwhile living' (1.ii.07, pNY). Fry had encountered Shaw as a socialist in the 1880s at Cambridge, before he became a playwright, and was set straight about art and justice. Later

Fry admitted that Shaw had been right about justice but he never took him seriously as an artist or aesthetic critic (*L*, II 633–4). Nor did Clive Bell, who thought his value lay in his attacks on the cant, convention and unreason found in the work of opponents like G. K. Chesterton ('Shaw', p. 292).

Bloomsbury's various involvements with Shaw took place mostly after their Cambridge years. Desmond MacCarthy's important dramatic criticism of Shaw's Court Theatre plays belongs to the Edwardian literary history of Bloomsbury. Leonard Woolf's Fabian period was in the Georgian years, when Shaw associated *Heartbreak House* with Virginia, who disagreed with Leonard about Shaw's importance (VW/*L*, II 529). The public argument between Shaw and Clive Bell over the ethics of *Back to Methuselah* was also in the 1920s. Bloomsbury's disgust with Shaw's fascist sympathies is part of the 1930s. No other contemporary spans the literary history of Bloomsbury in the way he did. Their agreements with his social criticisms and their disagreements with his solutions and his notions about the purpose of art help to clarify their distinctive modernism.

There were no other playwrights read or seen by Bloomsbury during their Cambridge years who had the interest for them of Ibsen or Shaw. There is surprisingly little comment on Oscar Wilde's plays. Strachey explained the homosexual meanings of *A Woman of No Importance* in a letter to Duncan Grant (MH/*LS*, pp. 357–8). Fry admired an English production of *Salome* (RF/*L*, I 267); so did MacCarthy, who disliked the play, however (DM/ 'Wilde'). Strachey was delighted with *Peter Pan* but thought the verse dramas of Stephen Phillips of little interest; Strachey hoped to be a dramatic poet, but not like Phillips. Maeterlinck's symbolic dramas were read by Forster and Leonard Woolf, who had ranked him so high as a poetic mystic. And presumably Virginia Woolf read Strindberg's *The Father* when Gerald Duckworth published a translation of it in 1898. (He brought out Ibsen's *Love's Comedy* in 1900.) One would like to have had her thoughts on Strindberg's treatment of a scholarly and military father, of an artist daughter's desire for education, of an almost patriarchal feminism, and of madness.

VI

Last in this survey are the modern English essays, biographies, histories, criticism and tracts that Bloomsbury read while at Cambridge. The importance of this reading for their development is reflected in the prose they themselves came to write, for more non-fiction was written in Bloomsbury than anything else.

Between Victorianism and modernism, non-fiction prose disappeared as a major literary form. Carlyle, Macaulay, Ruskin had no successors. Among the best writers of English prose after them are the three principal writers of the Bloomsbury Group, yet they are not their heirs. For some critics today the prose of Pater and Wilde, and perhaps Beerbohm and Symonds, constitutes the best non-fiction in English after the great Victorians. Bloomsbury did not really think so, but they read them attentively at Cambridge, along with the essays of Swinburne, Meredith, Butler, James and, of course, Leslie Stephen. The epistemological and ethical differences between the English aesthetes' impressionism and Bloomsbury's should be clearer after the Group's philosophical education at Cambridge has been described.

When Roger Fry read Pater's *Miscellaneous Studies* in 1898, he found the appreciations fine and imaginative but regretted all the mistakes Pater had made about the pictures. Fry hoped that Berenson, once he got over his theories, would be able to make similar discriminations in more accurate detail (*L*, I 171–2). Pater does not even appear on the great-writers tripos list of 1902. The year before, Strachey had read Pater 'wildly' and with loathing, complaining in a letter to Leonard Woolf that Pater's style was 'Death itself' (19.iii.01, pT). Leonard Woolf, however, admitted a partiality for Pater's hot-house prose, especially the famous concluding paragraph of *The Renaissance* (20.iii.01, pT). But late in life he stated that Bloomsbury felt Pater's style ridiculous in its self-conscious preciosity (Interview, 1966). In the 1920s, Virginia Woolf admired that style in an essay on the modern essay, and quoted from the famous portrait of the Mona Lisa that Yeats would anthologise as a poem. But she added ambiguously that the only one reading Pater any more seemed to be Conrad (*CE*, II 43–4).

Oscar Wilde is also missing from the tripos list, and there is no other record of anyone in Bloomsbury reading him at Cambridge. He was important as an aesthetic martyr to Fry (VW/ *RF*, p. 211), who late in life felt he had not done justice to Wilde, though he had always admired 'The Soul of Man under Socialism' (*L*, II 601). Considerably more important as an influence on Bloomsbury's writings was Max Beerbohm – the 'prince' of modern essayists, Virginia Woolf called him (*CE*, II 46). But the writings of his most admired by Bloomsbury were published after their Cambridge years. So was Edmund Gosse's autobiography. Another later-Victorian essayist, Augustine Birrell, was the father of one of Bloomsbury's younger followers. Virginia Woolf admired his *Obiter Dicta*, and wrote to him that she put them next to Stephen's *Hours in a Library* on her shelf (*L*, IV 76). But in 'The Modern Essay' she somewhat devastatingly mused on the great gulf that lay between an essay Birrell had written on Carlyle and 'the essay which one may supposed Carlyle would have written upon Mr Birrell' (*CE*, II 45). The very popular Robert Louis Stevenson was no more liked in Bloomsbury as an essayist than as a story-teller, partly because of his popularity. Forster thought the domestication of Pan was the result of Stevenson's influence, and he deplored 'the whole congregation of writers' who had imitated his sweetly written essays, prating 'of freedom and liberty after him till those holy and invisible things have become coated with their breath' (pKC). G. K. Chesterton was certainly read by Leonard Woolf, who met him and his brother at St Paul's. The even more prolific Hilaire Belloc was read too in Bloomsbury but the beliefs and biases of such men did not make them congenial writers for anyone in Bloomsbury.[3]

After Pater, and of course Ruskin, the nineteenth-century writer on art that several members of the Group appear to have read at the beginning of the twentieth was John Addington Symonds. William Morris had apparently no direct influence on Bloomsbury in either his poetry, his fiction or his essays; his group art (including printing) was well known to them, of course, and his socialism was familiar in Cambridge through the work of Edward Carpenter and others. Symonds had been published by Stephen in the *Cornhill*; one of Strachey's aunts was his sister, and after his death Virginia Woolf became close friends with his daughter Madge. But the greatest influence of Symonds's writings in Bloomsbury was on Fry, who learned about Renaissance art from him in Italy in the 1890s. Fry grew to dislike Symonds's style, but his books, said Virginia Woolf in her biography, had 'the root of the matter in them' (*RF*, p. 73). Fry also came to feel that Symonds, like Pater, was too much of an amateur art critic – and at this point in her biography of him Virginia Woolf commented that Fry himself remained an amateur in writing compared to Pater or Symonds (pp. 99, 106), or even, it might be added, Clive Bell. The discontinuity here in the history of English literature and art criticism is again notable. Would there ever be another professional art historian or critic who was also a literary artist?

Symonds for his part found the young Roger Fry quite attractive and confided in him, thus advancing Fry's sexual education too. Symonds rather shocked him with his advocacy of homosexuality, and Fry described him in a letter as 'the most pornographic person I ever saw but not in the least nasty . . .' (VW/*RF*, p. 75). Symonds's *A Problem in Modern Ethics*, privately published the year Fry met him in 1891, certainly circulated in Cambridge. Strachey, who also disliked Symonds's writing, and Forster, who reluctantly saw Italy partly through Symonds's works, must both have known of the book.

Strachey, Forster and others in Bloomsbury also knew the work of another English writer on homosexuality at the time, Edward Carpenter. Again there were biographical connections with Bloomsbury. Carpenter, ironically, was the clergyman Trinity Hall appointed as a fellow to replace Leslie Stephen. He lasted until 1874, when he too resigned from his fellowship and the clergy to take up various social and sexual causes, including socialism, anarchism, suffragism, free love, spiritualism, vegetarianism and homosexuality (Hynes, *Edwardian Turn*, p. 150). Like Symonds he was also an advocate of Walt Whitman, but the writings of Carpenter that attracted most attention were books such as *Love's Coming of Age* and *Homogenic Love*. In Bloomsbury both Fry and Forster came under Carpenter's considerable personal influence through Lowes Dickinson. That the influence was as much personal as intellectual suggests again the difference between the King's and Trinity strands of Bloomsbury at Cambridge. Leonard Woolf, who might have been interested in Carpenter's socialism, never mentions him, and Lytton Strachey, according to Forster, always greeted his name 'with a series of little squeaks' (*M*, p. 238). But Carpenter's was also an important literary influence, as Forster showed in the last of his

Edwardian novels, *Maurice*. Carpenter's main impact on Forster happened a decade after Cambridge. The posthumous publication of *Maurice* has led some recent critics to emphasise Carpenter to the diminishment of other influences on Forster at Cambridge, joining him with Pater and others (but not Strachey very much) in an English homosexual literary tradition that Forster is seen to continue. Such connections do not take sufficiently into account other aspects of the Apostolic tradition in which Forster was educated at Cambridge.

The mention of Lowes Dickinson and the Apostles brings in another group of non-fiction prose-writers, whom Bloomsbury were more profoundly influenced by than any other modern writers they read during their Cambridge period. These writers were the philosopher Apostles Dickinson, McTaggart, Russell and Moore. Their personalities, ideas and words belong to the philosophical education of Bloomsbury, that was as important to the Group's early history as their literary education at Cambridge.

Part Three
Cambridge: Philosophical Education

7 Philosophy and the Cambridge Apostles

I

Bloomsbury's undergraduate love of literature was matched only by their passion for philosophy. Even Virginia Woolf, pursuing her education as a private student in London, studied Plato in Greek. So fundamental was philosophy to the development of Bloomsbury that a literary history of the Group must be to some extent a philosophical history too. The ahistorical criticism devoted to the Bloomsbury writers has largely ignored the actual philosophical context of their work. Yet the need of critic after critic to relate Forster's or Virginia Woolf's fiction to some system of ideas known to the critic but not the writer at least shows an awareness that Bloomsbury's writing is grounded in some basic philosophical presuppositions. This, of course, is true of other modern writers, but the philosophical environment of Virginia Woolf, Forster and Strachey differs from that of, say, Joyce or Lawrence, Yeats or Eliot, in two interesting respects: the particular philosophical tradition the Group was involved in, and the way they shared their philosophical concerns with one another.

Philosophy, it has been noted, began at home for the Stephens and for Keynes, and it was basically the same philosophy of Cambridge utilitarianism. Keynes eloquently summed it up as a philosophical tradition and extended it down through Bloomsbury's education in the Preface to *A Treatise on Probability*:

It may be perceived that I have been much influenced by W. E. Johnson, G. E. Moore, and Bertrand Russell, that is to say by Cambridge, which, with great debts to the writers of Continental Europe, yet continues in direct succession the English tradition of Locke and Berkeley and Hume, of Mill

161

and Sidgwick, who in spite of their divergences of doctrine, are united in a preference for what is matter of fact, and have conceived their subject as a branch rather of science than of the creative imagination, prose writers, hoping to be understood. (*CW*, VIII 1)

Perhaps the principal reason why critics of Virginia Woolf and Forster continue for the most part to ignore the philosophical ideas that were closest to these authors is the critical belief that the tradition of thought described by Keynes is, as he seems to imply, irrelevant if not inimical to the creative imagination. There does seem to be a paradox here. How could empirical, scientific philosophies of fact, logic and common sense have appealed to prose-writers hoping to create imaginative literature that would be felt as well as understood? There were certainly elements in Cambridge philosophy that Lytton Strachey found absurd, Forster incomprehensible, and Virginia Woolf deadly, yet out of that philosophy came Bloomsbury's basic intellectual values and premisses. Had Thoby Stephen died before he went to Cambridge, had Virginia not married Leonard Woolf, had Strachey gone to Oxford, had Forster not been an Apostle, then Bloomsbury would have had no philosophical history, nor even perhaps a literary one either. To put it positively, the Bloomsbury Group's preoccupations with states of consciousness, with analytic methods of reasoning, with what is real, unreal, and ideal, with love and beauty, with means and ends in themselves, with mystical experiences, with the meanings of time and history, with the psychology of patriarchs and matriarchs, with the interactions of the human and the natural – all were shaped by Cambridge philosophy. They learned their art at college by reading, talking and listening, says Virginia Woolf in her important late essay 'The Leaning Tower':

What did they talk about? Here is Mr Desmond MacCarthy's answer as he gave it, a week or two ago, in the *Sunday Times*. He was at Cambridge just before the war began and he says: 'We were not very much interested in politics. Abstract speculation was much more absorbing; philosophy was more interesting to us than public causes. . . . What we chiefly discussed were those "goods" which were ends in themselves . . . the

search for truth, aesthetic emotions, and personal relations.'   (*CE*, II 167)

An understanding of Cambridge philosophy at the turn of the
century and how it was transmitted to Bloomsbury blunts the
paradox of a rationalistic philosophy providing the intellectual
foundations of an imaginative literature. The Cambridge
philosophers mentioned by Keynes (to whom could be added his
own father) were, as he says, in that tradition of British empiricism whose eighteenth- and earlier-nineteenth-century history
had been largely written by Leslie Stephen. Its nineteenth-
century development up through the work of Henry Sidgwick
could be fairly described as utilitarian. There is, for instance, a
fine utilitarian flavour to the term 'moral sciences' that since the
mid nineteenth century described the tripos subject of study of
non-ancient philosophy. The *OED* defines the moral sciences as
'a branch of academic study including psychology, ethics, political and economic science, and in fact all that is now commonly
understood by the term "philosophy"'. This is not a bad
description of the Cambridge philosophy Bloomsbury absorbed,
for it singles out ethics, political economy and psychology (by
which was meant epistemology and the philosophy of mind); the
omission of metaphysics also helps to identify Cambridge's
characteristic philosophical temper. Only one branch of
philosophical study that Bloomsbury was much concerned with
is missing: namely, aesthetics, which was usually subsumed
under that other normative field, ethics.

Other philosophical strands besides the utilitarian were, of
course, present in Bloomsbury's Cambridge philosophical education. German Idealism[1] was formidably present in the thought
of J. M. E. McTaggart, who also belonged very much in the
British tradition. More important was Greek Idealism. After
G. E. Moore, Plato is the most influential philosopher in
Bloomsbury. He was crucially important for Moore as well, and
it would not be difficult to trace some of the Platonic elements in
his thinking back through the eighteenth-century British
philosophers he admired to the seventeenth-century Cambridge
Platonists. Plato and Plotinus were fundamental to the philoso-
phy of Lowes Dickinson, and Plato has clearly left his mark on
Bertrand Russell's thought. Dickinson, McTaggart, Russell and
Moore were the primary Cambridge philosophical influences on

Bloomsbury. For all the differences between them in doctrine, character and achievement, they were basically in agreement about philosophical values. If they disagreed about the meanings of fact and common sense, they were nevertheless united in their respect for logic and truth. All belonged to the now notorious Cambridge Conversazione Society, alias the Society, alias the Apostles, to which all Bloomsbury's males belonged except Thoby Stephen, Clive Bell and Duncan Grant. Cambridge philosophy as Bloomsbury learned it came through the brothers and the traditions of the Apostles, to which a number of distinguished nineteenth- and twentieth-century philosophers have belonged. (In addition to those already mentioned there were F. D. Maurice, W. K. Clifford, A. N. Whitehead, Ludwig Wittgenstein, F. P. Ramsey and R. B. Braithwaite.)

To understand Bloomsbury's philosophical education at Cambridge, we need to examine the nature of the Cambridge Conversazione Society around the turn of the century and then look at the significance for the Group of four remarkable philosopher Apostles.

II

No one in Bloomsbury studied the moral sciences at Cambridge. They got their modern philosophy like their modern literature, by themselves. Discussion here was even more important than in literary study, and the Apostles constituted the most important discussion society in which Bloomsbury was educated philosophically. The records of that education in the form of papers written for the Apostles and also for the Sunday Essay Society will be considered among Bloomsbury's Cambridge writings in Chapter 11. What made the Apostles so much more influential than any of the other student societies was not just the intellectual distinction of its members: the organisation of the Society and the purposes of its discussions were also crucial. The Cambridge Conversazione Society was a secret group (hence all the aliases) limited to twelve active members, who combined strong friendship with serious intellectual discussion. The brothers, as the members referred to one another, remained in touch after Cambridge through annual dinners, and many of them continued to attend meetings when they were in Cambridge. The Apostles saw themselves as an intellectual, even a spiritual, elite. In their discussions and conversations, their old friendships, exclusivity and self-confidence, their wit and high seriousness, their criticism of conventional values and behaviour, the Apostles were the most important group precedent for Bloomsbury. 'I shall be one of those people', Virginia Woolf wrote in her diary on the verge of her success as a novelist and critic in 1924, 'who are, so father said, in the little circle of London Society which represents the Apostles, I think, on larger scale.' And then characteristically she went on to ask, 'Or does this no longer exist? To know everyone worth knowing. I can just see what he meant; just imagine being in that position – if women can be' (*D*, II 319).

One of the most important features of the Society is that it was not just an undergraduate group. Apostle dons frequently attended the weekly meetings and others came up from time to time to read papers or participate in the discussions that followed. Thus it was that Leonard Woolf and Lytton Strachey first met in discussion their future Bloomsbury friends Roger Fry, Desmond MacCarthy and E. M. Forster, as well as the dons or fellows Dickinson, McTaggart, Russell and Moore. Philosophy was not the only topic of discussion, however. When Roger Fry was elected in 1887 he described the Apostles to his mother as 'a society for the discussion of things in general' (VW/*RF*, p. 49). What the Society meant to Bloomsbury was a function of its subjects and methods of discussion as well as the friendships of the members. To appreciate this it is necessary to glance at the history of the Society from its early Victorian origins to the advent of Strachey and Keynes.

The early years of the Cambridge Apostles have been well documented by Peter Allen, who has noted the continuity of the Apostles' influence 'in the history of the liberal intelligentsia from the eighteen-twenties down to Bloomsbury' (p. viii). Theological, social and educational issues were the most important ones for the Victorian Apostles, especially under the influence of F. D. Maurice and his Christian socialism. With Maurice the Apostles changed from 'a rather ordinary essay society into an instrument for the spiritual regeneration of its members' (Allen, p. 70), and it remained this way through its Bloomsbury period, although its spiritual aims changed, of course. Even in Maurice's time there were ideological divisions in the Society between the 'muddy mystics' and the Benthamites as to whether social improvement were better effected by spiritual or by political means (Allen, p. 36).[2]

But more important than the particular points of view that were argued about in the Apostles was their belief that one learned from opposing opinions. Intellectually it was more blessed to receive than to give, to understand the ideas of others rather than to make one's own prevail. A basic principle was that the opinions of a brother constituted only the superstructure of his personality; they might change or be disregarded by other brothers without impairing the esteem or affection they had for him (Allen, p. 154). This helps explain the strong group feeling in the Society as well as its mixture of highly distinguished and apparently quite insignificant minds. Yet there was a danger here – and in the history of Bloomsbury itself – of emphasising the personal and discounting the intellectual. Because the interest in the origins of Bloomsbury has been primarily biographical and literary, the intellectual aspects of their early history have been unrecognised or unemphasised, as will be seen in the chapter on Moore, for example. Even Allen describes the Apostles as spiritually degenerating into the 'narcissistic elitism' of Lytton Strachey, though this is not borne out by the Apostle papers or correspondence of the time. Truth was as important to Strachey and his friends as to their predecessors, though of course it was not the same truth. They devoted more energy to personal relations than their Victorian brothers; nevertheless, 'the one essential Apostolic quality' for them, as Strachey wrote to Leonard Woolf after Cambridge in 1907, was 'the importance of truth' (1.viii.07, pNY). Charm, decency, sincerity, lovableness, beauty were all very important and sometimes they obscured for Strachey and others the quality of their brothers' minds and characters, yet in principle it was truth more than anything else that the Apostles sought. To minimise their intellectual concerns devalues this pursuit of truth.

From its inception the Society had been very critical of the kind of education that Cambridge offered. The Apostles' formal education had undergone a substantial transformation in the last half of the nineteenth century yet they still found their courses of study dispiriting. The term 'Apostles' was used at Cambridge to describe the last twelve students in the pass-degree examination results (Allen, p. 12). 'They fail to pass their Examinations, because they say, that success is failure & they despise success', Virginia Woolf mocked her Apostle friends while also revealing a basic Bloomsbury conviction about success (QB/*VW*, 1 206). Not all Apostles, not even all Bloomsbury ones, did that badly in exams, but most of them who wrote about their education agreed that at Cambridge it really took place in the Society instead of in tutorials, lectures or examinations. Alfred North Whitehead, to take a relatively contemporary example remote from Bloomsbury, wrote in his autobiography how the exclusively mathematical training at Cambridge was invaluably supplemented for him by Platonic dialogues in the Society with Sidgwick, Maitland, Jackson and Verrall (pp. 7–8). The educational importance of the Society for Bloomsbury is reflected in the number of their tutors and lecturers – Jackson, Verrall, Duff, Dickinson, Wedd, Browning, McTaggart – who were Apostles. The dominant Apostle among these older brothers was Henry Sidgwick, and his is still the best account of what the Society meant to its members.

III

According to Lytton Strachey, who did not admire him, Henry Sidgwick brought the Society out of the Middle Ages, presumably because he shifted its discussions from theological matters, in which they had been modernisers, to ethical subjects (26.iii.06, Grant/pBL). Sidgwick himself embodied the modernising Apostolic spirit in his efforts as an educational reformer. He resigned his Trinity fellowship, like Leslie Stephen, because of its religious requirements; they were abolished and Sidgwick remained at Cambridge to become the most influential don in the cause of women's education and an early advocate of the university teaching of English literature.

Sidgwick was also the best Cambridge philosopher of his time. His great achievement was *The Methods of Ethics*, which expanded the utilitarian end of happiness to accommodate the intuitionist ideal of perfection (Schneewind). What Sidgwick found irreconcilable without some kind of religious sanction were the claims of ethical egoism, and after a lifetime of speculation he had still not made up his mind about the necessity of religious belief. G. E. Moore thought ethical egoism self-contradictory, and he criticised Sidgwick for thinking the introduction of God would remove the contradiction (*PE*, pp. 100–4). Nevertheless *Principia Ethica* owes more to *The Methods of Ethics* than to any other single work of moral philosophy. Moore found Sidgwick's clarity and common sense very sympathetic ('Autobiography', p. 16). He took from Sidgwick the very influential idea that good was indefinable (*PE*, p. 17). Moore's criticisms of Bentham's and Mill's utilitarianism are quite similar to Sigwick's; but there are fundamental differences, too, between Sidgwick's utilitarian conception of ends and Moore's more Platonic one. *Principia Ethica* is a much more elegant philosophical work, less than half the Victorian length of *The Methods of Ethics*. Strachey summarised the influence of Sidgwick's book on Moore's (who was nicknamed 'the Yen') in a letter to Leonard Woolf in 1904: 'It is a vast vegetable mass of inert ponderosity, out of which the Yen had beaten and welded and fused his peerless flying machine. Don't you think Sidgwick contains the embryonic Moore?' (MH/*LS*, p. 226). Strachey's metaphor is historically apt; 1903 saw the publication of *Principia Ethica* and the Wright brothers' flight at Kittyhawk. Modernism in philosophy was not seen as an isolated phenomenon by Bloomsbury.

Henry Sigwick's account of the Apostles has been quoted over and over as the best description of what the Apostles taught and expected of themselves. The Apostolic spirit, he wrote, was

the spirit of the pursuit of truth with absolute devotion and unreserve by a group of intimate friends, who were perfectly frank with each other, and indulged in any amount of humorous sarcasm and playful banter, and yet each respects the other, and when he discourses tries to learn from him and see what he sees. Absolute candour was the only duty that the tradition of the society enforced. No consistency was demanded with opinions previously held – truth as we saw it then and there was what we had to embrace and maintain, and there were no propositions so well established that an Apostle had not the right to deny or question, if he did so sincerely and not from mere love of paradox. The gravest subjects were continually debated, but the gravity of treatment, as I have said, was not imposed, though sincerity was. In fact it was rather a point of the apostolic mind to understand how much suggestion and instruction may be derived from what is in form a jest – even in dealing with the gravest matters.   (*Memoir*, pp. 34–5)

Sidgwick wrote this at the end of his life and it was quoted in old age by another Apostle, Leonard Woolf, who remembered that 'our discussions, our intellectual behaviour in 1903 were in every conceivable way exactly the same as those described by Sidgwick' (*S*, pp. 150–1). Sidgwick continued, in a part of his memoir not quoted by Leonard Woolf,

No part of my life at Cambridge was so real to me as the Saturday evenings on which the apostolic debates were held; and the tie of attachment to the society is much the strongest corporate bond which I have known in life.'   (p. 35)

So it was for Bloomsbury at Cambridge. Their accounts of the Apostles continue to discuss the Society's value in terms or reality and unreality, as Sidgwick did. In Apostolic jargon, an embryo is a potential Apostle who either turns into an abortion or is born into the Society and becomes real. Those people and things outside the Society are merely unreal phenomena. When an active member resigned from the Society, he did not return to unreality but took wings and became an angel. Most of the terminology here is an ironic melange of Christian Idealism and homoerotic parthenogenesis, but the code words 'real' and 'unreal' remained important for Bloomsbury.

The philosophical and Apostolic continuity between the Society of the later nineteenth and early twentieth century is unmistakable. So are the sharp discontinuities in attitudes towards religious belief and personal relations. Moore found Sidgwick's personality unattractive ('Autobiography', pp. 16–17). When Sidgwick's *Memoir* was posthumously published in 1906, Maynard Keynes, who had known him well as a family friend and assisted with the proofs of a late edition of his *Principles of Political Economy*, wrote to Strachey how depressing he found the *Memoir*. 'He never did anything but wonder whether Christianity was true and prove that it wasn't and hope that it was', Keynes exaggerated, and then speculated,

I wonder what he would have thought of us; and I wonder what we think of him. And then his conscience – incredible. There is no doubt about his moral goodness. And yet it is all so dreadfully depressing – no intimacy, no clear-cut crisp boldness. Oh, I suppose he was intimate but he didn't seem to have anything to be intimate about except his religious doubts.   (RFH/*JMK*, pp. 116–17)[3]

What Sidgwick thought of Moore, at least, has been recorded. 'So far as I have seen his work,' he wrote three years before *Principia Ethica*, 'his *acumen* – which is remarkable in degree – is in excess of his *insight*' (Schneewind, p. 17). At times Moore thought so too.

Strachey included Sidgwick (he was the only Apostle) in a list of twelve people he was considering in 1912 for the book that eventually became *Eminent Victorians* (MH/*LS*, pp. 508–9). The year before, he concluded his next-to-last Apostle paper with a characteristic, ironically exaggerated description of the eminent Apostles who were Sidgwick's contemporaries – a description that epitomises the differences in Apostolic personal relations between Sidgwick's time and Moore's, Keynes's and Strachey's:

> Oh dear! the gay horror of those letters of our brothers Pollock, Verrall, and Jackson! The brave concealment of tragedy! The profound affection just showing, now and then, with such a delicacy, between the lines. . . . What a world, what a life, passing in these dimnesses! I see once more the bleak and barren plain, and the dreadful solitary castles, with their blinds drawn down.   (*RIQ*, p. 127)

IV

The changes that the Cambridge Conversazione Society underwent after Sidgwick are bound up with the ascendancy of the Apostles Dickinson and McTaggart, then Russell and Moore. To understand their importance for Bloomsbury, it is useful to sketch the changes that took place in the Apostles around what might be called its Bloomsbury period. These changes primarily involved two recurrent preoccupations of the Apostles: the selection of new members and the choice of topics for discussions. Whitehead once recalled at a meeting of the Apostles that, when he had been an active member in the 1880s, there had been at least a dozen and sometimes as many as seventeen brothers at a weekly meeting, all presenting different points of view vigorously.[4] Lowes Dickinson was the next Apostle to be elected after Whitehead; at first he disliked the Society's 'phenomenal' discussions of such subjects as 'The Devil in Literature' or 'Women and Smoking'. A published example of the kind of topic Dickinson had in mind is Walter Raleigh's 1882 Apostle paper 'Is Sense of Humour or Personal Integrity More Potent for Pleasure to its Owner?' Raleigh argues against 'that abortion, the optimist' and for the humorous pessimist who attains both aesthetic pleasure and a view of the moral universe through his perception of life's incongruities (pp. 1–16). Dickinson thought himself largely responsible for the change in the Apostles to a smaller, more intimate Society concerned with topics that often bore directly on personal relations. At one point in the Society's history, Dickinson remembered, the only active members were himself and his close friends McTaggart, Nathaniel Wedd and Roger Fry, who was elected in 1887 (21.iii.05, LS/pT). It was nearly ten years before the next Bloomsbury Apostle, Desmond Mac-Carthy, joined the Society; during that time, however, Russell, Moore and the Trevelyans had all become members.

While Dickinson changed the atmosphere of the Apostles' discussions, McTaggart and his Idealism dominated the Group intellectually until he was replaced by the young Moore. His importance in the history of the Apostles was described in a blasphemous analogy by Lytton Strachey, who wrote to Leonard Woolf that Bishop Tomlinson (the founder of the Society) was the Father, Sidgwick the Son, and Moore the Holy Ghost of the Apostles (25.v.05, pT). During Moore's time the Society became both more personal and more analytic. With Russell and Moore the discussions had become more technically philosophical and remained so after Moore left Cambridge in 1904. Desmond MacCarthy described the direction of the changes that started with Dickinson in an Apostle paper of 1900 that took its title from Henry James's latest novel. 'Is this an awkward Age?' argues that the *Zeitgeist* has made the Society more exclusive, affectionate, psychological and analytic, and less tolerant, dramatic, imaginative, reticent and rule-bound. 'They did not think less *of* their friends,' he wrote of the previous generation of Apostles, 'but they thought less about them, not less of friendship, but less of intimacy' (Levy, p. 224). The intensified intimacy and analysis of the Society coincided with a decline in the number of new members that the brothers agreed to elect. This 'barrennness' of the Society, as MacCarthy called it, was accompanied by an increased interest of the Apostles in homosexual relations.

E. M. Forster was elected to the Society in 1901, his last year at King's. He seems not to have enjoyed its meetings until several years later, when, under the influence of Strachey and Keynes, less demanding philosophical subjects were pursued. Forster felt he owed a great deal to the Apostolic discussions of sexual matters (PNF/*EMF*, i 77–9). In his biography of Lowes Dickinson, however, he stressed the general moral effect of university discussion societies like the Apostles (he preserves its secrecy) on both Dickinson and himself. Truth not victory is the end of its discussions; the members 'do not feel diffidence too high a price to pay for integrity', and that may be why Cambridge men have not had so great an impact on world affairs as those from Oxford. No one, Forster wrote, who has felt the power of societies like the Society,

> will ever become a good mixer or a yes-man. Their influence, when it goes wrong, leads to self-consciousness and superciliousness; when it goes right, the mind is sharpened, the judgement is strengthened, and the heart becomes less selfish. There is nothing specially academic about them, they exist in other places where intelligent youths are allowed to gather together unregimented, but in Cambridge they seem to generate a peculiar clean white light of their own which can remain serviceable right on into middle age.' (*GLD*, p. 55)

In February 1902, a year after Forster's election, Lytton Strachey became an Apostle, along with J. T. Sheppard, and they were followed in October by Saxon Sydney-Turner and Leonard Woolf. The last of Bloomsbury's core members to be elected was Maynard Keynes in February 1903. Then no other Apostles were chosen for two years. The difficulties attendant upon choosing new embryos for birth into the Society are displayed in an unnoticed remarkable Apostolic–Bloomsbury text among Lytton Strachey's papers at the University of Texas. The document is a questionnaire in Strachey's handwriting, entitled 'Quaestiones Gothicae', and drawn up in December 1902, after the elections of Sydney-Turner and Leonard Woolf. Addressed to 'The Trinity' of Trinity – Sydney-Turner, Leonard Woolf and Lytton Strachey himself – it concerns the possible election of Thoby Stephen, nicknamed 'the Goth'. Among the questions posed and answered are those asking if boredom is a reason against election, if lack of intelligence matters (assuming there is such a lack), and if 'magnificence' could make up for lack of interest. The answers given are all favourable to Stephen, including one that says nothing would give the Trinity more pleasure than his election. But it was not to be. The last question of the text consists simply of Moore's name followed by two question marks. A manifest interest in the pursuit of truth still seems to have been a necessary Apostolic quality, at least for the Trinity College wing of the Society. Perhaps if Thoby Stephen had been a Kingsman he would have been elected.

Strachey remained an active member of the Apostles for ten years (longer than anyone else except Sydney-Turner and James Strachey), and Keynes was active for seven of those years. Homosexuality came more to influence the election of new brothers and the topics chosen for discussion in the Society during their time. Bertrand Russell claimed that after his time as an active Apostle there was a long conflict between Strachey and G. M. Trevelyan; Strachey won and as a result 'homosexual relations among the members were for a time common, but in my day they were unknown' (*Autobiography*, I 74). Enough is now known about the Apostles to question both parts of Russell's statement.[5] 'The higher sodomy', as it was called, existed among the Victorian Apostles. With Strachey, Keynes and others a lower sodomy was embraced, but it is still not clear how common homosexual relations were among the Apostles. The struggle between Strachey and Keynes to sponsor the beautiful but supposedly unbright Arthur Hobhouse, the first Apostle to be elected since Keynes two years before, certainly suggests that homosexual feelings had become dominant in the Society. This time Strachey lost. His brilliant description in the Society of Keynes's paradoxical values might be viewed as a criticism of current Apostolic values, for which Strachey was partly respons- ible: Keynes, he says, 'is a hedonist and a follower of Moore; he

is lascivious without lust; he is an Apostle without tears' (MH/
LS, p. 252). Homosexuality remained an important element in
the Apostles. The combination of intensely felt ideas and friend-
ships was still in evidence in the 1930s, when the spy Apostles
Guy Burgess and Anthony Blunt mixed homosexuality with
Marxism in the Society (Boyle, pp. 72–4).

Russell also thought, following Keynes's famous memoir on
Moore's influence, that along with homosexuality there was a
change in the Society's subjects of discussion, philosophy and
politics being replaced by introspective analyses of shades of
feeling (*Autobiography*, I 70–4). There does appear to have been a
change after Moore, also noted by Forster but approvingly, in
the areas in which truth was pursued through the Society's
discussions. This is reflected in the correspondence of Keynes
and Strachey during the Edwardian years. Keynes once complained that they were being too lazy and ineffectual. Strachey
replied,

> Our great stumbling block in the business of introducing the
> world to Moorism is our horror of half-measures. We can't be
> content with telling the truth – we must tell the whole truth;
> and the whole truth is the Devil. . . . It's madness of us to
> dream of making dowagers understand that feelings are good,
> when we say in the same breath that the best ones are
> sodomitical.'   (MH/*LS*, pp. 211–12)

But one Apostle at Cambridge during this time has denied that
the Society ceased to discuss tough philosophical questions.
James Strachey thought that his brother's biographer, Michael
Holroyd, had misrepresented the Apostles's discussions:

> When I was a brother, Maynard, Norton and Hawtrey . . .
> had constant hard headed arguments about such things as
> sense-perception or truth or internal relations; and White-
> head, Sanger, Russell and Moore turned up often enough to
> affect the sort of conversation. . . .'   (MH/*LS*, p. 239)

The development that took place in the Apostles' discussions
from before Dickinson's time until after Strachey's and Keynes's
can be seen from another published Apostle paper, written in
1925 by the young philosophical genius Frank P. Ramsey. It

discusses brilliantly why there are no subjects left to discuss in the Society. All topics come down to shop or private lives. The former (which include science, history, politics, philosophy) have to be left to experts because they are too technical for general discussion, while the latter (which include the still primitive fields of aesthetics and psychology) come down to comparing feelings. Ramsey then offers *his* feelings about the universe, which does not frighten him as it did Pascal or Russell, because he sees it not drawn to scale but in perspective from his point of view ('Epilogue', pp. 287–92). Ramsey is thus what Raleigh would have called an optimist, but of an intensely analytical, self-aware, and personal kind that MacCarthy's 'Awkward-Age' paper had foreseen at the turn of the century.

In a brief account of modern English literature, a critic asked, 'What was the gain and loss to English civilization when the Cambridge of Russell and Keynes succeeded the Cambridge of Maitland and Sidgwick?' (Robson, p. 103). In figuring up this account it might be argued, for a start, that the work of Keynes and Russell has had a longer and deeper influence on the ideas of future generations than Maitland's and Sidgwick's. Nor is it obvious that the Society's (and Cambridge's) development from Raleigh to Ramsey is a matter for regret. But no simple comparisons or short sketches of the shifts in opinions and personalities among the Apostles will answer the question. To understand what the Cambridge Conversazione Society meant to Bloomsbury and therefore to the English civilisation of their time, we must look more closely at the works and lives of the four Apostles who educated Bloomsbury in philosophy at Cambridge and afterwards.

8   Dickinson and McTaggart

I

Goldsworthy Lowes Dickinson and John McTaggart Ellis McTaggart were older than Bertrand Russell and G. E. Moore, born in the 1860s instead of the 1870s, and their Apostolic philosophical significance for the literary history of the Bloomsbury Group preceded Russell's and Moore's more modern influences. Dickinson's wide-ranging liberal enthusiasms and McTaggart's conservative intellectual rigour – which illustrate again the King's and Trinity aspects of the Society – were balanced in close friendship until the First World War. Both were attracted to mysticism, but their philosophical attitudes toward it were very different. McTaggart wrote characteristically, 'All true philosophy must be mystical, not indeed in its methods, but in its final conclusions' (*Dialectic*, p. 259). Dickinson wanted philosophy to be mystical in its methods too.

Though Dickinson was the most literary of the four Apostles who shaped Bloomsbury's philosophical education, his importance now appears even more faded than McTaggart's because of Dickinson's mixed character. If anyone told him that the mixed was also the confused, he would not deny it, for he did not see how anyone could help being confused in this universe ('Dialogue', p. 19). Yet Dickinson exerted a considerable influence on the Kingsmen of Bloomsbury: on Fry, with whom he had been in love; on Forster, who wrote his biography and called him 'my friend and master' (*GLD*, p. 200); and also on Keynes, through his establishing with Marshall the economics tripos at Cambridge. The change to a more intimate Society that occurred with Dickinson's ascendancy among the Apostles in the late 1880s was not accompanied by any lessening of interest in politics, which was Dickinson's subject at King's, or philosophy, which was McTaggart's at Trinity. Instead these subjects began to be treated without the customary Victorian reticence and earnestness. Dickinson's most famous Apostle paper was entitled 'Shall We Elect God?' It describes a meeting in heaven of the Apostles Goethe, Hegel, Turgenev and Hugo (the Society enjoyed making honorary Apostles of their heroes) in which the brothers decide not to elect God to the Society because they do not like what they have heard about Him. Then God turns up and proves to be the individual Ideal of each of the Apostles. The paper's 'peculiar mixture of honesty and idealism', in Forster's words (*GLD*, p. 62), is utterly characteristic of Dickinson and indicates why his importance is hard to fix.

In his biography of Dickinson, written in the 1930s, it was still hard for Forster to represent Dickinson's mixed nature, because his own honesty and idealism kept encroaching on each other. The amusing epilogue to *Goldsworthy Lowes Dickinson* sums up the problem by invoking Mephistopheles (with whom Dickinson was quite familiar through his love of Goethe), who asks why there is a need for the biography Forster has just written. In the discussion that follows, the Devil asks if Dickinson was great as a human being, writer, humanitarian or thinker. Although Forster succeeds in answering only the first one satisfactorily, the questions provide a useful framework in which to examine Dickinson's importance for Bloomsbury.

II

Lowes Dickinson's reputation outside of Cambridge was as a man of letters, yet Bloomsbury did not value him highly as a writer. His most widely read works were *The Greek View of Life* (1896), an account mainly of the values of Greek literature; *Letters from John Chinaman* (1901), a twentieth-century, anti-imperialist version of Goldsmith's *The Citizen of the World*; and *A Modern Symposium* (1905), a dialogue dedicated to the Apostles in which spokesmen for science, anarchy, poetry and business contend. His most substantial work was *The International Anarchy* (1926), an account of the coming of the First World War; his most imaginative, *The Magic Flute* (1920), a 'fantasia' based on Mozart's mythology. Three of his other works were also dialogues: *The Meaning of Good* (1901), *Justice and Liberty* (1908) and *After 2000 Years* (1930). The dialogue was Dickinson's preferred literary form because he could represent points of view without having to resolve them. 'Dialogue is argument and discussion purged of its chaos and its intemperance', he wrote at the end of his career ('Dialogue', p. 1). He conceded that there could be a conflict between the dialogue's subject and its drama, but this does not occur in his dialogues, because Dickinson was more interested in content than form. The first of his dialogues, *The Meaning of Good*, does have some dialectical interchange among the slightly characterised speakers; there is no real interaction, however, and the book ends with the telling of a dream of friendship. *A Modern Symposium* is not really a dialogue at all but a series of speeches, and *Justice and Liberty* is completely dominated by one of the three speakers. *After 2000 Years* is more dialectically Platonic, as one would expect in a discussion between Plato and a young man in the Elysian fields, but it still lacks the Platonic dialogue's argumentative energy.

As novelists Virginia Woolf and Forster were impatient with the dialogue form in Dickinson's works. Virginia Woolf recognised their subtlety and melody but found the form too restrictive, and she urged Dickinson's friend R. C. Trevelyan, whose poetry is rather like Dickinson's prose, to 'dismiss the dead . . . and deal with Monday and Tuesday . . .' (*L*, v 293). Forster more neutrally distinguished in his biography between the dialogue-writer, who 'begins from within, and then proceeds to the oddities which make up the visible man', and the novelist, 'who hopes by recording the surface to indicate the forces beneath it' (*GLD*, p. 59). It was Dickinson's intention, however, to remain with internal abstractions. He wrote to a friend, 'I care only for fruitful and vital handling of the eternal commonplaces or else for a new insight that will really help someone to "internal freedom", as Goethe said' (*Autobiography*, p. 151).

The eternal commonplaces of Dickinson's books, letters and talks provoked Virginia Woolf, in the midst of struggling with the documents for her biography of Roger Fry, to an often-quoted outburst:

> Goldie depresses me unspeakably. Always alone on a mountain top asking himself how to live, theorising about life; never living. Roger always down in the succulent valleys, living. But what a thin whistle of hot air Goldie lets out through his front teeth. Always live in the whole, life in the one; always Shelley & Goethe, & then he loses his hot water bottle; & never notices a

face, or a cat or a dog or a flower, except in the glow of the universal. This explains why his highminded books are unreadable. Yet he was so charming, intermittently. (*D*, IV 360)

This is a telling account of a friend who had delighted her by writing that *The Common Reader* was 'the best criticism in English – humorous, witty and profound' (VW/*L*, III 182); later he rhapsodised about *The Waves* in a letter that she thought stated exactly what she was trying to do (EMF/*GLD*, pp. 192–3). Dickinson was an acute appreciator of his friends' writings, even if they could not appreciate his. This was part of his charm and integrity.

One of the difficulties Dickinson's Bloomsbury friends had with his writings was their prose style. When Dickinson complained about the tedious repetition of Leonard Woolf's prose in *After the Deluge*, Virginia Woolf replied (in her diary) that she detested the 'currency, plausibility & general first class aspect' of Dickinson's classically smoothed-out prose (*D*, IV 30). His style is lucid and fluent, a version of the plain style cultivated by Cambridge philosophers from Stephen to Moore, yet there is an absence of force in Dickinson's prose, an absence of the struggle for meaning that appears in the best Cambridge writing. Forster admitted to finding it hypnotic at times and thought 'a thin veil of melancholy . . . interposed between him and the paper as soon as he sat down to write' (*GLD*, p. xxi). Something of the *fin-de-siècle* remained in Dickinson's writing up through the 1920s.

Roger Fry's literary misgivings about Dickinson's work derived from the complete disagreement between the two friends about the significance of form in art. Dickinson was the son of a successful painter; nevertheless, Fry was convinced he had 'no sympathy or understanding for art' (VW/*RF*, p. 205). He did not believe that art was for the sake of itself, not even the music for which he and Forster cared so deeply. Music has its meaning not in form alone but in the way it fuses our abstract concepts and blind sensations, he wrote in a brief dialogue that anticipates Forster's use of Beethoven in *Howards End* (p. 354). Forster never completely agreed with Fry or Dickinson about form's significance or insignificance. In aesthetics he seems closer to Dickinson, however, than to Fry, who once wrote to Dickinson that he was developing a theory, which he knew Dickinson would have, maintaining that content in poetry 'is merely direct-tive of form' (*L*, 1 362). Fry, along with Bloomsbury, differed from Dickinson also in preferring French to German literature, though here again Forster is closer to Dickinson than others in the Group.

III

A suitable epitaph on Dickinson's value as a writer and humanitarian social reformer might be the phrase 'the league of nations', which he possibly coined (EMF/*GLD*, p. 136). Still, his interest in political economy was influential on Bloomsbury, starting with Fry and continuing on through Forster, Leonard Woolf and Keynes. Only Bertrand Russell's influence can com-pare with it. *A Modern Symposium*, which Forster called 'the Bible of Tolerance', and its continuation, *Justice and Liberty*, give a good notion of the Cambridge liberal-socialist origins of Bloomsbury's political attitudes before the First World War. Dickinson's com-bination of ideas from Mill, Arnold and Edward Carpenter was not particularly original, but it expressed a distinctive series of concerns which conservatives thought too socialist and socialists too idealistic. The Webbs, for example, disapproved of a concep-tion of good based on beauty and love rather than 'the social value of an institution or law' (EMF/*GLD*, pp. 223–4). Fry and Forster retained the essentials of Dickinson's liberal socialism throughout most of their careers; Leonard Woolf and Keynes left his politics for tougher forms of socialism and liberalism in the great worlds of the colonial service and the Treasury.

While discussing remedies for the 'social anarchy' of their time, the speakers in *Justice and Liberty* agree in their debate to ignore what Dickinson came to call the 'international anarchy'. This shows why Dickinson grew so dissatisfied with the conclu-sions of his Edwardian dialogues. The First World War depre-ssed him deeply and redirected his energies for more than a decade. McTaggart turned reactionary with the war and Russell radical, but it is characteristic of Dickinson that he became neither a patriot nor a pacifist.[1] After a detailed examination of the events leading to the war, Dickinson concluded in *The International Anarchy, 1904–1914* that there was not a trace in them of the purposes the warring nations said they were fighting for. The simple moral of the book is that we must have international government, because war is incompatible with civilisation and the international anarchy makes war inevitable. Forster thought the book a work of art, comparable to a Bach fugue (*GLD*, p. 161). Today not even historians read it. Dickinson also participated in groups (including the Fabians with Leonard Woolf) that were working towards the formation of the League of Nations, but withdrew when he saw the shape the League was taking. His disillusionment is prefigured in an unfinished dialogue, influenced maybe by Keynes's *The Economic Consequences of the Peace*, about the Wandering Jew at the Versailles Conference. The Jew with his experience of the Roman Empire shows in his conversations with Clemenceau and Lloyd George how empty their honourable motives are. 'A nation is nothing but a name for the chronic rancours of men', he maintains. 'The only reality is real men and women' (*Autobiography*, pp. 21–2, 227). With its specificity of description and intensity of emotion, 'The Wandering Jew' may well be the best dialogue Dickinson wrote.

'Is he important as a thinker?', Mephistopheles asks Dickinson's biographer, who replies,

> Some say that he is, but the majority endorse his own verdict, and according to that he ranks as a Cambridge philosopher below either McTaggart, Moore or Bertrand Russell, and takes no place in the philosophic hierarchy of the past. (EMF/*GLD*, p. 200)

The *DNB* aptly describes Dickinson as a 'philosophic writer', rather than a philosopher. In what might be called his philosophical values, however, Dickinson was very much part of the Cambridge scene. His fellowship dissertation was on Plotinus. McTaggart converted Dickinson to Hegel for a while, but in his memoir of McTaggart Dickinson admitted to putting up with 'a good deal of more or less unintelligible ratiocination in order to get imaginative, or imaginary, inspiration' (*McTaggart*, p. 35). Roger Fry, too, confessed he could not understand his friends' metaphysical discussions at Cambridge, and 'settled for collecting the small approximate facets of truth within my reach'.

Later he came to see Dickinson and McTaggart ensnared in the subtleties of their own ideas (*L*, II 596).

Dickinson did not remain an Idealist. His historical studies were inspired not by 'the Hegel of Eternity, but the Hegel of Time' (*Autobiography*, p. 142). But it is not clear that he became a philosophical Realist with Moore and Russell. In *The Meaning of Good* he rejected McTaggart's ideas but then found he had been guilty of Moore's naturalistic fallacy – 'a phrase which always amuses me, for it suggests some kind of unnatural vice'.[2] *The Meaning of Good* is as different from *Principia Ethica* as the amenities of a dialogue are from the rigours of a treatise. 'What a brain that fellow has!' Dickinson moaned about Moore to R. C. Trevelyan in 1898:

> It desiccates mine! Dries up my lakes and seas and leaves me an arid tract of sand. Not that *he* is arid – anything but: he's merely the sun. One ought to put up a parasol – I do try to, one of humour, but it has so many rents in it. Oh dear! Surely I once had some rivers? I wish you were here to water me. All poets water. They are the rain. Metaphysics are the sun: between them they fertilize the soil.'   (EMF/*GLD*, p. 92)

Dickinson's lament marks an important change in the development of the Apostles and modern philosophy.

In their ethical ideals Lowes Dickinson and G. E. Moore are closer to each other, and to McTaggart as well, whose *Studies in Hegelian Cosmology* appeared the same year as *The Meaning of Good* and acknowledged Dickinson's help. All agree the *summum bonum* is to be found in states of mind having to do with love. Moore includes in the Ideal the consciousness of beauty, but for Dickinson art is only partially ideal, because as the creation of man it is defective. Not until the late dialogue *After Two Thousand Years* did he add art and truth to love in his Ideal. The immortal longings of both Dickinson and McTaggart appear in their Ideals, but there are none in Moore's. Dickinson is perhaps fathest from Moore (but not McTaggart) in his writings on religion and immortality. They clearly show him to be the transitional figure Forster described as holding nineteenth-century opinions in a modern way (*GLD*, p. 99). He believed science and religion could be reconciled, but his Arnoldian conception of religion was one without 'ecclesiasticism' and without revelation. 'Truth is a matter of science, religion of imagination and feeling', he once wrote (*Letters*, p. 141).

Lionel Trilling has described Dickinson as Arnold's spiritual descendant if anyone was (*Arnold*, p. xi), and Forster, in a way, can be seen as Dickinson's. Unlike Forster, Dickinson was appalled by his experience of India, finding China a far more humanely spiritual land, but his travel report on India reads like a background study for *A Passage to India*. 'No impression remains more vivid with me of my visit to India', he wrote, 'than that of the dominance of nature, and the impotence and insignificance of man.' It was one of the ironies of history, he saw, that 'of all the western nations the English are the least capable of appreciating the qualities of Indian civilisation, and the most capable of appreciating its defects' (*Letters*, pp. 50, 52). Dickinson liked Greek civilisation best, and *The Greek View of Life* is probably his most influential book. Here too Dickinson's view is permeated by late Victorian cultural assumptions. He celebrated Platonic homoerotic love in the book, but, despite the writings of Nietzsche and, in his own university, Frazer and Harrison, Dickinson concerned himself only with the reasonableness of the Greeks. Euripides interested him more than Sophocles. In almost the last thing he wrote, Dickinson alluded to 'the more primitive beliefs that festered beneath the surface' of Greek religion (*Letters*, p. 100) – that verb shows his feelings about Greek irrationality. The Greek ideal for him was again the unity, the whole, that Virginia Woolf had disliked in his thinking. It was the good, the beautiful and the whole, rather than the true, that Dickinson admired in the writings of Goethe, Shelley and, most of all, Plato. He was, said Nathaniel Wedd after his death, 'the latest Cambridge Platonist' (p. 175).

IV

In response to Mephistopheles's prodding, Forster justifies his biography of Dickinson by describing its subject as 'beloved, affectionate, unselfish, intelligent, witty, charming, inspiring'. These were the qualities of Dickinson's personal significance for Bloomsbury. But the Devil astutely replies, 'Yes, but that is neither here nor there, or rather it was there but it is no longer here' (*GLD*, p. 199). Forster's book is the final answer to

Mephistopheles. Through the art of biography *Goldsworthy Lowes Dickinson* makes his personal qualities 'here', and its success can be measured by the fact that it is more widely known now than any of Dickinson's own books. Why, then, are Dickinson's ideas and writings worth mentioning in a literary history of Bloomsbury's early years? The answer is given in Forster's epilogue. Blinded by arithmetic and deaf to poetry, the Devil always assumes, says Forster, that a man is just the sum of his qualities. But Forster, as an Apostolic brother of G. E. Moore, knows that these qualities can fuse into a whole (p. 201). For Bloomsbury too, the whole that was Lowes Dickinson includes his dialogues and other political writings as well as the charm inherent in his writings, conversation and friendship, a charm Forster said was structural (p. 84). Dickinson had the maieutic gift that he so admired in Socrates. 'I owe an immense amount to his influence and his extraordinary sympathy', Roger Fry wrote to Vanessa Bell after Dickinson's death (3.viii.32, pKC).

Dickinson once admired a biography of Oscar Browning because it was 'quite unsparing and completely sympathetic' (EMF/*GLD*, p. 27). Forster's is this too, but a more contemporary Mephistopheles might not find it unsparing enough. Perhaps he would try, as some critics have in posthumous assessments of Forster, to reduce Dickinson's achievement to his homosexuality. Dickinson's deepest affections were homosexual, and Forster's biography – with its reticent asides on what the 'sensitive' will understand (p. 63) – needs to be supplemented, for a fuller understanding of Dickinson's character, with his own posthumously published autobiography, which goes into detail about such things as his shoe-fetishism. The concealing of Dickinson's sexuality in Forster's biography and the unveiling of it in the autobiography may have the effect of making his homosexuality seem more important than it really was. A saner response, perhaps, was the verdict Dickinson received after the war from the Apostles, following his reading to them of a two-hour homosexual dialogue: 'what a fuss over nothing' (*Autobiography*, p. 18).

Fry wrote to Vanessa Bell after Dickinson's death that he thought homosexuality finally made Dickinson closer to Forster than to him. Dickinson himself preserved in his autobiography (p. 100) a couplet of McTaggart's, in imitation of J. K. Stephen, on the different sexual proclivities of his two friends:

When the Frys shall cease from Rogering
And the Dickers sod no more.

Certainly Dickinson's attitude toward women was one of his
limitations. There are no women speakers in any of his dialogues,
of course. Forster ascribed Dickinson's support for the education
of women to his 'suicidal sense of fairness', and quotes Dickinson's murmuring at the 'aspiring and uninspiring spinsters'
touring King's, 'Oh dear, what is to happen to them? . . . I don't
know and they don't know. . . . Oh dear! What they want is a
husband!' (*GLD*, p. 88) – to which Virginia Woolf answered in a
note to *Three Guineas*, ' "What they wanted" might have been the
Bar, the Stock Exchange, or rooms in Gibbs's Buildings, had the
choice been open to them' (p. 282). Shortly afterwards, while
struggling with the problems of Fry's biography and the reti-
cences his rogering required, Virginia Woolf seems to have
agreed with Mephistopheles that Forster's biography was 'quite
futile' (*D*, IV 247). Fry himself, however, thought *Goldsworthy
Lowes Dickinson* desperately difficult to do and beautifully done
(RF/*L*, II 691).

A teacher and friend of great charm, a philosophic writer, a
humanitarian political economist, Lowes Dickinson was also
part of a Cambridge intellectual and moral tradition that is best
described in his own words. He wrote them after the deaths of
the Apostles and Bloomsbury friends C. P. Sanger and Frank
Ramsey. Keynes quoted them again in writing of both men, and
the passage continues to be cited as an eloquent statement of
what Cambridge represented for Bloomsbury.

> It does not become a Cambridge man to claim too much for
> his university, nor am I much tempted to do so. But there is, I
> think, a certain type, rare, like all good things, which seems to
> be associated in some peculiar way with my alma mater. I am
> thinking of men like Leslie Stephen, . . . like Henry Sidgwick,
> like Maitland, like one who died but the other day with all
> his promise unfulfilled. It is a type unworldly without being
> saintly, unambitious without being inactive, warm-hearted
> without being sentimental. Through good report and ill such
> men work on, following the light of truth as they see it; able to
> be sceptical without being paralysed; content to know what is
> knowable and to reserve judgment on what is not. The world

could never be driven by such men, for the springs of action lie deep in ignorance and madness. But it is they who are the beacon in the tempest, and they are more, not less, needed now than ever before. May their succession never fail![3]

V

John McTaggart Ellis McTaggart belongs to this Cambridge tradition too, though in mind and body he was the most unprepossessing of the four Apostles who formed Bloomsbury's philosophical education. The very redundancy of his name seems symbolic. His sidling gait appeared to illustrate the principle of the Hegelian dialectic he spent so much time expounding that spirit does not develop in a straight line. In the mad tea-party of Trinity, this physically inept, shy, yet formidable philosopher was the Dormouse to Russell's Mad Hatter and Moore's March Hare (Wiener, pp. 194–6). (Lowes Dickinson with his Chinese cap looked like the Carpenter – Martin, p. 119.) He was, said Dickinson, 'the most curious combination imaginable of Dr Johnson, Hegel and Robert Browning' (EMF/*GLD*, p. 60). McTaggart's adult life was spent as a fellow of Trinity, and his philosophical career illustrated F. H. Bradley's definition of metaphysics as the giving of bad reasons for what we believe on instinct (Bradley, p. xiv). From the first privately printed statement of his philosophy, *The Further Determination of the Absolute* (1893), to the final, posthumously published excogitation more than thirty years later in the concluding volume of *The Nature of Existence*, McTaggart never modified his fundamental belief in an absolute of timeless, mystically loving selves. It followed from this absolute that our ordinary life is almost completely misperceived. Birth and death, time and space were all unreal. Love existed, but not matter; immortality but not God. He was an ontological Idealist, he said in a summary of his philosophy, but also an epistemological Realist, because truth is a relation of correspondence not coherence ('Ontological Idealism', p. 251).

How could such a philosopher be anything but a figure of fun for Bloomsbury at Cambridge? A bit of doggerel by Lytton Strachey might be thought to sum him up:

McTaggart's seen through God
And put him on the shelf;
Isn't it rather odd
He doesn't see through himself.

(MH/LS, p. 170)

Most things about McTaggart were odd, but the way he saw through God intrigued Bloomsbury and fascinated philosophers. His influence came initially through the Apostles and his friendships there. Eventually, the thoroughness of his thought and the nature of his absolute gave him a place in the philosophical revolution that occurred in Cambridge at the turn of the century, and therefore a place in the literary history of Bloomsbury.

According to Dickinson again, McTaggart was the chief inspiration of the Apostles in the late 1880s (*Autobiography*, p. 92). One of his papers, now lost, entitled 'Violets or Orange Blossom?' and apparently having to do with a justification of homosexual love, was preserved for many years by the Society (EMF/*GLD*, p. 62; Levy, p. 103). Fry, Dickinson and Wedd were his closest contemporaries among the Apostles, and, when Russell and then Moore joined the Society, McTaggart's was the most powerful philosophical influence. Forster said he did not know McTaggart (Stone, p. 60), which is surprising but MacCarthy certainly did and once maintained he was the last philosopher to try to comprehend the whole universe (EMF/*GLD*, p. 61). Strachey and Leonard Woolf came to know McTaggart after his Apostolic influence had waned, when his mind 'seemed to have entirely left the earth for the inextricably complicated cobwebs and *O altitudos* of Hegelianism' (LW/*S*, p. 132). But he was not forgotten. Strachey was reported to have discussed the merits of McTaggart's philosophy on his death bed (MH/*LS*, p. 1053).

McTaggart's influence on Bloomsbury came primarily through Russell and Moore. Russell was persuaded by him to become a Hegelian for a while and dedicated his second book to McTaggart. Moore was persuaded by Russell to take up philosophy after listening to Moore's shocked attempts to answer McTaggart's arguments for the unreality of time (Moore, 'Autobiography', p. 14). Moore in turn helped convert Russell from Idealism to Realism. Eventually Russell came to feel that McTaggart's intellectual influence on his generation was bad

(*Portraits*, p. 71), but like Moore he remained permanently in McTaggart's debt for the lucid rigour of his philosophical method and style. Moore considered McTaggart his most influential teacher, partly because he saw more of him at the Apostles than any of his other, older teachers. 'Perhaps the most valuable lesson which his pupils learned from him', Moore wrote in *Mind* after McTaggart's death, 'was the importance and difficulty of trying to get quite clear as to what you hold, and of distinguishing between good and bad reasons for holding it.'

Moore also recognised in his obituary McTaggart's 'great distinction as a writer of English' ('Death', p. 271). At least one historian of philosophy has asserted that the revolution in philosophical style brought about by Moore and Russell owed its new simplicity and clarity largely to McTaggart (Quinton, p. 261). A passage from McTaggart distinguishing between those recurrent Bloomsbury preoccupations, reality and goodness, exhibits this new style well:

> It is absurd to ask whether reality or goodness be the more fundamental. Each is supreme in its own sphere, and the spheres are so different that they cannot come into conflict. What is real is real, however bad it is. What is not real is not real, however good it would have been. On the other hand, what is good is good, however unreal it is. What is bad is bad, however real it is. And so it is our duty to be humble in judging of reality, and imperious in judging of goodness. For what is real is real, however we may condemn it. But on the other hand, what we condemn – if we condemn rightly – is bad, even if it were the essence of all reality. (*Dogmas*, pp. 65–6)

This was written three years after *Principia Ethica* and reads like an excerpt from it. Bloomsbury's writing owes more than a little to this philosophical plain style, which is very different from the elegant prose of the other great English Idealist who was McTaggart's contemporary, F. H. Bradley. It is tempting to see in these two philosophers the different intellectual styles of Cambridge and Oxford.

The exacting thoroughness of McTaggart's Idealism is manifest in his developing the whole metaphysical system of *The Nature of Existence* from two premisses: (1) something exists; (2) what exists is differentiated. The second premiss involves the crucial principle of what he called 'determining correspondence', which has to do with the infinite divisibility of substance. 'Or maybe substance can be composite, / Profound McTaggart thought so . . .', Yeats wrote in 'A Bronze Head' (*Poems*, p. 382; Jeffares, p. 499). But philosophers, including Moore and C. D. Broad, the author of an exhaustive commentary on McTaggart's system (to which I am much indebted here), have found this principle very obscure – not 'woolly', to use a favourite word of McTaggart's, but obscure nevertheless (Moore, 'Autobiography', p. 19).

VI

The character of McTaggart's philosophy was more accessible to Bloomsbury in the one work he directed at the common reader. *Some Dogmas of Religion*, brought out by Forster's publisher in 1906, is a work of what today might be called religious deconstruction. The paradoxical nature of McTaggart's thought appears in the negative conclusions of his dialectic and the hope of his mystical absolute of love. Mill and Spinoza are the principal philosophical sources here. McTaggart argued, like Leslie Stephen, that the believer has to choose between God's benevolence and his omnipotence. The argument from design, if valid, reveals an incompetent or malevolent designer; free will can exist, but only in morally ruinous ways for theology.[4] The hash that McTaggart makes of traditional religious dogmas in his book could only have delighted Leonard Woolf, Strachey, Fry, Forster, Clive Bell and the Stephens, not to mention Dickinson, Russell and Moore. But how far Bloomsbury accepted his vision of religious love is not very easy to tell.

In *Studies in Hegelian Cosmology*, published by Cambridge University Press in 1901, when five of the future members of Bloomsbury were undergraduates at Trinity, McTaggart wrote, 'the use of philosophy lies not in being deeper than science, but in being truer than theology – not in its bearing on action, but in its bearing on religion. It does not give us guidance. It gives us hope' (p. 196). Neither the Apostles nor Bloomsbury accepted this restricted conception of philosophy, but both groups were responsive to the one enduring hope that McTaggart's metaphysics produced: a community of timelessly loving selves.

Most of them would have accepted McTaggart's definition of religion as a state of mind best described as 'an emotion resting on a conviction of a harmony between ourselves and the universe at large', but they would hardly have agreed that 'no man is justified in a religious attitude except as a result of metaphysical study' (*Dogmas*, pp. 3, 292). McTaggart's is a philosophy of love, like Plato's and even, in a sense, G. E. Moore's in *Principia Ethica*. His absolute Idealism contrasts clearly with that of F. H. Bradley, which T. S. Eliot was to find so interesting. Bradley's absolute is undifferentiated and its finite centres are isolated; McTaggart's is a mystical pluralism of loving, immortal selves, a differentiated unity made logically possible by the principle of determining correspondence. This vision of a loving collectivity was inspired by the Apostles and in turn inspired them and through them touched Bloomsbury. Virginia Woolf read some McTaggart when she was preparing to write Fry's biography and was 'surprised to find how interesting mystic Hegelianism is to me' (*L*, vi 6). It does not seem to have mattered that McTaggart illustrated his ideal of love with Dante's *Vita Nuova* or Tennyson's Apostolic *In Memoriam* (*Nature*, ii 149), or that he found his mystical experiences best expressed in Browning's *Saul* (Dickinson, *McTaggart*, pp. 92–4).

Toward the end of his life McTaggart told a friend, 'The longer I live, the more I am convinced of the reality of three things: – truth, love and immortality' (Dickinson, *McTaggart*, p. 77). Where Russell, Moore and Bloomsbury parted from McTaggart, and Dickinson too perhaps, was with the last of these. The chief argument against immortality, McTaggart argued in *Some Dogmas of Religion*, was bodily death. A belief in immortality required, therefore, a demonstration of the unreality of temporally contingent matter. This McTaggart thought he had accomplished in the famous demonstration of the unreality of time that so shocked the young Moore. The argument is based on ingenious distinctions between events that are contradictorily described as being past, present or future, and events timelessly described as earlier or later. What is needed to account for apparent (but really timeless) change is a series of increasingly inclusive perceptions (*Nature*, ii 9–31). Critics of Virginia Woolf and Forster have occasionally sought connections between McTaggart's denial of time and the fiction of Virginia Woolf or Forster (see Fleishman, 'Woolf', for example), but the disconnections are much more obvious. Mystical moments in their novels are transitory, physical nature utterly real, the past enduring, the future unknowable, and death quite final. McTaggart's Ideal also lacks the beauty that belonged to Moore's and Bloomsbury's and was inherent in the material realities of nature and art. Small wonder that Roger Fry lost interest in his friend's metaphysics.

McTaggart's politics were as full of paradoxes as his philosophy. He exalted loyalty to institutions and to country, yet was a free-trader and supporter of female emancipation. The radical Wedd thought McTaggart's Idealism was indifferent to social injustice, which was seen as an imperfect manifestation of an evolving good (Dickinson, *McTaggart*, p. 110). I. A. Richards, a former pupil of McTaggart as well as of Moore, described McTaggart as 'a big-scale dreamer' (*Complementarities*, pp. 258, 288). C. D. Broad nevertheless found a 'thinness' in McTaggart's Idealism when compared with the great systems of Leibniz, Spinoza, or of course Hegel, whose applications of philosophy to art, history, politics and religion were ignored in McTaggart's Hegelianism:

> He knew little of science and he cared nothing for history. And so, except for certain valuable material provided by his emotional life, there was little but straw to be cut by the exquisitely fashioned dialectical machinery of his mind. (Broad, ii 789–90)

Similar criticisms have sometimes been made of Moore's philosophy too, but then he was not offering to explain the nature of existence.

In the end McTaggart was an object lesson for Russell, Moore and Bloomsbury in how philosophy should not be done. For them his Idealism was not, in McTaggart's own words, humble enough in judging reality. Philosophies such as his brought Moore and his followers to defend common sense and detach their dearest hopes from a dependence on Idealistic metaphysics. Yet the Apostles and their friends respected McTaggart's intellectual passion and his Ideal of loving selves. At his funeral McTaggart's favourite passage from Spinoza was read out: 'A free man thinks of death least of all things; and his wisdom is a meditation not of death but of life.' These are also the last words of Virginia Woolf's biography of Roger Fry, who had them read at his funeral too.

9 Russell

Bertrand Russell's role in the philosophical education of Bloomsbury was, like Dickinson's, Moore's and even McTaggart's, both personal and intellectual. Like theirs, his influence on the Group began with the Apostles. Personally, Russell meant less to Bloomsbury than Dickinson or Moore, yet as a personality he became the most famous of the Apostles. This fame easily leads to misinterpretations that overemphasise his personal involvement with Bloomsbury and underestimate his intellectual significance for them. The variety and complexity, not to mention longevity, of his thinking were unequalled by anyone of his time. Russell's impact on Bloomsbury extends far beyond the Cambridge years, when he and Moore made their philosophical revolution, to the Great War when Bloomsbury strongly supported Russell's crusading pacifism, and on into the 1920s and 1930s when Russell's social, historical and popular philosophical writings were more appealing than the work in logic and epistemology that they had originally found so interesting.

In his two full-length autobiographical works Russell drew a clear distinction between his personal and his philosophical developments. He says relatively little about his philosophical work in *The Autobiography of Bertrand Russell* (1967–9), originally written in 1931 and then supplemented with letters and later autobiographical essays to cover the last forty years of his life. In 1959, however, Russell devoted a book to his work entitled *My Philosophical Development*. What he meant by philsophy in that work was essentially logic and epistemology; there is virtually no discussion of his extensive ethical or social writings. In trying to understand the particular nature of Russell's value for Bloomsbury, it is worth following the distinctions he made between his life and his technical and non-technical philosophy. Beginning with a short account of his place among the Apostles, we shall go on to a consideration of his Edwardian work in logic and epistemology; then turn to ethical and social philosophy that influenced Bloomsbury mainly during the First World War; and conclude with a look at Russell's criticisms of Bloomsbury, which will take us back to the Apostles again. Russell's popular philosophical and historical writings after the war continued to be read in Bloomsbury but they were not of the same consequence for the Group's development as his work before the 1920s.

Yet Bloomsbury's interest in Russell cannot be completely compartmentalised. Russell the reformer, the moralist, the educator, the writer; Russell the lunatic, the lover and the poet – all these need to be compact in our historical imagination with Russell the philosopher, or we shall never understand his unique significance. His brilliance of mind was an essential aspect of his personality; the attention that the Group gave to his social thought was not unrelated to his authority as a mathematical logician. And, while it is impossible, in a literary history at any rate, to avoid oversimplifying the thought of a philosopher whose work reaches from *The Principles of Mathematics* to *The Conquest of Happiness*, it may be possible to indicate something of the intellectuality that intrigued his contemporaries. 'He has not much body of character', Virginia Woolf said in her diary in 1924, while wondering if he disapproved of her:

> This luminous vigorous mind seems attached to a flimsy little car, like that on a glinting balloon. His adventures with his wives diminish his importance. And he has no chin, & he is dapper. Nevertheless, I should like the run of his headpiece. (*D*, II 295)

This headpiece fascinated Bloomsbury.

II

Russell's philosophical influence among the Apostles was tied to Moore's. All the Bloomsbury Apostles except Fry – the only member of the Group mentioned by Russell as a Cambridge friend (*Autobiography*, I 63) – encountered Russell as a mathematical philosopher and fellow of Trinity who confirmed and augmented Moore's philosophy. Russell had turned to philosophy in his last year as a student at Cambridge, disgusted with the trickery of mathematical teaching, which he had nevertheless mastered. As with other Apostles, his real education began in the Society; Whitehead, McTaggart and Moore were the principal philosophical influences on him at Cambridge. Under McTaggart's influence Russell and Moore, who was two years behind Russell at Trinity, became Idealists for a time. Then Moore, as Russell once put it, 'found the Hegelian philosophy inapplicable to chairs and tables, and I found it inapplicable to mathematics; so with his help I climbed out of it, and back to common sense tempered by mathematical logic' (*Basic Writings*, p. 35).

Russell's development from the Idealism of McTaggart and F. H. Bradley to the Realism of Moore can be traced in the Apostle papers he wrote in the 1890s. None was considered as remarkable in the Society as some by Dickinson, McTaggart or Moore, but it is revealing to watch Russell's progress from his first paper, in which he said that political questions are basically undecidable without a Hegelian theory of history, to a later paper in which he rejected McTaggart's and Bradley's dichotomy between appearance and reality along with the consolations of a metaphysics irrelevant to human experience. Sixty years later Russell allowed this paper, entitled 'Seems Madam? Nay, It Is', to be published in *Why I Am Not a Christian*. One of Russell's earlier papers argued in 1894 for the election of women to the Apostles on the grounds that freedom of discussion would be inimical to love, and furthermore that their participation would assist the discussions of metaphysical and sexual questions, because the juggernaut of McTaggart's absolute was of no use in deciding questions other than those of pure reason; besides, Russell ended, somewhat contradicting his earlier point, the attitudes of the Apostles to one another were far from intellectual anyway. (In the ensuing vote Moore agreed that women should be elected but thought Russell's argument specious; Dickinson voted against women, and McTaggart was absent – Levy, pp. 128–9.) In his last Apostle paper Russell turned his attention completely to Moore's philosophy and argued with him about the value of matter in the experience of beauty (*Cambridge Essays*).

In the books Russell was writing at the end of the nineteenth century and the beginning of the twentieth, the stages of his progress from Idealism to Realism are clearly evident. The Kantian analysis of geometry that he dedicated to McTaggart was followed by a study of Leibniz in which Moore's influence began to appear, and in his third philosophical book, *The Principles of Mathematics*, published in the same marvellous year for Cambridge philosophy as *Principia Ethica*, Russell announced,

> On fundamental questions of philosophy, my position, in all its chief features, is derived from Mr. G. E. Moore. I have accepted from him the non-existential nature of propositions . . . and their independence of any knowing mind; also the pluralism which regards the world . . . as composed of an infinite number of mutually independent entities. . . (p. xviii)

With such principles Russell said he was able to show that mathematics and logic were identical, and he spent the next ten years doing so with Whitehead, the result of which was *Principia Mathematica*. Keynes, the only member of Bloomsbury qualified to understand Russell's discoveries in symbolic logic (and whose work on probability Russell later used) thought in retrospect that *The Principles of Mathematics* supplied 'in spirit' a method for treating the material of *Principia Ethica*, and he gave as illustrations rather absurd problems in ethical mensuration that the Apostles played with (*CW*, x 438–9). What Keynes may have meant was that Russell's aim to analyse the fundamental concepts of mathematics and deduce them from a small number of logical concepts was related to Moore's analysis of the fundamental concepts of ethics that also derived them from a few elementary concepts. Both rely, for instance, on indefinability to establish their respective principles.

None the less, at the end of his career Moore thought that all Russell owed him were mistakes, while he had been influenced by Russell more than any other philosopher ('Autobiography', pp. 14–16). For Bloomsbury, however, it was the thought and character of Moore that dominated the Apostles when Russell was an active member and later. Leonard Woolf likened a philosophical argument between them to a race between the tortoise and the hare – only this time Russell was the hare (*S*, p. 134). Strachey wrote to Leonard Woolf that he thought the secret of Russell's ineffectiveness in the Society was his insignificance as a speaker, an activity having more to do with character than with intellect in the Apostles (21.iii.05, pT). In one respect Russell was more Apostolic than Moore: he was more amusing. Leonard Woolf did not think he had ever heard Moore say a witty thing (*S*, p. 134). Nor were Russell and Moore, despite their intense concern with each other's ideas, especially close friends. Russell thought, correctly, that Moore disapproved of him (Clark, p. 97), and James Strachey has suggested that he was jealous of Moore's dominance among the Apostles. (MH/*LS*, p. 165). MacCarthy, Lytton Strachey, Leonard Woolf and Keynes were all closer to Moore in the Society than Russell was. They all appear to have valued personal relationships more highly than he did. From time to time in the Apostles during its Bloomsbury period there was discussion as to whether the love of truth and knowledge was as high an ideal as the love of beauty and the love of love. Russell definitely thought so. His supreme goods were abstract: the certainty of mathematics or the intellectual love of God. These he idealised more than personal relations and aesthetic enjoyments. Russell was also less tolerant of homosexuality than Moore and other heterosexuals in the Society. For some time he was unaware of its existence among the Apostles; later he exaggerated its prevalence.

Still, for all the devotion to Moore in Bloomsbury, there was no doubting Russell's genius. Again, Leonard Woolf, the proudest intellectual in the Group and the most worshipful of Moore, testified that Russell had the quickest mind of anyone he had ever known (*S*, p. 134). Russell also knew more about logic and mathematics than anyone in the Society at this time except Whitehead. It is also possible that the absence of close Bloomsbury relationships with Russell may have enhanced their appreciation of his writings, which, in the decade after *Principia Ethica*, extended for them the relevance of Moore's epistemology, analytic methods and – for a time – ethics.

III

'Revolt into Pluralism' was the title Russell gave the chapter in *My Philosophical Development* dealing with his and Moore's rejection of Idealism at the beginning of the twentieth century. Idealism's subjectivity was the focus of Moore's attack; for Russell it was the monism that made mathematics impossible. Later Russell realised there were mistakes in this new Realism, but he thought Moore still agreed with the negative part of their revolution, 'the doctrine that fact is in general independent of experience' (p. 54). Pluralism remained a basic assumption of Bloomsbury's philosophical outlook. Conceptual analysis, not metaphysical synthesis, was the proper method of philosophy for them, philosophy being virtually synonymous with the analysis of ideas. And along with analysis went an appreciation of the analytic virtues of clarity and simplicity.

The kinds of analysis Russell and Moore did early in their careers were as different as mathematics is from ethics. Two logical paradoxes related to his work on *Principia Mathematica* made Russell philosophically famous in his thirties. Here the most important influences on Russell were Peano and Frege rather than McTaggart or Moore. In analysing the first paradox Russell developed his theory of descriptions, which used propositional functions as a modern Ockham's razor to show that non-existent entities such as golden mountains or round squares could be talked about without assuming, as phenomenologists such as Meinong had, that somewhere such non-existing entities existed. This metaphysical issue has literary implications. Russell's theory of descriptions showed, as he put it later, 'that, in analysing a significant sentence, one must not assume that each separate word or phrase has significance on its own account' ('Mental Development', pp. 13–14). Russell's other discovery concerned an analysis of the biblical paradox of the Cretan liar who said truly that all Cretans always lied. Russell evolved a theory of types that distinguished between first- and second-order propositions, but later agreed with Ramsey's criticism that systemic and linguistic paradoxes needed to be distinguished.[1] For those of the Group who could not follow Russell into symbolic logic, his work at least showed the power of philosophical analysis to clarify without metaphysics paradoxes of language. Roger Fry, for example, who in 1905 edited Sir Joshua Reynolds's discourses before the Royal Academy, turned to Russell early for help in analysing what Reynolds meant by beauty as the common form (*Reynolds*, p. v).

The values inherent in the pursuit of mathematics Russell

expressed for Bloomsbury in an essay written originally in 1902 but published in 1907 as 'The Study of Mathematics' in the *New Quarterly*, the first of Desmond MacCarthy's magazines. It was on the appearance of this essay that Strachey wrote to Russell,

Oh! – I shall have this engraved on my tombstone –

HE KNEW MOORE AND RUSSELL

and nothing more.   (Russell, *Autobiography*, i 197)

Strachey particularly liked the comparison of the understanding of mathematics with the emergence of an Italian palace out of the mist before a traveller. Whether Strachey also agreed with Russell that mathematics was superior to literature because its generality was greater is another matter, but he and Bloomsbury would have liked the aesthetic point, which is related to Moore's notion of an organic whole, that 'an argument which serves only to prove a conclusion is like a story subordinated to some moral which it is meant to teach: for aesthetic perfection no part of the whole should be merely a means' (*Mysticism*, p. 56). 'The Study of Mathematics' is one of the more Platonic of Russell's works, idealising a timeless realm to be contemplated by pure reason beyond this vale of tears. In their early Realism, Russell and Moore were persuaded of the independence of propositions as well as material things from knowing minds; these are combined in Russell's essay into a transcendent, if not transcendental, intellectual consolation:

The contemplation of what is non-human, the discovery that our minds are capable of dealing with material not created by them, above all, the realisation that beauty belongs to the outer world as to the inner, are the chief means of overcoming the terrible sense of impotence, of weakness, of exile amid hostile powers. . . .   (*Mysticism*, p. 55)

Virginia Woolf made the heroine of her second novel, modelled on Vanessa Bell, into a mathematician rather than a painter. The conflict of *Night and Day* might be expressed in these words of Russell's. Eventually Katherine Hilbery's education and love make her more humanly diurnal, less Platonically nocturnal. So with Russell, who lost his enthusiasm for mathematics when he realised under Wittgenstein's impact that it consisted of tautologies. Russell called this stage of his philosophical development 'The Retreat from Pythagoras' (*Philosophical Development*, p. 208).

But Russell never retreated from analysis. His continuing importance as a philosopher for the Bloomsbury Group is manifest in his analysis of the nature of perception. 1912 was an *annus mirabilis* for the Home University Library series, with the publication of Russell's *The Problems of Philosophy*, Moore's *Ethics* and Strachey's *Landmarks in French Literature*. Russell's book has been well described as 'the manual of the empiricist and realist revival' (Braithwaite, p. 237). No other work sums as lucidly and concisely the conception of philosophy that Bloomsbury took from Russell and Moore; none illuminates so well the intimations of epistemology to be found in the Group's criticism, biographies and fiction. Many of his ideas were taken, Russell acknowledged, from Moore's unpublished lectures of 1910–11, and some also came from Keynes's unpublished work on probability – but it was *The Problems of Philosophy* that made them all easily accessible to Bloomsbury. The value of philosophy is still in the end Platonic and mystical, the union of mind with the universe, but its methods are unrelentingly analytical. Problems, the title announces, are the province of philosophy. Questions not answers are its concern, because 'questions enlarge our conception of what is possible, enrich our intellectual imagination and diminish the dogmatic assurance which closes the mind against speculation' (p. 161). The enrichment of the intellectual imagination, for which Bloomsbury honoured all its philosophical mentors at Cambridge, took place in philosophy through the exercise of its essential function, criticism (p. 149). This is what distinguishes philosophy from science as well as from art. The problems of *The Problems of Philosophy* have to do with the way things and truths can be known. Russell took Moore's term 'sense data' to describe the contents of awareness, then he influentially discriminated between our direct knowledge by acquaintance and our indirect knowledge by description, which made use of his discoveries in symbolic logic. There were also discussions of induction (helped by Keynes), of *a priori* knowledge, and of the theory that a belief's truth depends on its correspondence with fact, not its coherence with other truths.

A number of ideas in *The Problems of Philosophy*, such as sense data, the difference between acquaintance and description in knowing, and the correspondence theory of truth stimulated Bloomsbury's intellectual imagination. Russell's book enacted for them an analytical and epistemological conception of philosophy that devalued some other contemporary philosophies, such as Bergson's. The year that *The Problems of Philosophy* was published Russell demonstrated how the critical function of philosophy could be used to expose the confusions of a metaphysics of time. In 'The Philosophy of Bergson' Russell pointed out how his theory of *durée* rested on 'the elementary confusion between the present occurrence of a recollection and the past occurrence which is recollected'. Bergson thought he was accounting for the difference between the present and the past, but all he was really doing was describing the difference between the present facts of perception and recollection. This was another illustration, Russell thought, of the confusion in a good deal of modern philosophy between the act of knowing and what is known, which was the original, essential distinction of Moore's Realism (*History*, pp. 807–8).[2] Perception and recollection, knowing and what is known, are also fundamental distinctions for the fiction of Forster and Virginia Woolf.

Two years after *The Problems of Philosophy* Russell published his last sustained work of technical philosophy before the war. *Our Knowledge of the External World* is usually referred to by that short title, but the rest of the title – *as a Field for Scientific Method in Philosophy* – indicates how Russell was moving away from more or less common-sense views of perception towards scientific ones. The problems of philosophy he was grappling with now were the relation of sense data to the time and space of mathematical physics; he was calling his philosophy 'logical atomism' and trying to explain our knowledge of the external world through points in space and instances in time – through 'private world' perspectives instead of the inferential analysis of *The Problems of Philosophy*. Russell dismissed in passing the anti-empiricist classical tradition in philosophy represented at the time by Bergson, 'whose extra-philosophical knowledge is literary' rather than scientific (*Our Knowledge*, p. 15). Moore's extra-philosophical knowledge was also literary not scientific, and he is not mentioned in the work. *Our Knowledge of the External World* is also the last of Russell's strictly philosophical books to interest Bloomsbury very much. It may have been this book that Fry wrote to Russell about, saying how mistrustful of metaphysics he was, yet how real and solid he found Russell's discussion, especially the parts having to do with infinity. Fry concluded with the question, 'Will you ever turn to Aesthetics or is that too complex even for your analysis' (7.iv.15, Russell Archives). It has also been suggested that Virginia Woolf's fictional representations of time and space owe something to Russell's constructions rather than Bergson's cruder ones (Hintikka, p. 9).

In *The Analysis of Mind*, given as lectures in London after the First World War to an audience that included Leonard Woolf, Russell was influenced by William James and the behaviourists with their denials of consciousness. He was now, as John Passmore notes, in violent reaction to 'the whole pattern of ideas within which his own and Moore's earlier theories had been worked out' (p. 238). Fry was again an enthusiastic reader, preferring it to any other metaphysics, including Moore's (24.i.22, Russell Archives). After *The Analysis of Matter* (1927), where he had again changed his position, Russell recorded in the disillusioned epilogue to his 1931 autobiography that he had come almost full circle philosophically, back to the subjectivity of Berkeley (*Autobiography*, II 160). He did not return to epistemology until the 1940s, when he developed new theories in response to the criticism of younger philosophers.

The twists and turns that brought Russell back to something like the subjectivity of Idealism were not much followed after the First World War in New Bloomsbury. Some of his popularisations of philosophy were read by members of the Group, however. *An Outline of Philosophy* delighted Fry; *Sceptical Essays* brought a fan letter from Clive Bell (Russell Archives); and Virginia Woolf cited *The Scientific Outlook* in *Three Guineas* (pp. 252–4, 326).

IV

The moral, social and political philosophy that Russell separated from his work in epistemology and logic interested Bloomsbury because of its scope and practical applications. Here Russell's influence became quite independent of Moore's for the Group. Throughout his extraordinary life he remained a touchstone of liberalism for them. His grandfather, after all, had been a Liberal prime minister, his parents were philosophical radicals, and John Stuart Mill had been his godless godfather. Russell's very first book, an analysis of German social democracy published in 1896, had included a critical exposition of Marxism quite consistent with his criticism of communism after his visit to Russia in 1919. Bloomsbury would have voted for Russell when he ran for Parliament in 1907 as a Women's Suffrage candidate; they agreed with his pacifism and opposition to conscription in the First World War and with his anti-pacifist opposition to Fascism in the Second; and those who were still alive after that war supported some aspects at least of his nuclear-disarmament campaign.

Russell emerged as a stimulating social thinker in Bloomsbury and beyond during the First World War with *Principles of Social Reconstruction*, his first widely read book. Most of Russell's earlier writings on religion and ethics had not the appeal of his technical work among the Apostles, because these writings were not as original. Dickinson and McTaggart on religion and Moore on ethics were more interesting, even for Russell. 'The Study of Mathematics' and its companion piece, 'A Free Man's Worship' – deplorably the most famous essay Russell ever wrote – were written before *Principia Ethica* and *Some Dogmas of Religion*, however, and attracted some attention among the Apostles. As a testament, 'The Study of Mathematics' has a certain authority because of Russell's achievements in mathematical logic, but 'A Free Man's Worship' seems little more than a *fin-de-siècle* prose hymn of stoic renunciation. Dickinson was impressed by the essay and persuaded Russell to publish it in the newly founded *Independent Review*, a journal controlled by Apostles which published the first reviews and essays of Strachey, Leonard Woolf, Forster and MacCarthy. (The editors rejected 'The Study of Mathematics'.) Roger Fry, who was more sympathetic to Russell than anyone in Bloomsbury, thought the article very fine but felt that in such a world indignation would be more justified than resignation (VW/*RF*, p. 118). And Russell himself came to regret the essay and wondered if he had been reading too much Milton and Taylor (*Portraits*, p. 212; *Autobiography*, I 150). He also appears to have been reading too much Pater: 'To abandon the struggle for private happiness, to expel all eagerness of temporary desire, to burn with passion for eternal things – this is emancipation, and this is the free man's worship' (*Mysticism*, p. 46). How remote the sentiments and the prose are from *Principia Ethica*, which appeared the same year, or even from the two reviews hailing Moore's book that Russell himself wrote. Russell's versatility as a stylist at this time is amazing and disturbing. When he wished, he could write the plain style with greater forcefulness than Dickinson, greater lucidity than McTaggart, and greater grace than Moore. Such prose was closer to Bloomsbury's idea of good writing than that of anyone else they knew in Cambridge.

The impetus behind 'A Free Man's Worship' was a mystical experience brought on by the illness of Whitehead's wife, with whom Russell appears to have been in love (*Autobiography*, I 146). Nearly a decade later, when he was in love with Ottoline Morrell, Russell began writing various works on religious topics again. One of these was an unpublished dialogue probably modelled on some of Dickinson's work. Part of another unpublished work appeared as an essay on the essence of religion, which Russell saw as fundamentally mystical in a Platonic rather than a Christian way; the only Christian religious elements worth preserving, Russell found, were worship, acquiescence and love (*Basic Writings*, p. 568). Bloomsbury would have accepted only the last, perhaps because it could include the other two. Forster, at eighty-three years of age, in an undelivered speech for Russell's ninetieth birthday, praised his impressive irreverence 'because it is a positive quality and not the negative of reverence, and because it is devoid of arrogance'; like Russell, he said, he also had no sense of sin or need of prayer, though he did feel an interest in thanksgiving, directed not to gods but to people (*CB*, p. 262).

Another essay of Russell's on mysticism written before the war has more bearing on Bloomsbury's philosophical education than most of his religious or ethical essays, because it attempted to reconcile mysticism with logic. Russell's definition of mysticism in 'Mysticism and Logic' as 'in essence little more than a certain intensity and depth of feeling in regard to what is believed about the universe' may not have been very helpful, but his examination of four basic mystical principles clarifies the associations of the visionary and the rational that many Bloomsbury works make. The first mystical principle, that intuition is superior to reason, is modified in Russell's conclusion that both harmonising reason and creative intuition are necessary; the second principle, that reality is monistic, is the only one of the four Russell cannot find some way of accommodating; the third and fourth principles, that time and evil do not really exist, are both fallacious for Russell, even though it is sometimes useful to think and act as if they were unreal. Russell's combination of the rational and the intuitive in 'Mysticism and Logic' was congenial to Bloomsbury's thinking; along with Russell and McTaggart they could conceive of a mystical pluralism. Time could at times be illusory, but its reality, including the reality of history, was, *pace* McTaggart, very real and important. In his logical analysis of the fourth principle of mysticism, however, Russell diverged from the ethics of Moore that Bloomsbury accepted. For Russell, evil could be considered illusory in some way because good as well as evil are subjective, merely the reflections of certain kinds of feelings we have. And the good should not be identified with the real, as in Plato, for this splits science and philosophy (*Mysticism*, pp. 12–13). It also split Russell and Bloomsbury.

Russell abandoned Moore's ethics in 1913 when Santayana published a criticism of *Principia Ethica* which argued that good might be indefinable but it was not unconditioned, not an intrinsic property independent of personal interests (*Winds*, pp. 141–3). Russell's original reviews of *Principia Ethica* had called the book brilliant and profound – especially the last chapter on the Ideal, which Russell agreed with his fellow Apostles in finding the best in the book. His only real criticism was of the chapter on ethics in relation to conduct, where Russell found Moore going too far in his consequentialist definition of 'ought' and suggested that it too might, like good, be indefinable. Nor was he as prepared as Moore and Bloomsbury to dismiss the whole deontological basis of Victorian moral philosophy. These criticisms may be reflected in the changes Moore made later in *Ethics*.[3] Russell tried to combine conscience and consequence types of ethical theory, calling them 'subjective' and 'objective', in the only substantial piece of ethical writing he did before the war – an essay, originally published in MacCarthy's *New Quarterly* and then retitled and reprinted as 'The Elements of Ethics' in his 1910 *Philosophical Essays*. In almost all the other main points of this essay Russell followed Moore's ethics closely; even the new title was the one Moore had given to the lectures that formed the basis for *Principia Ethica* and which Russell had read in typescript. Until he reversed himself under Santayana's criticism and abandoned objective for subjective ethics, Russell's moral philosophy was, like his epistemology, basically an extension of Moore's thought as far as Bloomsbury was concerned. When Russell's ethics became subjective, so in a sense did his epistemology in *Our Knowledge of the External World*. There is no discussion of the relativity of moral judgements in *Principia Ethica*; for the Bloomsbury Apostles, Plato's identification of the good with the real was perhaps implicit in Moore's basing his ethics on a realistic epistemology.

Russell came to believe that the only objective elements in ethics were political ones, and at the end of his life he felt deeply frustrated at 'the impossibility of reconciling ethical feelings with ethical doctrines' (*Autobiography*, III 34). Moore too at the end of his career was uncertain about whether 'good' had merely emotive meanings ('Reply', p. 554). In Bloomsbury's Cambridge and during the decade that followed there were no doubts. After Russell changed his mind, it was his social and political rather than his ethical writings that continued to interest most of Bloomsbury.

V

Russell was more closely involved with members of Bloomsbury during the First World War than at any other time, before or after. His active pacifism split the Society, particularly dividing Dickinson and McTaggart, but he had the approval of the Bloomsbury Apostles as well as Dickinson when he lost his lectureship at Trinity. The lectures he then gave in London early in 1916 and published under the title *Principles of Social Reconstruction* (badly translated as *Why Men Fight* by his American publisher) are among the most important of his writings for Bloomsbury because of the scope of their concerns, the genius of the lecturer, and the times in which they were written. Under the shock of the greatest public catastrophe of their lives, Bloomsbury paid attention to what the brilliant logician of *The Principles of Mathematics* had to say in the *Principles of Social Reconstruction*.

The principles Russell develops for the reconstruction of society are based on a theory of impulse. There are two fundamental kinds of impulse – possessive and creative. Social reconstruction should aim at liberating, vivifying the latter and diminishing the former by developing, first of all, an organic common purpose to counteract the overdeveloped individualism in our society. Syndicalism Russell sees as the form of socialism capable of achieving this for the government of the state, but there must also be world government to end the international anarchy that caused the war. As for individuals, they must learn to revere necessary authority and the spirit of life in others. The egoism of romantic love must be broken down, and there should be a Platonic harmonising of our instinctual, intellectual and spiritual lives. Both individual and community growth must be fostered, and a philosophy or religion developed that will incarnate such an ideal as God, truth or beauty, so that out of the war's destruction may come hope for a rebirth.

This sketch cannot do justice to the sweep of Russell's synthesis, but it may suggest his eclectic combination of liberal socialism, Lawrentian love, Platonic psychology and Spinozistic religion. The various themes of *Principles of Social Reconstruction* recur in different forms throughout Russell's extensive output of social and political writing over the next half century. His socialism did not remain syndicalist; his ideas on education, marriage and morals grew more permissive; and his psychology became more behavioural. But along with Bloomsbury he continued to see modern history in terms such as those in the titles of two of his later works, *Freedom and Organization* (1934) and *Authority and the Individual* (1949). Bloomsbury kept on reading and even occasionally reviewing his later popular and historical works, but none seems to have had the impact on the Group's development as his writings just before and during the war. The Group clearly approved, for example, of the destructive analysis of current social principles of state, war, property, education, marriage and religion – each the subject of a chapter – that preceded Russell's reconstruction in the book. 'It is splendid the way he sticks at nothing', Lytton Strachey wrote to Ottoline Morrell after attending Russell's lectures; 'Governments, religions, laws, property, even Good Form itself – down they go like ninepins – it is a charming sight!' (MH/*LS*, pp. 621–2). The Apostles had been engaging in piecemeal analyses of the social order for a long time but none had done so publicly with the completeness that Russell managed, which made brother Apostles like Forster think the *Principles of Social Reconstruction* a 'brave and splendid book' (PNF/*EMF*, II 46).

When it came to Russell's reconstructive principles, there was not as much agreement in Bloomsbury. The elite concept of civilisation being developed by Clive Bell was remote from guild socialism. Leonard Woolf's and even Roger Fry's socialism were closer to Russell's, and all agreed with Dickinson that world government was imperative for any post-war reconstruction. But what would Leonard Woolf, who attended the lectures, or Keynes have thought of the absence of any class analysis in Russell's discussions? Despite his early familiarity with Marx, Russell never mentions him in his lectures. One can imagine what Virginia Woolf, who attended at least one of the lectures, would have thought of Russell's ego-breaking, procreative theories of marriage or his confident assertion that the movement for the emancipation of women 'is not far from complete triumph' (p. 156). Strachey must also have had misgivings about Russell's notions of marriage, but he remained enthusiastic about the lectures, finding them 'very grand; one feels one had always thought something like that – but vaguely and inconclusively'. The way Russell put them together, they were 'solid and shining. . . . I don't believe there's anyone quite so formidable to be found just now upon this earth' (MH/*LS*, p. 622). Forster, writing to Russell from Egypt, was more reflective and critical:

> For a time I thought you would shake me out of my formula – that though of course there is a connection between civilization and our private desires and impulses and actions, it is a connection as meaningless as that between a word and the letters that make it up. But the formula holds. The war will only end through exhaustion and nausea. All that is good in humanity must be sweated and vomited out together with what is bad.   (PNF/*EMF*, ii 46)

That Forster, just six years after *Howards End*, could not connect the individual with civilisation says something not only about the war but also about Russell's reconstructive principles. In his disillusionment Forster sounds a little like D. H. Lawrence, with whom he was more sympathetic than anyone else in Bloomsbury. Forster saw the disconnection between personal renewal and social reconstruction in Russell's philosophy, but he was unwilling to give up liberty for the kind of community that Lawrence's philosophy called for.

Keynes also recognised the disjunction between the individual

and society in Russell's social thought and related it to Lawrence. In 'My Early Beliefs' Keynes depicted Russell among the
Apostles and elsewhere as sustaining

> simultaneously a pair of opinions ludicrously incompatible.
> He held that in fact human affairs were carried on after a most
> irrational fashion, but that the remedy was quite simple and
> easy, since all we had to do was to carry them on rationally. A
> discussion of practical affairs on these lines was really very
> boring. And a discussion of the human heart which ignored so
> many of its deeper and blinder passions, both good and bad,
> was scarcely more interesting.   (*CW*, x 449)

The context of Keynes's remarks, which certainly apply to
Principles of Social Reconstruction as a discussion of practical affairs,
was his criticism of the Moorean Apostles' unrealistically
rational conception of human nature – a conception that justified
a little Lawrence's attack on Keynes and his friends. The subject
of Keynes's important memoir was the influence of Moore's
ethics on the Apostles, and it belongs to the next and last chapter
of Bloomsbury's philosophical education. But it also became the
basis for the account of Keynes, Strachey and their Apostolic
generation that Russell wrote in 1952 and then worked into the
Autobiography. This, along with Russell's other reactions to
Bloomsbury, brings us finally back to Cambridge and the personal relations of Russell and the Group.

VI

Russell criticises the Apostolic generation of Keynes and
Strachey for abandoning the Victorian idea of progress, for
indulging themselves in 'the passionate mutual admirations of a
clique of the elite', and for degrading Moore's ethics to what he
quite inaptly described as 'girls-school sentimentalizing' (*Autobiography*, I 70–1). Russell was almost frightened by Keynes's
arrogant brilliance, but he thought his work valuable.[4]
Strachey's *Eminent Victorians* made Russell laugh in prison yet he
attacked Strachey's style and veracity. When Russell originally
published his recollections of Keynes and Strachey in the *Listener*, he provoked a reply from E. M. Forster, who asked why

Russell bothered to reminisce so ungenerously about Strachey since he so disliked him (SPR/*BG*, pp. 406–7). Perhaps because of Forster's complaint, Russell did not include the reminiscences in *Portraits from Memory*, but later he put them in his autobiography and added some paragraphs that finally refer to a central, but unstated, issue underlying both Russell's dislike of Keynes and Strachey, and Lawrence's revulsion with Cambridge. Strachey 'is diseased and unnatural', Russell wrote to Lady Ottoline in 1912, adding with a priggishness that is almost ironical, 'and only a very high degree of civilization enables a healthy person to stand him' (Darroch, p. 128). It is now quite clear from Russell's and Lawrence's letters that, despite their differences over the values of intellectuality and blood-consciousness, they were agreed in disliking homosexuality, though for different reasons. Lawrence found the homosexuality of Duncan Grant, Keynes and David Garnett threatening; Russell thought it sterilising (Rosenbaum, 'Keynes'). This is all part of Bloomsbury's Georgian, not Victorian, literary history, but it also explains why Russell was not as close to Bloomsbury as Dickinson or Moore. The deep, blinder passions of the heart that Keynes found Russell unable to take account of kept him from understanding the full impact of *Principia Ethica* on Bloomsbury, despite his thinking the chapter on the Ideal the best part of the book. Russell, unlike the other philosophical teachers of Bloomsbury in the Apostles, had no close relationships with Bloomsbury of the kind he had at various times with Wittgenstein, Lawrence, T. S. Eliot and even Katherine Mansfield. The relationship with Wittgenstein actually caused something of a rupture with the Apostles when Russell tried to dissuade him from joining and then Keynes intervened; Wittgenstein became an Apostle briefly, and just before he resigned Strachey was called upon to explain the Society to him (MH/*LS*, 515–17).

Keynes and Strachey were, of course, aware of Russell's disapproval. During their years as Apostles, Keynes once wrote to Strachey how shocked Russell would have been at their correspondence – how unsurprised he would be when Keynes finally died of syphilis (22.xi.05, JMK/pKC). In 1919 Strachey wrote to Virginia Woolf that he had met him again at Lady Ottoline's Garsington: 'Bertie worked his circular saw as usual. I've never been able to feel at ease with him, and I can only suppose that he dislikes me – pourquoi?' (*LVWLS*, p. 80). Part of the answer was that Russell disliked the 'pose of cynical superiority' that he thought Strachey had made fashionable at Cambridge ('Mental Development', p. 9). It is ironic that Russell of all people should complain of Strachey's cynicism. MacCarthy wrote to Russell in 1917 that he thought *him* too 'symmetrically cynical' in his writings, like La Rochefoucauld, and that this may have affected Russell and Moore's relations (5.i.17, Russell Archives). Russell's letters to Ottoline Morrell during the war show that he thought Strachey too passive a pacifist. Actually Strachey supported his friends' conscientious objections and maintained his own, as well as composing a leaflet for the No-Conscription Fellowship and, of course, writing *Eminent Victorians*, with its criticism of the world order that had helped bring about the war. And, in addition to his dislike of Strachey's sexuality, Russell also appears to have been jealous of Ottoline Morrell's considerable fondness for him.

Russell summarised what he saw as his relation to Bloomsbury in a letter written from prison to Lady Ottoline about an anonymous, hostile review of Siegfried Sassoon's poems. The review was written by Middleton Murry, but Russell thought it came from Bloomsbury.

Ouf! I hate all the Bloomsbury crew, with their sneers at anything that has live feeling in it. *Beastly* of them to be down on S. S. They put up with me because they know I can make any one look ridiculous – if I had less brains and less satire, they would all be down on me – as it is, they whisper against me in corners, and flatter me to my face. They are a rotten crew. I wish you had more congenial 'friends'. (1.viii.18, Russell Archives)

Certainly Bloomsbury and just about everyone else who knew Russell were aware of how deadly his circular-saw intellect could be. They openly admired his mind and were amused, not always as openly, at the extraordinary figure this genius seemed to cut. Indeed, cutting images appear in various descriptions of him, such as Margot Asquith's comparison of him with a knife: 'you can never see him edge on. He has to be turned flat' (Clark, p. 242). Yet Russell rarely appears as the flat, ironic symbol in Bloomsbury's writings that he does in the fiction of Lawrence and Huxley or the poetry of Eliot and Campbell. Bloomsbury was nevertheless familiar with the paradoxes of his character – a logician who laughed and was lecherous, an Alice-in-Wonderland figure wandering in the modern waste-land (Rosenbaum, 'Russell' and 'Cannan').

But just who made up the rotten Bloomsbury crew that Russell thought friends of Lady Ottoline Morrell? Not Roger Fry, who had quarrelled violently with her yet remained friends with Russell. Nor Desmond MacCarthy, who also kept up his friendship and had written with Russell's aunt a memoir of Lady John Russell. Not E. M. Forster, who was in Egypt and whose novels Russell quite liked. It probably included Keynes, whose *Economic Consequences of the Peace* Russell thought moral and clever. Perhaps Strachey too, whose *Eminent Victorians* Russell was delighting in. Probably Russell's Bloomsbury included Clive Bell as well, to whom Russell was soon to write asking for an educated layman's opinion of the *Introduction to Mathematical Philosophy*, which he had written in prison.[5] (Clive Bell later remarked, qualifying a little Moore's influence on all Bloomsbury, that Russell, 'though no one has ever called him "Bloomsbury", appeared to be a friend and was certainly an influence' – *OF*, p. 133.) Maybe the Woolfs were also of the crew, to whose Hogarth Press Russell and his third wife submitted in the 1930s their edition of the letters and diaries of Russell's parents, which were then published in two volumes as *The Amberley Papers*.

Apart from the familiar confusion as to whom 'Bloomsbury' encompassed, then, Russell's denunciation reveals that the personal and the intellectual remained separated in his and the Group's relationships. And *The Amberley Papers* suggests a final difference between Russell and Bloomsbury. There were Russells in Bloomsbury long before there were Stephens or Stracheys. The dukes of Bedford were Bloomsbury's landlords, and the squares and streets that the Group inhabited bore names associated with the Russell family – Bedford, Tavistock, Woburn and Russell itself. Bertrand Russell was not – like all of Bloomsbury, like all of the Apostles they knew – middle-class. He was an aristocrat, and this was one of his bonds with Ottoline Morrell, whose behaviour also intrigued Bloomsbury. (Vita Sackville-West was another.) One of the biblical texts Lady John Russell taught her grandson that he remembered all his life was 'Thou shalt not follow a multitude to do evil' ('Mental Development', p. 5). This background sustained him in his reforming crusades during the First World War and after the Second. Bloomsbury saw in the aristocracy a freedom from criticism and from the dreary self-consciousness of middle-class conformity. But the freedom could lead to irresponsible contempt. The anti-semitism, for instance, that Russell expresses in his autobiography and elsewhere was accurately described by Leonard Woolf (who rarely seems to have noticed it in others) as 'aristocratic anti-semitism' ('Autobiography of Russell', p. 345).

VII

When he was twenty-two, Russell had a Hegelian vision of two series of books he might write, one about the philosophy of the sciences and another on social questions. 'I hoped that the two series might ultimately meet in a synthesis at once scientific and practical', he recalled in his autobiography, and thought to some extent that they did (i 125). Later Russell agreed that there was no necessary connection between the two in his work, though there was a psychological one ('Reply', ii 727). For his Bloomsbury readers and others there was also a psychological connection in the sense that they hoped his analytical genius could provide wisdom in ethical and social matters. And, if Bloomsbury was ultimately disappointed in the discrepancies between Russell's logical and moral intelligence, there was still wisdom in what he said at the beginning of *My Philosophical Development* about what had been the only constant preoccupation of that development: 'I have throughout been anxious to discover how much we can be said to know and with what degree of certainty or doubtfulness' (p. 11). It was the scope, the subtlety, the versatility of this quest rather than its results that impressed Bloomsbury, whose admiration for Russell's thought, if not his character, was an illustration of the truth of the last sentence in his *A History of Western Philosophy*: 'In abandoning a part of its dogmatic pretensions, philosophy does not cease to suggest and inspire a way of life.'

10 Moore

'Why dont you contribute to the Queen's dolls House, Virginia?' 'Is there a W. C. in it, Vita?' 'You're a bit hoity toity, Virginia.' Well, I was educated in the old Cambridge School. 'Ever hear of Moore?' 'George Moore the novelist?' 'My dear Vita, we start at different ends.' (VW/*L*, III 85–6)

I

Unlike Russell's influence, the profound significance of George Edward Moore's philosophy and character for the literary history of Bloomsbury will not take us far from Cambridge. Moore, as he was called by his friends – the monosyllable somehow symbolising the incisive simplicity of his genius – was unquestionably the most important philosopher and Apostle for the Group. Yet, ever since the brilliant memoir in which Maynard Keynes undertook to describe how Moore shaped the early beliefs of himself and his friends, there have been disagreements within and without Bloomsbury about the nature of Moore's influence.

Keynes used his meeting with D. H. Lawrence in Cambridge in 1915 as a departure point for analysing what Moore's disciples learned from him, and he finds that they adopted his religion, which involved attitudes towards themselves and the ultimate, and ignored his morals, which involved attitudes toward the outside world and the intermediate. 'Nothing mattered except . . . timeless, passionate states of contemplation and communion, largely unattached to "before" and "after".' His followers developed, with the help of Russell's work, a method that calculated the precise value of the states of mind, and thus they became Utopian immoralists, repudiating conventional morality and traditional wisdom and adopting a pseudo-rational conception of human nature that resulted in superficial judgements and

214

feelings. But, if the fundamental intuitions of *Principia Ethica* about the value of love, beauty and knowledge were not enough, Keynes was convinced that they had nevertheless liberated his friends and himself from the economic overvaluations of Benthamism and Marxism, and also from the conventional Victorian notions of moral obligation (*CW*, x 436–46).

Russell, as noted in the last chapter, cited Keynes's memoir as evidence of how Keynes himself, Strachey and others distorted and diminished Moore's ethics. Leonard Woolf, however, authoritatively challenged Keynes's interpretation in his autobiography *Sowing*. He pointed out that Keynes was conflating two quite different periods of time: the Cambridge years, when they were undergraduates; and the period just before the war, when they no longer took *Principia Ethica* as a practical guide to life. Leonard Woolf also flatly disagreed that they had ever ignored Moore's morals and adopted only his religion. To be sure, they were not as socially conscious before the First World War as all the younger generations were afterwards, but both Moore and his followers were, he insisted, 'fascinated by questions of what was right and wrong, what one *ought* to do . . . and argued interminably about the consequences of one's actions, both in actual and imaginary situations' (*S*, pp. 148–9).

Quentin Bell, who was at the Memoir Club meeting the summer before Munich at which Keynes read his memoir, argues that 'My Early Beliefs' was in part a sermon against the Marxism of several younger members of the Club. This helps to explain why Keynes set his meeting with Lawrence just before the First World War. Bell also suggests that Lawrence's hostility to Cambridge was the result of homosexual jealousy rather than disgust with the results of Moore's influence (Q. Bell, *Bloomsbury*, pp. 46–53). The publication of the full text of the letter Lawrence wrote David Garnett about Cambridge after meeting Keynes there, together with a letter of Moore's about Lawrence's visit, show quite clearly that Lawrence was repelled by, if not jealous of, Keynes's homosexuality (Rosenbaum, 'Keynes'). Finally Richard Braithwaite, a later Cambridge philosopher and Apostle, developed Leonard Woolf's criticisms by 'derhetoricising' Keynes's memoir. He noted that Moore's morals were quite familiar already to Keynes through the utilitarianism of his father's philosophy, whereas Moore's religion, which rejected utilitarian hedonism, was exhilaratingly new to Keynes (pp. 242–6).

Faced with all the differing views of Moore's influence that Keynes's 'My Early Beliefs' has given rise to, the biographer of Moore's early years concluded that Moore's influence was 'not importantly doctrinal at all, but *personal*'. Bloomsbury's admiration and love for Moore's character, according to this theory, kept them from realising that his influence was personal not philosophical, and concealed from them that his philosophy was already implicit in the utilitarian beliefs of the Stephen, Keynes and Strachey families (Levy, p. 7).

No one familiar with the Cambridge origins of Bloomsbury has ever doubted that G. E. Moore exerted an immense personal influence on his contemporaries through the pure and passionate integrity of his mind and character. But to see this influence as merely personal rather than as a combination of the personal and the philosophical, however useful it may be for a biographer, makes little sense in terms of literary or intellectual history.[1] Moore cared intensely about philosophical ideas. How could he have so profoundly influenced his brother Apostles – intellectuals with minds as tough as Leonard Woolf's or Keynes's – without making them also care about these ideas? If Moore's importance is simply or even primarily a matter of his character or personality, why is it that Leonard Woolf and Keynes and Strachey and MacCarthy and Clive Bell all were mistaken in believing, early and late, that their ideas about ethics, perception and truth were essentially Moore's ideas? Moore's philosophy can be viewed as a representative Cambridge body of utilitarian and Platonic thought, and many of Moore's influential ideas are also to be found, as the preceding chapters here have shown, in such Apostolic philosophers as Sidgwick, Dickinson, McTaggart and Russell. But Moore's talk and writing were the actual contexts in which most of Bloomsbury received these ideas, just as it was Moore's personal and intellectual fusion of them that became permanently part of Bloomsbury's thinking. The evidence for this in the Group's autobiographical writings, fiction, biography and criticism is extensive.

The problem remains, however, of why Moore's influence has been controversial – why his followers have disagreed about the influence and why biographers and critics have so often misunderstood, ignored, denied or personalised it. The explanations are to be found in the nature of Moore's philosophy and the intimate way it was transmitted to Bloomsbury through the Apostles. Moore had no philosophical system. As he said at the end of *Principia Ethica*, 'to search for "unity" and "system," at the expense of truth, is not, I take it, the proper business of philosophy, however universally it may have been the practice of philosophers' (p. 222). Moore's general conception of philosophy is close to Russell's in its realistic epistemology, anti-metaphysical pluralism and analytic methods, although Moore was more concerned to reconcile philosophy with common sense than with science. Yet Moore's analyses can be very abstruse. He has been well described as the philosopher's philosopher (Passmore, p. 203). One of the paradoxes of twentieth-century English culture is that his thinking had greater significance for the literature of his country than had that of any other contemporary philosopher. In Bloomsbury that significance was inseparable from his influence on the Apostles. Moore's thought and character shaped Bloomsbury's beliefs about the nature of consciousness, perception and even perhaps mysticism, about the distinctions between right and good, about the importance of personal relations as well as public affairs, about the functions of criticism and the value of art. The shaping began when Moore was an undergraduate Apostle in the 1890s, absorbing, modifying, refuting the ideas of older philosopher Apostles such as Sidgwick, Dickinson, McTaggart, even Russell, and then influencing the younger Apostles who followed, starting with MacCarthy and continuing on into the twentieth century with Forster, Strachey, Woolf and Keynes. Fry alone among the Bloomsbury Apostles escaped Moore's influence at Cambridge, if not later. Originally through discussions in the Society that were then carried on outside, Moore's philosophical ideas and methods became familiar to the Society through the papers he read, the lectures he gave in London, the articles he was publishing in *Mind*, and finally the book he brought out in 1903. It is often assumed that only *Principia Ethica* among Moore's works was relevant to Bloomsbury, and, in the wake of Keynes, only its last chapter, on the Ideal. But Moore's ethics is not completely separable from his philosophy of mind or his analytic techniques. And the Group's interest in his work did not end in 1903. The

books, articles and lectures Moore produced throughout the
Edwardian years and into the 1920s continued to be read, heard
and discussed in Bloomsbury.

In a long essay written at the end of his life, in reply to a series
of articles on his philosophy, Moore divided his responses into
three categories: ethics, sense perception, and philosophic
method ('Reply', p. 535). These are useful distinctions through
which to examine Moore's large share of Bloomsbury's
philosophical education, because his ethics (including his aesthetics), which were so important for Bloomsbury, presuppose an
epistemology and a methodology. These are essential to a proper
understanding of Moore's importance. The methodology may be
the best place to begin, for there Moore's personal influence is
clearest.

II

'Methodology' seems too portentous a term to describe a
philosophic method that was not systematised or even very
self-conscious. Moore's method arose out of a persistent quest for
clear, exact meaning and may have had its origins in his
intensive literary training. Russell came to philosophy from
mathematics (T. S. Eliot thought it 'a public misfortune' that
Russell lacked a classical education – *Essays*, p. 434), but Moore
was trained as a classicist. Latin and Greek translation had
absorbed his attention before he changed to philosophy in his
third year at Trinity; Russell thought this work led him 'to
attach enormous importance to verbal precision' ('Influence',
p. 756). One of his classics teachers said Moore 'could construe
through a brick wall' (R. C. Trevelyan, p. 163), and his
philosophical genius might be seen in his ability to construe
propositions through philosophical brick walls. He is a great
philosophical translator, as it were, seeking clear meaning from
the opaque utterances of other philosophers. Not content simply
to show that their texts are philosophically corrupt, he assumes
they have meaning and strives to construe it correctly and
precisely. For the nascent writers of Bloomsbury this was a
valuable literary discipline.

Moore's philosophical construing often begins with the formulation of exact questions. The opening sentence of *Principia Ethica*

perfectly exemplifies the analytic questioning that was at the centre of his philosophic method:

> It appears to me that in Ethics, as in all other philosophical studies, the difficulties and disagreements, of which its history is full, are mainly due to a very simple cause: namely to the attempt to answer questions, without first discovering precisely *what* question it is which you desire to answer.   (p. vii)

After Lytton Strachey had read *Principia Ethica* he wrote to Moore that its destruction of all ethical writers from Aristotle through Christ to Spencer and Bradley was a small achievement

> compared to the establishment of that Method which shines like a sword between the lines. It is the scientific method deliberately applied, for the first time, to Reasoning. Is that true? You perhaps shake your head, but henceforward who will be able to tell lies one thousand times as easily as before? The truth, there can be no doubt, is really now upon the march. I date from Oct. 1903 the beginning of the Age of Reason.   (MH/*LS*, pp. 206–7)

Strachey's hyperbole notwithstanding, what this scientific method was, beyond the asking of precise, analytic questions, is not all that clear. Keynes remembered Moore's questioning as 'a method of discovery by the instrument of impeccable grammar and an unambiguous dictionary. "What *exactly* do you mean?" was the phrase most frequently on our lips' (*CW*, x 440). Leonard Woolf agreed this was the 'divinely cathartic question' in his Cambridge as in Socrates's Athens (*BA*, p. 25). But the method Leonard Woolf describes was more like a psychological third-degree derived from Plato and Henry James than an astringent dialectical discipline.

Moore professed not to understand what Strachey, Keynes and Leonard Woolf meant by his method (White, p. 757). Analytic questioning in his philosophy is closely related, however, to a common-sense conception of the world which clarifies a little what Bloomsbury took to be Moore's method. Appeals to common sense run throughout Moore's philosophic writings, the most famous being 'A Defence of Common Sense', which he contributed in 1925 to a collection of statements by philosophers defining their philosophies. (By contrast McTaggart's was entitled 'An Ontological Idealism' and Russell's 'Logical Atomism' – *Contemporary British Philosophy*.) Moore argues in this essay that any philosopher who disagrees with the simple truth of a common-sense statement such as 'The earth has existed for many years past' is confusing the question of whether we understand this sentence's meaning with the question of whether we are able to analyse this meaning correctly ('Defence', p. 198). The distinction is basic to Moore's method and to his influence on Bloomsbury, not to mention analytic philosophy. An analogous distinction, developed in the late 'Proof of an External World', emphasised the difference between having conclusive evidence for something and being able to prove it. 'I have no exquisite reason for't,' Moore might have said with Sir Andrew Aguecheek, 'but I have reason good enough' (*Twelfth Night*, II.iii.145–6).

In 'My Early Beliefs' Keynes amusingly maintained that, when Moore's dialectic dominated the Society, force of character counted for more than intellectual subtlety (*CW*, x 438–40). Moore's philosophic method was certainly connected with his simplicity and single-mindedness in the Apostles. Russell in his *Autobiography* compared Moore's inspired genius with Spinoza's deeply passionate intellect (I 64), and the comparison is more illuminating if one thinks of Russell as a latter-day Leibniz.[2] Leonard Woolf thought Moore the only great man he had ever known in ordinary life, and he compared him with saintly sillies like Tolstoy, Dostoevsky and even his wife (*S*, p. 131). Moore could be lovably charming in his shy, unaffected way, but he could also be fierce and ruthless in the pursuit of truth. His personality is implicit in his lucid, honest and at times painfully awkward prose, so bespattered with italics in places that it reminded Keynes of Queen Victoria's writing (*CW*, x 440). At school Moore remembered that he was criticised for his bland, childlike writing and given Saintsbury's *Specimens of English Prose Style* as a corrective ('Autobiography', p. 7). The childlike simplicity never completely disappeared from his style, though the blandness did.

For the brothers of the Society the purity of Moore's candour and the tenacity of his mind made him quintessentially Apostolic – except for his lack of wit. His dialectic, unlike Socrates's, had little irony in it. But his influence could still be inhibiting.

Desmond MacCarthy was Moore's closest friend in Bloomsbury, and Leonard Woolf believed this hindered MacCarthy's writing:

> The best, said the Greeks, is the enemy of the good. The vision of the best, the ghostly echoes of *Principia Ethica*, the catechism which always begins with the terrifying words: 'What exactly do you *mean* by *that?*', inhibited Desmond. When he wrote 'seriously', he began to labour, and the more he tinkered with what he wrote the more laboured and laborious it became. (*BA*, p. 138)

Leonard Woolf himself felt the restraining effect of Moore, and applied it, with some exaggeration, to Bloomsbury, telling the Memoir Club that, 'just as one hesitated in Moore's rooms at Cambridge to say anything amusing that was not also profound and true, so in Bloomsbury one hesitated to say anything true and profound unless it was also amusing' (SPR/*BG*, p. 122). The old truth-telling of Stephen and his contemporaries lived on in Moore and his contemporaries. A consequence of Moore's standards of precise meaning was that the conversation of his disciples was punctuated with periods of silence; conversation was too important to be made. After Moore left Cambridge in 1904, Strachey wrote to Keynes that he felt a kind of Moorish orthodoxy had grown up in the Apostles 'which makes impossible the discussion of big things & too difficult the little ones!' (8.x.05, JMK/pKC).

Moore agreed at the end of his career that as a philosopher he had been a better questioner than answerer ('Reply', p. 677). This was clearly part of his value for Bloomsbury. If sometimes his demand for analytical clarity and integrity paralysed his followers, it could also liberate their thinking. The distinction E. M. Forster, who was not close to Moore, liked to make between a mystery and a muddle has the spirit of Moore's analysis behind it.

III

Turning now to Moore's philosophy of sense perception, we may see how his precise, analytic, common-sense questioning seemed to release his Apostolic followers from epistemological prisons into the world of everyday experience that his ethics then helped them evaluate. When Moore returned to Cambridge as a lecturer in 1911, his subject was designated as psychology, though it had nothing to do with the experimental or therapeutic aspects of that field. 'Philosophy of mind' was the way Moore preferred to describe his work at Cambridge ('Autobiography', p. 29), and that is the best description of his concern with the nature of consciousness and its relation to external nature. As an undergraduate Moore was apparently a Lucretian materialist and sceptical empiricist, but under the powerful influence of McTaggart he became an Idealist like Russell, studied Hegel and Bradley, and then wrote an unsuccessful fellowship dissertation on Kant because he was the philosopher Moore most agreed with at the time. While working on his second, successful dissertation, Moore says he realised in analysing a passage from Bradley that the meaning of an idea was 'something wholly independent of mind. I tried to argue for this position, and this was the beginning, I think, of certain tendencies in me which have led some people to call me a "Realist" . . .' ('Autobiography', pp. 20–2).

In 1899 Moore published some of his dissertation as an essay on the nature of judgement in *Mind*. This marked the beginning of his and Russell's Realist revolution in philosophy. Initially their Realism was compatible with Plato's Idealism, if not McTaggart's or Bradley's. Moore wrote to MacCarthy that it pleased him to think the philosophy of his essay was 'the most Platonic system of modern times' ('Moore Papers', p. 86). Russell described the effect of this new philosophy on himself and Moore more dramatically:

> With a sense of escaping from prison, we allowed ourselves to think that the grass is green, that the sun and stars would exist if no one was aware of them, and also that there is a pluralistic timeless world of Platonic ideas. The world, which had been thin and logical, suddenly became rich and varied and solid.   ('Mental Development', p. 12)

From a monistic mentalism maintaining that anything's reality depended upon its existence as thought of some kind, Moore and Russell became dualists. They accepted both immaterial consciousness and the independent existence of material objects as ideas. Truth was now to be discovered in the correspondence of inner awareness and outer reality, not in the coherence of beliefs. Russell, it may be remembered, found Idealism inconsistent with mathematics; for Moore, Idealism was incompatible with his unshakable conviction that common-sense reality existed apart from our perceptions of it. Russell, again, has well described Moore's attraction to Realism:

> What I think at first chiefly interested Moore was the independence of fact from knowledge and the rejection of the whole Kantian apparatus of *a priori* intuitions and categories, moulding experience but not the outer world. (*Philosophical Development*, p. 12)

The relevance of all this to Bloomsbury's Cambridge education in philosophy can be seen in the famous essay Moore published in *Mind* in 1903. 'The Refutation of Idealism' is second in importance only to *Principia Ethica* in Bloomsbury's early literary history. It exemplified, first of all, the power of Moore's philosophic method. By asking, in effect, what *exactly* Idealists meant by saying *esse est percipi*, to be is to be perceived, Moore is able to show that the copula of that statement is fatally ambiguous. In Moore's example, if a colour and the perception of a colour were identical, then saying that a colour was being perceived would be the same thing as saying a colour is a colour. Obviously something more than a mere statement of existence is meant by saying that a colour is being perceived. Moore therefore concludes that Idealists are actually distinguishing between the act of perception and the object being perceived while they are identifying them. Moore's separation of the acts and objects of consciousness, as he later called them, is basic to his Realistic philosophy of mind (*Main Problems*, pp. 16–17). He rejects Idealism because he can find no good reason for denying the existence of reality apart from our perceptions of it, and he is not a Materialist because he can find no good reason for denying the existence of consciousness apart from the reality of which it is conscious.

Certain aspects of Idealism and empiricism, if not Materialism, are nevertheless inherent in Moore's Realism. He wrote in 'The Refutation of Idealism' that he was not denying that reality was spiritual; he devoutly hoped it was, but the hope did not entail a belief that reality's existence depended upon its being perceived (p. 3). And Moore's life-long preoccupation with epistemological problems is clearly in the English empirical tradition. During the first post-impressionist exhibition in London in 1910–11, Moore gave a series of lectures in which he replaced the subjective word 'sensation' with 'sense-data', a term he coined to describe 'things *given* or presented by the senses' (*Main Problems*, p. 30). Moore spent much of the remainder of his philosophical career struggling to define the status of sense-data, and was finally uncertain how they were related to material reality. But, for all his empiricism, Moore's common sense rejected the sceptical arguments of Hume about the limits of knowledge. His criticsm of Hume's philosophy appeared in MacCarthy's *New Quarterly*, and the next year was incorporated in his London lectures, in which he attacked the philosophical subjectivity of both idealists and empiricists. These lectures considerably influenced Russell's *Problems of Philosophy*, but because Moore did not publish them until 1953, it was Russell's book that popularised their philosophical Realism in the Georgian years. (Santayana suggested that a more accurate title for Russell's book might have been 'the problems which Moore and I have been agitating lately' – *Winds*, p. 112.)

Particularly important for Bloomsbury's work, especially Virginia Woolf's, was the conception of consciousness that Moore's philosophy of mind assumed. It is Moore's dualistic account of awareness and sense-data, rather than William James's, Bergson's, Husserl's or Freud's theories of consciousness, that underlies the preoccupation with perception in her writing.[3] In her fiction everything that states of mind consist of – the self, the past and the present, colour, nature, beauty, love, knowledge, other minds, even mystical moments – is presented to 'diaphanous consciousness', as Moore tentatively described it ('Refutation', p. 25). In these states of mind, however, this diaphanous awareness, difficult as it is to fix, has to be distinguished from what it is aware of. To be is not simply to be perceived; impressionism, whether Monet's or Pater's, is not enough. Moore's epistemology is, as it were, post-impressionist, and the recurrent ocular imagery of his examples made Moore's philosophy of mind more available to novelists, painters, biographers and critics, for whom art was passionate perception.

When in the 1920s Moore reprinted 'The Refutation of Idealism', he acknowledged that it was very confused but included the essay in *Philosophical Studies* anyway, because of its fame. Certainly it was well known in Bloomsbury, both for what Moore analytically refuted and for what he maintained and implied about consciousness and reality. Bloomsbury found in Moore's refutation of epistemological Idealism an affirmation of the independent, common-sense existence of ideas, of other people and of external nature. Reality in his philosophy was as it generally appeared to be – pluralistic, temporal, material, but also spiritual, because it included immaterial minds. In works such as Forster's *The Longest Journey*, Strachey's *Eminent Victorians* and Virginia Woolf's *Jacob's Room*, Moore's refutation of Idealism was transposed into a criticism of the egocentric and altruistic meanings of Victorian idealism. Moore's Realism was seen as a life-enhancing, modern alternative to these idealisms. The philosophical criticism that Moore made of nineteenth-century Idealism and Materialism was extended by Bloomsbury into critiques of the tasteless, mindless materialism of Victorian and Edwardian literature and art. Leonard Woolf's description of the purifying effect of Moore's method on Bloomsbury's writing and painting indicates the wide significance his philosophy had for Bloomsbury:

> Artistically the purification can, I think, be traced in the clarity, light, absence of humbug of Virginia's literary style and perhaps in Vanessa's painting. They have the quality noted by Maynard in Moorism, the getting rid of 'irrelevant extraneous matter'. (*BA*, p. 25)

G. E. Moore once had a nightmare, according to Keynes, in which he was unable to distinguish propositions from tables. Even awake, he could not, Keynes thought, 'distinguish love and beauty and truth from the furniture. They took on the same definition of outline, the same stable, solid, objective qualities and common-sense reality' (*CW*, x 444). The purity of Moore's integrity, his wholeness, made his epistemology of a piece with his ethics. It was not a coincidence that 'The Refutation of Idealism' was published in the same year as the book that Bloomsbury called their bible.

IV

The impact of G. E. Moore's *Principia Ethica* on the Apostles and their friends was quite extraordinary. Russell's reviews called it brilliant and profound. Strachey dated the beginning of the Age of Reason from its appearance in October 1903 (see p. 219). Keynes thought only *Principia Ethica*'s readers possessed the rudiments of a true ethics (RFH/*JMK*, p. 114). Even E. M. Forster, who never read it, was influenced by the book through his fellow Apostles: its seed 'fell on fertile if inferior soil', he wrote late in life, 'and I began to think for myself. . . .' ('How I Lost', p. 263). Outside the Apostles, Sydney Waterlow, a Trinity man and friend of Old Bloomsbury, attempted to organise a manifesto out of Moore's thought with essays by various friends, including Russell and Moore himself, to be published in a place like the *Independent Review* (Levy, pp. 251–8). Clive Bell declared the book's influence on Bloomsbury to be 'immense' (*OF*, p. 133). Duncan Grant found the meaning of good such a constant topic of conversation among his Bloomsbury friends that 'eventually, I, a mere painter, asked my mother for a copy of *Principia Ethica* for a birthday present in order to read the author in the original – a book I still possess' ('Where Angels'). Virginia Woolf, who read the book in 1908 and found Moore 'so humane in spite of his desire to know the truth', still thought in 1940 that *Principia Ethica* was 'the book that made us all so wise and good' (*L*, I 364; VI 400). Again, however, it is Leonard Woolf who best describes the impact of *Principia Ethica*. His hyperbole reflects the mood of Moore's disciples at Cambridge.

> The tremendous influence of Moore and his book upon us came from the fact that they suddenly removed from our eyes an obscuring accumulation of scales, cobwebs, and curtains, revealing for the first time to us, so it seemed, the nature of truth and reality, of good and evil and character and conduct, substituting for the religious and philosophical nightmares, delusions, hallucinations, in which Jehovah, Christ, and St Paul, Plato, Kant, and Hegel had entangled us, the fresh air and pure light of plain common-sense.   (*S*, p. 147)

Moore's influence on the Apostles, which had begun almost a decade before, culminated in *Principia Ethica*. 'It would be too much to say that Moore dethroned McTaggart, who was essentially undethronable', Forster observed in his biography of Dickinson, 'but he did carry the younger men by storm. . . .' (*GLD*, p. 92). Here for the world to see was the published evidence of Moore's wisdom and goodness. *Principia Ethica* is the single most important work in Bloomsbury's Cambridge education, but it is a difficult work whose complex significance has been repeatedly oversimplified by critics and biographers of Bloomsbury. To appreciate properly its immense and enduring importance for the Group's literary history, it is necessary to look at more than just the last chapter; the organising ethical principles that the book sets forth also need to be understood. The simplest way to do this might be to begin with the summaries of the most important truths and common errors that Moore gives at the end of his book – summaries that reveal the twofold, affirmative and critical nature of Moore's ethical revelation for Bloomsbury. Moore sums up the positive principles of his ethics as follows:

> That things intrinsically good or bad are many and various; that most of them are 'organic unities', in the peculiar and definite sense to which I have confined the term; and that our only means of deciding upon their intrinsic value and its degree, is by carefully distinguishing exactly what the thing is, about which we ask the question, and then looking to see whether it has or has not the unique predicate 'good' in any of its various degrees: these are the conclusions, upon the truth of which I desire to insist.

The question of intrinsic value is one of the two essential questions in ethics, Moore continues; the other – 'What ought we to do?' – is about the values of means rather than ends and must not be confused with the first question, though its answers necessarily depend upon it. Then Moore lists the negative principles of *Principia Ethica*:

> The practice of asking what things are virtues or duties, without distinguishing what these terms mean; the practice of asking what ought to be here and now, without distinguishing whether as means or end – for its own sake or for that of its results; the search for one single *criterion* of right or wrong, without the recognition that in order to discover a criterion we

must first know what things *are* right or wrong; and the neglect of the principle of 'organic unities' – these sources of error have hitherto been almost universally prevalent in Ethics. (p. 223)

Principia Ethica's originality lies not in any one of these principles, most of which were familiar to Cambridge philosophers of Moore's time, but in the rigour with which, from the book's epigraph and dedication to its culminating Ideal, Moore combined these principles into his own organic whole.

The epigraph of *Principia Ethica* is Bishop Butler's famous 'Everything is what it is, and not another thing.' Some philosophers have expressed alarm that a work of ethics has a tautology for its motto, but in the book the quotation is applied to the principle of organic unity, which holds that organic wholes are what they are – wholes – and not sums of their parts. The teachers and followers to whom the book is dedicated made up a kind of organic unity of their own in the Apostles, some of whose members were to belong to that organic unity known as the Bloomsbury Group.

In the important Preface to *Principia Ethica* Moore begins to exemplify Bishop Butler's saying by stating that precise questions must precede the search for answers and then drawing the most fundamental distinction of his book – that between questions of means and questions of ends. Moore's entire ethics and Bloomsbury's are based on this distinction. He argues here that ethical questions about ends – about things that ought to exist for their own sakes – are matters of unprovable intuition, whereas questions of means – actions we ought to perform – are not at all intuitional but capable of being proved according to their results in attaining intuited ends. The ethics of the Victorian intuitionalists have been reversed here. They had held that the rightness or wrongness of an action involved ineluctable intuitions about the nature of duty. Moore, however, confines intuition to his ethical ends and is uncompromisingly utilitarian in the insistence that right and wrong apply only to the consequences of actions. But he was hardly utilitarian in his intuited ends. Moore's intuitional consequentialism is also very different from the vitalistic self-realisation ethics of modern writers such as Shaw and D. H. Lawrence. (Strachey was once asked by a Christian at Cambridge if he maintained that the end of existence was self-realisation, and he replied, 'That certainly would be the *end*' – CB/*OF*, pp. 29–30). For Bloomsbury, questions about self-realisation had to do with ethical means, which were to be evaluated according to the ends they aimed at, and not as ends in themselves.

After establishing the essential difference between means and ends, Moore spends the first chapter of *Principia Ethica* in a discussion of the nature of good. Three subsequent chapters are spent refuting various types of ethical theories, and the last two chapters discuss ethical means and ends, respectively. Thus half the book is devoted to clearing away ethical confusions, and half to establishing 'the fundamental principles of ethical reasoning' (p. ix). *Principia Ethica* offered not conclusions to be accepted but principles of how to think about value and how to act upon these principles. This was its permanent significance for Bloomsbury.

Chapter 1 of *Principia Ethica* is on that endlessly debated Bloomsbury subject, the meaning of good. Involved are three distinct principles fundamental to the moral assumptions of Bloomsbury's literary work. The first is Moore's indefinable, non-natural conception of good. Attempts to define this ultimate reference for definitions of value produce what Moore rhetorically calls 'the naturalistic fallacy'. This was the phrase that so amused Dickinson with its innuendo of vice, but Moore probably derived it from Ruskin's pathetic fallacy'. Ruskin's fallacy is committed when human characteristics are attributed to inanimate nature, Moore's naturalistic fallacy when natural characteristics are attributed to intellectual entities. Good, according to Moore's formulation, is not natural because it is atemporal. Attempts to equate good with pleasure, happiness, self-fulfilment or the like all must fail, because the goodness of these things remains an open question: we can still ask whether happiness and the rest are good, which shows they cannot be the same thing.

Moore's very influential conception of good has been much debated in modern moral philosophy. In the literary history of Bloomsbury, however, its importance is to be seen in the way an intuited, indefinable, immaterial, and timeless conception of ultimate value was at the centre of the ethics Bloomsbury learned at Cambridge. Unlike Dickinson, McTaggart, and Russell, Moore appears not to have had any mystical experiences, but one of his late Apostle papers tries to describe, through an associative method he called 'literary', a quasi-mystical notion of rebirth (Cambridge papers). In the philosophic method of *Principia Ethica* there was no defining the indefinable. Yet there are affinities, as Keynes noted, between the Cambridge influences of Platonism, neo-Platonism and Moorism on Bloomsbury, and Fry once called such followers of Moore as Leonard Woolf mystics (VW/*RF*, p. 270).

The second fundamental Bloomsbury ethical principle expressed in the first chapter of *Principia Ethica* was Moore's consequentialist claim that 'good' was the ultimate ethical term, and that 'right' correctly described only means to good ends. All talk, therefore, of duty or virtue referred simply to means whose moral value depended upon the ends they were directed toward. Here Bloomsbury saw Moore's analysis as a radical refutation of the Victorian moralists' efforts to obscure the merely instrumental value of virtues like patriotism and chastity. Indeed, it was too radical for Russell, under whose criticism Moore limited his claim in *Ethics* to the assertion that good and right were 'logically equivalent' ('Reply', pp. 558–9). But that too was useful for Bloomsbury's criticism of Victorianism.

The third basic principle of Moore's first chapter is not to be found, as the others are, in Plato, Kant or Sidgwick. This is the principle of organic unity, which Moore defines as a whole whose value 'bears no regular proportion to the sum of the values of its parts' (p. 27). The most valuable of these organic wholes, Moore argues in his last chapter, are states of mind involving beauty and personal relations, but the evaluative principle of organic unity applies to all such wholes, whether they are good, bad or indifferent. Their values are what they are as wholes, not as sums of their parts. With this notion of a whole, Moore can avoid the reductive Benthamite calculations of goods, which the naturalistic fallacy had shown were not simply matters of pleasure or pain. But why Moore called these wholes organic is unclear. He says they are not Hegelian (pp. 30–1) and they are not Coleridgean either. (In *Ethics* Moore dropped the adjective and just called them wholes.) Nevertheless, the principle of organic unity, like the naturalistic fallacy, has implications for Bloomsbury's formalist aesthetics.

V

In the second, third and fourth chapters of *Principia Ethica* Moore uses his analytic method, Realistic epistemology and ethical principles to criticise naturalistic and metaphysical systems of ethics. Evolutionism, hedonism and egoism are all rejected in the philosophies of Spencer, Mill and Sidgwick. Hedonism is refuted with Plato's argument that pleasure alone cannot be good because memory and therefore consciousness are also required for it (pp. 87–9). Metaphysical ethics Moore refutes by distinguishing again between existence and perception, between thought and truth; he vigorously attacks the claim that we cannot separate something's being good from our preferring it, or between something being true and our thinking it true. With this separation, Moore believed, Kant's whole Copernican revolution collapsed (pp. 132–3). Yet Kant's terminology was still preserved in the Apostles, with their talk of phenomena and reality, and some of it carried over into Bloomsbury with their talk of reality as a realm of things-in-themselves by which phenomenal appearances and means were to be understood and evaluated.

Then in the controversial last two chapters of *Principia Ethica* Moore returns to the two basic ethical questions with which he began. 'Ethics in Relation to Conduct' discusses what we ought to do; 'The Ideal' considers what things are good in themselves to a high degree. The penultimate chapter was the one Keynes said Bloomsbury paid no attention to, though his own work on probability carefully criticised it. Moore is his most consequentialist in relating ethics to conduct. Our duty, he argues, 'can only be defined as that action which will cause more good to exist in the Universe than any possible alternative' (p. 148). Leonard Woolf remembered the interminable discussions with his friends at Cambridge about the consequences of conduct in imaginary and real situations (*S*, p. 149). These may have been partly the result of Moore's surprisingly conservative general conclusion about the difficulties, not to mention impossibilities, of calculating the consequences of actions, especially over indefinite periods of time: 'the individual can . . . be confidently recommended *always* to conform to rules which are both generally useful and generally practised' (p. 164). In philosophical jargon, Moore is a rule-utilitarian here, but, according to Keynes, the immoralism of himself and his friends stemmed from their act-utilitarianism: 'we entirely repudiated a personal liability on us to obey general rules. We claimed the right to judge every individual case on its merits. . . . We repudiated entirely customary morals, conventions and traditional wisdom' (*CW*, x 446). (Moore put his

finger on the exaggeration here by noting in his own copy of
Keynes's *Two Memoirs* that conventions and wisdom were
'utterly different things' – Levy, pp. 157–8).

A year after the publication of *Principia Ethica* Lytton Strachey
wrote to Leonard Woolf in Ceylon that he now realised that
Christ had preached a doctrine of ends but had produced an
anarchic result by entirely ignoring means (29.iv.04, pT).
Keynes seems to be saying something similar about the way
Bloomsbury took Moore's doctrine. The evidence of Keynes's
own Cambridge writing, as well as Strachey's and Leonard
Woolf's, does not tend to support Keynes's recollection, but
there is no doubt that the ends discussed in the last chapter of
Principia Ethica were of supreme importance to himself and his
fellow Apostles.

The evolution of Moore's conception of the Ideal makes its
importance clearer. The very first paper Moore wrote for the
Apostles was entitled 'What End?' and the answer given was
'pleasure'. Under the influence of the Apostles, Moore's Ideal
became permanently Platonised. Dickinson, McTaggart and
Russell all agreed around the turn of the century that the Ideal
involved loving states of mind, though there was some disagreement as to whether these states also included the contemplation
of goodness, truth and beauty. Moore's second Apostle paper
maintained that love – homosexual or heterosexual – was the
aim of life, though the young puritan admitted it included the possibly disagreeable element of copulation. In subsequent papers
he developed his Platonic Ideal by criticising lust, self-love and
masturbation. In 1898 Moore gave a series of lectures at the
London School of Ethics and Social Philosophy, one of whose
directors was Leslie Stephen; they were entitled *The Elements of
Ethics* and became the basis for *Principia Ethica*. Moore concluded
in these lectures that the Ideal had been best described by Plato
and Aristotle as 'Θεωρία or a feeling of contemplation of all that
is true and beautiful and good' (Rosenbaum, 'Moore's *Elements*',
p. 223). And in his first published ethical essay on the value of
religion, which was originally a lecture at the same school,
Moore asserted that, because there is no evidence one way or
another for the existence of God, religious emotion and worship
would lose little of their effectiveness if directed toward ideal
objects in literature and people worthy of all our affection
('Value', p. 98). Matthew Arnold's influence is acknowledged in

the essay, but more interesting is its direct anticipation of the aesthetic experience and love that become the ultimate ideal ends of *Principia Ethica*.[4]

Moore wrote the last chapter of *Principia Ethica* in the spring before the book was published, and its plan was suggested to him in conversation with a friend – perhaps H. O. Meredith, who was a close friend of Forster's (Moore, 'Autobiography', p. 25; Levy, p. 215). 'The Ideal' addresses the second fundamental question of ethics: what ought to *be*. On its answers depends the first question: what ought we to *do*. By 'Ideal' Moore means 'good in itself to a high degree' (p. 184). The greatest of these goods he describes in a famous sentence: 'By far the most valuable things, which we know or can imagine, are certain states of consciousness, which may be roughly described as the pleasures of human intercourse and the enjoyment of beautiful objects' (p. 188).

It is a little surprising, given the simplicity of Moore's Ideal, how often it has been misunderstood. Occasionally Moore has been called an Idealist, which confounds epistemological and ethical Idealism. Sometimes it is stated that personal affections and aesthetic enjoyments are the only goods in *Principia Ethica*, though Moore explicitly states that there are 'a vast number of different things, each of which has intrinsic value . . .' (p. 27), in addition to all the things that have instrumental value. Knowledge, for example, can be a great instrumental good and also of considerable intrinsic value, if not as much as affection or aesthetic appreciation. And Moore never maintained that intrinsic value consisted merely of states of mind. Consciousness is, of course, a necessary condition of intrinsic value, but it is hardly a sufficient one.

The indefinable nature of good and the intuitive character of intrinsic value make the Ideal impossible to prove or disprove. It is a matter of self-evident intuition. But Moore does have a method for discarding inadequate Ideals: he isolates absolutely what might be considered good in a high degree and then inquires what its value would be if it existed completely alone for ever. This method of isolation brings out the difference between instrumental and intrinsic goods as well as demonstrating the importance of organic unity. The isolation, for example, of a beautiful object no one could ever be aware of shows that it has little or no value in itself; the same is true of a state of consciousness that is not conscious of anything. But combined, the consciousness of a beautiful object can be something of very high value – but a value that is not, however, the additive result of its two essentially valueless components. This example also illustrates the organic unity of analysis and intuition in Moore's own moral philosophy that made it such a revelation for Bloomsbury.

Moore's ethical Ideal is also, clearly, an aesthetic Ideal, which made *Principia Ethica* even more exciting for the young Bloomsbury Apostles who were hoping to become writers. Moore's interest in aesthetics appears in his Apostle papers and Sunday essays, a number of which various Bloomsbury Apostles, including Fry, heard. In an early one entitled simply 'Aesthetics', Moore began by accepting Kant's separation of aesthetic sensation from volition or cognition and went on to argue for an expressive theory of art similar to the one Tolstoy would make famous in *What Is Art?* a few years later. Both doctrines reappear in the aesthetics of Fry and Bell. In later papers Moore attacked the theories of both aesthetes – called 'art-fanatics' by Moore – and philistines, because both make art's value primarily instrumental: the aesthetes by emphasising art's expressive or symbolic nature, and the philistines by insisting on art's mimetic aspects. (Moore had not yet developed his notion of an organic whole here.) He uncompromisingly insisted that the value of art, whatever else it might be, was also intrinsic, and this too became a fundamental assumption of Bloomsbury's aesthetics.

Moore's aesthetics in *Principia Ethica* analyses both personal affections and the asethetic enjoyments into the elements of emotion, cognition, true belief and beauty. Errors in emotion produce mistakes in taste, while those of cognition result in mistaken judgements. Here was material for those endless discussions in which Moore's followers tried to calculate the comparable value of affectionate and aesthetic states of mind. True belief was also centrally involved in these scholastic analyses, and it led Moore to some naïve conclusions about the nature of art. Moore's profound belief in common-sense reality was offended by the aesthetes' separation of nature and art, and he asserted in *Principia Ethica* that 'a just appreciation of nature and of real persons may maintain its equality with an equally just appreciation of the products of artistic imagination, in spite of the greater beauty of the latter' (p. 200) – to which Clive Bell responded in the margin of his copy of *Principia Ethica*, 'Has the author any definite idea of what he means when he speaks of the products of artistic imagination. Why is a landscape by Crome to be considered as an *object less real* than Mousehold Heath?' (*Bloomsbury Word and Image*, p. 14). It was a relief for Bell to write in *Art* – whose ideas of significant form and aesthetic emotion owed so much to *Principia Ethica* – that Moore no longer believed inanimate nature a good in itself (*A*, p. 111).

Beauty in Moore's analysis of the Ideal is defined as 'that of which the admiring contemplation is good in itself' (p. 201).[5] Found in both personal relations and aesthetic experience, this notion of beauty looks rather like Platonic love. And, by defining beauty in terms of good, Moore is able to bring all his criticisms of the naturalistic fallacy in ethics to bear on aesthetics, where, he says, the fallacy is just as common. Like the good, beauty is intuitive, indefinable, non-natural in the sense of being timeless, and can belong to organic wholes. The discussion of organic wholes leads Moore to distinguish between classic and romantic styles in art, the former aiming at the greatest value for the whole and the latter the greatest value for some part. He thought that 'the distinctively *aesthetic* temperament' tended to prefer the classical style as he had defined it, and Bloomsbury agreed.

The last part of the last chapter of *Principia Ethica* is about positive evils. Like their Ideal opposites, they too can be organic unities and mixed goods, which may be good or bad on the whole or as a whole. ('Good on the whole' and 'good as a whole' were almost code phrases in Bloomsbury.) Moore's quite fierce puritanism occasionally emerges here, as when he justifies, in a passage cited by Keynes, vindictive punishment as part of a mixed good, or when lasciviousness is ranked with cruelty as a great intrinsic evil.

Maynard Keynes thought that, beautiful as they were in their ideality, the basic intuitions of *Principia Ethica* were too few and too limited to fit mature experience. He particularly complained about the timelessness of Moore's Ideal, arguing that the value of organic unities had, among other things, to be considered temporally (*CW*, x 436, 444). Leonard Woolf did not agree with Keynes that Moore's ethics excluded political or social action at Cambridge or later, but one might wonder how far Leonard Woolf would have gone along with Moore's flat assertion that the Ideals of personal affections and aesthetic enjoyments were not just 'the rational ultimate end of human action' but also 'the sole criterion of social progress' (p. 189).

Moore left the Ideal out of his *Ethics*, which was published almost a decade after *Principia Ethica*. In his autobiography he preferred the later work because it was clearer and had fewer invalid arguments, yet, when *Principia Ethica* was reprinted in 1922, Moore wrote that he was 'still in agreement with its main tendency and conclusions' (p. xii). So was Bloomsbury.

VI

Principia Ethica was the climax of Bloomsbury's Apostolic philosophical education. When as an old man Forster wanted to describe the Cambridge of his autobiographical novel *The Longest Journey*, he identified it as 'the Cambridge of G. E. Moore which I knew at the beginning of the century: the fearless uninfluential Cambridge that sought for reality and cared for truth' (*LJ*, p. lxviii) – uninfluential, that is, in the great world, but not in Bloomsbury. The passionate lucidity and purity of Moore's thought and character were embodied, for Bloomsbury, in *Principia Ethica*. His intensely felt and argued distinctions between the acts and objects of consciousness, between analytic and intuitive knowledge, between instrumental and intrinsic value, between parts and wholes, combined with a love of affection and beauty that distilled for the Apostles and Bloomsbury the best of Greek, German and English philosophy. Moore's representative philosophical ideas – representative because many of them are also to be found in the Cambridge philosophy of Sidgwick, Dickinson, McTaggart and Russell, among others – remained among the fundamental philosophical assumptions of Bloomsbury's writings, even for those who were not Apostles or did not go to Cambridge. A year before her death, Virginia Woolf used a measuring metaphor to describe how Cambridge men such as her father, Dickinson and Moore, for all their disturbing lack of imagination, provided her with an enduring standard of intellectual integrity:

> If I am in the same room with other types, like Harold Nicolson or Hugh Walpole, I have my Cambridge intellectual yard measure handy; and say silently: How terribly you fall short. How you miss the mark, here and here and here. But at the same time I am seduced; and feel that my measure has been proved faulty. The Harold Nicolsons and the Hugh

Walpoles give me colour and warmth; they amuse and stimulate me. But still I do not respect them as I respect George
Moore. (*MB*, p. 109)

Moore's great importance for Bloomsbury has slowly been
recognised, but they were not the only writers he influenced. His
brother and son were the poets T. Sturge and Nicholas Moore.
Sturge Moore made G. E. Moore's philosophy known to his
friends William Butler Yeats and Wyndham Lewis. Yeats hated
what he took to be the Realism of Moore and Russell, and his
correspondence with Sturge Moore (published together with
some footnotes by G. E. Moore) is an amusing episode in the
interrelations of modern English literature and philosophy
(*Yeats and Moore*).[6] Lewis took Moore as something of an ally
in *Time and Western Man* and again in *Men without Art*, where,
ironically, he attacked Virginia Woolf because he thought her
work expressed Bergson's *durée* rather than Moore's dualistic
conception of time, which is what her fiction actually assumes.
Earlier T. E. Hulme, who thought Moore's philosophy could be
reconciled with Bergson's, believed there was support for the
criticism of humanism and romanticism in Moore's critiques of
empiricism and in what Hulme took to be his objective ethics
(*Speculations*, pp. 39, 62). But a more enduring influence of Moore
on English literature outside of Bloomsbury may have been in
the work of I. A. Richards, who studied philosophy under Moore
for seven years and then reacted negatively to his influence ever
after. 'He could hardly ever believe that people could mean what
they said; I've come to think they hardly ever can say what they
mean', was Richards's summary (*Complementarities*, p. 257).
There were more than just antithetical connections between
Moore's philosophical analysis and Richards's critical principles
and practice, but this is a matter that belongs to Bloomsbury's
literary history in the 1920s, when Richards attacked the formalist aesthetics of Bell and Fry.
      Moore's greatest literary influence, however, was on Blooms-
bury. For all of them except Fry perhaps, Moore was the most
important modern thinker. Yet, with the exception of Keynes,
none in the Group took a professional interest in philosophy.
Young Bloomsbury wanted to be writers, and this long excursion
to Cambridge has attempted to describe how their education in
modern writing and ideas came to some extent through the

classics and history they formally studied at King's and Trinity, but more through independent reading and discussions in groups like the Apostles. There was also independent writing – Apostle papers and other society essays, as well as poems, plays, and parodies. An account of these Cambridge texts, as well as the memoirs Bloomsbury wrote of Cambridge, concludes the Victorian literary history of the Bloomsbury Group.

Part Four
Cambridge Writings

11 Memoirs, Apostle Papers and Other Essays

I

Bloomsbury wrote about Cambridge throughout their literary careers. Two of Forster's novels, *The Longest Journey* and *Maurice*, are centrally concerned with Cambridge, and the fragment 'Arctic Summer' sensationally ends there. *Goldsworthy Lowes Dickinson* is a Cambridge biography, while a number of Forster's essays and memoirs return to Cambridge subjects and friends. In Virginia Woolf's work, some of the most expressive rooms in *Jacob's Room*, *A Room of One's Own*, *The Waves* and *Roger Fry* are Cambridge rooms. Keynes's *Essays in Biography* includes several Cambridge lives. Four of the subjects in Strachey's *Portraits in Miniature* are of Cambridge men.

These Cambridge writings as well as the different kinds of memoirs that the Group wrote about Cambridge belong to later periods of Bloomsbury's literary history. But there are also various unpublished or posthumously published non-academic pieces – Apostle papers, essays of one kind or another, poems, plays, parodies – that were written at Cambridge, for their own sake, for friends, for undergraduate societies, or occasionally for Cambridge periodicals. These texts are primarily interesting for their display of the literary and philosophical education that the Group received at Cambridge. With them the literary history of Bloomsbury at Cambridge can be concluded.

Before considering these writings, we should finish describing the published and unpublished Cambridge memoirs that have been so valuable for the reconstruction of the Group's university education. These memoirs exist in very different states and forms: short and lengthy fragments, finished essays, rather intimate Memoir Club papers, full-dress autobiographies, critical discussions, memorial tributes. Taken together, their Cambridge visions of encounters with one another's personalities, ideas and influence reveal the beginnings of Bloomsbury.

II

Clive Bell once remarked in a Memoir Club paper written toward the end of the Second World War that the Club was turning into a seminar for the study of Bloomsbury's origins (pTC). This was not really a new development; almost from its inception the Memoir Club heard papers about Bloomsbury's Cambridge beginnings. The Cambridge memoirs have survived in various forms: fragments by Forster and MacCarthy; actual Memoir Club papers by Keynes, Grant, Virginia Woolf, Vanessa and Clive Bell; and reworked, expanded essays and autobiographies by Clive Bell again and Leonard Woolf. Only Strachey and Fry, the first members of the Group to die, left no memoirs of Trinity or King's, although Fry did leave a visual record of his Cambridge in portraits of Dickinson, McTaggart and Edward Carpenter, and later of Russell and Forster. Fry also designed the masthead for the short-lived *Cambridge Fortnightly*, which he edited with Nathaniel Wedd and E. F. Benson (Laing, *RF*, p. 237). It represented the light of Cambridge in 'a tremendous sun of culture rising behind King's College Chapel' (VW/*RF*, p. 56).

E. M. Forster's fragment on the origins of Bloomsbury is one of the most amusingly revealing of the Group's Cambridge memoirs. He recalls first hearing Strachey's extraordinary voice in the rooms of that non-Bloomsbury Apostle G. M. Trevelyan, whom Forster described as a moral force without influence. The meeting with Strachey was not followed up, because Forster felt too inexperienced 'to risk knowing a person with a voice, like that'. He met Duncan Grant later in another Apostle's rooms, and Forster began to be haunted by his paintings with their slight but unfulfilled 'promise of pornography'. A meeting with Clive Bell in London turned into a quarrel over the worth of the Second Empire, Bell defending its civilised values and Forster attacking its inequality. The failure of rapport had slight consequences for Bloomsbury, Forster thought, but his discovery of Roger Fry was rather momentous. Before becoming an Apostle, Forster had heard Fry lecture at Cambridge on Venetian art.

(Strachey heard Fry on Florentine art in 1900 and found him interesting, if a little abstruse – MH/*LS*, p. 148.) Having read Ruskin, Forster felt a proprietary interest in Venice, yet seldom had he listened to more enjoyable and profitable lectures. And, as Fry began to lecture less on influence and more about form, Forster's initiation into Bloomsbury's formalism began:

> There were hints of the coming reign of Mass and Line, and of Treatment, that undying worm. 'It's not the Subject that matters, it's the Treatment.' Roger didn't say this at the time, nor may he ever have said it, nor may anyone in Bloomsbury exactly have said it, yet it may fairly be called the Bloomsbury undertone. . . .   (pKC)

How audible this undertone was in Fry's lectures at the turn of the century is a question, but Forster thought he heard it at Cambridge, before anyone else in Bloomsbury.

Forster remembered another Cambridge encounter that had critical implications for Bloomsbury. In a brief published tribute Forster recalled reading a paper at the King's literary society, the Apennines, and having it pulled apart by several auditors, including 'a quiet, dark young man with a charming voice and manner, who sat rather far back in the room, and who for all his gentleness knew exactly what he wanted to say and in the end how to say it' (SPR/*BG*, p. 156). This was Desmond MacCarthy, who a little later with G. E. Moore presumably voted to elect Forster to the Apostles. Looking backwards, Forster saw MacCarthy as the kind of critic who always sat rather far back in the room and knew his own mind – an Affable Hawk even at Cambridge.

Desmond MacCarthy's own Cambridge memoirs are typically scant and incomplete. For a while he thought Cambridge might be his spiritual home before deciding he did not have one, not even in Bloomsbury (*M*, p. 173). Like the rest of Bloomsbury he was educated at Cambridge, as he said, 'by my friends – and myself' rather than by his teachers (p. 205). MacCarthy converged on Bloomsbury from three different approaches, he recalled. The first was through meeting Clive Bell on a train to Cambridge in 1901; he enjoyed vicariously his companion's opulence, his 'eager and enjoying temperament', which reminded him of his time at Cambridge. It turned out, of course, that they had friends in common, including the younger Apostles like Lytton Strachey, who provided MacCarthy with his second approach to Bloomsbury (pp. 173–5). MacCarthy's memoir breaks off before he describes the third approach through meeting the Stephen sisters at home in London. But elsewhere, in a critical discussion of Strachey (which Virginia Woolf quoted in 'The Leaning Tower'), MacCarthy described the Cambridge spirit of his and Strachey's Apostolic generation, with its talk of good ends in themselves; he went on to describe how Russell and Moore had replaced McTaggart and were followed in turn by Strachey himself, whose influence fixed the attention of his younger contemporaries not on abstract reasoning, as McTaggart, Moore and Russell had done, but on human relations, on 'psychological gossip' (p. 41).

MacCarthy's account of the Apostles anticipates to some extent the most widely known of all Bloomsbury's Cambridge memoirs, but he does not mention Keynes. In 'My Early Beliefs' Keynes has little to say about his personal relations with Bloomsbury beyond labelling Strachey a Voltairean, Woolf a rabbi, Bell 'a gay and amiable dog', Sydney-Turner a quietist, Forster 'the elusive colt of a dark horse', and himself a non-conformist (*CW*, x 435). And, besides conflating two quite different periods of Bloomsbury's history, Keynes omits from his Memoir Club paper an important early belief that is also missing from all the other published Bloomsbury memoirs of Cambridge. Keynes taxed his contemporaries for ignoring the vulgar passions in their rational Moorean ethics, while he ignored, in his memoir at least, the vulgar passion of homosexuality, which so preoccupied him and many of his brother Apostles.

If Clive Bell was 'a gay and amiable dog' at Cambridge, he thought Keynes could have known this only by hearsay, for they were not friends at Cambridge and met only after his marriage to Vanessa in 1907. Clive Bell's Cambridge memoirs, published and unpublished, are almost as extensive as Leonard Woolf's, which they usefully complement because Clive Bell was not an Apostle. That is why he did not meet Keynes earlier, or Roger Fry. (Virginia Woolf thought it was not until 1910 that he brought Fry into Bloomsbury as 'the most interesting person he had met since Cambridge days' [*MB*, p. 197], but Vanessa remembered seeing Fry at Cambridge early in the century, having dinner with him at Desmond MacCarthy's after Leslie

Stephen's death, and then meeting him at Cambridge with Clive Bell in 1908, after which time he began to be a 'real person' to her [VB/pAG].) Not being an Apostle, Clive Bell thought, as was noted in the chapter on Bloomsbury's Cambridge literary education, that the first foundation stone of Bloomsbury was laid at Trinity by the Midnight Society (see p. 129). The second, according to his unpublished memoir of Bloomsbury, was laid when Thoby Stephen invited him home to meet his sisters. His friendship with Thoby kept the Cambridge origins of Bloomsbury from being completely Apostolic, and Strachey used to pretend that Clive and Thoby were in love with each other. 'Buggery was just coming in as we were going out', Bell wrote with more candour than he could in the published recollections of *Old Friends*; both Stephen and Bell laughed at the homosexuality of their friends, which Thoby labelled 'the Singalese vice', apparently alluding to Leonard Woolf's accounts of Ceylon. Clive Bell even claimed to know what Moore had said on the subject: 'You will all agree, said the great dialectician, that it is ridiculous to copulate with a woman, wherefore *a fortiori* it is ridiculous to copulate with a man' (pTC). In his published memoirs, Bell was more serious about Moore, calling him 'the dominant influence in all our lives' at Cambridge and, as some maintained, ever afterwards (*OF*, p. 28). Certainly his influence on Clive Bell's writings was deep, which shows that Moore's influence on Bloomsbury did not come only from Apostles.

Clive Bell's memoir of Lytton Strachey suggests that their relationship was partly based on a shared interest in the visual arts. Like Strachey's other friends, Clive Bell was influenced by Strachey's enthusiasm for the Elizabethans and Pope. But Bell and Strachey also met occasionally in the National Gallery or the Fitzwilliam Museum, and one of Bell's earliest attempts at aesthetics was the result of Strachey's wondering what the uninitiated thought of a Degas reproduction Bell had on his door (*OF*, p. 29). Nevertheless, Strachey's taste in painting remained incorrigibly literary, and he later asked Clive or Vanessa to try persuading Duncan Grant to paint beautiful pictures instead of making post-impressionist 'coagulations of distressing oddments' as he was then doing (*OF*, p. 134).

One last piece of Cambridge autobiographical writing by Clive Bell is worth some attention, and that is a late, unpublished fragmentary novel called 'Vocation'. In the early pages of this experimental mixing of fiction and Bloomsbury fact, the narrator describes how one Reginald Palgrave, a wealthy Trinity undergraduate, discovers in the course of some military pursuits that he has a vocation to write. Palgrave turns literary, invites Lytton Strachey and the narrator to tea, is elected to the X Society, buys the *Cambridge Review*, 'in which we had all written', reads *Principia Ethica*, venerates Moore, laughs at McTaggart, and gets a second in history, like the autobiographical narrator, who observes, 'An Apostle I do not think he ever became, but I am not in a position to be sure' (pTC). 'Vocation' trails off in Edwardian London, but there is enough of it to indicate that, interesting as this combination of genres is, Clive Bell did not miss his vocation as a novelist.

III

Cambridge does not enter into Leonard Woolf's autobiographical fiction, but the hundred pages he devoted to it in *Sowing* are, as the preceding chapters here have shown, the fullest account of what Cambridge meant to Bloomsbury, because he describes both the personal relations and what he calls 'the historical psychology of an era' that helped condition these relations (p. 162). It conditioned Bloomsbury as well, which Leonard Woolf once described, in an unpublished note on the Group, as not in fact a group 'but a company of personal friends whose residential roots were in Bloomsbury and their spiritual roots in Cambridge' (pS).

Leonard Woolf remembered, after his careers in Ceylon and London, that his first impression of Trinity College was that of a jungle. But after meeting Saxon Sydney-Turner, with whom he shared rooms for three years, then Lytton Strachey and Thoby Stephen, the place became an intellectual garden of delights. Clive Bell was not, Leonard Woolf thought, an intellectual like his other Bloomsbury friends when he came to Trinity, but he became one as a devoted follower of Stephen and Strachey. This is not exactly Clive Bell's view in *Old Friends*; he appears, at any rate, to have been closer friends with Thoby than anyone else in Bloomsbury, sharing with him a non-Apostolic nonchalance about intellectual argument and an appreciation of country pastimes. They were the most worldly in their set, Bell remembered, smoking cigars and talking about hunting; Sydney-Turner was the most learned, Strachey the most mature – and Leonard Woolf the most passionate and poetical (*OF*, p. 27), which is not exactly the self-image projected in *Sowing* either. Yet Leonard Woolf's portraits of Bell as a blood turned intellectual, of the cocooned Sydney-Turner, the arrogant, diffident, ribald and passionate Strachey, the monumental Thoby Stephen, the lovable, wilful Keynes, the pure genius of Moore, and of the himself – intense, tremulous, by turns elated and depressed – make Leonard Woolf's memoir an absorbing literary text. There are also briefer glimpses in *Sowing* of two other members of Bloomsbury, who appear as comets moving in and out of the solar system of Moore's Apostolic friendship: Forster, nick-named 'the Taupe' by Strachey, because he travelled under-ground intellectually and emotionally, popping up suddenly with some perceptive remark, and MacCarthy, the brilliant talker and promising novelist (pp. 171–4). Finally there were the beautiful and rather frightening Stephen sisters, whom Woolf met in Thoby's rooms under the chaperonage of their Newnham aunt. 'Stephenesque' is the term used to describe the monolithic character of the Stephens by one who would marry into the family and become in his own Woolfian way just as monolithic (pp. 182–4).

Leonard Woolf's *magnum opus* was a study of Europe after the French Revolution in which he tried to trace connections bet-ween personal and what he called 'communal psychology'. Though he abandoned the work after *Principia Politica* in 1953, he was still interested in these psychological connections when he began his autobiography several years later. Among his intellec-tual Cambridge–Bloomsbury friends (he had another circle of non-intellectual friends, whom he discusses at some length in *Sowing*) Leonard Woolf found not the Moorean religion and morals of Keynes's memoir, but three profound and passionate early beliefs: in the value of friendship, of literature and music (but not art), and of truth. These interacting beliefs, stimulated by Swinburne and Whitman, James and Butler, Meredith and Ibsen, Moore and Russell, produced a communal spirit of revolt against Victorianism. But the symbolic example of the need for revolt that Leonard Woolf gives in *Sowing* was not a Victorian, literary or philosophical matter, nor one of personal relations. It was political: the martyrdom of Dreyfus (pp. 159–62). For

Woolf, of course, it was personal, because, as he wrote at the end of *Sowing*, '. . . nearly all Jews are both proud and ashamed of being Jews' (p. 196). Being Jewish in the time of Dreyfus meant that Leonard Woolf could not be as indifferent to politics as Keynes thought they all were. And, if the Dreyfus Affair was noticed much among Leonard Woolf's Cambridge friends and brother Apostles, his Jewishness must have helped make it so.

On one aspect of the revolt against Victorianism at Cambridge Leonard Woolf is as silent as Keynes. When he was criticised in 1968, along with a number of other biographers and autobiographers, for saying nothing about 'sexual deviation' among the Apostles, Leonard Woolf replied, first, that, since he was not a homosexual himself, it was irrelevant to his personal relations; second, that it was irrelevant to the subjects of *Sowing*; and, third, that, when he wrote the book 'it was still unusual to reveal facts which might be painful to living people, unless it was absolutely vital to mention them' (Rees; LW/'Case'). Only the last reason is really convincing. Strachey's and Keynes's sexuality affected all their personal relations at Cambridge and was a crucial aspect of the value of Cambridge friendship that *Sowing* celebrates. Yet one result of the possibly unavoidable reticence of Leonard Woolf and others is that the sexual mores of Cambridge in Bloomsbury's time have been taken to be more homogeneously homosexual than they actually were.

Virginia Woolf's recollections of the Cambridge Apostles in her Memoir Club paper on Old Bloomsbury were not written for publication and therefore she could be maliciously frank and funny about the brothers' sexual preferences. Later she wrote more seriously in 'A Sketch of the Past' that the Apostles were among those invisible presences that influence our lives but are never analysed in memoirs (see above, p. 83). In 'Old Bloomsbury' Virginia Woolf did analyse them a little, showing that she too was interested in the Group's communal psychology. For her, Bloomsbury's first, monastic chapter began not in the Midnight Society or the Apostles but at the Thursday evening gatherings in Gordon Square of Thoby's Cambridge friends. Clive Bell appeared to her there as a combination of sun god, romantic poet, and horseman; Lytton Strachey as an elongated, cultivated eccentric who might become a great poet; Leonard Woolf as a 'violent, trembling misanthropic Jew'; and Sydney-Turner as a prodigy of learning who always spoke the truth (*MB*, pp. 187–8). Thoby idealised his friends, most of whom his sisters had already met at Cambridge, and Vanessa recalled how he tried to persuade his disdainful half-brother Gerald Duckworth to publish these geniuses (SPR/*BG*, pp. 76–7). What was talked about on those Thursday evenings, both sisters agree, were subjects from *Principia Ethica*. Virginia Woolf's metaphor for these conversations was a bull fight:

> The bull might be 'beauty', might be 'good', might be 'reality'. Whatever it was, it was some abstract question that now drew out all our forces. Never have I listened so intently to each step and half-step in an argument. Never have I been at such pains to sharpen and launch my own little dart. And then what joy it was when one's contribution was accepted.   (*MB*, pp. 189–90)

But these early Bloomsbury versions of Apostolic discussions were crucially different from those at Cambridge in one respect: love had no place in them. Only years later, in the second chapter of Bloomsbury's history, after the Group had lost some of its innocence, did Virginia Woolf discover why these discussions were so 'astonishingly abstract'.

> I knew there were buggers in Plato's Greece; I suspected – it was not a question one could just ask Thoby – that there were buggers in Dr Butler's Trinity [College], Cambridge; but it never occurred to me that there were buggers even now in the Stephens' sitting room at Gordon Square. . . . I did not realize that love, far from being a thing they never mentioned, was in fact a thing which they seldom ceased to discuss.   (p. 194)

The society of buggers had advantages for a woman, but one could not show off there. In time, however, thanks to the wit and honesty of Lytton Strachey, love came to be discussed in mixed company and with such happy results that even Leslie Stephen's daughter thought her father might have hesitated before calling Thoby's Cambridge friends blackguards – his favourite term for sexual miscreants (p. 197).

Virginia Woolf's attitude towards those invisible presences, the Cambridge Apostles, remains ambivalent in her writing. She loved Cambridge, and she loved mocking it, as her parody of the Society that is discussed in the next chapter shows. E. M.

Forster, who was ambivalent about Virginia Woolf's feminist ambivalences, cherished a fantasy that she once hoaxed Cambridge by taking a degree disguised as Orlando (*2CD*, p. 239). She might have been accompanied there, as she was in the *Dreadnought* hoax of the Royal Navy, by Duncan Grant, the only man of Bloomsbury's original members who did not go to university.

Grant became such close friends with Lytton and James Strachey, Keynes and other Apostles that he was made a kind of adopted brother of the Society, according to an unpublished memoir of Grant's, so that his friends and lovers might continue their Apostolic conversations in his presence. Grant's memoir Club paper is entitled, with Apostolic and Forsterian allusiveness, 'Where Angels Fear to Tread'. Grant's attitude toward the Apostles is one of slightly bewildered amusement at their secret antics. He knew that the effect of the Society on Lytton Strachey had been very great. At Trinity Strachey discovered that he was capable of intimate friendships with men very different from himself, his wit contending with their charms; although these men included Thoby Stephen and Clive Bell, it was ultimately the Society, according to Grant, that made Strachey a writer by keeping him from becoming a scholar. Yet, because of their secrecy, Grant could never really understand the Apostles. Sheppard once left the Society's book in one of his drawers, but he could make no sense out of its rigmaroles and was embarrassed over how to return it. He also claimed not to understand how the handsome but phenomenal Hobhouse had become an Apostle. Less tongue in cheek, Grant noted that the secrecy of the Apostles hurt some of the Apostles' friends, like Francis Birrell. The Society, he thought, with its exclusive brotherhood, mock symbolism and Saturday-night conclaves, also served Strachey, Keynes and others as a substitute for religion. And of course there was the dominance of Moore – the young men's prophet, Vanessa Bell called him (SPR/*BG*, p. 77) – and all the talk was about the meaning of good, so that even Grant was persuaded to read *Principia Ethica*. But, 'as to the Real Meaning and Significance of being a Cambridge Apostle', he was unable, he says at the end of his memoir, to form any just conclusion ('Where Angels'). Duncan Grant was able, however, to leave some visual impressions of Cambridge in the wall panels he painted with Vanessa Bell in Keynes's rooms at King's after the war. Eight elongated figures, four nude males and four clothed females, stand there as amusingly ambiguous personifications of various Cambridge triposes (Shone, pp. 234–7).

IV

In the literary history of Bloomsbury, 'the Real Meaning and Significance' of the Cambridge Apostles that eluded Duncan Grant is more particularly exhibited in the Group's extant Apostle papers than anywhere else. These texts are the best evidence that the role of the Society in Bloomsbury's education was not just personal but substantively intellectual. They show that the candid pursuit of truth, which Sidgwick identified with the spirit of the Apostles, remained so with the Bloomsbury Apostles, even though the kinds of truth pursued became more introspective and intimate. The Apostle papers of six members of Bloomsbury appear to have survived. They have to do with philosophy – the beautiful, the true, the good, the real; with literature and painting; with politics; with personal relations; and, of course, with the Society itself. The interest of these papers lies primarily in their anticipations of ideas and attitudes to be found in the Group's later work, but their genre, as shaped by Apostolic custom, also had its effect on the Group's subsequent writings. Usually an Apostle paper was a brief, humorous yet serious attempt to answer a general, sometimes riddling, question that had been selected at the previous meeting. The question could be turned into almost anything in the course of the paper, while the discussion that followed and concluded with a vote could be on quite another question that had emerged. A paper written for the Society was thus an audience-oriented essay that presented an argument for discussion by the brothers, the purpose of the whole exercise being truth rather than victory. Apostle papers differed from other Cambridge-society essays chiefly in the group self-consciousness that their writers and hearers shared. They transmitted this to Bloomsbury, where the custom continued of reading papers to a group of friends in order to create truthful, intimate, amusing, inquiring conversation.

The oldest Bloomsbury Apostle papers are Roger Fry's. Nearly a dozen unpublished ones survive among his papers at King's College. The last one, however, was written some time after Fry had discovered Proust during the First World War. Typically entitled 'Do We Exist?' it is the closest Fry came to writing a memoir of his Apostolic education. As an Apostle in the late 1880s Fry recognised, in the company of McTaggart, Dickinson and Wedd, his incapacity for metaphysical dialectic, but this did not keep him from making a practical philosophy out of Epicureanism and Taoism that combined pleasure with humility in a life of the present moment. The question of his sceptical title is answered, Fry thinks, in the experience of love. Our egos are linked to the external world through Proustian configurations of sensation and memory; this is the real moral world of reciprocal human relations and not the ethical one of individual bodies whose rights preposterously exercise us. In one of his earliest Apostle papers, Fry also preferred Epicureanism to mysticism, Pater's Marius to his Marcus Aurelius. In another he criticised the Idealist as always something of an egoist, and made a case for the objectively minded man. The general drift of these papers is antinomian. In one interesting anticipation of a later Bloomsbury concern, entitled 'Ought We to Be Hermaphrodite?' Fry paused over the 'terrific thought' that no woman has ever existed or can exist as long as the Society admits only males to Apostolic reality; he then argues from Plato to biology that we are divided in soul as well as body, living in parts and particulars which are united not in the individual but in the eternal One – an unusual conclusion in Fry's writings.

In his Apostle papers and other Cambridge writings Fry was much concerned with art, of course. A paper entitled 'Mr Westcott or Mr Whistler' avoids the points of view of both the impressionist artist and the Kingsman bishop because Romanticism is declining into obscurity and sodomy, while morality has become Wordsworth's 'Stern Daughter of the Voice of God' – whom Fry reminds the brothers they decided with Dickinson some time ago not to elect. Fry seeks instead a synthesis (remarking, 'Hegel like murder will out') of the two kinds of art his paper is about: the pure or aesthetic, and the expressive or symbolic. This distinction was a popular one of the time and turns up later in G. E. Moore's Apostle papers.

What makes Fry's Cambridge essays on art especially noteworthy in his development and Bloomsbury's are his efforts to justify his own work in science and art against the Idealistic metaphysics of Dickinson and McTaggart. He denied in one paper, for example, that the artist had to be a physiologist, because the facts of experience had nothing to do with physiology; Pan and Apollo still lived. Yet science and art were not irreconcilable. There are hints in Fry's Cambridge papers that he considered them both to be not phenomenal, and therefore Apostolically unreal, but phenomenological. Roger Fry's unsuccessful fellowship dissertation on art was entitled 'Some Problems of Phenomenology with Its Application to Greek Painting', and it examined the extent to which Greek painters were familiar with 'that science which deals with impressions made upon us by external objets in their entirety' (pKC). Fry avoids here and elsewhere the metaphysical question of the reality behind these impressions. The life-long interest in the epistemology of beauty that characterises his criticism, as much as does the 'Bloomsbury undertone' Forster heard at Cambridge, was an interest not in beauty itself but in the perception of beauty. The year before he died Fry began his lectures as Slade Professor of Art at Cambridge (he was the only member of Bloomsbury ever to be a professor there) with a plea for the academic study of art history that urged students to analyse their sensations rather than worry about the objectivity of beauty (*LL*, pp. 1–21). Some forty years earlier, in an Apostle paper, he had rejected Plato's absolute standard of beauty and avoided the philistine caprice of *de gustibus* to argue against McTaggart that beauty inheres in the way we order our perceptions. Fry cited here and elsewhere in his Apostle papers the work of a philosopher of science who had been at King's as an undergraduate and then as a fellow in the 1880s. Karl Pearson's *The Grammar of Science*, first published in 1892, is an attempt to free science from metaphysics by arguing that the real world science studies is the phenomenal one of consciousness, not the transcendental one of things-in-themselves. In Pearson's argument that science tries to describe our perceptual experience rather than explain it, Fry may have found a justification for his scientific as well as his aesthetic interests, and particularly for the impressionism that attracted him shortly after Cambridge.[1]

Fry's first art-teacher was the English impressionist Francis Bate, and Fry's first art review, which appeared in the *Cambridge Review* in 1893, was critical of a book on modern painting for failing to appreciate the genius of Monet. The author of the book was that other George Moore – the novelist – whom Fry praised, with qualifications, for an 'artist's view of art' which allowed Moore to attack the sentimental influence of subject on art (RF/'Modern Painting', pp. 211–14). Moore responded by urging Fry to develop his ideas on impressionism for the *Fortnightly Review*. He did so in a long essay called 'The Philosophy of Impressionism' which was never printed (Spalding, *RF*, p. 44). Fry argued in this culmination of his early unpublished writings on art that the impressionist owes allegiance not to any external facts, but only to the truth of his own visual impressions. What then of Keats's aesthetic equation? For Fry the art of the impressionist is to be defended on grounds of beauty, not truth. The artist has no obligation to scientific accuracy, yet in a way he resembles Pearson's kind of scientist, conceiving nature as a storehouse of experimental combinations of line, tone and colour. The artist's only duty to nature is to reject the unsuccessful combinations. 'The only excuse for a picture's being truthful', Fry concludes with Wildean succinctness, 'is that it is nevertheless beautiful' (pKC).

Virginia Woolf wrote that art for the Apostles in Roger Fry's time was the art of literature, 'and literature was half prophecy. Shelley and Whitman were to be read for their message rather than for their music' (*RF*, p. 51). This is not completely true of Fry's Cambridge writings. His developing aestheticism was stimulated more by painters than by writers, though he remained very literary in his aesthetic interests. 'The Philosophy of Impressionism' has an epigraph from Flaubert, and there are references in his Apostle papers and other Cambridge essays to Romantic and Victorian writers from Blake to Symonds. More than anyone else in Bloomsbury, Fry believed the arts were unified, and this had important implications for his first biographer.

V

Because Roger Fry was older and because he was more interested in art and science than philosophy, he brought into Bloomsbury a Cambridge intellectual outlook essentially independent of G. E. Moore's influence. Indeed, Fry found Bertrand Russell's philosophy more interesting than Moore's. But the next oldest member of Bloomsbury, Desmond MacCarthy, was closer to

Moore than anyone else in the Group, and this may initially have been his strongest tie with Bloomsbury. Only two of MacCarthy's Apostle papers have survived, both preserved by Moore among his own papers. 'Is this an awkward Age?' has already been mentioned, (see above, pp. 171–2). James's *The Awkward Age*, which had appeared the year before, in 1899, is the story of a young girl's coming to maturity in a very self-conscious group and at a time of transition to the modern age. MacCarthy alludes to the novel in his conclusion that the Apostles had always been 'a collection of affinities', and in the new age these affinities had changed from interests or capabilities to more personal relations. He thought the shift part of the *Zeitgeist*, to be seen in such places as the impressionistic criticism of art. Mac-Carthy did not disapprove of this change, for he felt 'the increased importance of persons as opposed to their opinions and qualities', which he found everywhere in the modern Awkward Age, made for increased sensitivity (Moore, Cambridge papers). MacCarthy's other Apostle paper, written earlier in 1900, displays this increased sensitivity to persons. It was on the traditional Apostolic topic of whether truth should be pursued at all costs. MacCarthy thought it should when applied to oneself but not necessarily in relations with others, whose well-being, like truth, was also an end. His paper illustrates again that the Society's increasingly self-conscious, analytic personal concerns, which began with Dickinson and were continued by Moore, Strachey and Keynes, did not preclude discussions of intellectual and moral substance.

E. M. Forster was elected to the Apostles in 1900. His papers may well have been Awkward Age ones too, but none that he wrote for the Society as an active brother is extant. All we have are characteristic Apostolic titles: 'Are crocodiles the best of animals?' and 'The bedroom, Brother?' (PNF/*EMF*, 1 75; *LJ*, p. xxxix). An important paper on the feminine note in literature was read to the Apostles in 1910 and then apparently rewritten for Bloomsbury's Friday Club; it belongs with the novels Forster was writing at that time and will be discussed with them. Another Apostle paper, also written in 1910, is relevant here, however. The subject was a fifteenth-century Roman 'Society' that eventually became the Academy of Rome. The paper begins autobiographically with Forster recalling that when elected he could not understand the Society's discussions of ethics, though he could hear them; now that the brothers have discovered literature, he can understand the discussions, but no longer hear them. Forster's antitheses lead him to ask what will happen when the Apostles discover history, and then to offer his paper as a contribution to that eventuality. 'Literature and History, if not the most effective weapons against authority, are the easiest to handle, and the Roman Academy discovered their power' (pKC). This is the moral of Forster's paper in the academy where he had learned to value literature and history.

Lytton Strachey was elected to the Apostles a year after Forster and then proceeded, as he acknowledged, to 'dominate' his generation at Cambridge (VW/*D*, 1 238). Strachey's Cambridge writings are more extensive than anyone else's in Bloomsbury. They include, in addition to essays for other societies, poems, plays and a fellowship dissertation, fifteen papers written for the Society during the decade he was active in it. Strachey's later Apostle papers belong to Bloomsbury's Edwardian literary history and need to be related to the criticism he was then publishing or to other Bloomsbury works, such as Forster's *The Longest Journey*, on which they occasionally comment. Clive Bell divided Strachey's Cambridge career into Trinity and King's periods, according to where he was living when at Cambridge (*OF*, p. 27). As an undergraduate he was at Trinity from 1899 to 1903, but afterwards he associated more with Apostolic friends such as Keynes and Sheppard at King's, his original Trinity brothers having all gone down. Strachey's Trinity writings, though not completely separable from his later King's work, can for the most part be considered alongside Bloomsbury's other Cambridge writings.

The first of the four surviving, unpublished Apostle papers Strachey wrote while at Trinity is a *tour de force* of the Apostolic genre. He takes the set topic, 'Ought the father to grow a beard?' and converts it with humour, self-awareness, and shocking frankness into a serious consideration of the limits of art. Strachey's argument is that anything is capable of artistic treatment if the artist places it in proper relation to reality. The aesthetic theory here is clearly related to the notion of organic unity in Moore's as yet unpublished *Principia Ethica* and is picked up again in Strachey's Edwardian Cambridge papers. 'Reality' – undefined because indefinable – is the quintessential Apostolic Bloomsbury predicate that aesthetically transforms whatever it touches. But what is so distinctively Stracheyan about this twenty-two-year-old Apostle's first paper is the illustration used to support the argument. Strachey maintained that 'forthing' (a euphemism for defecating suggested by the location of the college toilets, in the fourth court) could be treated artistically by considering the charm it exerts in reminding us of our material humanity:

> The thought of every member of the human race – the human race which has produced Shakespeare, and weighed the stars – retiring every day to give silent and incontestable proof of his material mould is to me fraught with an unutterable significance. There, in truth, is the one touch of Nature which makes the whole world kin! There is enough to give the idealist perpetual pause! There – in that mystic unburdening of our bodies – that unanswerable reminder of mortality! (*SS*, p. 19)[2]

The paper is a remarkable prevision of Strachey's paradoxical serious and comic, honest and hyperbolic, ironic rhetoric. (It also anticipates what would be happening in modernist literary works such as Joyce's *Ulysses* nearly twenty years later.) But after all its arguments for aesthetic frankness – even envisaging a naked Prince Consort in the Albert Memorial – Strachey concludes that a bearded father's curling hair, symbolic of the virility we cut off, decently conceals the loathsome spectacle of naked facial flesh. This too prefigured Strachey's development.

Lytton Strachey's second paper for the Apostles was on politics. It begins with an approving discussion of how liberalism has succeeded in emancipating conscience from force, the final outcome of the Dreyfus case being the latest example, and proceeds to describe a new gulf that is dividing 'the artist from the socialist, the intellectual from the demagogue, the illuminist from the sentimentalist'. Then, in an attack on liberalism – particularly as represented in the Apostles by G. M. Trevelyan – Strachey complains that moral and political freedom have increased our happiness but lessened our range of action. The paper is called 'Christ or Caliban?' and in it Strachey rejects what he amusingly feels is the liberal hedonism of the former for the anarchy of the latter (pST). The argument is rather confusing, but the performance is noteworthy again for its allusions and for its advocacy of an individualism beyond utilitarianism.

The other two surviving papers that Strachey read to the Society as an undergraduate are slighter. One picks up some of the themes of 'Christ or Caliban?' and argues for a Romantic discarding of timid dignity for the freedom of knowing people intimately. At the end of the paper, however, Strachey wonders, like MacCarthy, if the Apostles specialise too much in knowing themselves and each other (pST). The last paper applies a means–ends analysis to the effect of death on one's view of life. Immortality is but an improbable possibility, and annihilation's eventuality affects action, Strachey finds. It would have been better not to have been born; when people realise this they will stop copulating. 'The universe will simply be hugely ignored' is the last, mock-Jamesian sentence (pST).

VI

The papers that Leonard Woolf and J. M. Keynes wrote for the Society do not presage their literary development as much as Strachey's do his, because the ironic essay was not their preferred mode of writing. Their Apostle papers have, nevertheless, a place in the literary history of Bloomsbury for their representations of the Group's literary and philosophical ideas at Cambridge.

The five Apostle papers preserved among Leonard Woolf's Monk's House papers at the University of Sussex share certain concerns with Strachey's and Keynes's, but their tones and emphases are very different. In them Leonard Woolf is more pessimistically serious, less brightly ironic and self-conscious. His first paper, like Strachey's, was on art. It attempted to define style not as the expression of thought, which Moore's close friend A. R. Ainsworth had argued in an earlier paper, but as something derived from the imagination that elaborates thought. Browne, Burton and Peacock provide the illustrations. Imagination is not further defined, and therefore the paper's approach to a more precise critical terminology fails. The very attempt reveals a quite different critical atmosphere from that in which Raleigh's *Style* appeared five years earlier, however, and the paper's rejection of style as just a function of thought is significant for Bloomsbury's aesthetic development.

Leonard Woolf cited his own second Apostle paper as evidence that Keynes had misinterpreted Moore's influence on the Apostles. It was entitled 'George or George or Both?' and written in May 1903, five months before the publication of *Principia Ethica*. The Platonic question posed by the title is whether the cave-dwelling political interests of George M. Trevelyan can be combined with the philosophical concerns of George E. Moore, who dwells in the light of the sun. Like Strachey's 'Christ or Caliban?' of the previous autumn, Leonard Woolf's paper is critical of Trevelyan's mode of political commitment. But Leonard Woolf advocated no anarchy. For him Moore must return to the cave and take up Trevelyan's political work: 'while philosophers sit outside the cave, their philosophy will never reach politicians or people, so that after all, to put it plainly, I *do* want Moore to draft an Education Bill' (*S*, p. 149). Waiting for the light of *Principia Ethica*, all Leonard Woolf can say of the Apostles' philosophy in the cave is that it is a broken-down scepticism. The problems of this scepticism for him are not the political ones of how to get what is wanted, but those of how to know what ought to be wanted. The subsequent political education of Bloomsbury consisted partly in reversing this idea and learning that the intractable problems of the world had to do more with means than with ends. Leonard Woolf is nevertheless right in *Sowing* to single out this paper as evidence that the Apostles of his time were not, as Keynes had claimed, indifferent to politics.

The three Apostle papers Leonard Woolf wrote after *Principia Ethica* all strongly bear its impress. One on the badness of sentimental states of mind analyses Othello's true pathos and Byron's false sentiment as complex organic wholes. Another argues that happiness is incompatible with the supreme value of personal relations, because those relations are never as satisfactory as we imagine they will be. In his last Apostle performance, just before he took wings for Ceylon in 1904, Leonard Woolf combined his pessimism and literary instances in a good example of a Bloomsbury Apostle paper. 'Embryos or Abortions?' is on that favorite topic, the continuation of the Society. Leonard Woolf seeks in a familiar means–ends analysis of the word 'reality' an answer to the question why so many Apostolic embryos turn into abortions. Reality inheres in certain things really good in themselves (the circularity here is admitted) and also in the relations that a thing or event has to the world. These relations Leonard Woolf describes as 'realities' as distinct from 'reality'. Embryos keep turning into abortions because they see the things and events of life only in their narrower, less real relations. Zola, for instance, describes things of no value, though they exist; Idealist writers describe things that do not exist at all. In the greatest literary works, such as *King Lear* or *Madame Bovary*, 'the things they represent really do exist, are complicated & important facts which I have called "realities"' (pS). The argument here is not very clear, deep or original, yet it indicates some of the meanings with which the Apostles and later Bloomsbury would invest the term 'reality'. In a few years Leonard Woolf and Lytton Strachey would be discussing in letters exactly what it was Forster meant by 'reality' in *The Longest Journey*. And much later the narrator of *A Room of One's Own* would be ironically anxious about its meanings, because 'philosophic words, if one has not been educated at a university, are apt to play one false' (p. 165).

Maynard Keynes thought he had written twenty papers in the eight years he was active in the Society (Levy, p. 262). As a don at King's he gave a number of them again and even wrote some new ones. Not all are germane to Bloomsbury's literary history, but those that are can be looked at together here, because, unlike Strachey's, they do not require as much context of the author's later writings. Many of Keynes's Apostle papers, now in the Marshall Library at Cambridge, are variations on the great *Principia Ethica* theme of means and ends. Keynes repeatedly seeks to reconcile their claims in a dualism of the physical and the mental, of states of affairs and states of mind, of appearance and existence, of doing and being. An early paper on truth argues that, of faith, hope and charity, the greatest is not charity, as Forster or Strachey might have held, but faith in the greatness of truth as both a means and an end. A long paper on aesthetics read in 1905 and again in 1912 tries to establish a distinction between goodness and fitness – the latter being in the realm of aesthetics, where the physical and the mental are indissolubly connected. Keynes asserted here that mental states alone are good, but in a later paper he argued more correctly that his misinterpretation of Moore ignored the principle of organic unities by making good entirely a property of consciousness. In a paper entitled 'The Method', the subject of which had exercised Leonard Woolf, Strachey and other disciples of Moore, Keynes criticised the Apostles for taking the good to mean essentially the pleasant, and suggested in a typically brilliant paradox that identifying good entirely with intrinsic goods might be another form of Moore's naturalistic fallacy.

Not all of Keynes's Apostle papers were elucidations or refinements of Moore. At least one, entitled 'Egoism', attacks Moore's treatment of that subject, arguing that there was no reason to suppose the universe's good was bound up with the individual's. Then Keynes rather dramatically summons up a vision of absolute good and recants: 'Who am I that I should talk about *my* good? I have committed a sin against the Holy Ghost' (pML). Another paper, on Moore's chapter 'Ethics in Relation to Conduct', criticises the logic of Moore's conservative reliance on general rules of conduct; Keynes introduces instead a notion of probability that anticipates his later treatise. The arguments that Keynes began to use in this paper may have helped free Moore's ethics from the last vestiges of Benthamism (Skidelsky, p. 153).

Two lighter papers written in 1908 claim that disembodied spirits, if they exist at all, are cold creatures; therefore we must hope for the resurrection after death of body as well as spirit. In the first paper, set in a picture gallery, Keynes narrates an encounter with a bodiless jinn looking for an appearance in which to embody himself – until Keynes persuades him that without an appearance he really has no existence at all. The second, set in Windsor Castle, is a dialogue between drawings of Prince Henry and Prince Rupert, in which Rupert persuades Henry that emotion, though it works through the mind, exists in the body. The paper may have been directed at Rupert Brooke, who, according to Keynes's note in the margin, was among the Apostles who heard the paper. In other essays for the Society Keynes returned to the importance of truth. The one punningly entitled 'Posterior Analytics' is not directly about sodomitical feelings but attacks the phenomenal notion that increasing self-consciousness and analysis are inimical to life and feeling. This Awkward Age subject is continued in the most wide-ranging Apostle paper that Keynes wrote. Its title is 'Modern Civilization', and its thesis deals with how the machine may have changed the nature of our duties. Keynes notices the increasing contrast between the private and public lives of even the Apostolic elect. The 'semi-personal' relations of the past have disappeared along with older duties. In the deeper intimacy that the Apostles now achieve, the new machine moralities are largely ignored. Keynes's conclusion is that, for those who live apart from the machine, Plato will remain the first and greatest prophet of ends; but, while 'the good is changeless and apart, the ought shifts and fades and grows new shapes and forms' (pML). The relation of this paper to the criticisms of Moore's influence in 'My Early Beliefs' is quite direct.

Finally, there is among Keynes's Apostle papers a late facetious one about a central symbol in Bloomsbury's painting and writing. In 'Can we consume our Surplus? Or The influence of furniture on Love', the Apostolic economist analyses the influence of rooms on lives. Keynes observes that he has spent most of his life in rooms at Eton's, King's and Whitehall that were as pompous as possible. 'The shape of rooms . . . seems extraordinarily important – to one's calmness and flow of ideas in work. . . . It is difficult to be at ease in very high rooms or in one which is crowded with a great variety of objects.' Trinity's rooms differ from those of King's, and those of one court at Trinity from those of another – not so much because of their outlooks as because of their shapes, which influence the course of our loves. 'Who could commit sodomy in a boudoir or sapphism in Neville's Court?' he asks. It is possible, Keynes goes on to speculate, that our rooms are effects rather than causes, and may be, like the poems and pictures we try to make, inadequate expressions of our feelings (pML). In the work of Forster, Strachey, Virginia Woolf, Vanessa Bell, Grant and Fry, the 'consuming' of rooms continues to symbolise ways of feeling, thinking and living.

Keynes's extra-curricular writing at Cambridge concentrated on his papers for the Society, though it was not the only important student organisation he was involved in; he also belonged to the Cambridge Union and eventually became its president. Among Keynes's first publication were Union debate reports, and he also wrote an undergraduate review of a volume of Acton's *The Cambridge Modern History* for the *Cambridge Review* in November 1903. This review with its early Bloomsbury irony is a mature performance for a twenty-year-old and prefigures some of Keynes's later writings about Americans. The United States was the subject of the volume, and Keynes had no complaint, as Strachey did later, with the historiography of the series (LS/*SE*, pp. 115–20). A chapter by Woodrow Wilson on state rights he thought one of the most interesting in the book, but his review had the most fun displaying the foolishness of Professor Barrett Wendell's 'The American Intellect'. As a reader of Hawthorne, Keynes could not accept Wendell's assertion that Fenimore Cooper was the only world-class American writer, and he learnedly observes that Wendell had reversed himself from an earlier book to claim now that Americans were more Elizabethan than the English. Then, under the immediate impact of Moore's 'The Refutation of Idealism', which appeared the same month as his review, Keynes complains that Wendell's thesis about idealism being the main American characteristic uses 'idealism' in eight different senses without giving any 'clear and definite meaning' to the word (*CW*, xi 507). Nevertheless, the undergraduate found the professor's chapter most illuminating about a phase of the American intellect – not in what he said about it, but in what his writing showed of it.

VII

The subjects of Bloomsbury's Apostle papers are in one respect quite uncharacteristic of the Society's traditional concerns. They are rarely about religious questions. Occasionally the papers of Fry, Strachey and Keynes touch upon them, but only in the course of discussing other things. Bloomsbury's attitude toward religion at Cambridge was one of indifference, but they could be provoked into ridicule and hostility. (Forster and Keynes were not close in Cambridge or in Bloomsbury, but they were on the same, opposing side in a 1903 King's controversy about a college mission in London.) Only one work of expository prose is to be found among Bloomsbury's Cambridge writings, and that is a brief, anonymous, polemical pamphlet written in 1904 by Thoby Stephen, whose voice elsewhere in the written records of the Group is almost as silent as Percival's in *The Waves*. The pamphlet, addressed to the freshmen of Cambridge University, is entitled *Compulsory Chapel* and described on the cover as 'An Appeal to Undergraduates on behalf of Religious Liberty and Intellectual Independence'. Its polemic is directed against compelling undergraduates who are atheists or agnostics to attend their college chapels. Stephen claims that the 1871 Universities Test Acts, which gave to men outside the Church of England the right to religious liberty, including full membership in the universities, applied not just to Roman Catholics and nonconformists but to all non-believers. Undergraduate apathy allowed the deans to enforce chapel attendance, states the pamphlet, whose peroration urges non-compliance for the very sake of religious liberty.

> To take a firm stand in this matter here is not only to free yourselves from the burden of a discipline that is inconvenient and degrading, but to strengthen the cause of religious liberty in the last English stronghold of religious intolerance. Believing this I appeal not only to Atheists and Agnostics, but to all friends of intellectual independence, and to those Christians – if such there be – who consider that compulsory worship is an indignity to themselves and to their creed. I ask all who hold such views to refuse steadfastly to submit to any discipline which attempts to enforce Chapel attendance. . . . I am pointing them to no forlorn hope, no quest for the impossible. The prize is ready to the hand of all but the sluggard and the craven. (pp. 7–8)

The rhetoric is heavy and old-fashioned, closer to Milton than Mill, yet there is no mistaking the tradition of liberal thought in which it stands. The arguments could easily have been Leslie Stephen's, though they lack his understated ironic wit. 'It's no good being dainty with Christians', the monolithic Thoby wrote to Leonard Woolf about another pamphlet in this chapel controversy, and there is nothing dainty about his (LW/*S*, p. 126). Yet his views, if not his style, reflect the religious attitudes of his Cambridge friends and his adoring sisters too. *Compulsory Chapel* also has the distinction in the Group's literary history of being the first in a series of Bloomsbury polemics, which eventually extended from *Art* and *The Economic Consequences of the Peace* to *Quack, Quack!* and *Three Guineas*.

12 Poems, Plays, Parodies

I

Although the principal medium of Bloomsbury's non-academic Cambridge writing was prose, as one might expect from their later careers, little of it was prose fiction. Discussion societies expected various kinds of informal essays, and after these the genres Bloomsbury usually practised were poetic and dramatic. What fiction they did write at Cambridge was mostly in the form of parody. Forster alone began an undergraduate novel. The traditional forms of Bloomsbury's literary beginnings thus reflect their conservative academic setting, however modern the contents of these texts were.

Only Lytton Strachey and Clive Bell appear to have written much verse after Cambridge, and it had little connection with the prose works that made them well known. But at Cambridge Bloomsbury put considerable effort into the writing of poetry, publishing it in the *Cambridge Review* and then in *Euphrosyne*, the anonymous 1905 collection that was largely the work of Sydney-Turner and Clive Bell. Their Cambridge verse can be more usefully considered in the Edwardian context of that volume. Among Leonard Woolf's and Lytton Strachey's papers, however, are collections of poems written during their time at Cambridge and not published in *Euphrosyne*, which contains only three poems by each. These unpublished – and in Strachey's case unprintable – poems are insubstantial literary works, but they help to convey the poetic interests of the Group at Cambridge and may suggest why Bloomsbury produced no serious poetry afterwards.

Most of Leonard Woolf's poems seem to have been written during his first two years at Trinity. They are derivative, *fin-de-siècle* expressions of vague mysticism or stoical pessimism in

265

Swinburnian metres. Their atmosphere is one of proud disillusionment, *Weltschmerz*, futility or failure. Love makes its appearance only in abstract dreams. The first poem in a collection
carefully copied into a notebook in September 1900 is called 'A
Failure' and describes, almost prophetically for Leonard Woolf's
coming career, how the world actually failed the so-called failure:

> For he sat in a Desert divine
> > A Sphinx to the petty & mean,
> And poured the ineffable wine
> > Of knowledge unknown unseen
>
> In the vain barren sands of the World. . . .

A blank verse poem on Judas in the same collection has him
standing at the throne of God, 'a witness to God's guilt / God's
curse & Heaven's & all that smiling throng's' (pS). In another
blank-verse monologue, obviously influenced by Browning, the
dying satirist Lucian – also a favourite author of Strachey –
admits he is no second Socrates and despairs of religion, philosophy, women, life.

Though Leonard Woolf ranges from blank verse to villanelles,
he is not as technically accomplished a poet as either Strachey or
Sydney-Turner. And, unlike their poetry, his is rarely about love.
The repression rather than the expression of strong feeling recurs
in them. A good example of the mood of many of his poems is the
central stanza of a poem sent to Strachey called "The C Minor'
(Bloomsbury seems to have been fond of this Beethovenian key;
Forster even wrote an essay on it – *2CD*, pp. 119–21):

> O god, the iteration of dead things,
> > The long dull stupid round, the hopeless wheel
> Of the stale present's resurrection,
> > The known & felt past we've to know & feel!
>
> > > (pS)

Leonard Woolf's poetry, like Strachey's, is mainly interesting for
what it says about the poet and his future writings. A striking
example, dated September 1901, is the monologue of a Jewish
pawnbroker convicted of manslaughter in a pub brawl. After a
prose introduction setting the scene of his unspoken defence,

tetrameter couplets express the pawnbroker's rage at how his race has been treated; he rejoiced when his victim yelled 'Jew' at him, for he 'saw the mystic desert gleam', found a sword in his hand, smote the brute, 'And felt the glow of battle rise / And dead Pride lift me to the skies'. The imagery of the speaker is theatrical (a sword in a Victorian pub), yet the poem may be the only contemporary Cambridge text of Leonard Woolf's to suggest he was not a completely assimilated Jew.

II

Leonard Woolf thought Lytton Strachey did not publish the verse he wrote throughout his life because it did not come up to the standards he expected of published poetry, and Moore's influence turned him in other directions (SPR/*BG*, p. 180). Those directions were all prose ones; even at Cambridge, where Strachey did publish nine of his poems,[1] his prose is more interesting. Another reason, of course, why some of his poetry remained unpublished was its erotic character. Strachey's poems are technically quite competent and also quite derivative; their language, even when gross, is unengrossing. The main models are Shakespeare, the Romantics, Swimburne, some nineties poets, and later, Pope. Of the Symbolists, Whitman, Browning and the Metaphysical poets, who creatively influence so much modern poetry, only the last two seem to have much impact on Strachey's work. Yet, in the articulate honesty of its concerns, Strachey's verse displays better than anyone else's the poetic milieu of Bloomsbury at Cambridge.

None of the poems that Strachey published in the *Cambridge Review* is about the present. One is a parody of Herrick, and all the others – about a cat, a seventh-century monk, summer, love, death, and the coming end of the world – take their subjects from the remote past or future. A Shakespearean sonnet entitled 'From the Persian', and taken from a sequence Strachey wrote, is about how one look at the beloved in heaven on the day of judgement contents the lover with the hell he deserves for wasting his youth and vainly trafficking with truth. Another sonnet, 'The Penultimates', describes those who saw the sun set before the apocalypse and thought the ghastly glory good because their tears made it shimmer beautifully.

The one poem published under Strachey's name during his lifetime is also about the past. 'Ely: An Ode' won the Chancellor's Medal, was declaimed by its author in the Senate House, and then published by the University in the *Prolusiones Academicae* of 1902. Pindaric in form with strophes and anti-strophes, but Horatian in historical content, the poem celebrates the beauty of Ely Cathedral together with its historical and poetical associations. A roll call of Cambridge poets is included, starting with Spenser and ending with Tennyson, the 'brother' who is still mourned. Tennyson was also Strachey's Apostolic brother, but the reference to him, like almost everything else in the poem, is conventional, dictated presumably by the requirements of the heroic-verse competition for the Chancellor's Medal. 'Ely' is a polished exercise in the English ode, and undistinctive as a Bloomsbury work except perhaps in one respect. The cathedral of the poem is described as 'the sanctuary of man and God', but only the human associations of the place are described in the ode.

The epigraph of 'Ely' is 'omnia somnia', and it could stand also for the dreaminess of the three separate collections of Strachey's private undergraduate verse to be found among the Strachey Trust papers. Much of this verse is erotic, sado-masochistic or scatological, and most of it is bad. There are some lines, though no poems, that have a certain lyric intensity or epigrammatic bite, but as a whole the poetry is now consequential only because Strachey wrote it, circulated it among his friends and preserved it. The first collection begins with a dedicatory poem of November 1902 to Leonard Woolf and Saxon Sydney-Turner; it asks them to accept these poems so that 'Some fool may find our members dead and wet, / And our brows crowned with fragmentary flowers'. This seems to describe the purpose of the verse, much of which might be classified as pornographic, because its affective intentions prevail over its aesthetic ones. But there is also a moral purpose in these poems to be as explicit as possible about sexual feelings. All concealments are stripped away – clothes from bodies, skin from flesh, flesh from bones. Love and gruesome death frequently accompany each other in the poems. Michael Holroyd thought they expressed the worst of Strachey's character, with their grossness, their lack of pathos or humour – a judgement which provoked James Strachey to complain, with some justice, that this was just the kind of shocked response Lytton's whole career had been devoted to criticising (MH/*LSBG*, pp. 61–3). The writing of this verse enhanced Strachey's Cambridge reputation for uninhibited frankness. Leonard Woolf and Sydney-Turner were also known for their truth-telling, but it is difficult to imagine either of them exhibiting such sexual self-awareness in their verse. Nearly half of Strachey's poems in this first collection are about erotic crucifixions of one kind or another. A sonnet on Rembrandt's *The Elevation of the Cross* describes the event as 'Unblenching lust's unparalelled [*sic*] stark hour / Culminant and victorious on the cross'. In another the poet walks in the garden of the soul and finds a tearful Cupid hung in the Tree of Knowledge along with the poet's own rotting corpse. A poem on the flaying of Marsyas dwells on the gory action and ends with Apollo raping one of the satyr's followers. 'The Death of Milo', which Holroyd chose to reprint, is a lighter, less sadistic, more scatological poem about the handsome Greek boxer caught fatally in a tree (*LSBG*, pp. 375–8). All these poems are set in the past, often in classical Greece or Rome. Some are deliberately humorous in their indecency. There is a parody, for example, of Tennyson's 'Frater Ave Atque Vale', where Tennyson had called Catullus 'tenderest' of Roman poets; in Strachey's version Catullus hears of this and replies in extremely rude Latin.

The second collection of Strachey's early unpublished verse is the sequence of twenty sonnets he may have written to J. T. Sheppard (MH/*LSBG*, p. 62). These differ from Strachey's studies in classical sadism, being mainly about a contemporary love affair. Death is still present throughout, and there are dreams of scatological sex in them. In one of the sonnets the poet, after comparing himself and his beloved with Marsyas and Apollo, among others, concludes self-mockingly, 'But one description our two selves unites – / We both, dear love, are Higher Sodomites' ('the higher sodomy' was a current Cambridge term for the platonic homosexuality that Strachey thought faint-hearted and Forster criticised in *Maurice*.). A related poem describes an evening of joined souls interrupted by the horror of an erection. These sonnets are not better poems than those in the earlier collection, but some of them are funnier and more realistic. The sequence's celebration of love is, nevertheless, completely serious. In the last sonnet the lovers part, but not without praising

The one God greater than all Gods shall be,
Love, high as heaven, and soundless as the sea,
Immense as life, and as supreme as death.

In the third collection of Strachey's verse are a number of
miscellaneous poems written at the end of his Trinity years.
Some are quite conventional, like one on a volume of Keats.
Others are not. 'Inscription for a Piss-Pot' again rhymes 'kiss'
with 'piss', as Strachey was fond of doing. A poem called 'In
Arcady' is an almost Forsterian story of a shepherd whom Pan
grabs by the ears and turns into a faun of savage loves. There is
an 'Etude quasi Sadiste' of Shakespeare being whipped for
poaching. Another poem reverts to earlier themes with an imperial speaker who makes love to a pouting slave boy then rapes
him; the poem is dated 'Dec.–Jan. 1903–4' and entitled
'Adrian', though there are no other indications that it might
somehow refer to Adrian Stephen. In these poems the contrast
occurs, again, between sexual fantasies set in the past and those
about current loves. The latter are aptly summarised in the final
refrain of one called 'Ménage à Trois':

These speculations may perplex
The votaries of the other sex,
But we, on our astounding heights,
Are nothing if not Sodomites.

(pST)

III

Strachey continued to write poetry throughout his life, but little
of his later verse was pornographic or even very erotic. How
seriously he took himself as a poet at Cambridge is not certain,
but in his twenties and thirties Strachey put considerable effort
into becoming a dramatist. The plays and dialogues he wrote as
an undergraduate are no more successful than his poems, but
they are more relevant to the criticism and biography in which
he finally found himself as a writer.

The earliest dramatic writing of Strachey's preserved among
the Strachey Trust papers is the first act of a blank-verse tragedy
about the aged Tiberius. Attempts at love and assassination

make up what action there is, and old age calls forth some good speeches by Tiberius and others. The most ambitious of Strachey's Cambridge dramatic efforts was a Renaissance tragedy, *The Duke of Ferrato*, more than three acts of which were completed under the stimulus of writing a play for the X or Midnight Society. A list of actors for the play and some correspondence with Leonard Woolf indicate that Strachey wrote the play with Trinity friends in mind. The author himself was to play the Duchess of Ferrato, a literary descendant of the Duchess of Malfi and the first of the noble dames to figure centrally in his writing. The Duke of Ferrato is her young son; her second husband, described as a 'parchment-worm', was to be acted by Sydney-Turner. The orator–conspirator plotting to overthrow the dukedom is named Leonardo and was, of course, to be played by Leonard Woolf. Thoby Stephen was to be Giulio, the hero. He arrives with an army to assist the revolution but falls in love with the Duchess and out of sympathy with Leonardo, whose love he has nevertheless attracted. Other members of the play-reading society also had roles in the drama, though not Clive Bell. Strachey's writing in the play, as in the Tiberius fragment, is rhetorical rather than dramatic. There are some good lines and images, but the pitched emotion of the characters is not really communicated. The literary interest of the play is limited to the demonstration of how some members of Bloomsbury and their friends enjoyed acting out aspects of their personalities and relationships. Private plays and costume parties continued to amuse Bloomsbury for decades.

Why Strachey's plays are so unsatisfactory may be explained in part by the theory of drama he elaborated in an undergraduate discussion-society paper entitled 'When is a Drama not a Drama?' (pST). Whether the theory was cause or consequence, it describes the plays he was writing at Trinity and may have been derived from the French classical drama of which he was so fond. Yet the theory is utterly un-Aristotelian in its argument that states of mind, not actions, are the essence of drama. A good dramatic plot, according to the theory, consists of two parts, in the second of which the minds of the characters are completely different from what they were in the first, and the change from one to the other is the dramatic culmination. The interest of the play lies in our discovering what the new state of mind is. Strachey's idea of drama owes much to Moore's philosophy (a play is good only if the characters' states of mind are interesting), and looks forward to Bloomsbury's later theory that literature is most valuably about characters' states of mind rather than their actions or environments. But the theory, as elaborated by Virginia Woolf, in particular, was applied to fiction, not drama. Strachey's plays fail, by his own criteria, because their characters' states of mind are not dramatically or psychologically interesting; they exist in speeches more than as characters speaking, and their changes are unconvincing. Another Trinity essay of Strachey's about conversation defined drama as 'conversation treated architecturally'; literature as a whole was largely the crystallisation of imaginary conversation fugally arranged in a balanced mixture 'of egotism and altriusm, of selfishness and affection' (pST). This Bloomsbury description of a conversational ideal again shows how Strachey's dramas fail. Their conversations are not sufficiently interrelated to create architectural, musical or dramatic form.

One serious, even humourless, modern play is to be found among Strachey's papers. Under the impetus of Ibsen, it would seem, Strachey abandoned his antique settings to write a play about an anarchist named Robert Alisoun who persuades his religious wife to blow up a capitalist's house and family. She commits suicide afterwards and he undergoes conversion before falling dead over her body. A wealthy couple converted to anarchism by Alisoun are left hopeless at the end of the play. As an indication of Strachey's hostility to fanaticism of any kind, *Robert Alisoun* is a not insignificant early text of Strachey's, but as a play it is dramaturgically and psychologically absurd. The writing fails to convey the intense emotional experiences the characters are supposed to be undergoing. *Robert Alisoun* is undated, and may have been written after Strachey left Cambridge; more mature than *The Duke of Ferrato*, it is still not the work of a promising playwright.

Almost all the rest of the quasi-dramatic or fictional texts Strachey wrote at Cambridge are satiric in one way or another. An exception is the 'Diary of an Athenian 400 B.C.', a Platonic dialogue – or, to be more precise, Platonic monologue – that describes the love of Agathon for Glaucon. Agathon says it is 'the love of Souls', not boys, which sounds like the higher sodomy (*RIQ*, p. 141). A number of other dialogues among Strachey's papers were inspired by Lucian's *Dialogues of the Dead*. Their humour lies in the yoking of unlikely figures such as Julius

Caesar and Lord Salisbury, Cleopatra and Mrs Humphry Ward, or Catullus and Tennyson again. The classical figures in these pairings are incredulous at the political, religious or literary attitudes of the Victorians. A few of Strachey's dialogues are autobiographical. One, for example, is a conversation in which G. M. Trevelyan confidently assures Strachey that 'the sexual question' does not come into their studies at all, because 'it's one of the best facts in modern English life that there are no women at University'. Strachey remains silent at this, 'not venturing a combustion' (*LSH*, p. 110). Homosexuality is the explicit subject of most of the rest of Strachey's undergraduate satires. He wrote three tales about a fourth-century Paterish Saint Evagrius, whose sexual experiences drive him into Christianity, and there the command 'Thou shalt not' makes him miserable. Two fragmentary stories, one of which has been published (*RIQ*, pp. 152–5), are about college homosexual affairs and depend for their effect, like Forster's shorter homosexual stories, on treating that love as if it were an ordinary subject for fiction.

Among the various parodies to be found in Strachey's early Cambridge writings are two Jamesian pastiches; in one an indirect proposal is signalled by the words, 'Has the Major sold his mare?', and in the other a sado-masochistic schoolboy relationship is narrated in the master's late style (*RIQ*, pp. 99–100, 143–50). (A third Jamesian pastiche, not a parody, is an obscure conversation called 'Tragedy' about an older man's futile love for a boy.) In a parodic 'First and Last Will and Testament', Strachey bequeathed, among other things, his body to be dissected, articulated and wired to McTaggart's lecture table, presumably to illustrate the reality of matter to the Idealist (*LSH*, pp. 107–8. There is also a sermon preached to the Midnight Society on Pilate's 'What is Truth?' A number of similar pieces were written and delivered by Strachey and his friends, acting the part of a preacher who, according to Virginia Woolf, 'annihilated the Christian faith in the doctrines that fell from his lips' (*QB/VW*, I 206). And in a long dialogue written for the Sunday Essay Society in reply to an attack on intellectual snobs by one Barnes (*MH/LSBG*, p. 67), Strachey presented the colloquies of an Arabian pilgrim named Senrab with men of various religions and philosophies. At the end Senrab confesses to the spirit of the Prophet that all the contradictory beliefs he had been maintaining were merely his grandmother's opinions (*pST*).

Lastly, there are two adaptations of Euripidean plays that

may have been suggested by Forster's earlier parodies of Aeschylus, all of which derive from the Apostle A. W. Verrall's well-known *Euripides the Rationalist*, published in 1895. Verrall saw Euripides as 'a soldier of rationalism after the fashion of his time, a resolute *consistent* enemy of anthropomorphic theology, a hater of embodied mystery, a man who, after his measure and the measure of his time, stood up to answer the Sphinx' (p. 260). Strachey admired the book and wrote to his mother in 1903 that he wanted to do a tragedy as sketched by Euripides (MH/*LS*, p. 189). In his first adaptation, Strachey put Ulysses into *Iphigenia in Aulis* along with Achilles, a stupid boy who prefers hunting and Patroclus to his intended Iphigenia; her sacrifice is interrupted by Artemis, who goes off in a grove with Patroclus, leaving the distinct suspicion that she is actually Achilles in disguise. The two-act fragment *Iphigenia in Taurus* has Orestes in love with an annoyed Pylades, who is trying to find a woman. In Strachey's interpretations, then, Verrall's rational Euripides has become a dramatist of homosexual farces.

IV

The most important writing E. M. Forster did as an undergraduate at Cambridge was the fragment of a novel now called 'Nottingham Lace', but its history belongs with his other attempts to write novels at the beginning of the century. Forster also wrote while at Cambridge nearly a dozen undergraduate pieces that were published in Cambridge magazines. They relate more directly to his early development than Strachey's do to his; in them Forster begins to connect through parody the present with the classics and history he had been studying. Jebb's popular translation of *The Characters of Theophrastus* seems to have inspired a number of Forster's parodies. The first two, published in the *Cambridge Review* in 1900, were Theophrastian treatments of Cambridge undergraduate walkers and cyclists. The walkers are classified according to their intellectual capacities; the solid thinkers go by the Trumpington road and the aesthetic ones by the Madingley road, where a few find the chalk pit of *The Longest Journey* 'folded off from the outer world' (*AE*, p. 46). For the King's periodical *Basileona* Forster wrote two more sketches under the heading 'The Cambridge Theophrastus', which was to be a guide for the inexperienced to University characters such as the stall-holder or the early mother and father who try to help their offspring start college. These very minor facetious texts show an interest in satirical stereotyping that was shared with other Bloomsbury writers such as Strachey and Leonard Woolf, who took their Theophrastus through La Bruyére as well as directly, and Virginia Woolf, who must have known Thackeray's *Book of Snobs* well.

All of Forster's early published Cambridge writings are satires except for the brief allegory 'The Pack of Anchises', in which Aeneas-like undergraduates shed their fathers and household gods in the course of their education. At the end the question is asked whether the fathers disposed of the gods or the sons disposed of both gods and fathers. Forster's concern with past gods and disposable fathers runs through his early writings. The first of his two tragic interiors – the best parodies Forster wrote at Cambridge – takes off Aeschylus's *Agamemnon*. The *Cambridge Review* praised the parody, that praise being the first critical attention his work had received (PNF/*EMF*, 1 73). The occasion for the parody was the triennial Cambridge Greek play (in Greek), but Forster was also satirising Verrall's view of Euripides. Verrall had argued that to appreciate Euripides's art properly we had only to understand his ideas, not believe them; he defended his own disbelief in Euripides's rationalism by pointing to his other work on Aeschylus. And it is Aeschylus whom Forster's parody turns into a rationalist, by dramatising the absurd events that occur indoors in his tragedies. The *Agamemnon* interior is a bourgeois farce in which Clytemnestra's fear of revolution leads her to fake his murder. After the apparent killing, the Chorus glories in its power of prophecy, Agamemnon fusses over the condition of the carpet in the house, Cassandra wails 'Wow! keep the bull from the cow!', Aegisthus tells them all to keep up appearances for the servants by flitting around the place like ghosts, and Clytemnestra wonders how they will get through the *Choephori*. At one point Agamemnon observes that the play might have been written by Euripides, and Clytemnestra suggests the author might have been 'Dr V*rr*ll' (*AE*, pp. 61–7). Forster's second parody is from the *Choephori*. Agamemnon and Cassandra are now disguised as ghosts; Agamemnon complains of the muddle while Clytemnestra maintains appearances for the sake of the Chorus and to prevent a revolution. The

Furies, however, turn out to be quite real (*AE*, pp. 68–76). The sequel is not as funny as the first parody, but both show Forster's talent for depicting the domestic absurd.

Forster published one more academic parody in *Basileona* on historical interpretation. 'Strivings after Historical Style' ridicules a series of Oxford textbooks by classifying and imitating their styles. There is the Dramatic Style, bristling with clichés; the Personal Style, mixing physical and psychological descriptions; the Critical Style of mixed metaphors; and the apocalyptically trite Cosmic Style. Forster's illustrations of these styles' pretentious pointlessness anticipate *1066 and All That*. Another unpublished satire of Forster's was written in verse on the subject of the London-mission controversy at King's, in which Keynes was also involved. The poem adopts the position of the 'Such' party, whose name originated when someone on the other side said the views of 'Nonconformists and such' should be heard; Forster then undermines all the parties until hooligans, typifying perhaps the human heart, wreck everything (PNF/ *EMF*, I 99–100). Forster continued to write a little satirical verse as well as other kinds of poetry from time to time, but like Strachey he published none of it.

To conclude this survey of Bloomsbury's Cambridge writings, it might help restore perspective a little by abandoning chronology to look at yet another satire, this time one by the Bloomsbury writer who has been largely absent from the discussions of the Group's literary and philosophical education at Cambridge. In 1920 or 1921 Virginia Woolf wrote a piece called 'A Society' and included it in *Monday or Tuesday*, the experimental stories and sketches that led to her modernist novels. When these works were reprinted with other stories in the posthumous *A Haunted House*, however, it and another brief sketch were omitted at her wish (*HH*, pp. 7–8). Virginia Woolf may have felt by 1940 that the satire of the Society in 'A Society' was too dated and inconsequential, while its feminism had been expressed much better in later works. But for her readers today it is the historical feminism that makes it the most prominent story in *Monday or Tuesday*. 'A Society' recounts at some length – it is the longest piece in the collection – the story of a young women's discussion group somewhat like the Apostles. (Forster had described a similar group in chapter 15 of *Howards End*, which appeared in 1910.) The group began out of the despair of one of the members, whose father left her a fortune on the condition that she read all the books in the London Library, whose president Leslie Stephen had been. The heiress discovers in this autobiographical nightmare of women's education that the books by men, such as A. C. Benson's *From a College Window*, are not any good, and this leads the women of the discussion society to investigate a world in which women have been bearing children while men have been creating books and pictures. Their inquiry is based on the Ideal of their society, which in mockery of *Principia Ethica* is that 'the objects of life were to produce good people and good books' (*CSF*, p. 120). Until they are satisfied how successful men have been at this, Lysistrata-like they will bear no more children. The quest of the Apostolic women takes in the British Museum, the Royal Academy, the Tate Gallery, Oxford, Cambridge and the Navy. There are allusions to the results of the *Dreadnought* hoax and to Virginia Woolf's recent dispute with Desmond MacCarthy over the intellectual status of women. The satiric form of 'A Society' is the old one of having an alien or outsider of some kind describe uncomprehendingly the customs of familiar institutions. The irony is thus double-edged, cutting at both the absurd behaviour of men in these places and at the enforced naïvety of the women observers. For example, the member of the society who visits Oxbridge finds the life of dons in the university reminding her of her aunt's cactus conservatory: 'There, on hot pipes, were dozens of them, ugly, squat, bristly little plants each in a separate pot. Once in a hundred years the Aloe flowered, so my Aunt said' (p. 122).

'A Society' is not a completely coherent story. The silly hilarity of the women vies occasionally with the absurd institutions of the men. But there are places in the writing where the trenchant wit and unexpected symbolism combine with the feminist quest for knowledge and an understanding of men to make 'A Society' a remarkable predecessor of *A Room of One's Own* and *Three Guineas*. The quest of the women in 'A Society' is broken off by the First World War; the question the women then seek to answer becomes the one Virginia Woolf will ask bitterly in the 1930s: why do men make war? The society finds its answer after the war in the education of men, for that is what had made them proclaim their intellectual superiority and demonstrate the opposite in their books, pictures and wars. The only solution the women of 'A Society' can envision, short of devising a way for men to bear children, is to teach little girls (like the one born after her mother had visited Oxbridge) to believe in themselves.

V

Yet to what extent did the men of Bloomsbury believe in themselves after Cambridge? Their reading and discussions clearly gave them an intellectual, moral and even aesthetic self-confidence that the women of the Group lacked at that time. In 1906 Virginia Woolf observed after reading *Euphrosyne* that the system of educating a girl at home preserved her 'from the omniscience, the early satiety, the melancholy self-satisfaction which a training at either of our great universities produces in her brothers' (QB/*VW*, I 205). The familiar idiom was apt: after Cambridge one went *down*. Among the men at Cambridge, Sydney-Turner and Maynard Keynes alone were unqualified successes academically, yet for them too the most valuable part of their education had been extra-curricular. The sowing, in Leonard Woolf's metaphor, had been wide and deep; the growing would be slow. Only E. M. Forster was at all visible in the early Edwardian literary landscape. Yet by the First World War, a decade or so later, Desmond MacCarthy had written an important book of dramatic criticism, Lytton Strachey had succeeded as a critic of English and French literature, Roger Fry and Clive Bell had written their most influential works on aesthetics, Leonard Woolf had published his two novels, and Virginia Woolf had become an established *Times Literary Supplement* reviewer while finishing, after six years and perhaps as many drafts, her first novel.

Notes

NOTES TO THE INTRODUCTION

1. These are Renato Poggioli's terms in *The Theory of the Avant-Garde*. ch. 2. Poggioli's entire account illuminates how Bloomsbury was and was not avant-garde.

2. Bloomsbury writers were closely associated at times with the *Nation* and the *New Statesman*, but the political and even parts of the literary halves of these periodicals were edited and written by journalists largely unassociated with the Group. Desmond MacCarthy edited two periodicals that might be considered small magazines, and, though both had Bloomsbury contributors, neither the *Speaker* nor *Life and Letters* could be called a Bloomsbury magazine.

3. Desmond MacCarthy can serve as an illustration of what is involved in determining the membership of Bloomsbury. Recently MacCarthy's son-in-law David Cecil has denied his connection with Bloomsbury: 'As he himself said, "Bloomsbury has never been a spiritual home to me"' (Cecil, 'Introduction', p. 15). Cecil omits the other half of the sentence from MacCarthy's Bloomsbury memoir, which is 'but let me add that I have not got one, although at Cambridge for a few years I fancied that I had'. MacCarthy goes on to call Bloomsbury a home away from home and note how he converged on the Group through the Apostles, Clive Bell and the Stephen sisters (SPR/*BG*, p. 28). To these connections could be added his association with Roger Fry, which led to his writing the introduction for the catalogue of the first post-impressionist exhibition. Like Strachey, MacCarthy was more closely involved in Old than New Bloomsbury, but in both he edited periodicals that depended on his Bloomsbury friends for contributions. One of Mary MacCarthy's purposes in founding the Memoir Club was, as with its precursor the Novel Club, to encourage her husband to write. That MacCarthy moved in other circles as well as Bloomsbury is not, of course, a sufficient reason for excluding him from the Group, because all the members had friends outside Bloomsbury. In his associations, his values and, most importantly, his writings, Desmond MacCarthy displays as many affinities with Bloomsbury as anyone in the Group, which is why Leonard Woolf, Raymond Mortimer and Quentin Bell, among others, include him in Bloomsbury.

NOTES TO CHAPTER 1: INTELLECTUAL BACKGROUNDS

1. The connection between Virginia Woolf and Caroline Emelia Stephen has been overdeveloped by Jane Marcus, who thinks that 'we need search no

further for the origins of Virginia Woolf's pacifism and mysticism' than her aunt's books (p. 27). The evidence is mostly indirect (though there are unmistakable indications of a dislike of her aunt's personality and writings in Virginia Woolf's early letters), and there are other, more obvious sources in Virginia Woolf's quite different mystical experiences, in her study of Plato, in the pacifism of the women's movement, in the anti-militarism of her father and in the Quaker heritage of Roger Fry, who influenced her so profoundly.

2. The interesting connections between Moore, Russell and phenomenologists, especially Franz Brentano with his influential concept of intentionality, have been set forth in Roderick Chisholm's *Realism and the Background of Phenomenology*.

3. Raymond Williams has described Bloomsbury's liberalism as a bourgeois ideology of pluralistic civilised individualism and noted some of the ironies of its current influence:

> Indeed the paradox of many retrospective judgements of Bloomsbury is that the group lived and worked this position with a now embarrassing whole-heartedness: embarrassing, that is to say, to those many for whom 'civilised individualism' is a mere flag to fly over a capitalist, imperialist and militarist social order; embarrassing, also, to those many others for whom 'civilised individualism' is a summary phrase for a process of privileged consumption.   (p. 63)

4. The essay, reprinted in *The Captain's Death Bed* and *Collected Essays*, reads 'in or about December, 1910', but the original Hogarth Essay text says 'on or about December, 1910'.

5. Pater was one of the few influential Victorian prose authors about whom Virginia Woolf did not write. In *The Absent Father: Virginia Woolf and Walter Pater*, Perry Meisel finds her silence an indication of Pater's importance for her. Some of the connections Meisel finds significant can also be located in the work of Virginia Woolf's present father, which Meisel does not examine; other similarities are to be found in the influence of such writers as Henry James and G. E. Moore, which Meisel also ignores while finding additional evidence for Pater's influence in the deep differences between his work and Virginia Woolf's.

NOTES TO CHAPTER 2: LESLIE STEPHEN

1. See Lowell's 'Verses Intended to Go with a Posset Dish to My Dear Little God-Daughter, 1882', as printed in Maitland (pp. 318–19), with its description of the gifts he wishes her – her father's wit, her mother's beauty – and the faintly ominous prophetic warning,

> I simply wish the child to be
> A sample of Heredity
> Enjoying to the full extent
> Life's best, the Unearned Increment, . . .

> Thus, then, the cup is duly filled;
> Walk steady, dear, lest all be spilled.

2. The typescript (Add. MS 61973 in the British Library) is a revised version of pp. 107–37 of 'A Sketch of the Past' in the first edition of *Moments of Being* (1976) and includes an additional twenty-seven-page section on Leslie Stephen and Hyde Park Gate. The typescript has been incorporated into the second edition of *Moments of Being* (1985), which is the text cited here.
3. Hardy thought Stephen's philosophy influenced him more than that of any other contemporary (F. Hardy, p. 100).
4. In *The English Utilitarians* Stephen wrote of Mill's *The Subjection of Women*,

> None of his writing is more emphatically marked by generosity and love of justice. A certain shrillness of tone marks the recluse too little able to appreciate the animal nature of mankind. Yet in any case, he made a most effective protest against the prejudices which stunted the development and limited careers of women. (III 281)

5. See Noel Annan's *The Curious Strength of Positivism in English Political Thought* and his Introduction to Stephen's *Selected Writings in British Intellectual History*; Leonard Woolf is not discussed specifically in these, but Annan's criticisms clearly apply to his work.
6. Two unreprinted essays in the *Cornhill* give Stephen's views on literature and morality quite clearly: 'Art and Morality' was written shortly after the publication of Pater's *The Renaissance*; 'The Moral Element in Literature' is a defence of the ideas in 'Wordsworth's Ethics' that Arnold had criticised.
7. Stephen's letters to his wife, now in the Berg Collection, reveal him to be unhappy with omissions he felt forced to make, and, in his *DNB* account of his grandfather James Stephen, he concealed the parentage of an illegitimate son.

NOTES TO CHAPTER 3: SOME VICTORIAN VISIONS

1. One reason why Forster seems not to have forgotten the details of Rooksnest is that he kept an account of it written when he was fifteen, just after leaving the house, and then continued more than a half century later. See the Appendix to *Howards End*.
2. When *A Nineteenth-Century Childhood* was reissued in 1948 (with an introduction by John Betjeman describing it as 'a work of genius'), Mary MacCarthy changed some of the fictitious titles and place names to their originals but kept the family name of Kestrell.
3. According to Keynes's mother, Florence Ada Keynes. Mark Rutherford portrayed John Brown in *The Revolution in Tanner's Lane* (F. A. Keynes, pp. 21–2).
4. In 1899 Virginia Woolf turned a copy of Isaac Watts's famous *Logick* into a palimpsest by pasting the pages of a fragmentary holiday diary into it, anticipating in a symbolic manner, perhaps, the way in which G. E. Moore's epistemology would underlie her later fiction. This Warboys diary

contains various kinds of writing, such as Ruskinian nature sketches (QB/*VW*, I 65–6) and another early satire, 'A Terrible Tragedy in a Duck Pond', which makes fun of the Duckworths' name by imagining its origin in the saving of a duck for a king (pNY).

5. Virginia Woolf's obituary is reprinted in Winifred Gérin's *Anne Thackeray Ritchie*, a good biography for the Victorian backgrounds of Virginia Woolf.

6. Spilka notes the connection between this passage and Virginia Woolf's suicide (p. 124).

7. Leslie Stephen's side of the correspondence is now in the Berg, and Julia Stephen's manuscripts are in the library of Washington State University, Pullman, Washington.

8. See Virginia Woolf's 'Nurse Lugton's Curtain' and 'The Widow and the Parrot' (*CSF*). One of Julia Stephen's stories has some faint connections with *To the Lighthouse*. In 'Emily Caunt', the name of a fairyland haven for animals imagined by Vanessa and Thoby when they were very young (according to a note on the manuscript), the boy who visits this land on a rocking horse has a sister named Lily; just before the visit he receives a toy sailing boat for his birthday, but is told that because of the fog it cannot be sailed on the Round Pond that day. An example of the pervasive social milieu of these stories, together with what must have been an allusion to Virginia, occurs in the beginning of a story about a monkey on a moor. A young child named 'Ginia' buries her shoes and stockings in the sand, and is likened to a bare-legged little beggar girl when she has to be carried home.

9. In 'A Sketch of the Past' Virginia Woolf also says he never went to Italy or stayed in Paris (*MB*, p. 115), but J. W. Bicknell, in an essay entitled 'Mr Ramsay was Young Once', notes that Stephen did in fact go to Italy on his honeymoon and also visited Paris as well as Germany.

10. In his life of Fitzjames Stephen, Leslie writes that their father 'could not bear to have a looking glass in his room lest he should be reminded of his own appearance. "I hate mirrors vitrical and human", he says when wondering how he might appear to others' (p. 51).

11. Virginia Woolf changed '*Common Reader* articles' to '*Literary Supplement* articles' in the revised version of her typescript, suggesting perhaps that she was able to remedy these manners in turning her *TLS* articles into *Common Reader* essays.

12. As she was finishing *Roger Fry* Virginia Woolf sought the opinions of Lydia and Maynard Keynes about the matter: 'About Roger. "Can I mention erection?" I asked. Lydia "What?" M [Maynard]. "Stiff" (their private word). No you cant. I should mind your saying it. Such revelations have to be in key with their time. The time not come yet' (*D*, v 256).

NOTES TO CHAPTER 4: HISTORY AND CLASSICS AT KING'S AND TRINITY

1. For an informative interpretation of Victorian Cambridge history, see Sheldon Rothblatt's *The Revolution of the Dons*.

2. The couplet as quoted is attributed by Wingfield-Stratford to Stephen

(p. 158), but L. P. Wilkinson, quoting a somewhat different version, says the author was G. A. Falk (*Kingsmen*, p. 35).

3. Sheppard's paper is quoted and discussed by Furbank, who believes it can be applied to Rickie and Ansell in *The Longest Journey* (*EMF*, I 104–7).

4. In the context of Bloomsbury, Maitland has been described as 'the father of the pluralist tradition in English political thought', whose awareness of the roles of social groups may have made Bloomsbury more acceptable (Crabtree, pp. 19–20).

NOTE TO CHAPTER 5: ENGLISH LITERARY LECTURES, READING AND ESSAYS

1. Leonard Woolf's outline is with his papers at the University of Sussex; copies of his list of mystics are in Lytton Strachey's papers at the University of Texas and Sydney-Turner's papers at the Huntington Library.

NOTES TO CHAPTER 6: MODERN READING

1. Stephen also appears to have been something of a misogynist. The first motion he proposed as founder of the Walpole debating-society at King's in 1891 was 'That the Female Sex stands in need of repression', and it was carried, with Oscar Browning and Lowes Dickinson in the minority (Wilkinson, *Century*, p. 151). This sentiment may also have been an aspect of anti-Victorianism, however.

2. Leslie Stephen knew Hardy's *Wessex Poems* (1898), but there is no evidence his children read it until later.

3. Clive Bell at Trinity once took to adjectivising Thoby Stephen's nickname as 'Gothic' until Thoby started to call him 'Belloc' (CB/pTC).

NOTES TO CHAPTER 7: PHILOSOPHY AND THE CAMBRIDGE APOSTLES

1. I have capitalised the words 'Idealism', 'Realism' and 'Materialism' when they refer to particular philosophies; uncapitalised, they are used in their more ordinary senses. I have also capitalised 'Ideal' when it refers to the Ideal in *Principia Ethica*, in order to distinguish it more clearly from other senses of the word.

2. Leslie Stephen's highly critical *DNB* life of Maurice approvingly records that he was described as a 'muddy mystic' by some people. Stephen also notes Maurice's affinities with Coleridge and the Cambridge Platonists. The Bentham–Coleridge Victorian dichotomy seems to have been manifested to some extent in the Apostles, and vestiges of it might be seen in the Society's later Trinity–King's divisions.

3. Keynes apparently knew nothing of Sidgwick's friendship with John Addington Symonds or of Symonds's relationship with Sidgwick's brother (cf. Grosskurth).

4. Whitehead's recollections of the Society, as well as those of Dickinson that follow, are described in a letter Strachey wrote to Leonard Woolf in Ceylon after an extraordinary meeting of the Society on 18 March 1905 (21.iii.05, pT). (Neither letter nor meeting have been mentioned in published biographies, memoirs or histories of the Apostles.) At this meeting J. T. Sheppard read a paper entitled 'Shall We Broaden Our Base?', in which he defended the Society's failure to elect more members. In the ensuing discussion, according to Strachey's letter, Keynes, Russell, Whitehead, Strachey himself, MacCarthy and Dickinson all spoke about the history and purposes of the Society in their time.

5. Trevelyan was not even an active Apostle at the same time as Strachey and Keynes, though his concern for politics continued to be reflected in Apostolic papers such as Leonard Woolf's on the two Georges, Trevelyan and Moore (see Ch. 11). A list of the Apostles from 1822 to 1914 with the dates that most of them joined and resigned from the Society is given in Levy (pp. 300–11).

NOTES TO CHAPTER 8: DICKINSON AND McTAGGART

1. When D. H. Lawrence came to Cambridge during the war as Bertrand Russell's guest to talk about solutions to the war, he particularly wanted to meet Dickinson, though later he described him along with Cambridge as England's disease, not its hope (*Letters*, III 49). It is likely that Lawrence read some of Dickinson's early work, such as *The Greek View of Life*, where at one point he describes how Aristophanes accused Euripides of 'lowering the tragic art by introducing – what? Women in love! The central theme of modern tragedy!' Dickinson goes on to quote in Frere's famous translation of *The Frogs* Aeschylus's disclaimer: 'Indeed I should doubt if my drama throughout / Exhibit an instance of women in love!' (p. 158).

2. Dickinson mistakenly says (and Forster repeats it) that *Principia Ethica* came out while he was writing *The Meaning of Good* in 1901, and that he tried rather futilely at the last moment to dodge the naturalistic fallacy (*Autobiography*, p. 164). *Principia Ethica* actually appeared two years after *The Meaning of Good*, but Moore had developed his ideas about the indefinability of good in a series of lectures on ethics given in London in 1898 and subsequently discussed in Apostle meetings (Rosenbaum, 'Moore's Elements'). Dickinson, of course, would have known of Sidgwick's *The Methods of Ethics*, which influenced Moore's formulation of the naturalistic fallacy.

3. Dickinson's remarks on Sanger first appeared in the *Nation and Athenaeum*, 22 Feb 1930, and were quoted by Keynes in the *Economic Journal* and again in the *New Statesman and Nation* (*CW*, x 325, 340). Noel Annan used them again recently to conclude his rewritten life of Leslie Stephen.

4. *Some Dogmas of Religion* brought McTaggart a fan letter from Thomas Hardy, who wrote that in *The Dynasts* he was trying to sketch a negative philosophy not all that different from McTaggart's. In addition to Hardy and Yeats, McTaggart also impressed two modern novelists in different ways. H. G. Wells mocked him in *The New Machiavelli* (1911) as Codger,

whose 'woven thoughts' lay across the narrator's perception of realities when he was his student at Cambridge (ch. 3). Wells's antipathy may have increased the admiration of one of his writer loves, Dorothy Richardson. In *Deadlock* (1921), the sixth novel of *Pilgrimage*, she represented McTaggart *in propria persona* as a lecturer in philosophy who influences the heroine towards a mystical individualism (ch. 7; C. Blake, pp. 57ff.).

NOTES TO CHAPTER 9: RUSSELL

1. For an excellent account of these paradoxes and Russell's technical philosophy as a whole, its relation to Moore's and to the development of modern analytic philosophy, see John Passmore's *A Hundred Years of Philosophy*, to which I am indebted throughout this account of Bloomsbury's philosophical backgrounds.
2. Russell's criticism of Bergson first appeared in the *Monist* in July 1912, and was reprinted as a pamphlet in 1914. When Russell came to write *A History of Western Philosophy*, he included it as the chapter on Bergson. Revising the history in 1961, Russell cut his discussion down because he no longer thought Bergson important enough to merit an entire chapter.
3. '*Principia Ethica*', in the *Cambridge Review* for 3 December 1903, is unsigned but obviously by Russell; his signed 'The Meaning of Good' appeared in the March 1904 issue of the *Independent Review*.
4. In Russell's account of the Apostles there is the same chronological confusion of the turn of the century with a period around the First World War as is to be found in Keynes's memoir. Russell, for example, describes Keynes at the time he was an undergraduate being besieged by the Vice-Chancellor about university business (*Autobiography*, I 71).
5. Clive Bell's reply to Russell's request is suspicious of a hoax (Russell Archives), but there was in his library at Charleston a copy of *Introduction to Mathematical Philosophy* inscribed 'with grateful acknowledgements / from Bertrand Russell'.

NOTES TO CHAPTER 10: MOORE

1. Keynes's recent biographer Robert Skidelsky is fully aware of Moore's influence and provides detailed evidence for it from Cambridge writings of Keynes overlooked by Levy (Skidelsky, I 133–60).
2. Stuart Hampshire's description of Spinoza and Leibniz suggests many of the parallels to Moore and Russell:

> Nearly equal in intellectual stature and always concerned with the same fundamental problems, the two philosophers were utterly opposed in temperament and ambition, and in their conceptions of the philosopher's role in society. Leibniz, multifariously active and accessible, organizing, power-loving, avaricious, was a courtier and politician, a man of encyclopaedic knowledge and many attainments; he was immersed in the public life of his time at every point, writing and publishing incessantly

on a great variety of subjects in response to some immediate need or request. . . . By contrast Spinoza was inaccessible, secluded, unworldly, and self-sufficient; his whole life was narrowly concentrated in constructing a single metaphysical system and in drawing moral implications from it, and even his political writings were studiously remote from the actual details of current affairs. Leibniz, with his prodigies of technical invention, has posthumously remained in the main stream of European logic and science, while Spinoza has always been islanded and has left no legacy of logical invention.   (pp. 233–4)

3. It is not surprising that critics have found Virginia Woolf's work amenable to phenomenological description. Franz Brentano, who developed the influential idea of the intentionality of consciousness, was a teacher of Freud's and Husserl's as well as an important influence on Moore and Russell (Passmore, pp. 202–6; Chisholm).

4. A number of Moore's Apostle and Sunday Essay Society papers are discussed in Levy, but not *The Elements of Ethics* or 'The Value of Religion' – lectures which are so important in the early development of his moral philosophy.

5. Monroe Beardsley has pointed out that Moore's definition is difficult to reconcile with his arguments against the value of beautiful objects unperceived by anyone – objects that Sidgwick thought valuable (p. 545).

6. Sturge Moore attended his brother's lectures in London in 1898, sending his detailed notes to G. E. Moore for criticism. G. E. in turn helped Sturge edit Shakespeare and translate various authors from the Greek, which Sturge did not know (Legge, pp. 97, 123). But G. E. Moore did not appreciate his brother's aesthetic criticism and complained to Leonard Woolf that the philosophy in it, like all bad philosophy, was vague, inconsequent and false, resembling a sermon whose purpose is 'to make you appreciate good things' (LW/S, p. 139).

NOTES TO CHAPTER 11: MEMOIRS, APOSTLE PAPERS AND OTHER ESSAYS

1. Linda Hutcheon has pointed out in *Formalism and the Freudian Aesthetic: The Example of Charles Mauron* how the influence of Claude Bernard's experimental methodology on Mauron may well have shaped Fry's later scientific views. But earlier, during the period of his *Vision and Design* essays for example, Fry appears to have been interested in Pearson's philosophy of science and then Bertrand Russell's as developed in *Our Knowledge of the External World*.

2. The quotation of this passage has been corrected from the manuscript, which, along with Strachey's other unpublished Cambridge writings, is in the possession of the Strachey Trust.

NOTE TO CHAPTER 12: POEMS, PLAYS, PARODIES

1. In addition to the seven poems listed in Michael Edmonds's bibliography of Strachey (pp. 75–6), there are two more almost certainly by Strachey:

'The Penultimates', signed 'G. L. S.' in the *Cambridge Review*, xxiii (28 Nov 1901) 102, and 'A Chinese Epitaph' signed 'Se Lig' (which, like 'Selig', the author of 'The Monk', was Strachey's first name spelled backwards) in the *Cambridge Review*, xxv (26 May 1904) 323.

Bibliography

This bibliography is divided into two parts: first, works by members of the Bloomsbury Group, then other works. The place of publication is London unless otherwise stated. Short title references used in the text are given in square brackets at the end of the entry.

1 WRITINGS BY THE BLOOMSBURY GROUP

Bell, Clive, *Art* (Chatto & Windus, 1914). [*A*]
——, '*George Bernard Shaw* by G. K. Chesterton', *Athenaeum*, 11 Sept 1909, pp. 291–2 ['Shaw']
——, *Old Friends: Personal Recollections* (Chatto & Windus, 1956). [*OF*]
——, Papers, Trinity College, Cambridge. [pTC]
——, *Pot-Boilers* (Chatto & Windus, 1918). [*PB*]
Bell, Quentin, *Bloomsbury* (Futura, 1974).
——, *Virginia Woolf: A Biography*, 2 vols (Hogarth Press, 1972). [QB/*VW*]
Bell, Vanessa, *Notes on Virginia's Childhood: A Memoir*, ed. Richard J. Schaubeck, Jr (New York: Frank Hallman, 1974). [*Notes*]
——, Papers, in possession of Angelica Garnett. [pAG]
Forster, E. M., *Abinger Harvest* (Edward Arnold, 1936). [*AH*]
——, *Albergo Empedocle and Other Writings*, ed. George H. Thomson (New York: Liveright, 1971). [*AE*]
——, *Aspects of the Novel and Related Writings*, Abinger Edition, xii, ed. Oliver Stallybrass (Edward Arnold, 1974). [*AN*]
——, *Commonplace Book* (Scolar Press, 1978). [*CB*]
——, 'E. M. Forster on his Life and his Books', interview with David Jones, *Listener*, 1 Jan 1959, pp. 11–12.
——, *Goldsworthy Lowes Dickinson and Related Writings*, Abinger Edition, xiii, ed. Oliver Stallybrass (Edward Arnold, 1973). [*GLD*]
——, 'How I Lost My Faith', *Humanist*, lxxviii (1963) 262–6.
——, *Howards End*, Abinger Edition, iv, ed. Oliver Stallybrass (Edward Arnold, 1973). [*HE*]
——, *The Longest Journey*, Abinger Edition, ii, ed. Elizabeth Heine (Edward Arnold, 1984). [*LJ*]
——, *Marianne Thornton: A Domestic Biography* (Edward Arnold, 1956). [*MT*]
——, *Maurice* (Edward Arnold, 1971). [*M*]
——, Papers, King's College, Cambridge. [pKC]

288

——, 'Recollectionism', *New Statesman and Nation*, 13 Mar 1937, pp. 405–6.

——, *Two Cheers for Democracy*, Abinger Edition, VI, ed. Oliver Stallybrass (Edward Arnold, 1972). [*2CD*]

Fry, Roger, *Last Lectures*, intro. Kenneth Clark (Cambridge: Cambridge University Press, 1939). [*LL*]

——, *Letters of Roger Fry*, ed. Denys Sutton, 2 vols (Chatto & Windus, 1972). [*L*]

——, 'Modern Painting by George Moore', *Cambridge Review*, XXII (June 1893) 417–19; repr. in *The Cambridge Mind*, ed. Eric Homberger *et al.* (Jonathan Cape, 1970) pp. 211–14. ['Modern Painting']

——, Papers, King's College, Cambridge. [pKC]

——, (ed.), *Sir Joshua Reynolds: Discourses Delivered to the Students of the Royal Academy* (Seeley, 1905). [*Reynolds*]

Grant, Duncan, Papers, British Library. [pBL]

——, ' "Where Angels Fear to Tread": A Memoir of the Apostles', Duncan Grant papers in possession of Henrietta Garnett. ['Where Angels']

Keynes, John Maynard, *The Collected Writings*, ed. Donald Moggridge and Elizabeth Johnson, 30 vols (Macmillan, 1971–). [*CW*]

——, Papers, King's College, Cambridge. [pKC]

——, Papers, Marshall Library, Cambridge. [pML]

MacCarthy, Desmond, *Criticism* (Putnam, 1932). [*C*]

——, *Experience* (Putnam, 1935). [*E*]

——, *Humanities* (Macgibbon & Kee, 1953). [*H*]

——, *Leslie Stephen* (Cambridge: Cambridge University Press, 1937). [*Stephen*]

——, 'Oscar Wilde and the Literary Club Theatre', *Speaker*, XIV (7 July 1906) 315–16. ['Wilde']

——, *Memories* (Macgibbon & Kee, 1953). [*M*]

——, *Portraits*, I (Putnam, 1931). [*P*]

——, Papers, Lord David Cecil. [pC]

MacCarthy, Mary, *A Nineteenth-Century Childhood* (Heinemann, 1924) [*NC*]; rev. edn, intro. John Betjeman (Heinemann, 1948).

Strachey, Lytton, *Books and Characters, French & English* (Chatto & Windus, 1922). [*BC*]

——, *Characters and Commentaries* (Chatto & Windus, 1933). [*CC*]

——, 'Ely: An Ode', *Prolusiones Academicae* (Cambridge: Cambridge University Press, 1902).

——, *Eminent Victorians* (Chatto & Windus, 1918). [*EV*]

——, 'A Frock-Coat Portrait of a Great King', *Daily Mail*, 11 Oct 1928, p. 10. ['Frock-Coat']

—— (signed 'G. L. S.'), 'From the Persian', *Cambridge Review*, XXIV (5 Feb 1903) 168.

——, *Landmarks in French Literature*, Home University Library of Modern Knowledge (Williams and Norgate, [1912]). [*LFL*]

——, *Lytton Strachey by Himself: A Self Portrait*, ed. Michael Holroyd (Heinemann, 1971). [*LSH*]

——, Papers, British Library. [pBL]

——, Papers, Robert H. Taylor Collection, Princeton University Library. [pP]

——, Papers, Humanities Research Center, University of Texas. [pT]

——, Papers, the Strachey Trust. [pST]

—— (signed 'G. L. S.'), 'The Penultimates', *Cambridge Review*, XXIII (28 Nov 1901) 102.

——, *Portraits in Miniature* (Chatto & Windus, 1931). [*PM*]

——, *The Really Interesting Question and Other Papers*, ed. Paul Levy (Weidenfeld & Nicolson, 1972). [*RIQ*]

——, *The Shorter Strachey*, ed. Michael Holroyd and Paul Levy (Oxford: Oxford University Press, 1980). [*SS*]

——, *Spectatorial Essays*, ed. James Strachey (Chatto & Windus, 1964). [*SE*]

——, *Virginia Woolf and Lytton Strachey: Letters*, ed. Leonard Woolf and James Strachey (Hogarth Press, 1956). [*LVWLS*]

Woolf, Leonard, *After the Deluge: A Study of Communal Psychology*, 2 vols (Hogarth Press, 1931 and 1939). [*AD*]

——, 'Autobiography of Bertrand Russell: Volume II', *Political Quarterly*, XXXIX (1968) 343–7. ['Autobiography of Russell']

——, *Beginning Again: An Autobiography of the Years 1911–1918* (Hogarth Press, 1964). [*BA*]

——, 'A Case for Treatment', *Encounter*, XXX (May 1968) 91. ['Case']

——, 'Coming to London', *Coming to London*, ed. John Lehmann (Phoenix House, 1959, pp. 27–35. ['Coming']

——, *Downhill All the Way: An Autobiography of the Years 1919–1939* (Hogarth Press, 1967). [*DAW*]

——, *Essays on Literature, History, Politics, Etc.* (Hogarth Press, 1927). [*E*]

——, *Growing: An Autobiography of the Years 1904–1911* (Hogarth Press, 1961). [*G*]

——, Interview, 20 June 1966.

——, Papers, University of Sussex. [pS]

——, *Principia Politica: A Study of Communal Psychology* (Hogarth Press, 1953). [*PP*]

——, *Sowing: An Autobiography of the Years 1880–1904* (Hogarth Press, 1960). [*S*]

——, *The Wise Virgins: A Story of Words, Opinions and a Few Emotions* (Hogarth Press, 1979). [*WV*]

Woolf, Virginia, *Books and Portraits*, ed. Mary Lyon (Hogarth Press, 1977). [*BP*]

——, *'A Cockney's Farming Experiences'* and *'The Experiences of a Pater-familias'*, ed. Suzanne Henig (San Diego, Calif.: San Diego State University Press, 1972).

——, *Collected Essays*, ed. Leonard Woolf, 4 vols (Hogarth Press, 1966–7). [*CE*]

——, *The Complete Shorter Fiction of Virginia Woolf*, ed. Susan Dick (Hogarth Press, 1985). [*CSF*]

——, *Contemporary Writers* (Hogarth Press, 1965). [*CW*]

——, *The Diary of Virginia Woolf*, ed. Anne Olivier Bell, assisted by Andrew McNeillie, 5 vols (Hogarth Press, 1978–84). [*D*]

——, *A Haunted House and Other Short Stories*, Uniform Edition (Hogarth Press, 1953). [*HH*]

——, *Jacob's Room*, Uniform Edition (Hogarth Press, 1945). [*JR*]

——, 'Lady Ritchie', *TLS*, 6 Mar 1919, p. 123; repr. in Winifred Gérin, *Anne Thackeray Ritchie* (Oxford: Oxford University Press, 1981) pp. 279–84.

——, *The Letters of Virginia Woolf*, ed. Nigel Nicolson and Joanne Trautmann, 6 vols (Hogarth Press, 1975–80). [*L*]

——, 'The Method of Henry James', *TLS*, 26 Dec 1918, p. 655.

——, 'Mr Henry James's Latest', *Guardian*, 22 Feb 1905, p. 339.
——, *Moments of Being: Unpublished Autobiographical Writings*, 2nd edn, ed. Jeanne Schulkind (Hogarth Press, 1985). [*MB*]
——, *Monday or Tuesday* (Hogarth Press, 1921).
——, *Orlando* (Hogarth Press, 1928).
——, Papers, University of Sussex. [pS]
——, Papers, Berg Collection, New York Public Library. [pNY]
——, *A Room of One's Own* (Hogarth Press, 1929). [*RO*]
——, *Roger Fry: A Biography* (Hogarth Press, 1940). [*RF*]
——, 'A Sketch of the Past', typescript, Add. MS 61973, British Library ('Sketch' TS)
——, 'The Schoolroom Floor', *TLS*, 2 Oct 1924, p. 609. ['Schoolroom']
——, *Three Guineas* (Hogarth Press, 1938). [*3G*]
——, *Virginia Woolf and Lytton Strachey: Letters*, ed. Leonard Woolf and James Strachey (Hogarth Press, 1956). [*LVWLS*]

2 OTHER WRITINGS

Allen, Peter, *The Cambridge Apostles: The Early Years* (Cambridge: Cambridge University Press, 1978).
Annan, Noel, *The Curious Strength of Positivism in English Political Thought* (Oxford University Press, 1959).
——, 'Editor's Introduction', *Leslie Stephen, Selected Writings in British Intellectual History* (Chicago: Chicago University Press, 1979) pp. xi–xxx.
——, 'The Intellectual Aristocracy', *Studies in Social History*, ed. J. H. Plumb (Longmans, Green, 1955) pp. 241–87.
——, *Leslie Stephen: The Godless Victorian* (Weidenfeld & Nicolson, 1984).
Arundell, Dennis, 'Lopokova as an Actress', *Lydia Lopokova*, ed. Milo Keynes (Weidenfeld & Nicolson, 1983) pp. 122–38.
Beardsley, Monroe, *Aesthetics: Problems in the Philosophy of Criticism* (New York: Harcourt, Brace, 1958).
Benson, A. C., 'Blanche Warre-Cornish', *London Mercury*, VIII (1923) 145–58.
Bicknell, John W., 'Leslie Stephen's *English Thought in the Eighteenth Century*: A Tract for the Times', *Victorian Studies*, VI (1962) 103–20. [Stephen]
——, 'Mr Ramsay was Young Once', *Virginia Woolf and Bloomsbury: A Centenary Celebration*, ed. Jane Marcus (Macmillan, forthcoming).
Blake, Caesar, R., *Dorothy Richardson* (Ann Arbor, Mich.: University of Michigan Press, 1960).
Bloom, Harold, 'Introduction: The Crystal Man', *Selected Writings of Walter Pater*, ed. Bloom (New York: Columbia University Press, 1974) pp. vii–xxxi.
The Bloomsbury Group: The Word and the Image, VII, exhibition catalogue (National Book League and Hogarth Press, 1976). [*Bloomsbury Word and Image*]
Boissevain, Jeremy, *Friends of the Friends: Networks, Manipulators and Coalitions* (Oxford University Press, 1974).
Boyd, Elizabeth French, *Bloomsbury Heritage: Their Mothers and their Aunts* (Hamish Hamilton, 1976). [*Bloomsbury*]
——, 'Luriana, Lurilee', *Notes and Queries*, CCVIII (1963) 380–1.

Boyle, Andrew, *The Climate of Treason*, rev. edn (Hodder & Stoughton, 1980).

Bradley, A. C., 'Poetry for Poetry's Sake', *Oxford Lectures on Poetry* (Macmillan, 1909).

Bradley, F. H., *Appearance and Reality: A Metaphysical Essay*, 2nd edn (Oxford University Press, 1969).

Braithwaite, R. B., 'Keynes as a Philosopher', *Essays on John Maynard Keynes*, ed. Milo Keynes (Cambridge: Cambridge University Press, 1975) pp. 237–46.

Broad, C. D., *Examination of McTaggart's Philosophy*, 2 vols (Cambridge: Cambridge University Press, 1933 and 1938).

Bussy, Dorothy Strachey ('Olivia'), *Olivia* (Hogarth Press, 1949).

The Cambridge Mind: Ninety Years of the 'Cambridge Review', 1879–1969, ed. Eric Homberger, William Janeway, Simon Schama (Jonathan Cape, 1970).

Cecil, David, Introduction to *Desmond MacCarthy: The Man and his Writings*, ed. Cecil (Constable, 1984) pp. 13–34.

Charteris, Evan, *The Life and Letters of Edmund Gosse* (Heinemann, 1931).

Chisholm, Roderick M. (ed.), *Realism and the Background of Phenomenology* (Glencoe, Ill.: Free Press, 1960).

Clark, Ronald W., *The Life of Bertrand Russell* (Jonathan Cape/Weidenfeld & Nicolson, 1975).

Colmer, John, *E. M. Forster: The Personal Voice* (Routledge & Kegan Paul, 1975).

Crabtree, Derek, 'Cambridge Intellectual Currents of 1900', *Keynes and the Bloomsbury Group*, ed. Crabtree and A. P. Thirlwall (Macmillan, 1980).

Dahl, Christopher C., 'Virginia Woolf's *Moments of Being* and Autobiographical Tradition in the Stephen Family', *Journal of Modern Literature*, x (June 1983) 175–96.

Darroch, Sandra Jobson, *Ottoline: The Life of Lady Ottoline Morrell* (Chatto & Windus, 1976).

DeSalvo, Louise A., '1897: Virginia Woolf at Fifteen', *Virginia Woolf: A Feminist Slant*, ed. Jane Marcus (Lincoln, Nebr.: University of Nebraska Press, 1983) 78–108.

Dickinson, G. Lowes, *After Two Thousand Years* (Allen & Unwin, 1930).

——, *The Autobiography of G. Lowes Dickinson*, ed. Dennis Proctor (Duckworth, 1973).

——, 'Dialogue as a Literary Form', *Essays by Divers Hands, Transactions of the Royal Society of Literature*, xi (1932) 1–19. [Dialogue']

——, *The Greek View of Life*, 23rd edn, Preface by E. M. Forster (Methuen, 1957).

——, *J. McT. E. McTaggart* (Cambridge: Cambridge University Press, 1931).

——, *Justice and Liberty: A Political Dialogue* (J. M. Dent, 1907).

——, *Letters from John Chinaman and Other Essays*, new edn, intro. E. M. Forster (Allen & Unwin, 1946). [*Letters*]

——, *The Meaning of Good: A Dialogue*, 4th edn (J. M. Dent, 1907).

——, *A Modern Symposium*, intro. E. M. Forster (Allen & Unwin, n.d.).

Dictionary of National Biography, ed. Leslie Stephen and Sidney Lee *et al.*, 22 vols (Smith, Elder, 1908–9) Supplements, 1901–   (Oxford University Press, 1912–   ). [*DNB*]

Edel, Leon, *Bloomsbury: A House of Lions* (Philadelphia: J. B. Lippincott, 1979).

Edmonds, Michael, *Lytton Strachey: A Bibliography* (New York: Garland, 1981).

Eliot, T. S., *Selected Essays*, new edn (New York: Harcourt Brace, 1950). [*Essays*]

——, 'Virginia Woolf', *Horizon*, III (1941); repr. in *The Bloomsbury Group*, ed. S. P. Rosenbaum (Toronto: University of Toronto Press, 1974) pp. 202–3. ['VW']

Fleishman, Avrom, 'Woolf and McTaggart', *ELH*, XXXVI (Dec 1969) 719–38.

Furbank, P. N., *E. M. Forster: A Life*, 2 vols (Secker & Warburg, 1977–8). [PNF/*EMF*]

——, 'Forster and "Bloomsbury" Prose', *E. M. Forster: A Human Exploration. Centenary Essays*, ed. G. K. Das and John Beer (Macmillan, 1979) pp. 161–6.

Garnett, Angelica, *Deceived with Kindness: A Bloomsbury Childhood* (Chatto & Windus, 1984).

Garnett, David, *Great Friends: Portraits of Seventeen Writers* (Macmillan, 1979).

Gathorne-Hardy, Robert (unsigned), *Cornishiana* (privately printed, 1937).

Gérin, Winifred, *Anne Thackeray Ritchie* (Oxford: Oxford University Press, 1981).

Gordon, Lyndall, *Virginia Woolf: A Writer's Life* (Oxford: Oxford University Press, 1984).

Gross, John, *The Rise and Fall of the Man of Letters: Aspects of English Literary Life since 1800* (Weidenfeld & Nicolson, 1969).

Grosskurth, Phyllis, *John Addington Symonds* (Longmans, 1964).

Hampshire, Stuart, *Spinoza* (Harmondsworth, Middx: Penguin, 1967).

Hardy, Florence, *The Life of Thomas Hardy: 1840–1928* (Macmillan, 1962).

Hardy, Thomas, *Complete Poems*, ed. James Gibson (Macmillan, 1978).

Harrison, Jane Ellen, *Ancient Art and Ritual*, rev. edn (Oxford University Press, 1951).

——, *Prolegomena to the Study of Greek Religion* (Cambridge: Cambridge University Press, 1903).

——, *Reminiscences of a Student's Life* (Hogarth Press, 1925).

Harrod, R. F., *The Life of John Maynard Keynes* (Macmillan, 1951). [RFH/*JMK*]

Hassall, Christopher, *A Biography of Edward Marsh* (New York: Harcourt, Brace, 1959).

Hicks, John, 'Thornton's Paper Credit', *Critical Essays in Monetary Theory* (Oxford University Press, 1967) pp. 174–88.

Hill, Katherine C., 'Virginia Woolf and Leslie Stephen: History and Literary Revolution', *PMLA*, XCVI (1981) 351–62.

Hintikka, Jaakko, 'Virginia Woolf and our Knowledge of the External World', *Journal of Aesthetics and Art Criticism*, XXXVIII (Fall 1979) 5–13.

Holroyd, Michael, *Lytton Strachey: A Biography*, rev. edn (Harmondsworth, Middx: Penguin, 1971). [MH/*LS*]

——, *Lytton Strachey and the Bloomsbury Group: His Work, their Influence* (Harmondsworth, Middx: Penguin, 1971). [*LHBG*]

Hulme, T. E., *Speculations: Essays on Humanism and the Philosophy of Art*, ed. Herbert Read (Routledge & Kegan Paul, 1960).

Hutcheon, Linda, *Formalism and the Freudian Aesthetic: The Example of Charles Mauron* (Cambridge: Cambridge University Press, 1984).

Hynes, Samuel, *The Edwardian Turn of Mind* (Princeton, NJ: Princeton University Press, 1968).

Jakobson, Roman, 'Two Aspects of Language and Two Types of Aphasic Disturbances', *Fundamentals of Language*, ed. Jakobson and Morris Halle (The Hague: Mouton, 1955) pp. 69–82.

James, Henry, *The Awkward Age* (Heinemann, 1899).

——, *The Art of the Novel: Critical Prefaces*, ed. R. P. Blackmur (New York: Charles Scribner's Sons, 1953). ['Prefaces']

——, *Letters*, IV: *1895–1916*, ed. Leon Edel (Cambridge, Mass.: Harvard University Press, 1984).

Jeffares, A. Norman, *A Commentary on the Collected Poems of W. B. Yeats* (Macmillan, 1968).

Johnstone, J. K., *The Bloomsbury Group: A Study of E. M. Forster, Lytton Strachey, Virginia Woolf, and their Circle* (Secker & Warburg, 1954).

Kenner, Hugh, *The Pound Era* (Berkeley, Calif.: University of California Press, 1971).

Keynes, Florence Ada, *Gathering up the Threads: A Study in Family Biography* (Cambridge: Heffer, 1950).

Keynes, Geoffrey, 'The Early Years', *Essays on John Maynard Keynes*, ed. Milo Keynes (Cambridge: Cambridge University Press, 1975) pp. 26–35.

——, *The Gates of Memory* (Oxford: Clarendon Press, 1981). [*Gates*]

Keynes, Milo (ed.), *Essays on John Maynard Keynes* (Cambridge: Cambridge University Press, 1975).

—— (ed.), *Lydia Lopokova* (Weidenfeld & Nicolson, 1983).

Kirkpatrick, B. J., *A Bibliography of E. M. Forster*, rev. edn (Rupert Hart-Davis, 1968).

——, *A Bibliography of Virginia Woolf*, 3rd edn (Oxford: Clarendon Press, 1980).

Laing, Donald A., *Clive Bell: An Annotated Bibliography of the Published Writings* (New York: Garland, 1983). [*CB*]

——, *Roger Fry: An Annotated Bibliography of the Published Writings* (New York: Garland, 1979). [*RF*]

Lawrence, D. H., *The Letters of D. H. Lawrence*, ed. James T. Boulton *et al.*, 3 vols to date (Cambridge: Cambridge University Press, 1979–).

Leavis, F. R., 'Keynes, Spender and Currency Values', *Scrutiny*, XVIII (June 1951); repr. in *The Bloomsbury Group: A Collection of Memoirs, Commentary, and Criticism*, ed. S. P. Rosenbaum (Toronto: University of Toronto Press, 1975) pp. 395–402.

Leavis, Q. D., 'Leslie Stephen: Cambridge Critic', *Scrutiny*, VII (1939) 404–15. ['Stephen']

Legge, Sylvia, *Affectionate Cousins: T. Sturge Moore and Marie Appia* (Oxford: Oxford University Press, 1980).

Levy, Paul, *Moore: G. E. Moore and the Cambridge Apostles* (Weidenfeld & Nicolson, 1979).

Love, Jean O., *Virginia Woolf: Sources of Madness and Art* (Berkeley, Calif.: University of California Press, 1977).

Lowell, James Russell, 'A Fable for Critics', *Poetical Works* (Boston, Mass.: Houghton Mifflin, 1890) III 5–95.

Maitland, Frederic William, *The Life and Letters of Leslie Stephen* (Duckworth, 1906).

Marcus, Jane, 'The Niece of a Nun: Virginia Woolf, Caroline Stephen, and the Cloistered Imagination', *Virginia Woolf: A Feminist Slant*, ed. Marcus (Lincoln, Nebr.: University of Nebraska Press, 1983) pp. 7–36.

Martin, Kingsley, *Father Figures* (Hutchinson, 1966).

Maurer, Oscar, 'Leslie Stephen and the *Cornhill Magazine*, 1871–82', *Texas Studies in English*, XXXII (1953) 67–95.

McTaggart, J. McT. E., *The Nature of Existence*, ed. C. D. Broad, 2 vols (Cambridge: Cambridge University Press, 1968). [*Nature*]

——, 'An Ontological Idealism', *Contemporary British Philosophy: Personal Statements*, ed. J. H. Muirhead, 1st ser. (Allen & Unwin, 1924) pp. 251–69.

——, *Some Dogmas of Religion* (Edward Arnold, 1906). [*Dogmas*]

——, *Studies in Hegelian Cosmology* (Cambridge: Cambridge University Press, 1901).

——, *Studies in Hegelian Dialectic* (Cambridge: Cambridge University Press, 1896). [*Dialectic*]

Meisel, Perry, *The Absent Father: Virginia Woolf and Walter Pater* (New Haven, Conn.: Yale University Press, 1980).

Merle, Gabriel, *Lytton Strachey (1880–1932): Biographie et critique d'un critique et biographe*, 2 vols (Lille, Université de Lille, 1980).

Moore, G. E., 'Autobiography', *The Philosophy of G. E. Moore*, ed. Paul Arthur Schilpp, 2nd edn (New York: Tudor, 1952).

——, 'Death of Dr McTaggart', *Mind*, XXXIV (1925) 269–71. ['Death']

——, 'A Defence of Common Sense', *Contemporary British Philosophy: Personal Statements*, 2nd ser., ed. J. H. Muirhead (Allen & Unwin, 1924) pp. 191–223. ['Defence']

——, *The Elements of Ethics*. See S. P. Rosenbaum, 'G. E. Moore's *The Elements of Ethics*'.

——, Papers, Cambridge University Library. [Cambridge papers]

——, 'The Papers of G. E. Moore', Sotheby's *Catalogue of Valuable Autograph Letters Literary Manuscripts and Historical Documents* (sale 17 Dec 1979) pp. 65–90. ['Moore Papers']

——, *Philosophical Studies* (Routledge & Kegan Paul, 1922).

——, *Principia Ethica* (Cambridge: Cambridge University Press, 1922). [*PE*]

——, 'The Refutation of Idealism', *Philosophical Studies* (Routledge & Kegan Paul, 1922) pp. 1–30. ['Refutation']

——, 'A Reply to my Critics', *The Philosophy of G. E. Moore*, ed. Paul Arthur Schilpp, 2nd edn (New York: Tudor, 1952) pp. 535–687.

——, *Some Main Problems of Philosophy* (Allen & Unwin, 1953).

——, 'Wittgenstein's Lectures in 1930–33', *Philosophical Papers* (Allen & Unwin, 1959).

——, 'The Value of Religion', *International Journal of Ethics*, XII (1901) 81–98. ['Value']

Moore, T. Sturge, *W. B. Yeats and T. Sturge Moore: Their Correspondence, 1901–1937*, ed. Ursula Bridge (New York: Oxford University Press, 1953). [*Yeats and Moore*]

'Olivia', *Olivia*. See Bussy, Dorothy Strachey.

The Oxford English Dictionary, ed. James A. H. Murray *et al.*, 13 vols (Oxford University Press, 1931); *A Supplement to the Oxford English Dictionary*, ed. R. W. Burchfield, 3 vols to date (Oxford University Press, 1972–).

Passmore, John, *One Hundred Years of Philosophy* (Duckworth, 1966).

Pearson, Karl, *The Grammar of Science* (Dent, 1937).

Poggioli, Renato, *The Theory of the Avant-Garde*, tr. Gerald Fitzgerald (Cambridge, Mass.: Harvard University Press, 1968).

Quinton, Anthony, 'Thought', *Edwardian England: 1901–1914*, Ed. Simon Nowell-Smith (Oxford University Press, 1964) pp. 253–302.

Raleigh, Walter, 'Is Sense of Humour or Personal Integrity More Potent for Pleasure to its Owner: An Address to The Apostles, 9th December 1882', *Laughter from a Cloud* (Constable, 1923) pp. 1–16.

——, *Style* (Edward Arnold, 1897).

Ramsey, F. P., 'Epilogue', *The Foundations of Mathematics and Other Logical Essays*, ed. R. B. Braithwaite (Routledge & Kegan Paul, 1931) pp. 287–92.

Rees, Goronwy, 'A Case for Treatment', *Encounter*, xxx (Mar 1968) 71–83.

Reynolds, Sir Joshua, *Discourses Delivered to the Students of the Royal Academy*. See Fry, Roger (ed.).

Richards, I. A., *Complementarities: Uncollected Essays*, ed. John Paul Russo (Manchester: Carcanet New Press, 1976).

Robson, W. W., *Modern English Literature* (Oxford University Press, 1970).

Rosenbaum, S. P., 'Bertrand Russell: The Logic of a Literary Symbol', *Russell in Review*, ed. J. E. Thomas and Kenneth Blackwell (Toronto: Samuel Stevens, Hakkert, 1976) pp. 57–87. ['Russell']

—— (ed.), *The Bloomsbury Group: A Collection of Memoirs, Commentary, and Criticism* (Toronto: University of Toronto Press, 1975). [SPR/*BG*]

——, 'G. E. Moore's *The Elements of Ethics*', *University of Toronto Quarterly*, xxxviii (Apr 1969) 214–32. ['Moore's Elements']

——, 'Gilbert Cannan and Bertrand Russell: An Addition to the Logic of a Literary Symbol', *Russell*, nos 21–2 (Spring–Summer 1976) 16–25. ['Cannan']

——, 'Keynes, Lawrence, and Cambridge Revisited', *Cambridge Quarterly*, xi (1982) 252–64. ['Keynes']

Rothblatt, Sheldon, *The Revolution of the Dons* (New York: Basic Books, 1968).

Russell, Bertrand, Archives, McMaster University, Hamilton, Ontario.

——, *The Autobiography of Bertrand Russell*, 3 vols (Allen & Unwin, 1967–9).

——, *The Basic Writings of Bertrand Russell: 1903–1959*, ed. Robert E. Egner and Lester E. Denonn (Allen & Unwin, 1961).

——, *The Collected Papers of Bertrand Russell*, i: *Cambridge Essays: 1888–99*, ed. Kenneth Blackwell *et al.* (Allen & Unwin, 1983). [*Cambridge Essays*]

——, 'A Free Man's Worship', *Mysticism and Logic and Other Essays* (Allen & Unwin, 1963) pp. 40–7.

——, *A History of Western Philosophy* (New York: Simon & Schuster, 1945). [*History*]

——, 'The Influence and Thought of G. E. Moore. A Symposium of Reminiscence by Four of his Friends', *Listener*, 30 Apr 1959 pp. 755–6. ['Influence']

——, 'The Meaning of Good', *Independent Review*, ii (Mar 1904) 328–33.

——, 'My Mental Development', *The Philosophy of Bertrand Russell*, ed. Paul Arthur Schilpp, 3rd ed 2 vols (New York: Harper & Row, 1963) i 3–20. ['Mental Development']

——, *My Philosophical Development* (New York: Simon & Schuster, 1959). [*Philosophical Development*]

——, *Mysticism and Logic and Other Essays* (Allen & Unwin, 1963). [*Mysticism*]

——, *Our Knowledge of the External World As a Field for Scientific Method in Philosophy* (Allen & Unwin, 1961). [*Our Knowledge*]

——, *Portraits from Memory* (New York: Simon & Schuster, 1956).

—— (unsigned), 'Principia Ethica', *Cambridge Review*, xxv (3 Dec 1903) literary supplement, pp. xxxvii–viii.

——, *The Principles of Mathematics*, 2nd edn (New York: W. W. Norton, 1964).

——, *Principles of Social Reconstruction*, 6th edn (Allen & Unwin, 1960).

——, *The Problems of Philosophy* (Oxford University Press, 1959). [*Problems*]

——, 'Reply to Criticisms', *The Philosophy of Bertrand Russell*, ed. Paul Arthur Schilpp, 3rd edn, 2 vols (New York: Harper & Row, 1963) ii 681–741. ['*Reply*']

——, 'The Study of Mathematics', *Mysticism and Logic and Other Essays* (Allen & Unwin, 1963).

——, *Why I Am Not a Christian and Other Essays on Religion and Related Subjects*, ed. Paul Edwards (New York: Simon & Schuster, 1957).

Santayana, George, *My Host the World* (New York: Charles Scribner's Sons, 1953;.

——, *Winds of Doctrine* (New York: Harper, 1957).

Schneewind, J. B., *Sidgwick's Ethics and Victorian Moral Philosophy* (Oxford University Press, 1977).

Shakespeare, William, *The Riverside Shakespeare*, ed. G. Blakemore Evans *et al.* (Boston, Mass.: Houghton Mifflin, 1974).

Shone, Richard, *Bloomsbury Portraits: Vanessa Bell, Duncan Grant, and their Circle* (Oxford: Phaidon, 1976).

Sidgwick, Henry, *A Memoir by A. S. and E. M. S.* (Macmillan, 1906).

——, *The Methods of Ethics*, 7th edn (Macmillan, 1907).

Skidelsky, Robert, *John Maynard Keynes: A Biography*, 1 vol to date (Macmillan, 1983–).

Spalding, Frances, *Roger Fry: Art and Life* (Berkeley, Calif.: University of California Press, 1980). [*RF*]

——, *Vanessa Bell* (Weidenfeld & Nicolson, 1983). [*VB*]

Spilka, Mark, *Virginia Woolf's Quarrel with Grieving* (Lincoln, Nebr.: University of Nebraska Press, 1980).

Steele, Elizabeth, *Virginia Woolf's Literary Sources and Allusions: A Guide to the Essays* (New York: Garland, 1983).

Stephen, James, *The Memoirs of James Stephen Written by Himself for the Use of his Children*, ed. Merle M. Bevington (Hogarth Press, 1954).

Stephen, J. K. (signed 'J. K. S.'), *Lapsus Calami* (Cambridge: Macmillan and Bowes, 1891).

Stephen, Julia (Mrs Leslie), *Notes from Sick Rooms* ed. Constance Hunting (Orono, Maine: Puckerbrush Press, 1980).

——, Papers, Washington State University, Pullman, Washington.

Stephen, Julian Thoby (unsigned), *Compulsory Chapel* (privately printed, n.d.).

Stephen, Leslie, *An Agnostic's Apology and Other Essays* (Smith, Elder, 1903). [*Apology*]

——, 'Art and Morality', *Cornhill Magazine*, xxxii (1875) 91–101.

——, *English Literature and Society in the Eighteenth Century* (Methuen University Paperbacks, 1963). [*English Literature*]

——, *The English Utilitarians*, 3 vols (New York: A. M. Kelley, 1968).

——, *History of English Thought in the Eighteenth Century*, 2 vols (New York: Harcourt, Brace, 1962).

——, *Hours in a Library*, 3rd ser., 3 vols (Smith, Elder, 1899). [*Hours*]

——, *Life of Henry Fawcett* (Smith Elder, 1885).

——, *The Life of Sir James Fitzjames Stephen*, 2nd edn (Smith, Elder, 1895). [*Fitzjames Stephen*]

——, *Mausoleum Book*, ed. Alan Bell (Oxford: Clarendon Press, 1977). [*Mausoleum Book*]

——, *Men, Books, and Mountains: Essays*, ed. S. O. A. Ullmann (Hogarth Press, 1956). [*Men, Books*]

——, 'The Moral Element in Literature', *Cornhill Magazine*, XLIII (1881) 34–50.

——, 'A New "Biographica Britannica"', *Athenaeum*, 23 Dec 1882, p. 850. ['Biographica']

——, Papers, Berg Collection, New York Public Library.

——, *The Science of Ethics* (John Murray, 1907). [*Science*]

—— (unsigned), *Sketches from Cambridge by a Don*, ed. G. M. Trevelyan (Oxford, 1932). [*Sketches*]

——, *Some Early Impressions* (Hogarth Press, 1924). [*Impressions*]

——, *Studies of a Biographer*, 4 vols (Duckworth, 1910). [*Studies*]

Stone, Wilfred, *The Cave and the Mountain: A Study of E. M. Forster* (Stanford, Calif.: Stanford University Press, 1966).

Swinburne, Algernon Charles, *Poems and Ballads. Atlanta in Calydon*, ed. Morris Peckham (Indianapolis: Bobbs-Merrill, 1970).

Trevelyan, G. M., *An Autobiography and Other Essays* (Longmans, Green, 1949).

——, *Trinity College: An Historical Sketch* (Cambridge: Trinity College, 1972). [*Trinity*]

Trevelyan, R. C., *Windfalls: Notes and Essays*, 2nd edn with additions (Allen & Unwin, 1948).

Trilling, Lionel, *Matthew Arnold* (Allen & Unwin, 1949).

Verrall, A. W., *Euripides the Rationalist* (Cambridge: Cambridge University Press, 1895).

Wedd, Nathaniel, 'Goldie Dickinson: The Latest Cambridge Platonist', *The Criterion*, XII (Jan 1933) 175–83.

White, Morton, 'The Influence of G. E. Moore. A symposium of Reminiscence by Four of His friends', *Listener*, 30 Apr 1959, pp. 757–8.

Whitehead, Alfred North, 'Autobiographical Notes', *The Philosophy of Alfred North Whitehead*, ed. Paul Arthur Schilpp (New York: Tudor, 1951) pp. 3–14.

Wiener, Norbert, *Ex-Prodigy* (Cambridge, Mass.: MIT Press, 1953).

Wilkinson, L. P., *A Century of King's* (Cambridge: King's College, 1980). [*Century*]

——, *Kingsmen of a Century: 1873–1972* (Cambridge: King's College, 1981). [*Kingsmen*]

Williams, Raymond, 'The Significance of "Bloomsbury" as a Social and Cultural Group', *Keynes and the Bloomsbury Group*, ed. Derek Crabtree and A. P. Thirlwall (Macmillan, 1980) pp. 40–67.

Wilson, J. Dover, *Leslie Stephen and Matthew Arnold as Critics of Wordsworth* (Cambridge: Cambridge University Press, 1939).

Wingfield-Stratford, Esmé, *Before the Lamps Went Out* (Hodder & Stoughton, 1945).

Wittgenstein, Ludwig, *Philosophical Investigations*, tr. G. E. M. Anscombe (Oxford: Blackwell, 1963).

——, *Remarks on Frazer's 'Golden Bough'*, ed. Rush Rhees (Retford, Notts.: Brynmill Press, 1979).

Woolmer, J. Howard, *A Checklist of the Hogarth Press: 1917–1938* (Hogarth Press, 1976).

Yeats, William Butler, *The Collected Poems of W. B. Yeats* (Macmillan, 1967). [*Poems*]

——, *W. B. Yeats and T. Sturge Moore: Their Correspondence, 1901–1937*, ed. Ursula Bridge (New York: Oxford University Press, 1953). [*Yeats and Moore*]

Young G. M., *Victorian England: Portrait of an Age* (Oxford University Press, 1936).

Index

References to writings are given under their authors or editors and cross-referenced only when unidentified in the text.